LeeWards
Complete
Library of
Needlecraft

FULLER & DEES
TIMES MIRROR

New York • Los Angeles • Montgomery

Contributors

Fuller and Dees

PRESIDENT
James Lueck

ART DIRECTOR
George Alexandres

PRODUCTION DIRECTOR
William Holmes
George Jenks

EXECUTIVE EDITOR
Carter Houck

PROJECT EDITOR
Nell McInnish

EDITORIAL STAFF
Phyllis Fenn
Carl Richardson
Pat Warner

LAY-OUT DIRECTOR
Nancy Crippen
Mary Veitch

PHOTOGRAPHER
Myron Miller

ILLUSTRATORS
Jacqueline Butler
Marilyn Heard Eubanks
Janice Culbertson
Debbie Benedict
Patrick Gibson
Eleanor Palmer

CONTRIBUTING AUTHORS
Claudia Manley
Knitting, Crochet
Designer, Assistant Editor and Writer for
Spinnerin Yarns

CONTRIBUTING EDITOR
John Bade (Hook Arts)

CREATIVE STAFF
Courtney Bede
Kathy Crowe
Martha Ann Crowe
Grace Harding
Joe Ann Helms
Marion Moffat
Sandy Singer

ACKNOWLEDGEMENTS
Brunswick Yarn Company
Lily Yarn Company
C.J. Bates & Son

© Fuller & Dees MCMLXXV
3734 Atlanta Highway, Montgomery, Alabama 36109
Library of Congress Cataloging in Publication Data
Main entry under title:

A Complete Library of Needlecraft
Includes index.
1. Needlework   2. Fancy work.   3. Textile crafts.
TT705.C75   746   74-32451

Complete Set ISBN 0-87197-085-6
Volume 1 ISBN 0-87197-086-4

Contributors

CARTER HOUCK

A writer and teacher of needlework, Carter Houck attended design school at Virginia Commonwealth College in Richmond. Since then she has worked for Singer Sewing Machine Company, Butterick Pattern Company and has written and edited for such magazines as Parents' and Lady's Circle Needlework.

MYRON MILLER

Myron Miller is the photographer responsible for the black and white diagrams and details, frontispieces and color photography. He also works with many of the needlework magazines, including Good Housekeeping and McCall's, and with many pattern and yarn companies.

JINNY AVERY

Jinny Avery's needlework talents cover all forms of stitchery, sewing and patchwork. The designer of many of the projects for embroidery, appliqué and patchwork, her needlework career includes teaching at every level.

JOHN BADE

John Bade has worked in the field of yarns, canvas and associated arts for many years. Having designed and written for several companies, most recently C.J. Bates & Son, he specializes in rug making.

CLAUDIA MANLEY

A teacher, designer, writer and editor, Claudia Manley wrote and edited the instructions for the knitting and crocheting chapters and worked the swatches used in the main text.

CECELIA TOTH

Presently the Needlework Editor of Good Housekeeping Magazine, Cecelia Toth has also worked as the Creative Director of the Sewing Notions Division of Scovill and as the Fashion Director at Milliken.

SHARON VALIANT

Many of Sharon Valiant's original design pillows, afghans, screens and macramé pieces have been photographed by several magazines. She has worked for Woman's Day and has written a booklet for Lady's Circle.

Introduction

An increasing number of people are expressing themselves in the many forms of needlecraft. Although few of these arts could be considered new, there has been a resurgence in their popularity. To understand fully the importance of this new interest in needlecraft fashion, it is necessary to look at some of its history.

There is no way to pinpoint the beginnings of the needle arts. However, the advent of machine-made clothing and textiles did not diminish the interest in hand-work; women who no longer had to spin their yarn had more time to knit or crochet. Fine silk fabrics and embroidery threads became available and affordable to almost everyone. Machine woven fabrics of the nineteenth century made a new type of quilt possible.

With the invention of the automobile and airplane, people laid aside their knitting needles, crochet hooks and quilting frames and found pleasure in travel. However, at some point in the last two decades, the reverse happened — the artistic value of needlework began to appeal to more and more people, especially the young.

The needle arts have regained popularity for several reasons. One is certainly the high cost of clothing and home decorations. The fuel shortage has caused a decline in traveling as a pastime, which in turn has caused a renewed interest in the home and home crafts. But perhaps the real reason is the feeling of satisfaction derived from creating a beautiful design. The more one learns to use originality in design, the more satisfying the work will be. This idea has played an important part in the creation and division of this book.

First, all of the areas of needlecraft to be included in these volumes were divided into similar categories. For example, all embroidery is so interrelated that there should be no restriction on which is Crewel, Cross Stitch or White Work. All of the information is in one place, available to be used in any of the many ways the artist wishes. Too many rules spoil the creativity.

Introduction

In knitting and crochet, many extra ideas beyond the basics were included. This makes it possible to create original designs instead of depending only upon suggested projects. It is possible to use the designs in this book as points of departure for individual styles. Many of the sweaters are in basic styles which can be easily changed by the use of a different sleeve or neckline.

Most of the designs that are included in the projects for embroidery, rug making, needlepoint, patchwork and applique are open to changes, variations and individual interpretations. One of the toy soldiers in the Guardsmen Three Rug would make a lovely applique design; many of the needlepoint designs can be expanded for larger items. All of the charted designs for needlepoint, rugs or cross stitch can be used for the other two techniques. The clothes in the sewing projects are so simple and have such large seamless areas that they can be attractively decorated with embroidery or applique.

Therefore, all of the basic ingredients are in this book. However, the rules do not restrict the reader's individuality. The result of such a plan is a colorful and highly usable group of projects with all the information necessary to create new ones.

Scan the book casually to gain a better knowledge of the various crafts as a group. There are interesting bits of history in the introductions to each section. The novice should read through the first steps and even try some of the stitches on a scrap fabric before attempting large-scale projects in a new craft. As you progress and learn new needle arts, use these volumes as handy references. Whenever you are puzzled by a technique in a commercial pattern, you will find a fuller explanation here.

The authors of the various sections are experts in their fields and know the kinds of questions that most often may occur to the novice. They have tried to answer them carefully in text and diagram.

Contents

Volume 1

Knitting, which involves interlacing yarn or thread into loops connected by needles, is one of the most popular forms of needlework. An ancient craft, it is still used primarily for making various types of clothing.

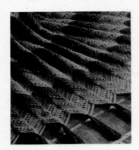

Crochet is an easily mastered hook art that had its origin in France and Ireland. Employing various types of threads, crochet has an endless number of uses, such as for clothing, wall hangings and other decorative purposes. New yarns, the use of larger needles, and contemporary designs have resulted in renewed interest in this versatile hobby.

Hook arts use different techniques to make lacy knotted fabrics, braids and edgings. It is ideal for children's and senior citizen's groups because one or many can work on the same project.

Volume 2

A rewarding and expressive kind of stitchery, embroidery can beautifully decorate fabrics by varying basic stitches and using colorful threads and yarns. Embroidery has come a long way from the early disciplined patterns and is now being used in freeform and abstract work to fit contemporary ways of living.

Needlepoint, once referred to as canvas work, is a form of creative needlecraft that has been traced back to Biblical times and is regaining its popularity in America. By applying groups of warp and weft threads to woven fabric, such as linen or canvas, designs can be made for pillows, wall hangings, mantle covers and carpets.

Contents

Introduction

Back through almost every period in history, there have been tradesmen making lace and fabrics by hooking and knotting threads. Not only women but men too — have plied these trades — and many still do in some parts of the world.

Almost everyone can recall a friend or relative who was never without knitting needles, crochet hooks or some other type of hook with which she created beautiful sweaters, afghans, mittens, and socks. Anyone who has envied these talented people will find in this volume information valuable to the beginner as well as the accomplished needlewoman. The knitting and crochet chapters are planned as lessons to take the beginner from the first slip knot to a completed project. For the person already familiar with the basics, there are advanced sections dealing with complex techniques and original designing. There are professional tips for the really avid knitter and crocheter who wants to perfect these skills.

The miscellaneous arts in the third chapter are mostly outgrowths of knitting and crochet. These are basically simple — in each project, there is only one technique to learn. The patterns are methods of joining lace and knitted cord to make afghans, shawls and garments of all kinds. An hour or so of practice should be enough for learning the fundamentals of these simple hook arts. Naturally, the more practice, the more perfect the project will be.

The projects in all of the chapters have been selected on the basis of their classic styling and timeless good looks. Some are simple enough for first attempts and others are challenges to the expert. There are specific learner's projects planned to make use of only the skills learned in the early sections of each chapter — such as the scarf made with one simple knitting stitch. A real beginner should try these before launching into the more complex projects that follow. Before purchasing the material required for any project, read the pattern instructions completely. Then, knit or crochet a sample piece to obtain the correct gauge and to determine the actual appearance of the pattern stitch. Because the size of the garment is determined entirely by the gauge, accuracy and some simple arithmetic are necessary.

Start with the art that most appeals to you. Work with the simple projects until proficiency in the art is obtained. Be sure to read the text of the chapter first in order to gain a working knowledge of the terms and phrases of the particular patterns.

Knitting

In man's quest for better, more practical and more beautiful textiles, the art of knitting was historically later than weaving. No one knows exactly when knitting first began since there is no actual record of any knitted fabric before 200 A.D. However, there are legends — one of which is that Christ's seamless garment was knitted. Indeed, seamless or tubular fabrics have been knitted for many generations.

The Arabs were responsible for the spread of knitting from the East (where it originated) to the Mediterranean coast of Europe. From there, it spread through northern Europe and eventually to America. As was the case with Macramé, it was the men—sailors and traders—who knitted. But in Europe, it became woman's art as well.

Both weavers and knitters formed guilds in the 15th and 16th centuries. And, the men who worked in the industry had to pass rigid tests to be accepted into the guild. In most of Europe, the men did the commercial knitting while the women knitted for their families. In the British Isles both men and women knitted commercially. These cottage industries still continue in some of the small isles today.

Some of the feats of the guild knitters before the industrial revolution are difficult for today's

Grandma's wooden needles and home dyed yarn were familiar articles in many 19th century living rooms like this one at Richmondtown Restoration in Staten Island, New York.

beginning knitter to comprehend. Most guilds required that a man design and knit several "masterpieces" within a limited time in order to be accepted as a Master Knitter. One generally required item in the test was a carpet approximately 6 feet by 5 feet intricately patterned in many colors. The finished effect of these carpets was much like that of a Persian rug.

Speed was of the utmost importance to commercial hand knitters. To make it possible to knit faster, many supports for the needles and other such aids were invented to take some of the strain off the hands. There are records of people knitting more than 200 stitches a minute on common knitting needles, using supports so that the hands were free to handle the yarn at high speed. Such methods can sometimes be seen in remote areas of England, Scotland, Ireland or Wales to this day.

Other innovations have been used to increase knitting speed and to make it possible to knit larger pieces. One that appeared in many forms was the knitting frame, a square or round frame with pins set all around. These most nearly resembled the knitting spools that children still use. Just as the child's spool makes a small tubular piece of knitting, the frames made a large tubular piece.

The first needles were shaped rather like long crochet hooks. But, the technique was that of knitting. Straight needles with smooth points probably appeared first in the thirteenth or four-teenth century. Early knitters made their own needles of bone, wood, ivory and many other materials. These were smooth and highly polished. There were no knob ends so small stoppers of wood or cork were necessary to keep the stitches from sliding off. The finest needles, barely more than wires, were used for knitting silk.

Wool has always been the principal yarn for knitting and it has been prepared and treated in many ways. People in fishing communities such as Ireland and the Aran Isles spun their yarn from a wool still containing its natural lanolin which enabled it to still shed water as it did on the sheep. In France and Austria some knitted garments are still felted after completion so that the yarn becomes matted together and thus impervious to wind and weather. Wool can be spun to be heavy enough for a coat or delicate enough for a baby's first sweater. Silk, linen and cotton have also been used for knitting. And now, synthetics are fast becoming the most popular yarns.

As the Puritan work ethic grew in the last centuries, knitting became a symbol of the woman whose hands were never idle. Women often kept a small piece of knitting in their pockets to work on in every spare minute. The terrible Madame Defarge in Tale of Two Cities even knitted while she watched the executions at the guillotine.

Today's busy woman often finds knitting a good tranquilizer, particularly in those frustrating moments of waiting in airports or traffic jams. Now that we are not usually concerned with knitting large carpets, most knitting can be put into a bag and taken along on vacations, business trips and for long waits in the doctor's office.

INTRODUCTION TO KNITTING

If you wish to learn to knit the correct way, you will find the Primer of Knitting just what you want. It presents the basic steps with diagrams necessary for you to learn in order to become a self-taught, confident knitter.

If you know the basic steps of knitting, you will find the advanced section filled with improved methods as well as the basic methods used in professional work. Many of these will give you new knowledge and more efficient methods for working.

LEFT-HANDERS

It was once believed that "left-handers" had a special problem in learning to knit. Experience has taught that "left-handers" can learn with the same instructions, diagrams and practice as the "right-handers."

Since all knitters need to use both hands almost equally in knitting, being left-handed usually is only a problem in the "left-hander's" mind. Any particular problems the "left-hander" feels are exactly the same problems of tension and lack of dexterity that the "right-hander" feels when first using needles and yarn. The "left-hander" can learn the same methods as others and to their advantage.

If, however, this seems impossible and becomes frustrating, try using a mirror in which to view the diagrams. This will reverse all the diagrams so that by reading *left for right* and *right for left* you will be able to proceed with hands reversed, using exactly the same materials as all others.

PRIMER

A beginner should practice each step using a Knitting Worsted-weight of yarn and a pair of 12-inch single-pointed needles, size No. 7 or 8. A bright color yarn is helpful in seeing the formation of each stitch.

Never go to a new step until *you* are convinced that you understand and have mastered the step you just completed. Check each step carefully. Be sure it is correct before you leave it.

Knitting is based on only two types of stitches. These are called the Knit Stitch and the Purl Stitch. All work is made from these two stitches or a combination of these.

Before we can learn to knit, we must first learn to place stitches on a needle. This is called "To Cast On Stitches."

GLOSSARY OF ABBREVIATIONS
SYMBOLS AND TERMS USED IN KNITTING

K. . . . . knit	sl. . . . . slip
P. . . . . purl	MC. . . . . .Main Color
st(s) . . . . stitch(es)	CC . . . . Contrasting Color
St st . . . . Stockinette stitch	dp. double-pointed
inc(s) . . . . increase(s)	psso . . . . pass slipped stitch
dec(s) . . . . decrease(s)	over knitted stitch
yo or o(s). . . . . yarn over(s)	sl, K, and pass . . . . Slip 1 stitch,
beg . . . . beginning	Knit 1 stitch, pass slipped stitch over
″. inch or inches	knit stitch
in(s) . . . . inch(es)	rnd(s). . . . . round(s)
tog . . . . together	sk . . . . skip
pat . . . . pattern	sc . . . . single crochet
rep . . . . repeat	dc . . . . double crochet
lp(s) . . . . loop(s)	

SYMBOLS AND TERMS USED
IN KNITTING

SYMBOLS

* (Asterisk): Indicates that work following the * is to be repeated the number of times indicated *in addition* to the first time.

* to * : Indicates that work between *s is to be repeated the number of times indicated *in addition* to the first time.

** (Double Asterisk): Used in the same way as *(Asterisk).

† (Dagger): Used in the same way as * (Asterisk).

() Parentheses: Indicate that what is enclosed in the () must be repeated the number of times indicated after the ().

[ ] Brackets: Indicate that what is enclosed in the [ ] must be repeated the number of times indicated after the [ ].

TERMS

Work Even: Work without increasing or decreasing any stitches.

Place a marker on needle: Slip a contrasting colored loop of yarn or a commercial ring marker on needle. Slip this marker from one needle to another on every row or round.

Mark Stitch: Tie a contrasting colored thread or place a safety pin on stitch.

Mark Row: Tie a contrasting colored thread or place a safety pin at beginning or end of row.

Bind off stitches at the beginning of the next two rows: Bind off the stitches at each side once.

The Multiple of a Pattern Stitch: This is the number of stitches which is necessary to work one repeat of a pattern.

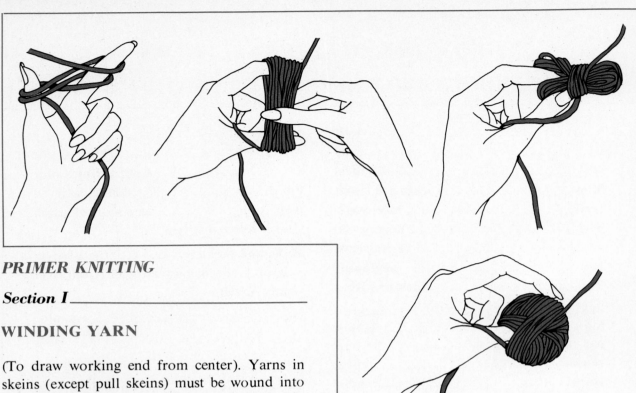

PRIMER KNITTING

Section I

WINDING YARN

(To draw working end from center). Yarns in skeins (except pull skeins) must be wound into balls before they can be used. Open a skein; slip the coils over the back of a chair or sit down and slip them over your knees. Break and discard the knotted piece of yarn holding the coils together. Take one end of the strand from the skein. Leaving a 12-inch end, wind yarn ten times around thumb and index finger of left hand forming a figure eight. Remove from fingers; fold in half and hold folded piece at center with thumb and second finger of left hand. Wind yarn *loosely* around thumb and two fingers fifteen times. Keeping thumb at center, remove yarn from fingers; turn ball one quarter turn. Continue to turn ball in order to keep a round shape. Be sure that the 12-inch end remains free. Wrap loosely until skein is converted into a pull ball. Wind final end around several wraps; secure with a knot. Draw yarn from center for working.

CASTING ON STITCHES

There are many ways of casting on stitches. We shall describe the two methods most often used and easiest to learn.

Method 1:

Step 1: Measure off a 20-inch length of yarn; do *not* break off. From this length, which we will call the "short end," we will cast on 20 stitches. *A good rule to follow in determining the length of the short end is to allow 1 inch for each stitch when using Knitting Worsted weight yarn; ¹/₂ inch for each stitch when using lightweight yarn.*

Step 2: Make a slip knot 20 inches from end of the short end of yarn; place loop on needle.

Step 3: Pull both ends gently, tightening the loop to fit needle easily. The loop should move freely back and forth on needle.

Step 4: Hold needle with first cast-on stitch in right hand; yarn from ball over index finger, under second finger and over third and fourth fingers. Place short end over left thumb; hold end of yarn *inside* left hand against palm with three fingers.

Step 5: Bring needle down in front of thumb, forming loop on thumb.

Step 6: Insert needle from left to right into loop on thumb.

Step 7: Pass ball end of yarn under and over point of needle.

Step 8: Hold yarn firmly in right hand; draw yarn through loop on left thumb with point of needle.

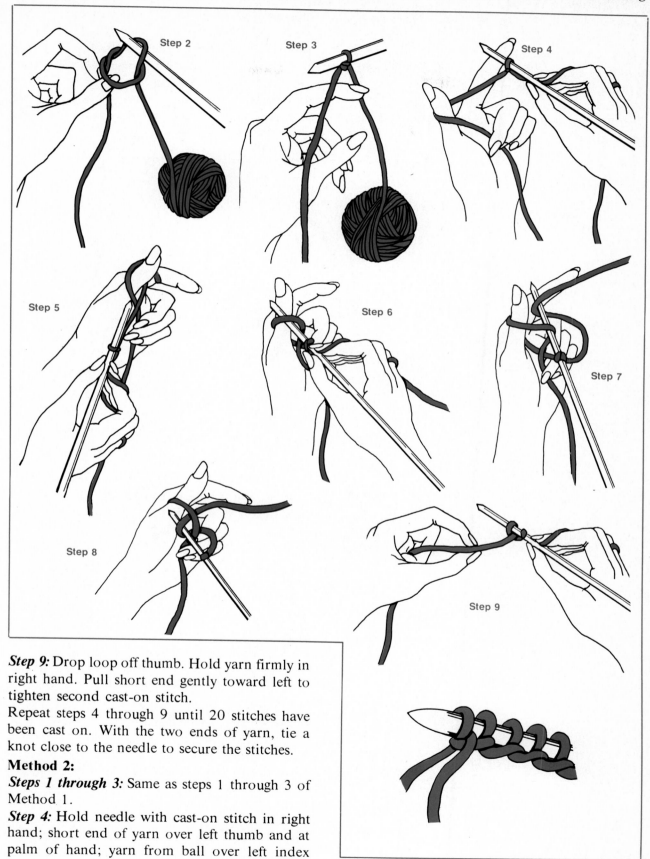

Step 9: Drop loop off thumb. Hold yarn firmly in right hand. Pull short end gently toward left to tighten second cast-on stitch.

Repeat steps 4 through 9 until 20 stitches have been cast on. With the two ends of yarn, tie a knot close to the needle to secure the stitches.

Method 2:

Steps 1 through 3: Same as steps 1 through 3 of Method 1.

Step 4: Hold needle with cast-on stitch in right hand; short end of yarn over left thumb and at palm of hand; yarn from ball over left index finger and at back of hand. Hold both ends of yarn between third and fourth fingers of left hand and *against* palm.

Step 5: Bring needle down in front of left thumb, forming a loop on thumb.

Step 6: Insert needle upward into loop.

Step 7: Pass point of needle from right to left under yarn on forefinger.

Step 8: Draw yarn from forefinger through loop with point of needle.

Step 9: Drop loop from thumb. Insert thumb under short end and draw loose end away from needle to tighten the stitch.

Repeat steps 5 through 9 until 20 stitches have been cast on. To secure stitches, tie a knot close to needle with two ends of yarn.

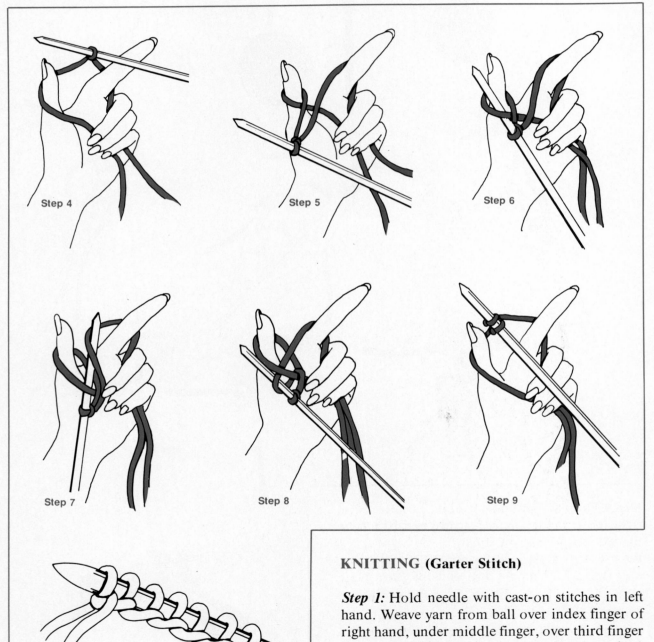

Step 4

Step 5

Step 6

Step 7

Step 8

Step 9

KNITTING (Garter Stitch)

Step 1: Hold needle with cast-on stitches in left hand. Weave yarn from ball over index finger of right hand, under middle finger, over third finger and under little finger. Always keep yarn at *back* of work.

Step 2: Insert right needle from left to right into front of first stitch on left needle until point of right needle is in back of left needle.

Step 3: Bring yarn under and over right needle.

Step 4: Bring point of right needle down and under left needle to front, thus drawing yarn through stitch on left needle.

Step 5: Slip original stitch from left needle: one knit stitch on right needle.

Repeat steps 2 through 5 until all stitches are on right needle — one row knitted.

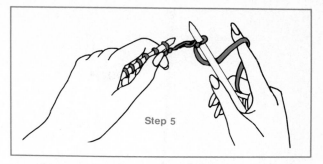

Step 5

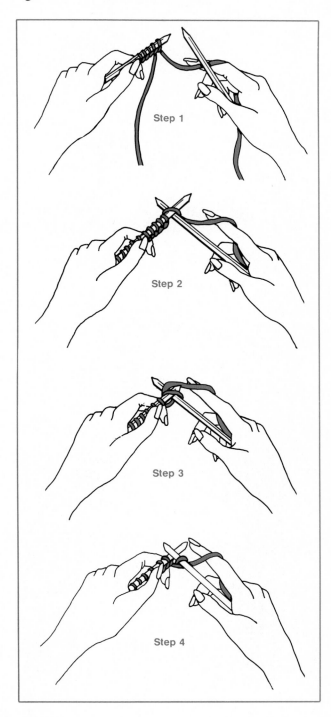

Step 1

Step 2

Step 3

Step 4

Step 6: Turn work around; place needle with stitches in left hand.

The stitches should not be too tight or too loose. Check to see if they slide easily on the needle.

Step 7: Examine the first stitch on left needle. This has a large loop hanging right below the needle. Do *not* knit in the large loop. It is *not* a dropped stitch. Knit only the stitches that are over the needle. Pull the large loop out of the way. Do not pull the loose yarn over the needle to the back of the work; this will make an extra stitch. Hold the large loop down and with the yarn at *back* of work, knit the first stitch. Continue to knit row after row of stitches to desired length. Concentrate on how each stitch is formed. This is the *front* or right side of a Knit stitch. This is the *back* or wrong side of a Knit stitch.

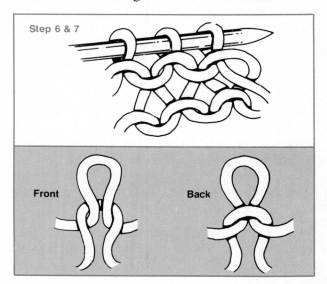

Step 6 & 7

Front   Back

Count the stitches to be sure there are the same number as the original stitches cast on. If there are less stitches, you have worked two or more stitches together or you have dropped stitches. If there are more, you have either worked the same stitch more than once or have knitted the strand between two stitches.

Garter Stitch

When several consecutive rows of stitches are knitted, the work is called "Garter Stitch" and both sides of the work are alike. Two rows form one ridge.

PURLING (Stockinette and Reverse Stockinette Stitch)

Step 1: Hold needles same as for knitting but always keep yarn at *front* of work.

Step 2: Insert right needle from right to left into front of first stitch on left needle until point of right needle is in front of left needle.

Step 3: Pass yarn from front to back over and around right needle and back to front.

Step 4: Bring point of right needle from front to back through first stitch; draw yarn through stitch on left needle. With right needle in back of left needle, slip stitch from left needle: — one purled stitch on right needle.

Repeat steps 2 through 4 until all stitches are on right needle. Purl several rows more; check to see how each stitch is formed.

Work a stockinette stitch sample as follows: Cast on 20 stitches. This will be counted as the first row or a Knit row. Purl 1 row, Knit 1 row. Continue to alternate 1 purl row and 1 knit row for 4 inches. The right side of Stockinette Stitch is the knit (smooth) side. The wrong side is the purl (ridged) side. When the purl side is used for the right side, this is called Reverse Stockinette Stitch.

To count rows: It is easier to count on the purl (wrong) side. *Every* row worked, knit or purl,

will form a ridge on the wrong side. Beginning at the last row worked, count down; include the cast on row as the last row.

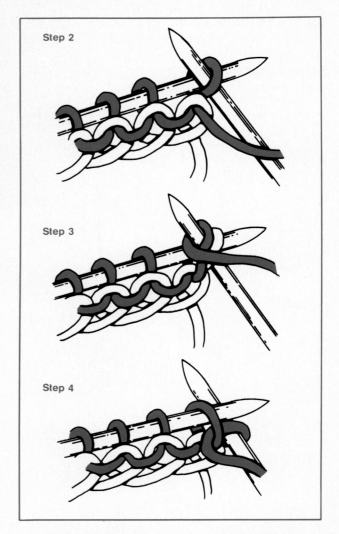

Step 2

Step 3

Step 4

Knit Side (right side)

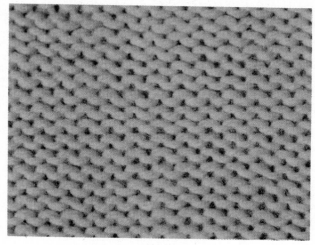

Purl Side (wrong side)

BINDING OFF

Step 1: Knit the first 2 stitches. (Or, if you should be purling, purl the first 2 stitches.)

Step 2: Insert point of left needle from left to right in front loop of first stitch on right needle.

Step 3: Lift the first stitch over the second stitch and over the point of right needle: one stitch bound off.

Step 4: Work (knit or purl) 1 stitch from left to right needle: 2 stitches on right needle. Repeat steps 2 through 4 until one loop remains on right needle. Break yarn, leaving an end only a few inches long. Draw end of yarn through loop on needle. Drop loop from needle.

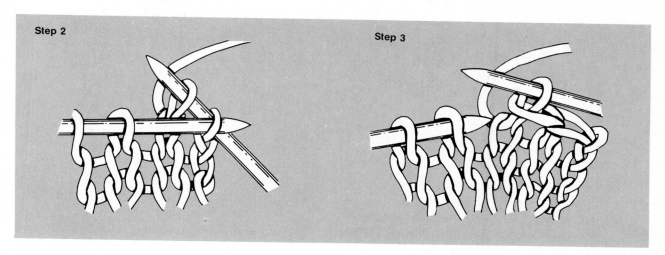

Step 2

Step 3

JOINING A NEW STRAND OF YARN

Join a new strand of yarn at beginning or end of row by making a slip knot with new strand around the previous strand. Draw slip knot close to edge of work. Weave in ends later along edge of work.

When joining is necessary in mid-row or mid-round, leave a 4-inch end on last strand. Leaving a 4-inch end on new strand, resume work with new strand. After several rows have been worked with new strand, weave in the ends on wrong side in opposite diagonal directions.

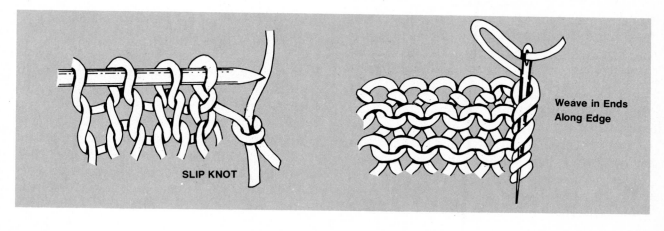

SLIP KNOT

Weave in Ends Along Edge

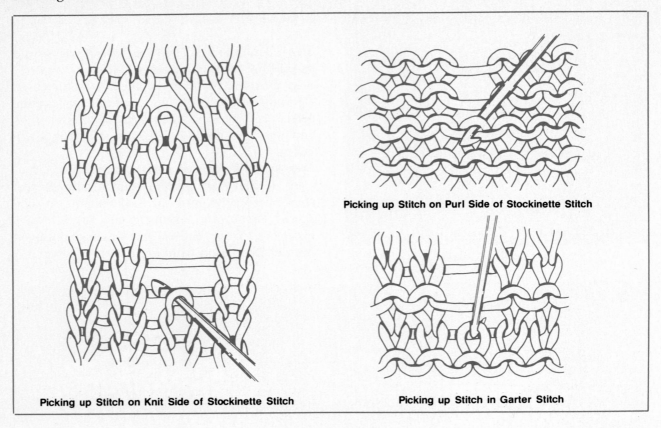

Picking up Stitch on Purl Side of Stockinette Stitch

Picking up Stitch on Knit Side of Stockinette Stitch

Picking up Stitch in Garter Stitch

PICKING UP DROPPED STITCHES

If a dropped stitch ravels down several rows, pick it up with a crochet hook as follows: on knit side of Stockinette Stitch, insert crochet hook through loop of dropped stitch from front to back of work.

Be sure stitch is not twisted. * Draw horizontal thread of row above through loop on hook. Repeat from * to last row. Place loop on knitting needle.

On purl side of Stockinette Stitch,* insert crochet hook through loop of dropped stitch from back to front; draw horizontal strand of the row below through loop on hook. Remove hook. Repeat from * to last row. Place loop on knitting needle.

To pick up a dropped stitch in Garter Stitch, * insert hook through loop of dropped stitch from back to front as illustrated on purl side of Stockinette Stitch. Draw horizontal strand of row below through loop on hook. (Garter Stitch illustration shows yarn drawn through loop.) Turn hook up; draw horizontal strand of the row above through loop as illustrated on knit side of

Stockinette Stitch. Remove hook. Repeat from * to last row. Place loop on knitting needle.

You may have worked several rows before noticing that a stitch has been dropped. If this happens and is not discovered immediately, there will not be enough yarn between the stitches to pick up the dropped stitch without making the work look very tight. This will cause the picked up stitch to show as a mistake at this point. The only way to correct this dropped stitch is to rip back. A dropped stitch cannot be picked up at the beginning or end of a row.

RIPPING KNITTING

Remove needle from work. Rip (draw strand to undo stitches) down to the row where the mistake appears. Rip next row 1 stitch at a time. With either side facing you, begin at the end where yarn is hanging. Insert a smaller size needle from *back* to *front* into the loop of the stitch just below the first stitch; carefully pull the yarn free from this stitch. Repeat in each stitch across the row until all stitches are on the smaller needle. This will prevent any stitches from being twisted. Work stitches off with original size needle.

MAKING FRINGE

Cut a piece of cardboard the same width as desired for the fringe length. Wrap yarn loosely around cardboard; cut at one end. Use the number of strands in instructions or as desired. Fold strands in half. Insert crochet hook from wrong side into stitch or row to be fringed. Draw folded loop through stitch or row. Draw cut ends (beginning and end of yarn strands) through loop and pull to tighten. Knot will be on right side.

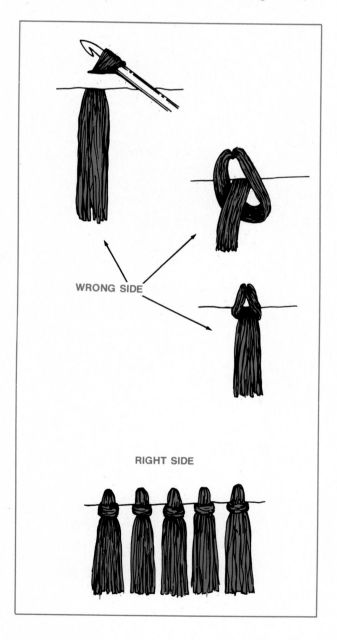

MAKING TASSELS

Around a piece of cardboard cut to specified measurements, wrap yarn the number of times required in the instructions. Draw a piece of the same yarn under the loops at the top of the cardboard and tie the strands together. Cut the loops at the bottom of the cardboard. Cut a small piece of the same yarn. Wrap it tightly several times around the strands about one inch from the fold. Tie the ends together and draw them to the middle of the tassel.

PROJECT — FRINGED SCARF (See page 67 for a fringed scarf that you can make now)

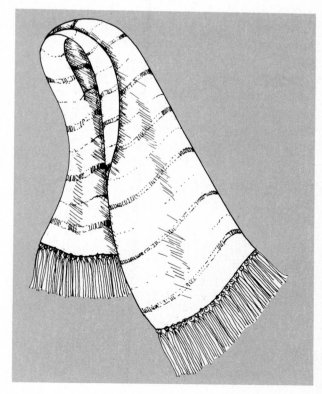

Section II

GAUGE

(What It Means — Why It Is So Important — How To Check It)

Every set of knitting instructions calls for a specific gauge. The stitch gauge is the number of stitches which equals 1 inch; the row gauge is the number of rows which equals 1 inch. This is determined by the weight of the yarn, the size of needles used and the way you control the yarn (called the tension).

The size of a garment is based on mathematical calculations according to the gauge given. You must always check your gauge before beginning your work. To do this, you knit a sample piece using the yarn and needles recommended.

To Make a Sample Piece: Cast on the number of stitches to measure 4 inches. Multiply the stitch gauge by 4, this will give you the number of stitches to cast on. Work 4 inches according to the row gauge given. Bind off.

To Measure Stitch Gauge: Place sample right side up on a flat surface. Do not stretch; pin flat if necessary. Place tape measure in a straight line across stitches, as shown. Place three pins (at beginning of tape, at 1-inch and at 2-inch marking), even if each pin does not come between 2 stitches. Remove tape. Unpin. Holding work, count stitches between two pins; make note. Count stitches between first and last pin. This gives the number of stitches which equals 2 inches; it may be an uneven number of stitches. Do not disregard the one-half stitch per inch.

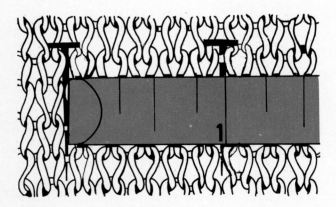

Gauge shows 5 stitches = 1 inch

Gauge in the illustration shows 5 stitches = 1 inch, 10 stitches = 2 inches. If there are fewer stitches to an inch than the gauge given, the work is too loose and a smaller size needle should be tried. If there are more stitches to an inch, the work is too tight and a larger size needle should be tried. The size of needles used is *not* important. The correct gauge is *very* important. *Never* try to change your gauge by working tighter or looser.

To Measure Row Gauge: Place sample wrong side up. Place tape measure as shown. Place three pins (at beginning of tape, at 1-inch and 2-inch marking). Count rows; make note. Gauge in the illustration shows 6 rows = 1 inch.

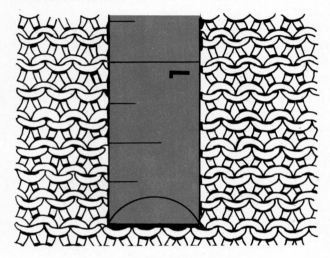

Gauge shows 6 rows = 1 inch

INCREASING (One Stitch on Knit Side of Work)

Method 1: Knit in *front* loop of stitch; *do not* drop from left needle. Knit in *back* loop of same stitch; drop stitch from left needle.

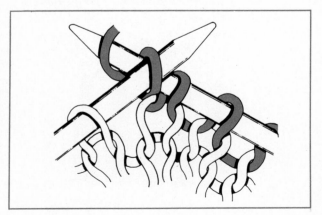

You will notice a purl-like stitch below your needle. This is correct , it is your increased stitch. This is the method most often used.

A stitch may also be increased on purl side by purling in front. Take the yarn between needles to back and knit in the back of the same stitch.

Method 2: Knit to point of increase. Insert left needle from front to back under the horizontal strand between the last stitch worked (on the

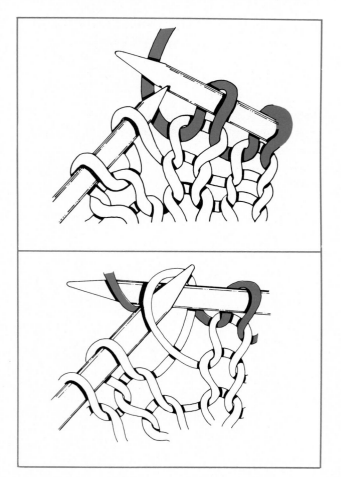

right needle) and next stitch to be worked (on the left needle). Knit through back loop of this strand, thus twisting the stitch and tightening. This method gives an increase less noticeable than Method 1.

DECREASING (One Stitch on Knit Side of Work)

Method 1: On the knit side of work, knit 2 stitches together through the front of the stitches (decrease will slant to the right). Knit 2 stitches together through the back of the stitches (decrease will slant to the left).

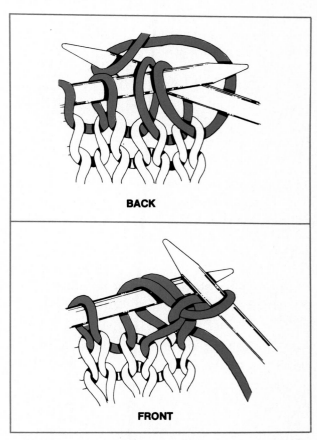

BACK

FRONT

Method 1

Method 2: Insert right needle in next stitch as to knit. Slip stitch from left to right needle without working the stitch; knit next stitch.

Pass the slipped stitch over the knitted stitch as in binding off. Directions for decreasing in this manner usually read: Slip 1, knit 1, pass slip stitch over knit stitch; or, slip 1, knit 1, psso; or, SKP. This decrease slants to the left.

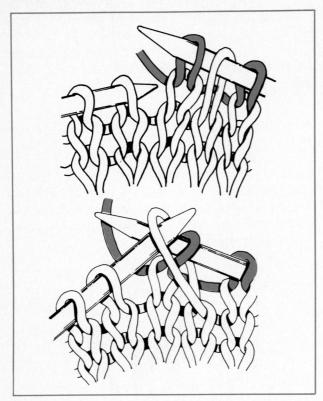

Method 2

Method 3: On the purl side of work, insert needle through 2 stitches as to purl; purl the 2 stitches together.

CASTING ON FOR RIBBING

This is accomplished by knitting the stitches onto the needle. This will give an elastic edge with no right or wrong side.

Make a slip knot, place on left needle (first cast-on stitch). Insert right needle in front loop of this

stitch; knit the stitch. Do *not* drop the stitch from left needle. Draw stitch out as shown. Insert point of left needle from left to right into back loop on right needle (right needle will be on top of left needle). Remove right needle: there are 2 stitches on left needle.

Insert right needle *between* the 2 stitches, knit a stitch. Place on left needle as before. Always inserting right needle *between* the last two stitches, cast on required number of stitches.

WORKING RIBBING

Ribbing is a combination of knit and purl stitches worked in the same row. The knit stitches are worked over the knit stitches; the purl stitches over the purl stitches. This forms vertical lines of knit and purl stitches.

Knit 1, Purl 1 Ribbing A: Worked on an even number of stitches.

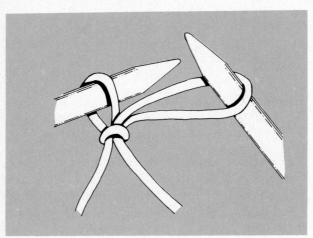

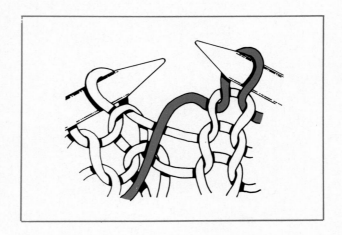

Row 1: Knit 1 stitch; bring yarn between needles to front of work; purl 1 stitch; take yarn between needles to back; knit 1 stitch; bring yarn to front again; purl 1 stitch. Continue to knit 1 stitch and purl 1 stitch alternately to the end of row. Turn work. Repeat Row 1 for desired length. Both sides of work are alike. To bind off in ribbing, knit the knit stitches and purl the purl stitches.

Knit 1, Purl 1 Ribbing B: Worked on an uneven number of stitches.
Row 1: Work same as Row 1 of A, but begin and end the row with knit 1 stitch.
Row 2: Beginning and ending row with purl 1 stitch, work same as in Row 1 of A.
Alternate these 2 rows for desired length. Bind off same as in A.

Knit 2, Purl 2 Ribbing C: Worked on a number of stitches divisible by four (8, 12, 16, 20, etc).
Row 1: Knit 2 stitches, purl 2 stitches; continue to knit 2 stitches and purl 2 stitches alternately to end of row. Turn work. Repeat Row 1 for desired length. Bind off as in A.

Knit 2, Purl 2 Ribbing D: Worked on a number of stitches which is divisible by 4, plus two extra stitches (10-14-18-22, etc).
Row 1: Work same as Row 1 of C but begin and end row with knit 2 stitches.
Row 2: Beginning and ending row with purl 2 stitches, work same as Row 1.
Alternate these 2 rows for desired length. Bind off same as in A.

Ribbing may be worked in any combination of knit and purl stitches, provided the correct multiple of stitches are on the needle.

K 2, P 2 Ribbing

WORKING SEED OR MOSS STITCH

Seed or moss stitch can be worked on an uneven or even number of stitches.

Method 1: Worked on an uneven number of stitches.
Row 1: Knit 1 stitch, purl 1 stitch; continue to knit 1 stitch and purl 1 stitch alternately to end of row. The last stitch will be a knit stitch. Repeat Row 1, thus knitting each stitch which appears as a purl stitch and purling each stitch which appears as a knit stitch.

Method 2: Worked on an even number of stitches.
Row 1: Knit 1 stitch, purl 1 stitch; continue to knit 1 stitch and purl 1 stitch alternately to end of

K 1, P 1 Ribbing

Seed or Moss Stitch

row. The last stitch will be a purl stitch.

Row 2: Purl 1 stitch, knit 1 stitch; continue to purl 1 stitch and knit 1 stitch alternately to end of row. The last stitch will be a knit stitch. Repeat rows 1 and 2, thus knitting each stitch which appears as a purl stitch and purling each stitch which appears as a knit stitch.

MEASURING WORK

Always lay article to be measured on a flat surface. Measure at center of work with a ruler or heavy tape measure.

MEASURING ARMHOLE

Mark the last row before bound-off stitches for armhole by running a colored thread for 3 inches across this row. Lay work on a flat surface. Measure up in a straight line from colored thread.

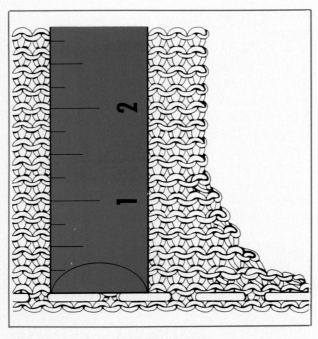

Measuring Armhole

BLOCKING TO MEASUREMENTS

Careful blocking often makes the difference between a beautiful professional knit garment and an amateurish or nonprofessionally blocked garment. *The most important elements are time and patience. Never hurry!* There are three acceptable

methods for blocking. Use the one which you prefer.

Method 1: Blocking Pieces Separately
Take as many actual measurements as possible. With the wrong side up, lay the piece flat on a padded pressing surface (old table pads, table or floor). Using rustproof T pins, pin edges about every 1/4 inch to padded surface, stretching to desired measurements. Lay wet cloth (sheeting or terry cloth wrung out in cold water) over the piece. Using a moderately hot iron, pat all over the cloth, allowing steam to go through cloth. (You may use a steam iron.) *Do not* run iron back and forth over cloth as in ordinary pressing. *Do not* allow weight of iron to rest anywhere on the piece. Leave piece pinned until thoroughly dry.

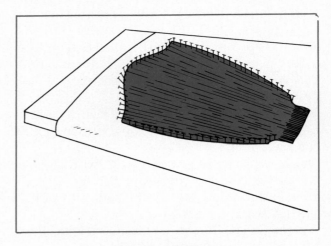

Blocking separately

It is advisable to fold large symmetrical pieces in half. Block to within 1 inch of fold; let dry. Remove pins and steam out fold. Also when two pieces are alike (fronts or sleeves), pin them together for blocking to keep the two pieces the same size. *Do not* block ribbed borders or raised pattern stitches. After seaming pieces together, steam seams.

Method 2: Blocking After Finishing
In cold water, immerse two terry cloth towels large enough to cover the garment. Wring towels as dry as possible. Lay one moist towel on blocking board or floor space; place garment on top. Shape garment to desired measurements. If stretching is necessary, pin with *rustproof* push pins. Cover garment with the other moist towel. Allow to dry thoroughly. You may steam slightly

through the top terry cloth towel to hasten drying, but *do not* press.

Method 3: To Block Acrylics After Finishing
Carefully wet entire garment. Take care to keep hands under garment so that it will not hang and stretch. Place wet garment flat on a large dry towel. Roll up towel; squeeze out extra moisture. Lay another large dry towel on a flat surface. Place garment carefully on towel; pat into desired shape and correct measurements. Leave until dry.

SEAMING

Method 1: Backstitch
Pin right sides of pieces together; keep edges even, match rows, and adjust width of seam for proper fit of garment. Backstitch seam, being careful not to draw stitches too tightly. Fasten end securely. The seam should be as elastic as the knitting.

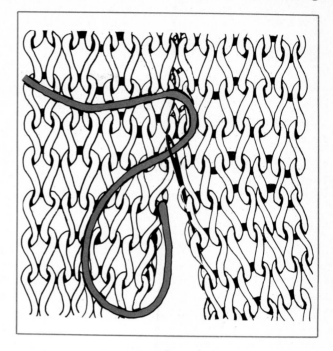

Weaving seams together

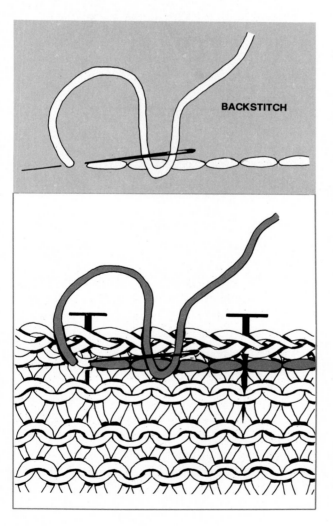

BACKSTITCH

Method 2: Weaving Seams
It is necessary to have two pieces with the same number of rows. Hold edges together with right sides toward you. Bring needle up through first stitch on left edge. Insert needle down through center of first stitch on right edge, pass under 2 rows; draw yarn through to right side of work. Insert needle in center of stitch on corresponding row on left side. Pass under two rows, draw yarn through as before. Continue to work from side to side, matching rows. Seam must be flat and as elastic as knitted pieces.

PROJECT — SLEEVELESS SLIP-ON
(See page 75 for a sleeveless slip-on you can make now)

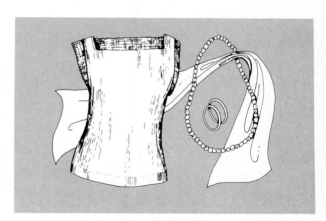

Section III

WORKING A CABLE

In addition to a pair of single-pointed needles, a double-pointed needle or a cable needle is required.

Cast on 12 stitches.

Row 1: Knit 2 stitches, purl 8 stitches, knit 2 stitches. This is wrong side of work.
Row 2: Purl 2 stitches, knit 8 stitches, purl 2 stitches.
Row 3: Knit 2 stitches, purl 8 stitches, knit 2 stitches.
Row 4: Purl 2 stitches, knit 8 stitches, purl 2 stitches.

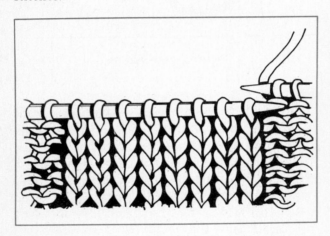

Row 5: Knit 2 stitches, purl 8 stitches, knit 2 stitches.
Row 6: Purl 2 stitches, slip next 4 stitches onto a double-pointed or cable needle; hold this needle at *back* of work.
Knit the next 4 stitches from left needle; knit the 4 stitches held on the double-pointed needle.

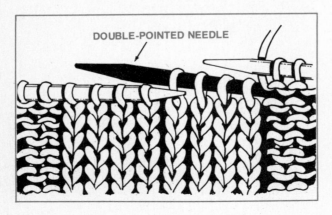

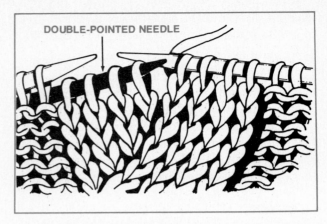

Take care to knit these stitches in the same order that they were slipped onto the double-pointed needle. A cable twist is made. Purl 2 stitches. Repeat these 6 rows.

Even Cable Twists

There are many types of cables. These vary according to the number of stitches in the cable, the number of rows between the cable twists and the manner in which the cable twist is worked. We shall describe the type having an even number of rows between cable twists.

An Even Cable Twist

Cast on 24 stitches.
Row 1 (right side): Purl 4 stitches, knit 6 stitches, purl 4 stitches, knit 6 stitches, purl 4 stitches. This is the right side of work.
Row 2: Knit 4 stitches, purl 6 stitches, knit 4 stitches, purl 6 stitches, knit 4 stitches.
Row 3: Work same as Row 1.
Row 4: Work same as Row 2.

Row 5: Purl 4 stitches, slip the next 3 stitches from left needle to a double-pointed needle; hold this needle at *back* of work. Knit the next 3 stitches from left needle. Knit the 3 stitches from double-pointed needle; take care to knit the stitches in the order they were slipped. You have twisted a cable: purl 4 stitches, twist a cable, purl 4 stitches.

Row 6: Work same as Row 2.
Row 7: Work same as Row 1.
Row 8: Work same as Row 2.
Row 9: Work same as Row 1.
Row 10: Work same as Row 2.
Repeat these ten rows for pattern. Cable is twisted every ten rows.

MAKING POMPONS

Step 1: Cut two cardboard circles 1¹/₂ inches in diameter for small pompon; 2 inches for medium; 3 inches for large. Cut hole in middle of the circles. Cut strand of yarn 6 yards long.

Step 2: Thread the cut ends into a blunt tapestry needle. Place circles together. Draw the needle through center, over the circles and through the loop formed by the fold in the yarn. Continue to wrap yarn over the circles and through the hole until yarn fills the center and the circles are completely covered.

Step 3: With sharp scissors, cut between the circles at the outside edge.

Step 4: Between the circles, wind two strands of yarn about 8 inches long. Tie securely.

Step 5: Remove circles. Attach pompons with yarn used for tying. Trim pompon evenly.

Note: If this length is not long enough to cover the circle, use a second length. If the original length is cut too long, it will fray.

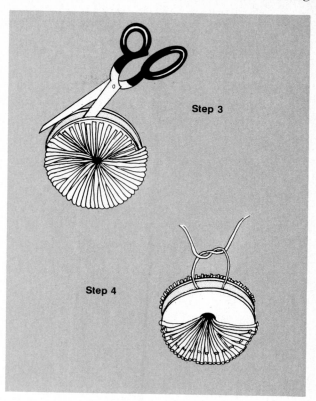

Step 3

Step 4

PROJECT — CABLED CAP (See page 76 for cabled cap that you can make now)

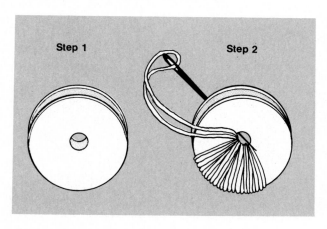

Step 1   Step 2

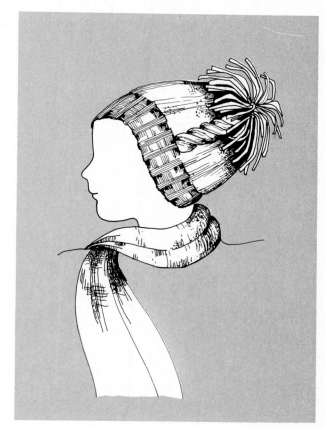

Section IV

WORKING YARN OVERS

When making a yarn over between knit stitches, bring yarn under right needle from back to front, then take yarn over right needle to back; knit next stitch.

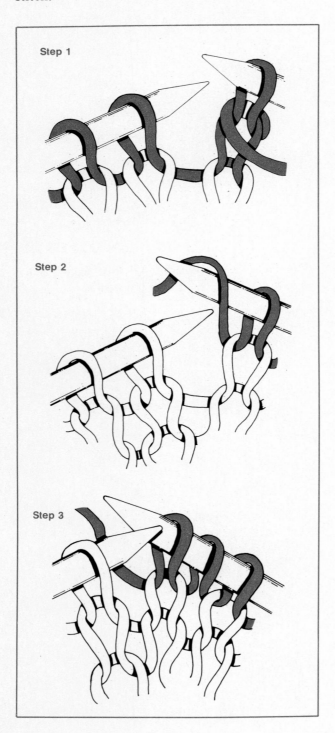

Step 1

Step 2

Step 3

When making a yarn over *before* a purl stitch, have yarn at *front* of work. Take yarn over right needle to back, then under right needle to front; purl next stitch.

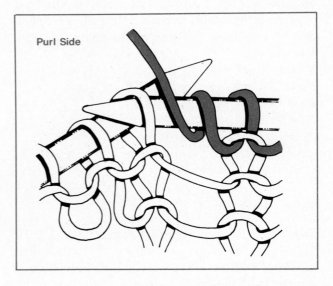

Purl Side

When making a yarn over between a purl stitch and a knit stitch, take yarn over right needle to back; knit next stitch.

The yarn over is used for lacy patterns, but it is also a method of increasing a stitch. This method forms a hole in the work.

PICKING UP STITCHES ON EDGES

Method 1: Use a needle one or two sizes smaller than needle used for body. With right side of work toward you, insert needle into edge of work; take yarn under and over needle. Bring

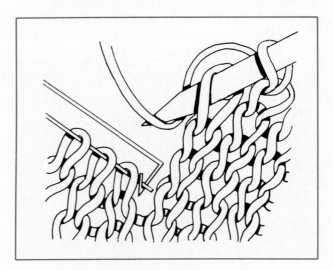

loop on needle through to right side of work; this makes a picked up stitch. When picking up stitches on bound-off or cast-on edge, pick up 1 stitch in each stitch, going under 2 loops when possible.

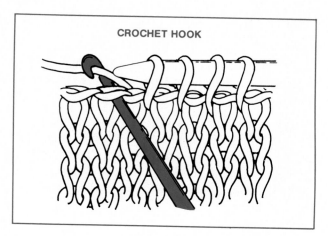

CROCHET HOOK

Method 2: Use a crochet hook. Draw new strand of yarn through edge. Place loop on needle. Continue to draw loop through each stitch or row until the desired number of stitches are picked up.

SETTING IN SLEEVES

Method 1: First Seam Shoulder, Sides and Sleeves

With wrong side of garment showing, divide armhole into four equal parts; mark with pins.

With right side of sleeve showing, divide the top of the sleeve into four equal parts; mark with pins.

Place the right side of garment and the right side of sleeve together. This can be accomplished by turning the garment wrong side out and the sleeve right side out. Pin sleeve to the armhole, matching the four pins.

Between the four sections, add additional pins to secure the two pieces. Join sleeve to sweater armhole using backstitch. Seam and ease in any fullness.

Method 2: Sew Shoulder Seams
With the right side of sleeve and right side of armhole together, pin the top center bound-off stitches of sleeve to the garment shoulder seam. First bound-off stitches of sleeve should match the bound-off stitches of armhole. Ease the re-

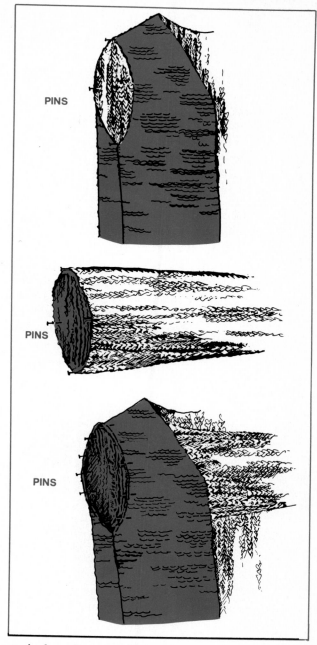

PINS

PINS

PINS

mainder of cap to fit armhole. Backstitch sleeve to armhole.

PROJECT — BABY CARDIGAN (See page 75 for a baby cardigan you can knit now)

ADVANCED KNITTING

Section V_____

WORKING ON CIRCULAR NEEDLES

When To Use Circular Needles:

If there are more stitches to be worked than will fit easily on a single-pointed needle, cast on stitches on circular needle. *Do not* join. Work back and forth the same as with two needles.

If tubular piece with no seams is desired, stitches are cast on the same as for single-pointed needle. Hold needle with end where first stitch was cast on in left hand, the end with ball attached in right hand. Look carefully to *be sure stitches are not twisted* on needle. All loops must be flat on top of needle with lower part of stitches at bottom of needle. Place a marker on the needle after last

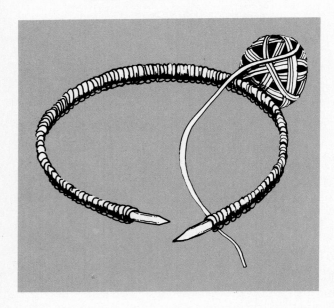

cast-on stitch (see page 13). With yarn at back, knit first stitch: this will join work. Knit every stitch on needle. This is called one round. Now slip marker which indicates end of a round. Continue to knit around and around slipping marker at end of every round. *This forms Stockinette Stitch* with the knit side outside, the purl side inside.

For a purl round bring yarn between points of needle and purl all stitches. *For Garter Stitch,* alternate a knit round and a purl round.

CAUTION: After first round has been worked, check again for twisted stitches. Twisted work cannot be corrected.

Alternate Method of Beginning Circular Knits: A second method is to work back and forth for a few rows or through a border pattern. Then join into a circle and knit around and around. This will give a piece of knitting that is wide enough to show that the material is not twisted. The edges of these first rows are later woven together to form a flat seam.

Length of Circular Needle To Be Used:

The length used must never be longer than the measured length of the stitches when worked. Example: Gauge is 5 stitches equal 1 inch; 100 stitches are cast on. We divide 100 by 5; work should measure 20 inches. It is necessary to use a 16-inch needle rather than a 24-inch needle because the longer length needle will stretch the stitches. It is often necessary to use more than one length needle for a single garment.

HEMMING IN STOCKINETTE STITCH

Method 1: With Turning Ridge on Right Side With the same size needle used for body of work, cast on stitches. Change to needle one size smaller. Work in Stockinette Stitch for the required depth of hem; end with a knit row. Knit next row on wrong side. This row is the turning ridge. Change back to original needles and begin with a knit row; for a pattern, begin with a right side row. Continue in Stockinette Stitch or Pattern.

Turning Ridge On Right Side

Method 2: With Turning Ridge on Wrong Side
With the same size needle used for body of work, cast on stitches. Change to needles one size smaller. Work in Stockinette Stitch to desired depth; end with a purl row. Purl next row on the right side. This row is the turning ridge. Change back to original needles; begin with a row for the wrong side. Continue in Stockinette Stitch or Pattern.

Method 3: With Picot Edge For Turning Ridge
Work on an even number of stitches. With the same size needles used for body of work, cast on stitches. Work in Stockinette Stitch to required depth; end with a knit row. Next row: K 1, * K 2 tog, yo; rep from *, end with K 1. This row is the turning ridge. Begin with a knit row. Continue in Stockinette Stitch or Pattern.

Picot Edge for Turning Ridge

Method 4: Without Turning Ridge
With the same size needles used for body of work, cast on stitches. Work in Stockinette Stitch for twice the depth desired; end with a purl row. Place a marker at the end of last row (see page 13). Continue in Stockinette Stitch or Pattern.

Without Turning Ridge

SEWING HEMS

Turn at the turning ridge or desired depth without ridge. Using yarn, over cast by picking up a single strand of the cast on stitch and one thread of every second body stitch. Be careful not to draw work or let stitches show on right side.

KNITTING HEMS TOGETHER

Any hem may be joined in this way. Work as given on page 32 until there are the same number of rows above the turning ridge as below the turning ridge, or, twice the depth of hem desired. End with a row worked from wrong side. Turn hem as to sew hem. Holding work in left hand, insert right needle into first stitch and into the corresponding cast-on stitch; knit these two stitches together. Continue until all cast-on stitches are joined to body stitches. Beginning work with a wrong side row, continue in Stockinette Stitch or Pattern. If circular needles have been used, begin work with right side row.

PROJECT — TURTLENECK SLIP-ON (See page 67 for a turtleneck slip-on that you can make now)

Section VI

MULTIPLE OF A PATTERN STITCH

"Multiple" refers to the number of stitches which is necessary for one pattern. The number of stitches on the needle should be evenly divisible by the number of stitches in the multiple. For example: if the multiple of a pattern is 4, the number of stitches to be worked could total 16, 24, 48, 116, etc. If the multiple of pattern is 4 plus two extra stitches, the number of stitches to be worked could total 18, 26, 50, 118, etc.

CASTING ON AT END OF ROW

Method No. 1: Knitting Stitches On
Insert right needle in first stitch on left needle. Knit 1 stitch. Do not drop stitch from left needle. Insert left needle from right to left into loop on right needle. Drop loop from right needle: 1 stitch cast on. Repeat until desired number of stitches are cast on.

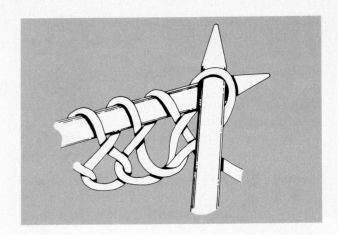

On next row, work the cast on stitches. Then work the next stitch *through* the back loop: this will tighten the stitch and prevent a hole. Work remaining stitches in the normal way.

Method 2: Using a Crochet Hook
Use a crochet hook large enough to work loosely. Insert crochet hook in the last stitch on right needle two rows below; draw up a loop. Make a loose chain of the number of stitches to be cast on. Remove the crochet hook; insert the free needle in the loop. Count this as first stitch. Pick up and knit or purl a loop in each remaining chain. Bring needle up to the last stitch of complete row. Continue to work across the stitches on left needle.

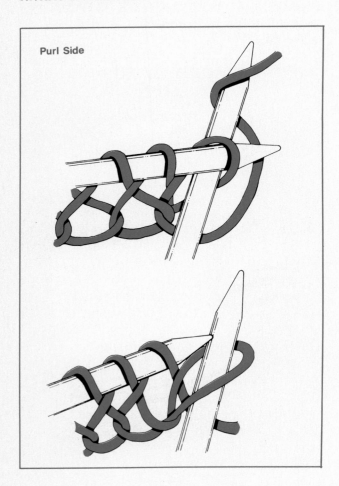

Purl Side

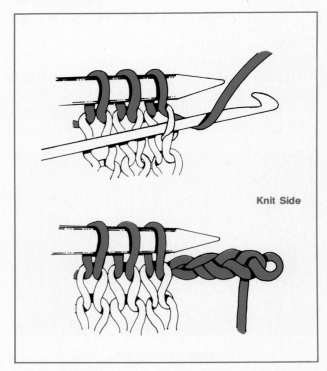

Knit Side

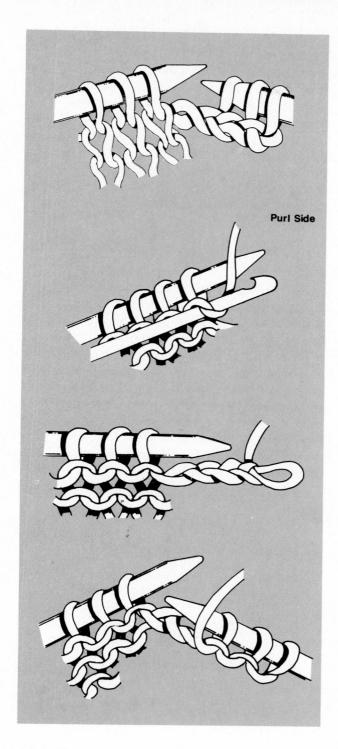

Purl Side

WORKING BUTTONHOLES

Knitted Horizontal Buttonhole in Two Rows

Instructions read: K 2 sts, bind off 3 sts, K 4 sts. Knit 2 stitches. It is necessary to knit 2 more stitches in order to bind off 1 stitch; * K 1 st, bind off 1 st; repeat from * once (3 stitches bound

off); 1 stitch is left at end of right needle; knit 3 more stitches: 4 stitches at end of buttonhole.

On next row, work to space left by bound-off stitches; turn work (yarn will hang from back of needle in left hand). Using Method 1 for casting on at end of row, page 34, cast on 3 stitches on needle in left hand. Turn work; work to end of row.

This buttonhole is the one most often used and should be hand finished.

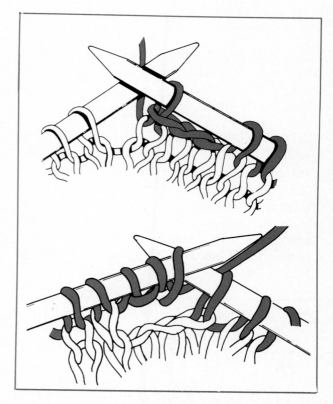

Knitted Horizontal Buttonhole In One Row:
Work the number of stitches designated. Insert right needle in next stitch as if to purl, slip stitch to right needle; bring yarn between needles and drop; slip the next stitch from left needle to right needle, * pass first slip stitch on right needle over second stitch, slip next stitch from left needle to right needle. Repeat from * until desired number of stitches are bound off. Slip the last stitch on the right needle back to left needle. Turn work. Bring dropped yarn between needles to *front*. Purling, cast on 1 stitch more than was bound off. Turn work. Slip first stitch from left needle to right needle. Slip extra cast-on stitch over this stitch; draw yarn tight. Slip last stitch on right

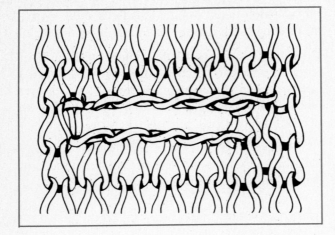

needle back to left needle. Work to end. It is not necessary to finish this buttonhole.

FINISHING BUTTONHOLES

Use the same yarn as was used in knitting; separate the plys if too heavy. Then, using the common stitch known as the "Buttonhole Stitch," work on top and bottom of buttonhole. To prevent stretching, it is wise to sew 1 stitch at each end of buttonhole over the 2 rows in which buttonhole was made. This is done in any machine-made buttonhole in your own clothing. Check to see.

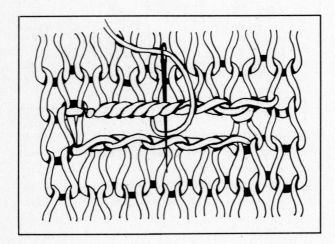

SETTING IN HORIZONTAL POCKETS

Pocket Lining: Cast on number of stitches desired for pocket width. Work Stockinette Stitch to desired depth. End with a knit row. Place stitches on a stitch holder. Work piece (in which pocket is desired) to proper depth before pocket

opening; end on wrong side. On next row, work to place where pocket opening is desired; bind off same number of stitches as on pocket lining. Or, if a border is to be worked on pocket opening later, slip the same number of stitches as on pocket lining to a stitch holder; then work pattern to end of row. On next row, work to pocket opening; place stitches of lining on left-hand needle, then work pattern across stitches of lining and remaining stitches of row. When this piece of garment is complete, sew free edges of lining in place.

WORKING DUPLICATE STITCH

Follow drawings for stitch placement. Thread tapestry needle with strand of contrasting colored yarn. Fasten yarn on wrong side of work. * From wrong side, insert needle into center of the lower point of a stitch; draw yarn through to right side of work. Insert needle at top right hand side of same stitch; pass under the two strands of yarn of stitch above. Draw yarn through at top left hand side of same stitch. Insert needle down into the center of same stitch from right side; draw yarn through to wrong side of work. Repeat from * until design is completed.

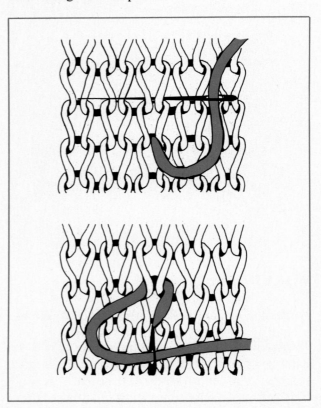

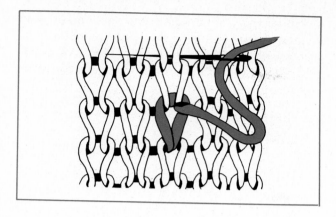

Duplicate stitch may be worked vertically or horizontally. Double duplicate stitch is worked in same way as duplicate stitch but over two stitches in adjoining rows.

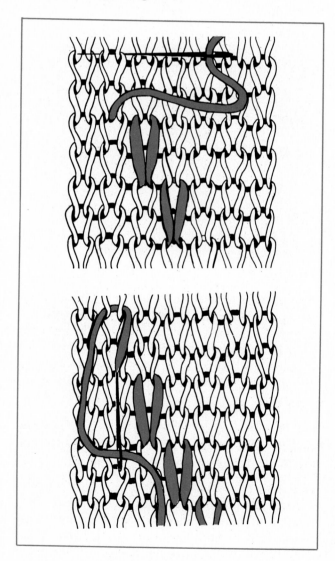

Double Duplicate Stitch

COLOR KNITTING FROM CHARTS

Always join yarns with a slip knot (see page 19). Each square on a chart represents 1 stitch and 1 row. Symbols or colors are used to show the specific color for each stitch. When changing colors, drop color just used to the back of work on knit rows; to the front of work on purl rows. Pick up new color from underneath the dropped color. This will twist yarns and prevent holes in work.

Read all knit (right side) rows from right to left; all purl (wrong side) rows from left to right. Begin to read the chart at lower right hand corner for Row 1 unless otherwise indicated; at left hand edge for Row 2.

Method 1: Knitting A Design Using Balls of Yarn (Stranding)
Colors not in use are carried across the back of the work. They should not be carried across more than 3 stitches in heavy yarn or 5 stitches in light yarn without dropping the color in use and picking it up again under color not in use. Tighten yarn enough to maintain gauge but leave loose enough so that work does not pucker. When work is completed, weave in ends on wrong side.

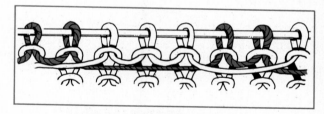

Stranding: Wrong Side of Work

Method 2: Knitting Design Using Bobbins
Colors are *not* carried across back of work. Each design is worked with a separate bobbin wound with correct color. Wind bobbins according to manufacturers instructions. Do not overcrowd bobbins. Join each color bobbin as needed and cut off, leaving an end to be woven in later when no longer needed. Enough yarn must be released from bobbin to handle yarn easily. Do not allow long lengths to hang from bobbins not in use: they will tangle. If this should occur, hold work up, allow to untangle and shorten lengths. When changing colors, be sure to twist yarns. When work is completed, weave in ends on wrong side.

Method 3: Fair Isle Knitting (Weaving)
Traditional "Fair Isle" designs rarely contain more than 2 different colors in a single row of knitting. However, all color knitting today is often called "Fair Isle" Knitting.

Fair Isle necessitates a special technique called weaving. This should be practiced before beginning a garment.

The color not used for a stitch may be carried on left hand as in "Continental" Knitting or Crochet. The yarn for the stitch is held in right hand. Change hands when changing yarn colors.

a. When weaving, the woven strand should alternate first "Above" then "Below" the next stitch. *Correct tension must be maintained.* This will prevent strand from being drawn too tight, causing work to pucker.

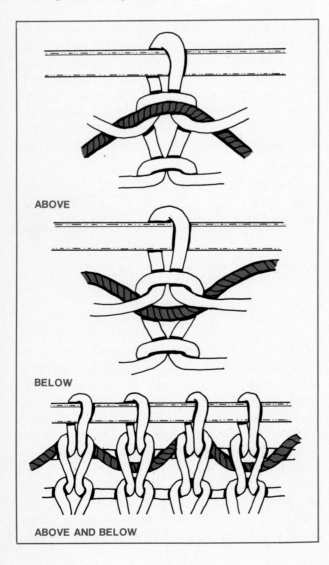

ABOVE

BELOW

ABOVE AND BELOW

b. Knitting a stitch with right hand and at same time weaving the left yarn "Above": The left hand is placed above the needle **(Fig. A),** while the right hand knits a stitch drawing only the right hand color through the stitch.

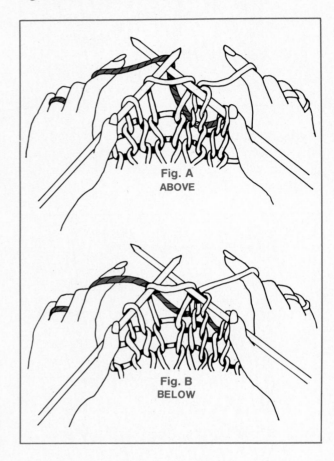

Fig. A
ABOVE

Fig. B
BELOW

c. Knitting a stitch with right hand and at same time weaving the left yarn "Below": The left hand yarn is held below the needle **(Fig. B),** while the right hand knits a stitch drawing only the right hand color through the stitch.

d. Purling a stitch with right hand and weaving the left yarn "Above": The purl stitch will be completed as shown by arrow in **Fig. C.**

e. Purling a stitch with right hand and weaving the left yarn "Below": The Purl stitch will be completed as shown by arrow in **Fig. D.**

To Finish Yarn Ends: Thread ends of yarn at ends of rows into a tapestry needle; run through ends of rows about 1¹/₂ inches. Fasten securely and cut. Thread ends of yarn within the body of the work into a tapestry needle. Weave in and out of the row on wrong side through matching color

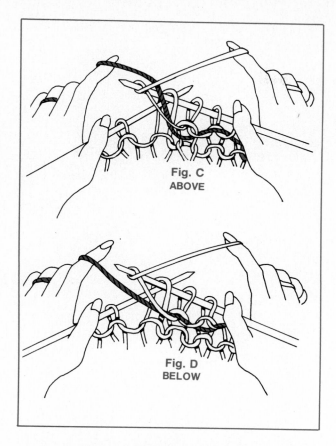

Fig. C
ABOVE

Fig. D
BELOW

stitches. Be careful that the yarn does not show on right side. Fasten securely and cut.

WEAVING TOP EDGES OF STOCKINETTE STITCH (Kitchener Stitch)

Stitches may be removed from needles before beginning to weave, or left on needles and removed as each stitch is woven to corresponding stitch.

It is necessary to have two pieces with the same number of stitches. Thread a blunt tapestry needle. Lay pieces to be joined close together, one

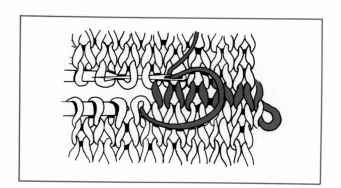

piece above the other. Inserting needle from *wrong* side, draw yarn through first stitch at right hand edge of *upper* piece. Insert needle from *right* side into first stitch on *lower* piece; bring up through next stitch on *lower* piece from *wrong* side; draw up yarn.

* Insert needle from *right* side into same stitch as before on *upper* piece; bring up through next stitch on upper piece from *wrong* side, draw up yarn. Insert needle from *right* side in same stitch as before on *lower* piece; bring up through next stitch; draw up yarn. Repeat from * until all stitches are joined. Fasten yarn securely. Be sure gauge of woven row is the same as knitted piece. Cut yarn.

WEAVING EDGES OF GARTER STITCH

Lay pieces to be joined close together, one piece above the other; upper piece with what appears to be purled side of last row facing you, lower piece with the knitted side of last row facing you. Inserting needle from *wrong* side, draw yarn through first stitch on *upper* piece; insert needle from *wrong* side into first stitch on *lower* piece; draw up yarn. Insert needle from *right* side into next stitch on *lower* piece; draw up yarn.

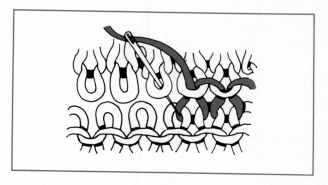

* Insert needle from *right* side into same stitch as before on *upper* piece; bring up through next stitch from *wrong* side, draw up yarn; insert needle from *wrong* side in same stitch as before on *lower* piece, draw up yarn; insert needle in next stitch from *right* side, draw yarn through. Repeat from * to end. Fasten off.

WEAVING RIBBING OF K 1, P 1

The two pieces to be woven must have the same number of stitches. It is necessary to have four

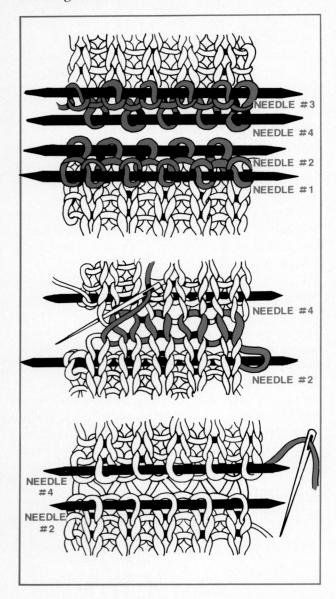

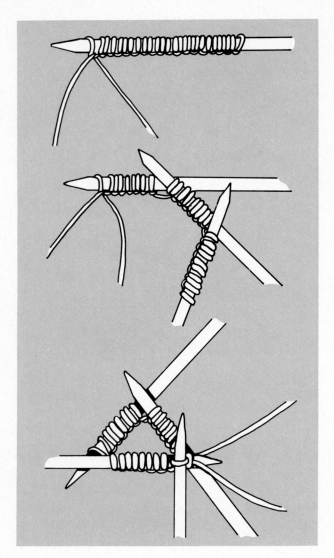

double-pointed needles the same size as used for the original work.

Slip all the knit stitches of one piece to needle No. 1. Turn work. Slip all remaining stitches to needle No. 2. Slip knit stitches of the other piece to needle No. 4. Turn work. Slip all remaining stitches to needle No. 3. Weave stitches of needles No. 1 and 3 together.

Turn work. Weave stitches of needles No. 2 and 4 together.

DOUBLE-POINTED NEEDLE WORK

Cast on all stitches on one needle if possible. Slip one third of the number of stitches to each of the two other needles, or cast on one third the number of stitches onto each of three needles.

Hold needles in left hand. Be sure stitches are not twisted as on circular needle, page 32. Place marker on needle after last cast on stitch to mark end of rounds. With free needle knit first cast on stitch to join.

Continue to work to end of first needle, then work several more stitches from second needle. Again with free needle, work stitches of second needle and several more stitches from third needle. Slip the end-of-round marker. Continue in this way to work around; always work several stitches from next needle to avoid loose thread.

PROJECT — SOCKS & MITTENS (See page 68 for socks and page 70 for mittens you can make now)

PROFESSIONAL KNITTING

Section VII _____

BODY MEASUREMENT CHARTS

Misses'

Misses' patterns are designed for a well-proportioned and developed figure.

Size	6	8	10	12	14	16	18	20
Bust	30½	31½	32½	34	36	38	40	42
Waist	23	24	25	26½	28	30	32	34
Hip	32½	33½	34½	36	38	40	42	44
Back Waist Length	15½	15¾	16	16¼	16½	16¾	17	17¼

Women's

Women's patterns are designed for the larger, more fully mature figure.

Size	38	40	42	44	46	48	50
Bust	42	44	46	48	50	52	54
Waist	35	37	39	41½	44	46½	49
Hip	44	46	48	50	52	54	56
Back Waist Length	17¼	17⅜	17½	17⅝	17¾	17⅞	18

Girls'

Girls' patterns are designed for the girl who has not yet begun to mature.

Size	7	8	10	12	14
Breast	26	27	28½	30	32
Waist	23	23½	24½	25½	26½
Hip	27	28	30	32	34
Back Waist Length Approx.	11½	12	12¾	13½	14¼
Height	50″	52″	56″	58″	61″

Children's

Size	1	2	3	4	5	6
Breast or Chest	20	21	22	23	24	25
Waist	19½	20	20½	21	21½	22
Back Waist Length Approx.	8¼	8½	9	9½	10	10½
Height	31″	34″	37″	40″	43″	46″
Finished Dress Length	17″	18″	19″	20″	22″	24″

Babies'

Babies' sizes are for infants who are not yet walking.

Age	Newborn (1-3 months)	6 months
Weight	7-13 lbs.	13-18 lbs.
Height	17″-24″	24″-26½″

Boys'

These size ranges are for growing boys and young men who have not yet reached full adult stature.

Size	7	8	10	12	14
Chest	26	27	28	30	32
Waist	23	24	25	26	27
Hip (Seat)	27	28	29½	31	32½
Neck	11¾	12	12½	13	13½
Height	48	50	54	58	61

Mens'

Men's patterns are sized for men of average build.

Size	34	36	38	40	42	44	46	48
Chest	34	36	38	40	42	44	46	48
Waist	28	30	32	34	36	39	42	44
Hip (Seat)	35	37	39	41	43	45	47	49
Neck	14	14½	15	15½	16	16½	17	17½

TAKING BODY MEASUREMENTS

1. Around the fullest part of the bust (with undergarments as worn); hold tape a little higher in back; take care to hold tape snugly but not tightly.

2. Around the natural waistline.

3. Around hips at fullest part; usually 7 inches below waistline for Misses' sizes, 9 inches for Women's sizes.

4. Across back of shoulders from armhole to armhole.

5. Across back from armhole to neck.

6. Lengthwise from waistline to underarm (1 inch below armpit).

7. From waistline to back of neck to give shoulder slant.

8. Around upper arm for sleeve.

9. From wrist to armpit for long sleeve.

10. From waistline to desired length for skirt.

WORKING FROM INSTRUCTION BOOKS

Numerous yarns are *interchangeable,* provided the same stitch gauge can be achieved with each. The yarns may be of the same type, both smooth or both nubby, or they may be of different types, one smooth and one nubby. If they are of different types the garment will have a different appearance, so the desirability should be considered when interchanging yarns. It is advisable also when interchanging yarns to compare the *yardage* of balls or skeins of both yarns; they may vary according to manufacture, temperature and humidity. Do *not* compare weight of balls or skeins of yarn; equal weight does *not* mean equal length. It is necessary to know the number of yards called for in the instructions (not the number of balls or skeins). Acquire not only the exact number of yards, but also an extra amount of yarn to assure enough to finish the work satisfactorily.

Usually the finished measurements are given at the beginning of the instructions. These measurements are the body measurements with an allowance for the fit of garment, depending on the style. If these measurements correspond to body measurements, plus the allowance you desire (at least 2 inches more than body measurements), you can select the desired size and follow the instructions.

If the measurements are not given, divide the number of stitches at bustline (back and front or fronts) by the gauge (number of stitches which equals 1 inch). Do the same for the waistline. You will then have the bustline and waistline measurements upon which the book's instructions are based.

Note: The body measurements as given in tabulation states that for sizes 10, 12, 14, bustline measurements are 32½, 34, 36 inches and waistline measurements 25, 26½, 28 inches.

Slip-on with back and front alike and no shaping for waistline

Instructions read as follows: Directions are written for size 10. Sizes 12 and 14 are in parentheses.
Gauge: 6 sts = 1 inch, 8 rows = 1 inch
Back: Cast on 104 (108-114) stitches. Work in Stockinette Stitch until piece measures 12 inches from beginning, or the desired length to underarm.

To arrive at bust measurement, divide 104 (108-114) stitches by 6. This will give 17¼ (18-19) inches for one-half the bust measurement or 34½(36-38) inches for the total bust measurement. An extra 2 inches has been added to body bust measurement for this style of garment.

If measurements check and the extra allowance of 2 inches over body bust measurement is satisfactory, begin work.

If measurements do not check but size is in same range as book size (Misses', Women's, etc.), add or subtract the number of stitches equal to the number of inches to be added or subtracted to the cast-on stitches.

Example: If body bust measurement is 31½ inches and a 2-inch allowance is satisfactory, ½ inch should be subtracted from both back and front. Three stitches or ½ of 6 stitches would be subtracted from the back and also from the front. With 101 stitches on each piece divided by 6, we have 16¾ inches or a 33½-inch garment bust measurement (a 2-inch allowance over body bust measurement).

If body bust measurement is 33½ inches, add 3 stitches or ½ inch to back and also to front. Then garment measurement will be 35½ inches, again 2 inches over body bust measurement.

If a pattern stitch is used, be sure that the multiple of stitches is correct.

Slip-on with back and front alike, but with fitted waistline

Instructions read as follows: Directions are written for size 10. Sizes 12 and 14 are in parentheses.

Gauge: 6 sts = 1 inch, 8 rows = 1 inch
Back: Cast on 96(100-106) stitches. Work in Stockinette Stitch, dec one st each side every ¾ inch (6 rows) 8 times. Work even until piece measures 7 inches from beg. There are 80(84-90) stitches on needle. Mark for waistline.

To arrive at waistline measurement, divide 80(84-90) by 6. This will give 13¼ (14-15) inches for one-half waistline or 26½(28-30) inches for the total measurement, again 2 inches extra added.

If a larger waistline measurement is desired, work fewer decreases and space them farther apart. If a smaller waistline measurement is desired, work more decreases and reduce the spaces between them.

When changing the instructions, write the changes in the book. Circle or underline all numbers to follow to prevent using the wrong numbers.

Some new terms will be found in instruction books. In knitting armhole, etc: Bind off 6 sts at beg of next 2 rows. This means bind off 6 stitches at each side once. This requires 2 rows of work.

Decrease or increase 1 stitch each side or each end. This means, unless otherwise stated, work first 2 stitches and last 2 stitches together to decrease; work an extra stitch in first and last stitches of the row to increase.

BEING YOUR OWN DESIGNER

How To Make The Correct Size Without Taking Body Measurements: Sometimes it is difficult to take your own or another's body measurements. Select a garment from your own or the other person's wardrobe that fits just the way the knit should fit. You can measure this and get all the important measurements; bust, hips, shoulder width, underarm seam length, sleeve width and length and any other necessary measurements. Make a note of all measurements.

How To Make The Correct Size When Taking Body Measurements: Take as many body measurements as possible. Make a note of each measurement. Decide if a tight or loosely fitted garment is desired. Take into account the style and type to be made. Make a swatch using the yarn for garment and the size of needles recommended for desired gauge or texture. Make a note of the gauge.

For An Average Slip-on For Misses' and Teens' Sizes: Add 1 inch over bust measurement for back and 1 inch for front, add 1/4 inch for each seam, more if a loosely fitted slip-on is desired.

For An Average Slip-on For Women's Sizes: Add 1 inch to back, 2 inches to front and 1/4 inch for each seam; more if a loosely fitted slip-on is desired. Also, front may be made 1 inch longer than the back and a half inch underarm bustline dart may be sewn in, or the extra length may be eased in at the bust.

For A Man's Slip-On: Chest measurement is used plus 1/4 inch for each seam.

For Children's Clothes: Garment should be loosely fitted; add 1 or more inches to back and front.

For An Average Cardigan for Misses' and Teens' Sizes: Add 1 inch over bust measurement to back; 1/2 inch plus width of borders and seams to each front, or more to fronts if a loosely fitted cardigan is desired.

To Figure Correct Number of Stitches and Rows For Each Measurement: Secure graph paper if possible. Figure instructions by multiplying the width measurement by the number of stitches which equals 1 inch; the length measurement by the number of rows which equals 1 inch. Place all information on graph paper; or draw outline of each piece and place information on outline.

To Figure Shaping For Slip-On (Back and Front Alike, Round Neck, No Back Opening, Long Sleeves): *Back or Front Armhole:* Subtract the number of stitches needed for the shoulder measurement from the total number of stitches at underarm. This gives the number of stitches to be bound off and decreased for armhole shaping. Usually one half the number of stitches are bound off for the two armholes or one-fourth for each armhole. The remainder of stitches are decreased every second row or every right side row. If the number is not even, the extra stitches are placed in the bound-off stitches.

Example: 70 stitches on needle, 48 needed for width of shoulders. $70 - 48 = 22$ stitches to bind off and decrease. Bind off 6 stitches at beginning of the next 2 rows. Decrease 1 stitch on each side every second row (or right side row) 5 times.

Back Shoulders: Two-thirds of the number of stitches on needle are usually allowed for the shoulders; one-third for back of neck. However, if shoulders are wider more stitches may be needed; if narrower, less stitches. Also, if there is no zipper opening, neck will need more stitches so

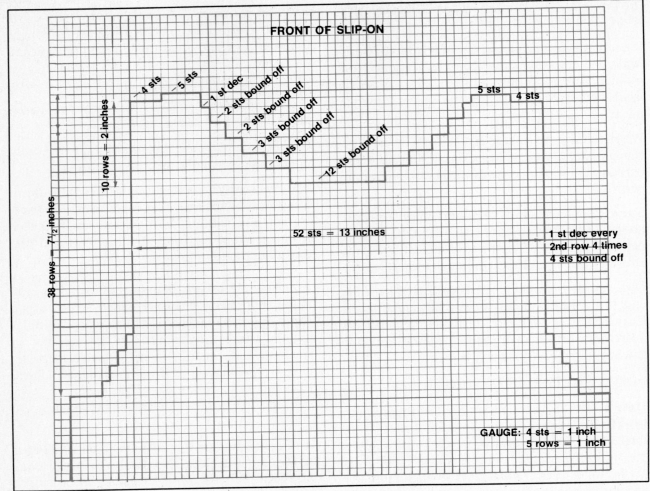

FRONT OF SLIP-ON

4 sts — 5 sts

1 st dec

2 sts bound off

2 sts bound off

3 sts bound off

3 sts bound off

12 sts bound off

5 sts — 4 sts

10 rows = 2 inches

38 rows = 7½ inches

52 sts = 13 inches

1 st dec every
2nd row 4 times
4 sts bound off

GAUGE: 4 sts = 1 inch
5 rows = 1 inch

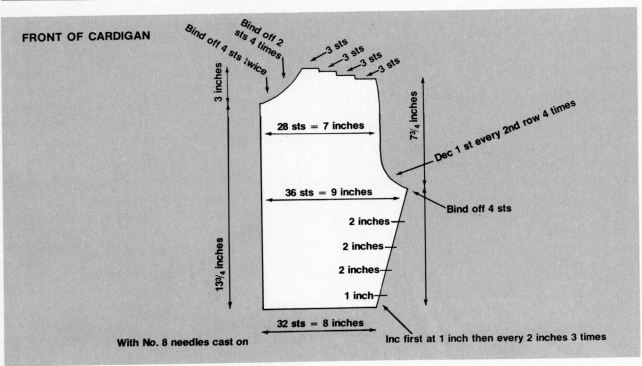

FRONT OF CARDIGAN

Bind off 4 sts twice

Bind off 2 sts 4 times

3 sts   3 sts   3 sts   3 sts

3 inches

28 sts = 7 inches

7¾ inches

Dec 1 st every 2nd row 4 times

36 sts = 9 inches

Bind off 4 sts

2 inches

2 inches

2 inches

1 inch

13¾ inches

With No. 8 needles cast on

32 sts = 8 inches

Inc first at 1 inch then every 2 inches 3 times

that it will fit easily over head; with zipper it will require fewer stitches. Also, shoulders should have at least a 1-inch slant (worked in an even number of rows).

Example: 48 stitches needed for width of shoulders. Neck should be at least 5 inches (20 stitches); 48 − 20 = 28 stitches for shoulders (14 stitches for each shoulder). We will use 6 rows for shaping. Bind off 5 stitches at beginning of next 4 rows; 4 sts at beginning of next two rows; 14 stitches bound off for each shoulder.

The 28 stitches will be placed on a stitch holder if a neck band is to be worked later, or bound off if the neck is to be finished without a band.

Front of Neck: Usually begins 2 inches below first row of shoulders. Subtract the number of stitches equal to 3 inches (center front stitches) from the number of stitches on needle after armhole shaping. If number does not divide evenly, add extra stitches to center-front number. Divide remaining number of stitches by two (gives number of stitches at each side of center stitches). Subtract the number of stitches of one shoulder from number of stitches at one side of center stitches. The remaining stitches have to be bound off or decreased before shoulder shaping is completed.

Example: 48 stitches on needle; 4 stitches = 1 inch, 5 rows = 1 inch. 48 − 12 = 36. 36 ÷ 2 = 18 stitches at each side of center stitches. 18 − 14 = 4 stitches to be bound off or decreased at one side of neck. One stitch is decreased at neck edge every second row 4 times, using 8 rows or 1½ in-ches. Then the 14 stitches are worked and the shoulder is bound off as on one side of back.

Sleeves: Determine the width desired at wrist (be sure it will stretch to go over hand) and is a multiple of the stitch to be used. Subtract number at wrist from number to be used at underarm. From total length to underarm, subtract at least 3 inches; all increasing should be completed at this point. Divide the number of stitches to be increased by two, as 1 stitch will be increased at each side on increase rows. Multiply the number of inches allowed for increases by the row gauge. Now divide number of rows by the number of times necessary to increase. If this is not even, adjust by alternating number of rows between increases.

To Shape Cap: There are many methods used, depending on the style of the garment and present-day styles. At the top of the cap there can be from 2 to 5 inches bound off, but a good rule is to leave 3 or 4 inches. When the length is finished to the underarm, the same number of stitches are bound off as on the back armholes. The length of the sleeve cap must be worked to fit into the size of the armhole.

Example: Width of sleeve is 12 inches. Gauge is 6 stitches = 1 inch, 8 rows = 1 inch (12 x 6 = 72 stitches). There are 6 stitches bound off at each side of armhole (72 − 12 = 60 stitches).
At top of sleeve we will leave 4 inches to bind off (4 x 6 = 24 stitches). Subtract these stitches (60 − 24 = 36 stitches).

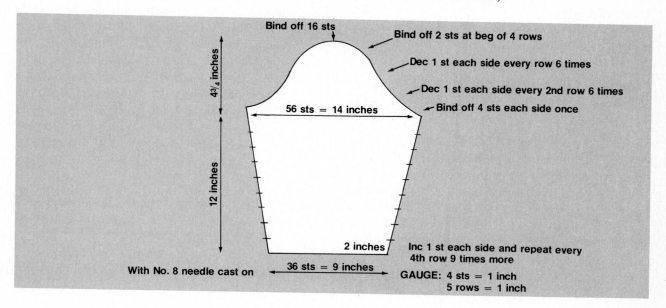

Bind off 16 sts

Bind off 2 sts at beg of 4 rows

Dec 1 st each side every row 6 times

Dec 1 st each side every 2nd row 6 times

Bind off 4 sts each side once

4¾ inches

56 sts = 14 inches

12 inches

2 inches

Inc 1 st each side and repeat every 4th row 9 times more

With No. 8 needle cast on

36 sts = 9 inches

GAUGE: 4 sts = 1 inch
5 rows = 1 inch

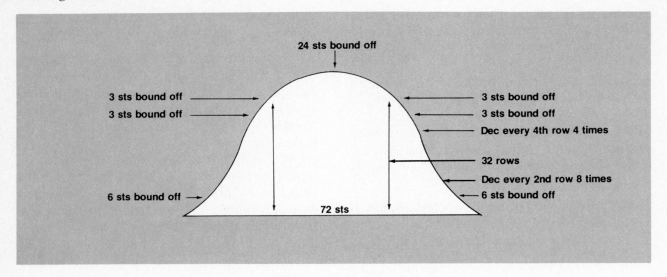

Just before our last bind-off to round top of cap, we bind off at each side the number of stitches which equals approximately ½ inch (3 stitches) for the number of rows which equals approximately ½ inch (4 rows); (3 x 4 = 12 stitches). Subtract these stitches (36−12 = 24 stitches). Therefore 24 stitches must be decreased in a given number of rows.

Armholes are 7 inches (in straight line) from first armhole bind-off to beginning of shoulder on both back and front (14 inches around).

From total of 14 subtract the 4 inches across top (14−4 = 10). Now subtract 1 inch at each side made from other bind off. (10−2 = 8). There are two sides to sleeve cap (8÷2 = 4). Row gauge is 8 rows equal 1 inch (4 x 8 = 32). Therefore, there must be 32 rows of decreases; 24 stitches to decrease, or 12 times to decrease.

Formula 1: If The Number of Stitches to be Decreased is a Smaller Number Than The Number of Rows:

Multiply the number of times to be decreased (12) by the lowest even number that will give a product larger than the number of rows (32) i.e., 12 x 4 = 48. Subtract the number of rows from the number just found (48−32 = 16). As there are two sides to decrease, divide by 2 (16 ÷ 2 = 8). This number (8) will be the number of times to decrease every second row (the lowest even number under the number used for multiplying). Subtract this number from the total times to

decrease (12−8 = 4). This represents the number of times (4) to decrease every fourth row (the number used for multiplying).

Check this as follows: Decrease 1 stitch on each side of every second row 8 times (16 stitches and 16 rows used). Decrease 1 stitch on each side every fourth row 4 times (8 stitches and 16 rows used); (16+8 = 24 stitches) and (16+16 = 32 rows). Your sleeve cap will fit your armhole.

Formula 2: If the Number of Stitches To Decrease is More Than Twice The Number of Rows in Which to Decrease:

Example: There are 62 stitches to decrease in 40 rows. Subtract the number of rows from the number of stitches (62−40 = 22). This will give you the number of times to decrease 1 stitch on each side *every* row. Subtract the number of times to decrease every row from the total number of times to decrease (31−22 = 9). This will give you the number of times to decrease every second row. Check this as follows: Decrease 1 stitch on each side every second row 9 times (18 stitches and 18 rows used). Decrease 1 stitch each side every row 22 times (44 stitches and 22 rows used). (18+44 = 62 stitches used) (18+22 = 40 rows used).

These two formulas may be used in the same way for skirts or V-necks when 1 stitch is decreased each side in a definite number of rows. The formulas may also be used to figure increases when 1 stitch is to be increased on each side in a definite number of rows.

Section VIII

WORKING SHORT ROWS IN STOCKINETTE STITCH

A short row is a row which is not worked to the end. Instructions will read: work a given number of stitches, "turn"; or, work to last given number of stitches, "turn." Leaving unworked stitches on left needle, turn work around.

At the beginning of a knit row, with yarn at back of work, slip 1 stitch as if to purl; at the beginning of a purl row, with yarn at front, slip 1 stitch as to purl. Continue to work the short rows as directed. Short rows are used to make work deeper and yet have ends remain the same length; as for collars, darts, shoulders, etc.

To Eliminate Loose Stitches and Close Holes: On knit side, knit to first hole or space. Insert left needle from front to back in center of the stitch 2 rows below the last stitch on right needle: this forms a stitch on the left needle. Knit 2 stitches together. Knit to the end, closing all holes in the same way. On purl side, purl to first hole. Insert left needle from purl to knit side in center of the stitch 2 rows below the last stitch on right needle: this forms a stitch on left needle. From back (right side of work), purl 2 stitches together. Purl to end, closing all holes.

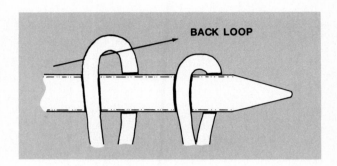

BACK LOOP

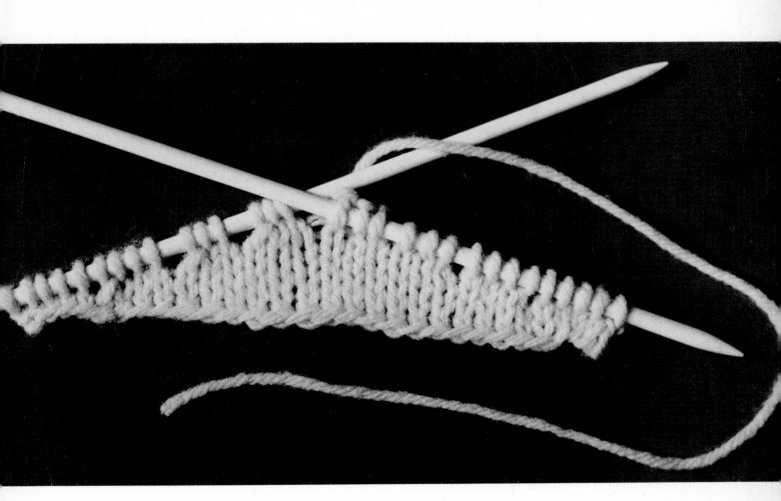

For Shoulder Shaping: Stitches are not bound off; leave stitches on needle. Using the short row method, close holes in work. Place stitches on stitch holders; one for each shoulder, one for back of neck. When back and front or fronts are completed, shoulder stitches can be woven together using the Kitchener Stitch. Or with the right sides of pieces together, bind off front and back shoulder at the same time by working 1 stitch from each piece together and binding off at the same time. Neck can be bound off or left on holders.

PICKING UP STITCHES ON FRONT EDGES

Number of Stitches Given: Use size of needle recommended. Divide one front in half, place pin at this point. Divide in fourths, then in eighths, placing pins at each point. Divide into smaller sections if desired. Divide the number of stitches to be picked up by the number of sections. With the right side of work toward you, begin at the lower edge of the first section. Insert needle in stitch (one or one-half stitch from edge) and draw a loop through. When front has no decreases, stay in same stitch or line. If there are decreases, stay in far enough so that there are no

holes. Pick up the number of stitches for one section. Check to be sure there are no holes and that the line is straight; then continue with same number of stitches in each section. When picking up stitches on other front, begin at top of this section and pick up as on first front. If ribbing is used, bind off with needle used for body and in rib pattern.

Number of Stitches Not Given: Use needle two sizes smaller than body of work. Divide front into sections and pick up 1 stitch in each row of first section as described above. Work pattern to be used for 1 inch. If work is satisfactory, rip and pick up all sections. If work is too full, reduce the number of stitches by skipping every fourth row. When satisfied that work will lie flat, proceed for entire front. If ribbing is to be used, be sure to stretch and block first section before ripping, as rib should be stretched out. Bind off with needle used for body in rib pattern.

DETERMINING THE NUMBER OF STITCHES TO PICK UP (Round-Neck Rib Band)

If ribbed border is used on lower edge, take measurement on 3 inches. Neckband must go easily over the head. Multiply the number of inches required (Misses' Sizes are usually 18 to 20 inches without stretching) by the number of stitches which equals 1 inch. This is the necessary number of stitches to pick up around the neck (includes the stitches on holders or stitches bound off for front and back of neck). When binding off for double neckband to be turned and sewn to neck edge, bind off knitting with needle used for body.

Section IX

WORKING WITH SEQUINS

To String Sequins on Yarn: Hold one strand of sequins with the right side of the sequin (inside of the cup) toward the ball of yarn. Tie thread on which the sequins are strung around the yarn (do *not* tie yarn around thread). Slide the sequins carefully over the knot onto the yarn. String no more than one strand (usually 1,000 sequins)

onto yarn at one time. When additional sequins are needed, cut yarn 4 inches from the last stitch worked at the end of a row and slide one more strand onto yarn.

Knitting Sequins (Right Side Row): Knit to the stitch for sequin; insert right needle into *back* loop of the next stitch. Slide the sequin close to work; knit the stitch drawing the sequin through the stitch to the front of work: one sequin worked. Knit the next stitch through *back* loop. There must always be a stitch knitted through the *back* loop after a sequin is worked.
Wrong Side Row: Purl all stitches. Be sure the sequin remains on the right side.

Care of Sequins: Never use an iron or steam on a garment with sequins. Sequin garments can be blocked between wet towels. Saturate a bath towel with water, then wring out as much as possible. Lay on a flat surface. Turn the garment inside out (sequins on the inside). Place on a damp towel and smooth into place. Pat garment

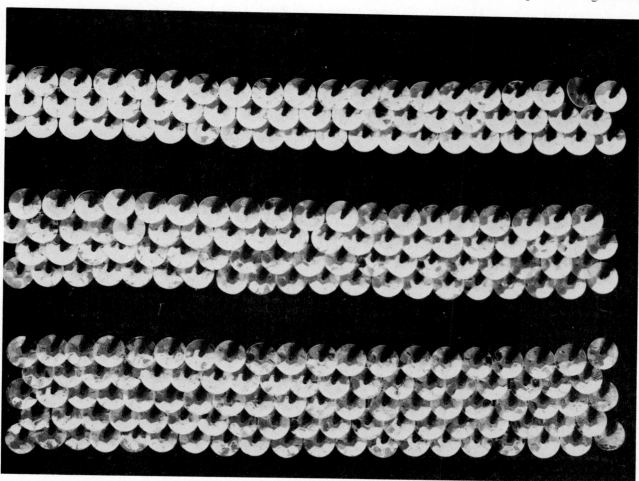

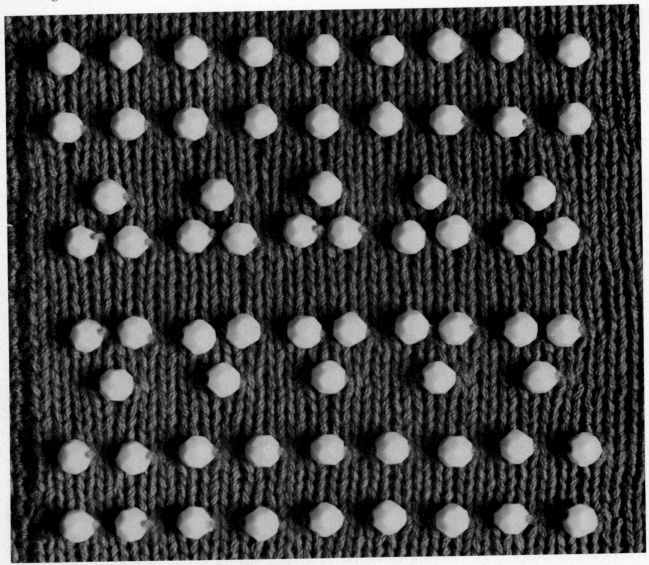

out to correct size. Saturate and wring out another towel. Place it on top of the garment. Leave until practically dry. Turn to right side and shake gently. Be sure no moisture clings to the sequins. Lay on a dry flat surface until completely dry. Hand wash gently in warm water with mild detergent. Do *not* machine wash or dry clean.

WORKING WITH BEADS

To string beads, use yarn that is the same size as the hole in the bead to be used. String the same as with sequins or thread a tapestry needle with yarn and string beads. When working in a design, use a separate ball of yarn for the beaded rows and break off when not in use.

Beads are knitted on right side rows. *Right Side Rows:* Knit stitches up to the bead stitch in the normal way. Bring yarn to front; slide bead close to needle; slip the next stitch, then knit the next stitch through the back loop. *Wrong Side Rows:* Purl all stitches, taking care that beads remain on the right side of work.

REVERSIBLE KNITTING IN TWO COLORS FOR FLAT KNITTING

To cast on, it is necessary to have three needles of the same size, as called for in the directions. With color A, cast on the total number of stitches needed. Leaving yarn attached, lay aside color A. With color B, cast on the same number of stitches on the second needle; leave yarn attached.

With left hand, hold needle with A stitches in front of needle with B stitches. The third needle will be used to work off the stitches.

Row 1: Place both A and B strands at back; with A strand, knit the first A stitch. Bring A and B between needles to the front; with B strand, purl the first B stitch. Take A and B between needles to the back; with A, knit the next A stitch; bring A and B between needles to front; with B, purl next B stitch. Continue in this way to the end. All stitches are on one needle. Always take both strands between needles when changing from knit to purl, or from purl to knit.

Row 2: Knit the B stitches and purl the A stitches. When the A stitches face you, the A stitches will be knitted and the B stitches purled. When the B stitches are facing you, the B stitches will be knitted and the A stitches purled.

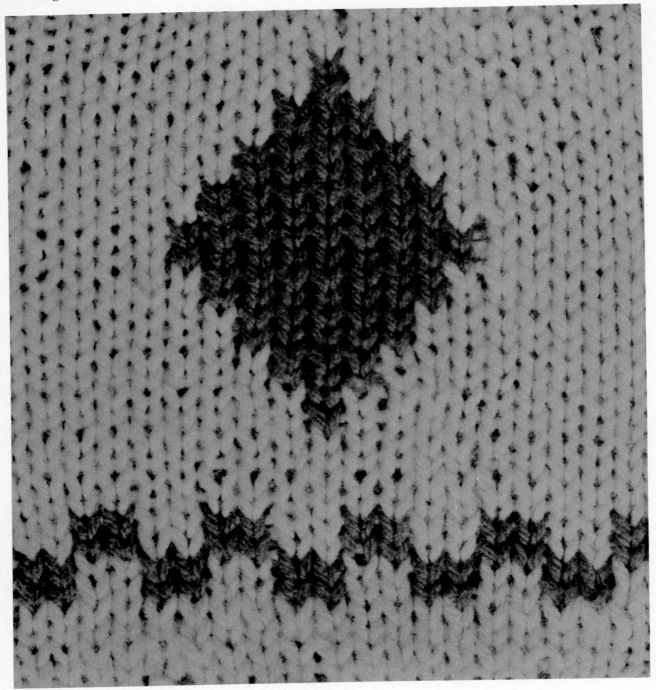

To reverse colors, with A stitches facing you, knit the first stitch with B. Bring yarn forward; purl the first B stitch with A. Continue in this way to the end of the row. All stitches are reversed. Always twist yarns as in color knitting.

The basic principle is that for a color stitch to show, that stitch must be knitted. Then, the next stitch must be purled to have it show on the reverse side. For every knit stitch in one color,

there must be a purl stitch in the other color. When colors are reversed, the two sides will be joined.

To bind off, place all A stitches on a double-pointed needle; all B stitches on another double pointed needle. Bind off A stitches with A and B stitches with B. To finish, weave all open edges together.

ALTERATIONS BY HAND

Separating A Knitted Piece Horizontally

If seams have been made, rip seams to desired length. If rib band will be used, allow for this length. Snip a thread in the middle of row at desired length, minus the length required for finishing.

Work from right to left with a crochet hook or a tapestry needle. Stitch by stitch, draw out the cut end to the right edge. Cut the end when a few stitches have been released, but leave at least 4 inches at the edge. Draw out end to the left edge in the same way. Carefully place stitches on a needle or a double strand of yarn.

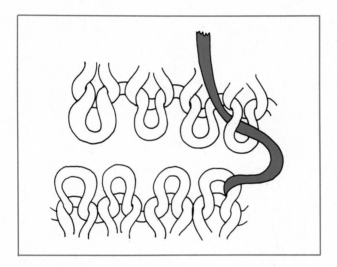

To Lengthen

Rib Band Knitted On: With needles two sizes smaller than the size used for the garment, rib to desired length and bind off in rib pattern.

Rib Band Woven To Major Section: With needles two sizes smaller than used for the garment, cast on the same number of stitches as on one section of garment. Rib to desired depth. Change to needles used for garment; work one row. Using Kitchener Stitch, weave pieces together.

To Shorten

Rejoin Rib Band: Separate the garment two rows above the ribbed band. Remove desired number of inches from the large piece. Using the Kitchener Stitch, weave ribbed band to the larger piece. If one piece has more stitches than the other piece, it will be necessary to decrease

the larger piece. Spacing evenly across the row, take two stitches together as in decreasing.

Hem: Separate piece at desired length. Place stitches on needle. Working first row from wrong side, knit one row for the turning ridge. Then, beginning with a knit row, work in Stockinette Stitch for 1 inch or desired depth of hem. Turn hem and sew.

Crochet Edge: Separate piece at desired length. With needles or crochet hook, bind off all the stitches. Work the desired crochet stitch on the lower edge for two rows.

ALTERATIONS BY MACHINE

In order to make alterations by machine, some knowledge of sewing is necessary. Turn garment inside out and baste to proper size. Work two rows of stitching on top of each other. Then work two more rows of stitching as close as possible to the first rows. Trim excess material, leaving a $1/4$ to $1/2$-inch seam.

IRISH FISHERMAN KNITS

These are a combination of two or more traditional patterns. When working with these knits, it is advisable to make a simple swatch of each pattern before beginning your project. Place markers between the patterns in a row to keep the patterns divided. The patterns are not difficult, but understanding a few basic techniques should be of great help.

The Twist Stitches

There are many ways of working Right and Left Twists, but the same abbreviations (RT and LT) are usually used regardless of the number of stitches being twisted. (Twist stitches are not Cable stitches.) In each set of instructions, details are given as to how each twist is worked. To understand how to work these various twists, study the diagrams.

Right Twist — *Method A*

Skip 1 stitch, knit next stitch through the front loop and leave it on the left needle (arrow shows how right needle is inserted — note that right needle remains on *top* of left needle).

Yarn is drawn down through the stitch. Knit the skipped stitch (instructions will specify whether

through the front or back loop); drop 2 stitches from the left needle. As you knit the skipped stitch, pull both original stitches from the left needle; the 2 twisted stitches are now on the right needle.

Right Twist — *Method B*
Skip 1 stitch, knit next stitch and leave on left needle (right needle is inserted through stitch to the back of work: it remains *under* the left nee-

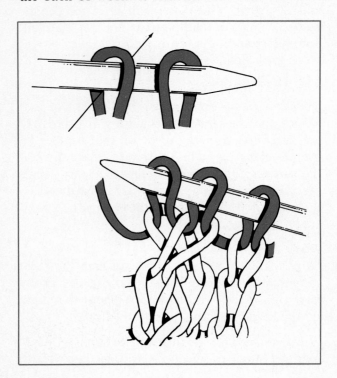

dle). Knit the skipped stitch and drop 2 stitches from needle (see Right Twist — Method A). Right Twist is then completed.

Left Twist
Skip 1 stitch, knit next stitch through the back loop (right needle is behind the left needle). The stitch is drawn through. Bring right needle back to the front and knit the skipped stitch (through front or back loop as specified in instructions); drop 2 stitches from left needle. A Left Twist is the reverse of a Right Twist: it slants toward the left.

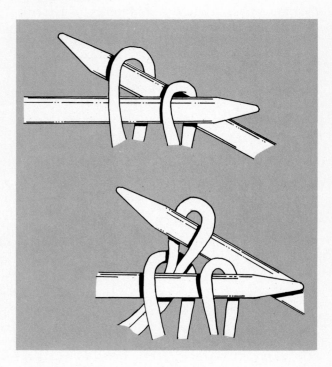

Purl Through Back Loop

Arrow in diagram shows the direction the right needle is inserted through stitch. Keep yarn in front of work; twist the right needle to go through the stitch as shown. Bring the point of

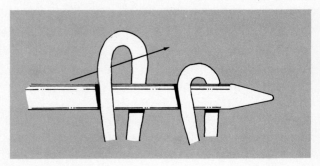

right needle back to the front *below* the left needle. Purl the stitch.

Popcorn Or Bobble

There are many different ways of working these, but the principle is usually the same. An increase of several stitches is made in one stitch (4 stitches are used in the example). Several rows are worked on just these stitches. Beginning with the 2nd stitch as shown (then the 3rd and 4th), the extra stitches are passed one at a time over the first stitch and then off the needle. One stitch remains.

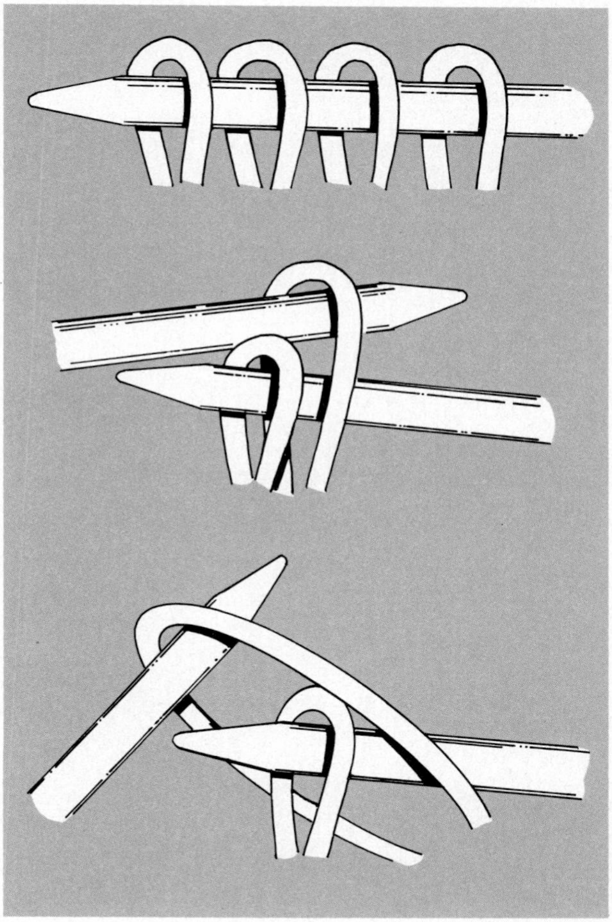

Section X

ADDITIONAL WAYS TO CAST ON, WORK AND BIND OFF

Improved Hems: With a contrasting color yarn, cast on the required number of stitches. Break yarn. Begin work with main color yarn. When work is complete, pick out cast-on row. This will leave a row of open loops. Turn hem and sew loops to wrong side of stitches. This gives a less heavy finish.

With a contrasting color yarn and crochet hook, make a chain of the required number of stitches. Break yarn. With main color yarn, pick up 1 stitch in each chain. Complete work and finish as above.

K 1, P 1 Rib With Elastic Edge (Children's Garments, Socks, Mittens, etc): With contrasting color yarn, cast on one-half the required number of stitches. Break yarn.

Row 1: With main color, * K 1, yo; rep from *, end with yo.
Row 2: K first stitch (the yo) through back loop, * with yarn at *front,* slip 1 st as if to P, take yarn under needle to back, K 1 st; rep from * to end.
Row 3: * K 1, bring yarn to front, sl 1; rep from * to end (the stitch which appears as a purl stitch will be slipped).
Row 4: * K 1, P 1; rep from * to end. Repeat Row 4 to desired depth for ribbing. Pick out cast-on row.

K 1, P 1 Double Band (Lower edges of body, sleeves, hems): Cast on and work the same as the first 3 rows of the above. Then continue to repeat Row 3 to the desired depth.

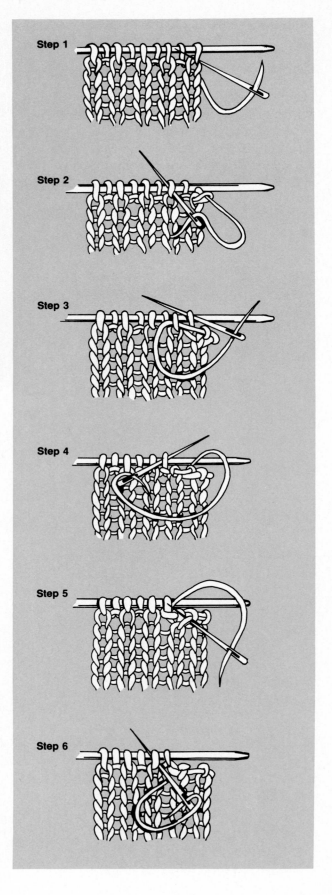

On the next row (which will be the wrong side) purl 2 stitches together across the row, again having the original number of stitches. Continue to follow pattern as given in instructions. Pick out cast-on row.

K 1, P 1 Double Bands For Necks: With smaller needles than those used for the body of the garment, pick up the desired number of stitches from the right side.

Row 1 (wrong side): * P 1, insert left needle from back to front under strand between last P st and next st on left needle, making a loop on left needle, P in front of this loop; rep from * to last 2 sts, P last 2 sts. This gives an even number of stitches.

Row 2: Same as Row 1 of K 1, P 1 Ribbing A (see page 24).
Rep this row for desired depth. Cut yarn, leaving a long end for binding off.

Binding Off Double Band: Thread yarn into a tapestry needle. Hold work with right side facing you. Follow steps 1 through 6 as shown in diagrams. Repeat steps 3 through 6 to the end. Tie off last pattern.

ADDITIONAL BUTTONHOLES

Vertical Buttonholes In Ribbed Or Garter Stitch Borders: Divide the number of stitches in the border in half if possible. If not, have the additional stitch before the separation for the buttonhole. Mark at division. Beginning at the side edge, work to marker; drop original ball (ball one) and join a 2nd ball of yarn (ball two). Work to front edge.

On next row with ball two, work to the opening; drop yarn. With ball one, work to the end. Continue in this way to work each section with its own ball of yarn for the depth required to fit the button snugly. End with ball one at the side edge.

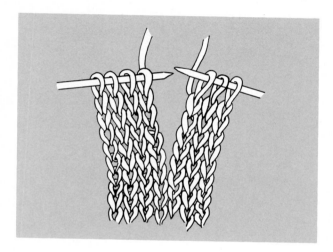

On next row, join by working all stitches with ball one. Break off ball two, leaving an end. When border is completed, weave in ends neatly on wrong side.

Working With Contrasting Color Yarn: Use a lightweight yarn. This buttonhole must always be worked on a right side row.

Work to the place where buttonhole is to be made. With contrasting color yarn, KNIT (do not work a pattern stitch) for the number of stitches necessary for the buttonhole. Place the contrasting color stitches back on left needle. Be sure ends will not pull out, but do not tie. KNIT the contrasting color stitches with the main color. Continue to work with main color to end.

On the next row, work to the buttonhole. Purl the buttonhole stitches; work to end. Continue work-

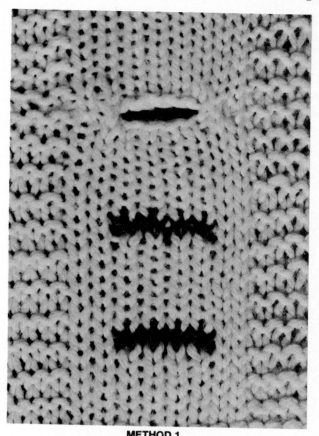

METHOD 1

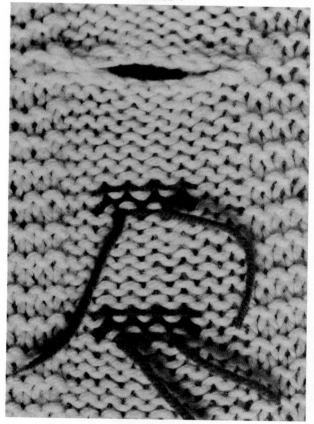

METHOD 1

ing all buttonholes in this way. When garment is finished, the buttonholes will then be finished. Do not remove contrasting color yarn.

Finishing: Select the crochet hook of the size necessary to keep the correct gauge while working a slip stitch (usually a size 2 for sport yarn-weight; size 1 for knitting worsted-weight).

Method 1 — Slip stitches will *not* show on the right side (Very good for medium and light-weight yarn): *Hold work with top of buttonhole at top of work, wrong side facing you.

Leaving a 3-inch end, make a slip knot with a strand of main color, and place the loop on hook.*Holding yarn on wrong side, insert hook in loop of 2nd stitch at top and to right of buttonhole (do *not* take hook through work to right side). Work a slip stitch, then work a slip stitch in the loop of next stitch: 2 slip stitches worked.* Inserting a hook from the wrong side, work a slip stitch in each main color loop where a contrasting color appears. Do *not* work in the contrasting color. Work a slip stitch in the loop of each of the next 2 stitches to the left of buttonhole. Cut yarn, fasten off and weave in ends. Turn work upside down and work bottom of buttonhole in the same way. Pick out contrasting color.

METHOD 2

Method 2 — Slip stitches will show on right side (Very good for heavier-weight yarn): Repeat between * s of Method 1.

Pick out contrasting color yarn. Be careful that open stitches do not drop. Continue to hold yarn on wrong side and insert hook from right to wrong side in first open loop of buttonhole. Work slip stitch. Inserting hook from right to wrong side, work slip stitch in each open loop. Then, from wrong side, work slip stitch in the *back* loop of the next 2 stitches as at the beginning of row. Cut yarn, fasten off and weave in ends. Turn work upside down and work bottom of buttonhole in same way.

METHOD 2

Cut-In Buttonhole: These buttonholes are made when the garment has been knitted without buttonholes. This allows you to space the buttonholes as desired, counting the rows between buttonholes. However, since these are not easy to work, practice buttonholes should be made before working on the finished piece. Mark the width of the buttonhole and the row where the buttonhole is to be made.

With small pointed scissors, cut a stitch at the center of buttonhole and pick out yarn to the edges of buttonhole. Place each loop, top and

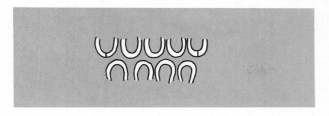

bottom, on a thread. Note there are two half loops at top and full loops at bottom. Finish buttonholes as buttonhole worked with contrasting color yarn.

If buttonholes are in fronts and facings, finish by working loops of double buttonholes together.

BUTTONS

Knit a piece of material in Stockinette Stitch, using a fine yarn; or, split a heavier yarn and use only one- or two-ply for knitting. Make a piece at least 1 inch larger than the button mold or the button to be covered. Cover the button as with fabric.

Crochet over a plastic ring a size smaller than desired size for button, usually ³⁄₈-inch ring. Use a fine or medium-weight yarn, or two-ply of a 4-ply yarn. Make a slip knot and place on hook. Work single crochets around the ring until it is completely covered. Count the number of stitches; use the same number for every button. Cut yarn, leaving an end for sewing the button on. Thread end with a tapestry needle and draw under each single crochet.

Pull tightly and the top edge will turn to center of ring. Secure the end with a few stitches. Sew to garment through center of button.

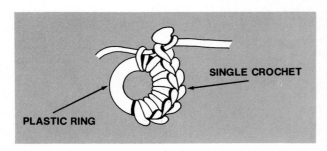

SINGLE CROCHET

PLASTIC RING

Make a ball to use for a button. With yarn, as for the plastic ring button, chain 3 stitches. Join with a slip stitch to form a ring.
Rnd 1: Work 6 sc in the ring. *Rnd 2:* 2 sc in each

sc, 12 sc. *Rnd 3:* sc in first sc, * 2 sc in next sc, 1 sc in next sc, repeat from * around: 18 sc. Continue to inc 6 sts in every rnd (Rnd 4 - 2 sc in every 3rd sc; Rnd 5 - 2 sc in every 4th sc) to approximate size for top of button. Work 1 rnd even. Stuff with yarn, cotton or button mold. Work around, skipping every 2nd st until ball is tightly closed. Fasten off and secure end.

KNITTED FRINGE

Use one, two or three strands of yarn, depending on thickness desired (cut shows 3 strands). With size needles for thickness of strands, cast on 10 sts (more if a deeper knot section or fringe is desired.
Row 1: Wrap yarn around free needle, P 2 tog, * wrap yarn, P 2 tog; rep from * to end.
Repeat Row 1 for desired length (edge to be fringed).
Next row: Bind off 4 or 6 stitches, depending on depth of knot section desired. Fasten off. Ravel out remaining stitches. Trim evenly to desired length or leave loops if desired.

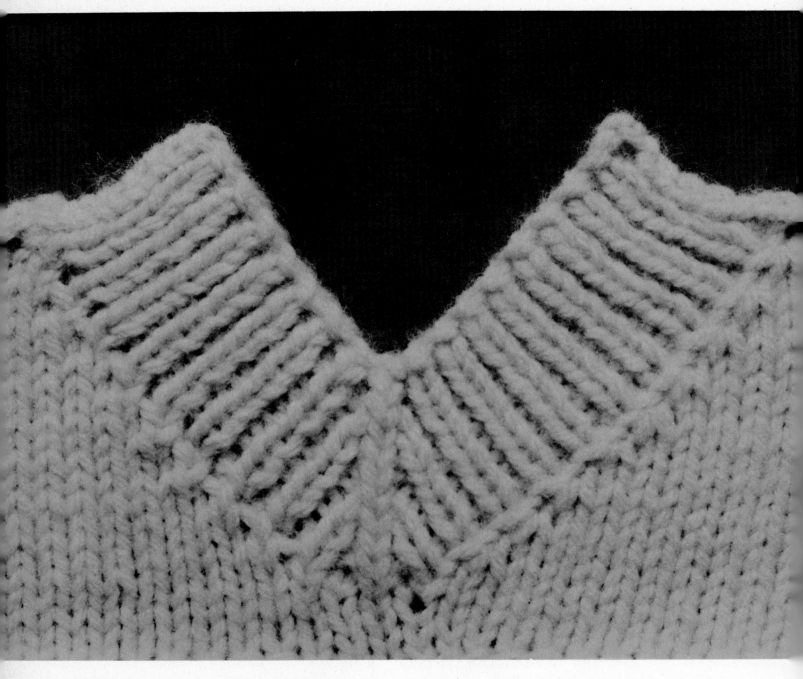

TO POINT UP A V-NECK RIBBING

From right side, beginning at left front shoulder, pick up stitch on shaped edge to center front, one stitch at center front and mark; pick up the same number sts on right front edge as on left.

Row 1 (wrong side): K 1, P 1 to center front stitch, P center stitch, beginning with K or P as stitch before center stitch, rib to end.

Row 2: Rib to 1 stitch before center stitch. Slip next st as to P, place center stitch on a cable needle; slip stitch from right needle back to left needle, insert left needle from back to front in stitch on cable needle and slip to left needle. K 3 together through *back* loops, rib to end.

Row 3: K the knit stitches and P the purl stitches. Repeat Rows 2 and 3 to desired depth end with a row worked from right side.
Bind off by knitting the knit stitches and purling the purl stitches.

KNITTED LACE

Use fine yarn or cotton and small needles.

Edging: Cast on 9 stitches.

Row 1 (right side): Sl 1, K 2, yo, K 2 tog, K 2, yo twice, K 2.

Row 2: Sl 1, K 1, K 1 more in yo, dropping 1 wrap of yo, P 1 in *back* of remaining wrap of yo, K 4, yo, K 2 tog, K 1.

Row 3: Sl 1, K 2, yo, K 2 tog, K 6.

Row 4: Bind off 2 sts, K 5, yo, K 2 tog, K 1. Repeat these 4 rows to desired length; end with Row 4. Bind off.

Edging: Cast on 10 stitches.

Row 1 (right side): Sl 1, K 2, yo, K 2 tog, K 1, yo twice, K 2 tog, yo twice, K 2 tog.

Row 2: Sl 1, K 1 in yo, dropping 1 wrap of yo, P 1 in *back* of remaining wrap of yo, K 1, K 1 more in yo, dropping 1 wrap of yo, P 1 in *back* of remaining wrap of yo, K 3, yo, K 2 tog, K 1.

Row 3: Sl 1, K 2, yo, K 2 tog, K 3, yo twice, K 2 tog, yo twice, K 2 tog.

Row 4: Sl 1, K 1, P 1, K 2, P 1, K 5, yo, K 2 tog, K 1.

Row 5: Sl 1, K 2, yo, K 2 tog, K 5, yo twice, K 2 tog, yo twice, K 2 tog.

Row 6: Sl 1, K 1, P 1, K 2, P 1, K 7, yo, K 2 tog, K 1.

Row 7: Sl 1, K 2, yo, K 2, K 11.

Row 8: Bind off 6 sts, K 6 sts, yo, K 2 tog, K 1. Repeat these 8 rows to desired length, end with Row 8. Bind off.

Insertion: Cast on 19 sts.

Row 1 (wrong side): Yo, K 2 tog, K 4, P 7, K 6.

Row 2: Yo, K 2 tog, K 1, yo, (K 2 tog) twice, K 5, sl 1 as to P, K 1, psso, K 1, yo, K 2 tog, K 2. (17 sts on needle).

Row 3: Yo, K 2 tog, K 1, yo, K 2 tog, K 8, yo, K 2 tog, K 2.

Row 4: Yo, K 2 tog, K 1, yo, K 2 tog, K 2, (yo, K 1) 3 times, yo, K 3, yo, K 2 tog, K 2. (21 sts on needle)

Row 5: Yo, K 2 tog, K 1, yo, K 2 tog, K 1, P 9, K 2, yo, K 2 tog, K 2.

Row 6: Yo, K 2 tog, K 1, yo, (K 2 tog) twice, K 7, sl 1, K 1, psso, K 1, yo, K 2 tog, K 2 (19 sts on needle).

Row 7: Yo, K 2 tog, K 1, yo, K 2 tog, K 1, P 7, K 2, yo, K 2 tog, K 2.

Repeat from Row 2 to desired length; end with Row 7. Bind off.

HELPFUL HINTS

When doubtful about how much yarn to leave for casting on, use two balls — one to form loops, the other to form stitches. When the desired number of stitches are cast on, break off one ball. To avoid tight bind-off, use a needle two sizes larger than the size being used for the garment.

If grosgrain ribbon is to be used for facings, be sure to wash it before using. Before cutting, allow for the turn in at the ends. Then allow 1 inch more than the length to be faced. Sew in loosely, allowing for the stretch in the knitted fabric.

If you have to use two dye lots in the same piece of work, use double-pointed needles so that you can work from both ends. Work one row of each dye lot alternately. A streak may show, but not as obviously as a complete change from one dye lot to another.

If work shows a mark where it has been left on the needle for more than a day or two, it will seldom come out. Rip two rows and discard the yarn. Begin working with new yarn.

KNITTING PROJECTS

SCARF

Designed and Created by Joe Ann Helms

Approximate Size 10 X 104 inches (without fringe)

MATERIALS — Brunswick Windrush (4-oz) 2 skeins each A, B and C

NEEDLES: "Susan Bates" No. 8 OR SIZE TO GIVE GAUGE

GAUGE: 5 sts = 1 inch, 9 ridges = 2 inches

Scarf is worked in Garter Stitch (K every row). With A cast on 50 sts. * K 16 rows A, join B, K 2 rows, Cut B, K 15 rows A; Cut A. K 16 rows B; K 2 rows C. Cut C, K 16 rows B; Cut B. K 16 rows C, K 2 rows A. Cut A, K 16 rows C. Cut C.* Rep between *s until 10 pats of 102 rows each have been completed. K 16 rows A. Bind off. Sew in ends.

Fringe: Wrap A around a 12-inch cardboard 72 times. B and C 64 times. Cut at 1 end. See How to knot fringe, page 21.

Beg with A, in first bound off st, * knot 1 strand in each of first 2 sts, B in each of 2 sts, C in next 2 sts; rep from *, end with A in each of last 2 sts. Fringe other end in same way. Trim evenly.

RAGLAN SLIP-ON WORKED ON CIRCULAR NEEDLE

Designed and Created by Joe Ann Helms

Instructions are for size 8. Changes for sizes 10, 12, 14 and 16 are in parentheses.

MATERIALS — Brunswick Germantown Knitting Worsted (4 oz) 4 (4-4-5-5-5) MC and 1 skein each Color A and Color B

NEEDLES: "Susan Bates" 24-inch and 16-inch 1 circular No. 7 and 1 pair No. 7 OR SIZE TO GIVE GAUGE

GAUGE: 5 sts = 1 inch, 6 rows = 1 inch

FINISHED MEASUREMENTS (in inches)
Bust 32 (34-36-38-40). Sleeve at underarm 12 (12$\frac{1}{2}$-13-13$\frac{1}{2}$-14)

With 16-inch needle and MC cast on loosely for neck edge 76 (84-90-92-104) sts.

Join, taking care not to twist sts. When sts become too crowded, change to larger needle. Place marker to indicate beg of rnd and slip marker every rnd.

Neckband — Rib in K 1, P 1 for 3 inches. Remove marker.

Rnd 1: K 1 (seam st), place marker on needle; K 28(31-32-35-38) for front, place marker; K 1 (seam st), place marker, K 12 for sleeve, place marker; K 1 (seam st), place marker; K 28 (31-32-35-38) for back, place marker; K 1 (seam st), place marker, K 12 for sleeve, place marker to indicate end of rnd. There are 4 seam sts with a marker at each side. Slip markers every rnd.

Rnd 2: * K 1 (seam st), inc 1 st in next st (K in front and back of st), K to 1 st before marker, inc 1 st in next st; rep from * 3 times, ending last rep inc 1 st in last st. There are 8 increases.

Rnd 3: Knit all sts. Rep rnds 2 and 3 until there are 22 (23-25-26-27) inc rnds and 260 (274-292-306-320) sts on needle. There are 72 (77-82-87-92) sts on back and on front; 56 (58-62-64-66) sts on each sleeve and 4 seam sts.

Divide as follows: K 74 (79-84-89-94) sts, leave yarn attached, place these sts on a stitch holder (front). With a new ball of MC and straight needles K 56 (58-62-64-66) sts for sleeve; place on holder for back next 74 (79-84-89-94) sts; place on another holder 56 (58-62-64-66) sts for 2nd sleeve.

Sleeve: At end of last row cast on 3 sts, P 1 row, cast on 3 sts. There are 62 (64-68-70-72) sts on needle. Work back and forth in St St (K 1 row, P 1 row) for 2 inches, end with a purl row.

Next row: K 1, K 2 tog, K to last 3 sts, sl 1 as to P, K 1, pass the sl st over the K st, K 1.

Next row: Purl.

Work St St for 8 rows.

Rep the last 10 rows 4 times more. Work on 52 (54-58-60-62) sts until sleeve measures 14$\frac{1}{2}$ inches, or 3 inches less than desired length, end with a P row. Drop MC.

Stripe Pattern: Join A and K 1 row, P 1 row, K 1 row, Cut A, pick up MC. P 1 row, K 1 row, Cut MC. Join B. (P 1 row, K 1 row) 3 times. Cut B. Join MC. P 1 row, then work St St for 6 rows more.

P next row on right side for turning ridge. Beginning with a P row work St St for 7 rows. Bind off as to knit. Place the sts of 2nd sleeve on straight needle to work the first row from the K side. Work same as first sleeve.

Body: Place sts of front on 24-inch needle, pick up attached yarn, cast on 6 sts. K across sts of back, cast on 6 sts. Place marker to indicate end of rnds. Join. There are 160 (170-180-190-200) sts on needle. K around until body measures 11 inches from underarm, or 3 inches less than desired length.

Striped Pattern: K 3 rnds A; 2 rnds MC; 6 rnds B; 7 rnds MC. Cut A and B. P next rnd for turning ridge. K 7 rnds. Bind off as to knit.

Finishing: Turn neckband in half to wrong side and sew loosely to neck edge. (Take care not to draw tightly.) Sew sleeve seams and sew cast-on st of sleeves to cast-on sts at underarm. Turn hems of sleeves and body to wrong side at turning ridge and sew. Steam if desired.

MAN'S SOCK WITH AUTO OR FRENCH HEEL

Instructions are for size 7½. Changes for sizes (8½-9½-10½-11½-12½) are in parentheses.

MATERIALS — Brunswick Fairhaven (1-oz) 2 skeins MC, 1 skein CC

NEEDLES: "Susan Bates" 1 set (4) each No. 1 and No. 3 OR SIZE TO GIVE GAUGE

GAUGE: 8 sts = 1 inch, 10 rows = 1 inch

On No. 1 needles, with MC cast on 64(68-72-76-80-84) sts. Divide sts on needles as follows: Needle No. 1 — 24(25-27-28-30-31); Needle No. 2 — 16(18-18-20-20-22); Needle No. 3 — 24(25-27-28-30-31).

Join and check carefully to be sure sts are not twisted on needles. Mark end of rnd and sl marker every rnd.

Work around in K 2, P 2 rib for 2 inches. Change to No. 3 needles. K all rnds for 1½ inches.

Begin Pattern — Note: When changing colors, pick up color to be used, under color previously used, twisting yarns to prevent holes.

Use a separate stand, bobbin, or ball of CC color for each of the 2 side patterns.

Rnd 1: Needle No. 1 — K to within 6 sts of end of needle, K 1 MC, join CC and K 1, K4 MC to end of needle;

Needle No. 2 — K with MC to end of needle; Needle No. 3 — K 4 MC, Join 2nd CC and K 1, with MC K to end of rnd.

Rnd 2: With MC, knit all sts.

Rnd 3: Needle No. 1 — K to within 6 sts of end of needle, K 1 CC, K 1 MC, K 1 CC, with MC, knit to end of needle;

Needle No. 2 — K with MC to end of needle; Needle No. 3 — K 3 MC, K 1 CC, K 1 MC, K 1 CC, with MC, knit to end of rnd.

Rnd 4: With MC, knit all sts.

Repeat these 4 rnds for side patterns.

Work until 1 inch from end of ribbing. Continue side patterns AND AT SAME TIME dec 1 st at beg and end of next rnd and rep decs every 1 inch 3 times more. There are 56(60-64-68-72-76) sts on needles. Continue to work patterns until 9 inches from end of ribbing or desired length to beginning of heel. Discontinue patterns and use MC only.

Auto Heel: K the first 14(15-16-17-18-19) sts of Needle No. 1, sl the last 14(15-16-17-18-19) sts of Needle No. 3 to end of Needle No. 1. Leave remaining 28(30-32-34-36-38) sts on Needle No. 2 for instep. Work back and forth on heel sts as follows: Sl 1, P 26(28-30-32-34-36), turn, sl 1, K 25(27-29-31-33-35). Turn. Sl 1, P 24(26-28-30-32-34), turn, sl 1, K 23(25-27-29-31-33). Turn. Continue working in St St, always slipping the first st and always knitting or purling 1 st less until 10(11-12-13-14-15) sts remain unknitted on each side of center 8 sts, ending with a P row. Turn and K back on the 8 center sts just purled. Insert left needle from the front to the back between the last st knitted and next (first unknitted st), forming a loop on left needle, K this loop and next (first unknitted st) together. Turn and P 9 sts, pick up a loop as before and P this loop with next st. Turn. Continue in this way to work 1 st more, picking up 1 loop at end and working loop together with next st until all sts are worked, ending with a P row. Turn. K 14(15-16-17-18-19) sts and leave sts on needle; K next 14(15-16-17-18-19) sts, pick up 4 sts on side of heel. (Needle No. 1); K across 28(30-32-34-36-38) sts of instep (Needle No. 2). With Needle No. 3 pick up 4 sts on side of heel and K across remaining 14(15-16-17-18-19) sts of heel.

Gusset — Rnd 1: Knit around.

Rnd 2: Needle No. 1 — K to last 3 sts, K 2 tog, K 1; Needle No. 2 — Knit; Needle No. 3 — K 1, sl 1, K 1, p s s o, K to end. Rep these 2 rnds 3 times more. There are 56(60-64-68-72-76) sts on needles.

Foot: K around until foot measures 6(6½-7-7½-8-8½) inches, or approximately 2 inches less

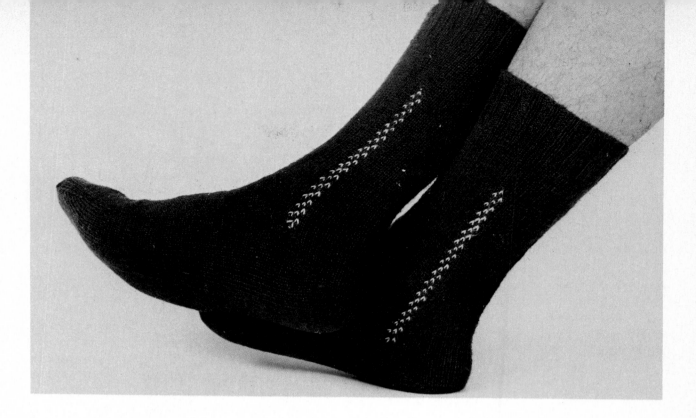

than desired length from back of heel to top of toe.

Shape Toe — *Rnd 1:* Needle No. 1 — K to within 3 sts of end, K 2 tog, K 1; Needle No. 2 — K 1, sl 1, K 1, psso; K to within 3 sts of end, K 2 tog, K 1; Needle No. 3 — K 1, sl 1, K 1, psso, K to end of rnd.

Rnd 2: Knit.

Rep these 2 rnds until there are 8(8-10-10-12-12) sts on Needle No. 2.

Place the sts from Needles No. 1 and No. 3 on same needle (be careful they are in order, not twisted). Break yarn, leaving a 5-inch end. Thread end into tapestry needle and weave sts together with Kitchener stitch as follows:

(I) Hold the needles side by side with the right sides out, *insert needle in the first st on the front needle, as though you were going to K. Let the st slip onto the tapestry needle, insert the needle in the second st on the front needle as if to purl. Pull the yarn through both these sts (one off and one on the dp needle).

(II) Drawing the yarn up close, but not tight, insert the tapestry needle in the first st on the back needle as if to purl. Let the st slip off the dp needle onto the tapestry needle. Insert the tapestry needle in the second st on the back needle as if to K. Pull the yarn through the 2 sts (one off and one on the dp needle). Repeat from * until all the

sts are woven, secure end. These are always two operations on each stitch with the loss of 1 st each time on each needle. Steam lightly.

French Heel: Mark the center back of the sock. Place 32 (32-32-38-38-38) sts at center back ($1/2$ at each side of center marking) on 1 needle for heel and remaining 40 (40-40-46-46-46) on needle to be worked later.

Working on Heel needle, K across sts dec 4 (2-0-4-2-0) sts evenly spaced 28 (30-32-34-36-38) sts.

Row 1: Sl 1, P to end.

Row 2: *Sl 1, K 1; rep from * to end. Rep these 2 rows for 2 (2-$2^1/_4$-$2^1/_4$-$2^1/_2$-$2^1/_2$) inches, ending with a P row.

Turn Heel: K 16 (17-18-19-20-21), this is half the number of sts, plus 2; K 2 tog, K 1, turn.

Row 1: Sl 1, P 5, P 2 tog, P 1, turn.

Row 2: Sl 1, K 6, K 2 tog, K 1, turn.

Row 3: Sl 1, P 7, P 2 tog, P 1, turn.

Continue in this way, always having 1 st more before dec and K 2 tog or P 2 tog on each side of hole until 16 (18-18-20-20-22) sts are on heel needle.

Next Row: K 8(9-9-10-10-11) and leave on needle. Needle No. 1 — K 8(9-9-10-10-11) the remaining sts of heel, with same needle pick up along side of heel piece 14 (15-16-17-18-19) sts.

Needle No. 2 — Work across 40 (40-40-46--46-46) instep sts. Needle No. 3 — Pick up along side of heel piece 14 (15-16-17-18-19) sts, with same needle, K the 8 (9-9-10-10-11) sts of heel.

Shape Instep — Rnd 1: Knit all sts.

Rnd 2: Needle No. 1 — K to last 3 sts, K 2 tog, K 1;

Needle No. 2 — Knit;

Needle No. 3 — K 1, sl 1, K 1, psso, K to end of needle.

Rep last 2 rnds until there are 72 (72-74-80-82-82) sts on 3 needles. Work even until foot measures 5 (6-7-8-9-10) inches.

Next Rnd: Dec instep sts at even intervals to 32 (32-34-34-36-36) sts.

Toe: Shape and weave same as Toe of Sock with Auto Heel.

LADIES' MITTENS

MATERIALS — Brunswick Germantown Knitting Worsted or Windrush (4-oz) 1 skein

NEEDLES: "Susan Bates" 1 set (4) double pointed No. 7 or SIZE TO GIVE GAUGE; and 1 cable needle

GAUGE (St St): 5 sts = 1 inch, 7 rnds = 1 inch

Right Mitten

Cuff: Cast on 40 sts and divide on 3 needles as follows: Needle No. 1 — 12 sts; Needle No. 2 — 13 sts; Needle No. 3 — 15 sts. Join. Check to be sure sts are not twisted on needles. Work around in K 2, P 2 ribbing for 2½ inches.

Hand — Rnd 1: Needle 1 — K 12 sts (thumb needle); Needle 2 — K 13; Needle 3 — K 1, P 2, K 4, P 2, K 6.

Rnd 2: K 26, P 2, K 4, P 2, K 6.

Rnd 3: Rep rnd 2.

Rnd 4 (cable rnd): K 26, P 2, Sl next 2 sts to cable needle, hold at ***front*** of work, K next 2 sts, K 2 from cable needle (cable twist), P 2, K 6.

Rnds 5 and 6: Rep rnd 3. Rep these 6 rnds for cable pattern, twisting cable every 6th rnd for entire hand.

Thumb Gusset — Rnd 7: Needle 1 — K 2, place a marker on needle, inc 1 st in next st, K 1, inc 1 st in next st, place a marker on needle, work to end of rnd. There are 5 sts between markers. Sl markers every rnd.

Rnds 8 and 9: Work even, knitting the K sts including the inc sts and purling the P sts.

Rnd 10: K 2, inc in next st, K 3, inc in next st, work to end of rnd. There are 7 sts in thumb gusset.

Rnds 11 and 12: Work even.

Rnd 13: Inc for gusset as before. There are 9 sts in gusset.

Rnds 14 and 15: Work even.

Rnd 16: Inc for gusset as before. There are 11 sts in gusset.

Rnds 17 and 18: Work even.

Rnd 19: Inc for gusset as before. There are 13 sts in gusset.

Rnds 20 thru 22: Work even.

Rnd 23: K 2, sl next 13 sts to a stitch holder (these will be worked later for thumb); cast on 3 sts on same needle with 2 sts, then continue to work to end of rnd. There are 40 sts on needles. Continue to work on these 40 sts until mitten, when tried on, fits to top of little finger or approximately 1½ inches less than total length desired for comfortable fit. Discontinue cable pat.

Shape Top: * K 6, K 2 tog; rep from * around — 5 decs. Rnd 2 and all Even-Numbered Rnds; Knit.

Rnd 3: * K 5, K 2 tog; rep from * around.

Rnd 5: * K 4, K 2 tog; rep from * around.

Rnd 7: * K 3, K 2 tog; rep from * around.

Rnd 9: * K 2, K 2 tog; rep from * around.

Rnd 10: * K 1, K 2 tog; rep from * around. Fasten off, leaving a 5-inch end. Thread end in to tapestry needle and run needle through sts on needles. Draw sts together tightly and secure on wrong side.

Thumb: Slip the 13 sts from holder to a needle, pick up 1 st in each of the 3 cast-on sts of hand. Divide the stitches on 3 needles. Join. Knit around until thumb measures approximately 2 inches, or desired length.

Next Rnd: * K 1, K 2 tog; rep from * 4 times, K 1. Fasten off and complete same as hand.

Left Mitten

Work same as Right Mitten to beg. of thumb and gusset.

Rnd 7: Work 4 sts of Needle No. 2, place marker, inc 1 st in next st, K 1, inc 1 st in next st, place marker, K 6.

Complete to correspond to right mitten.

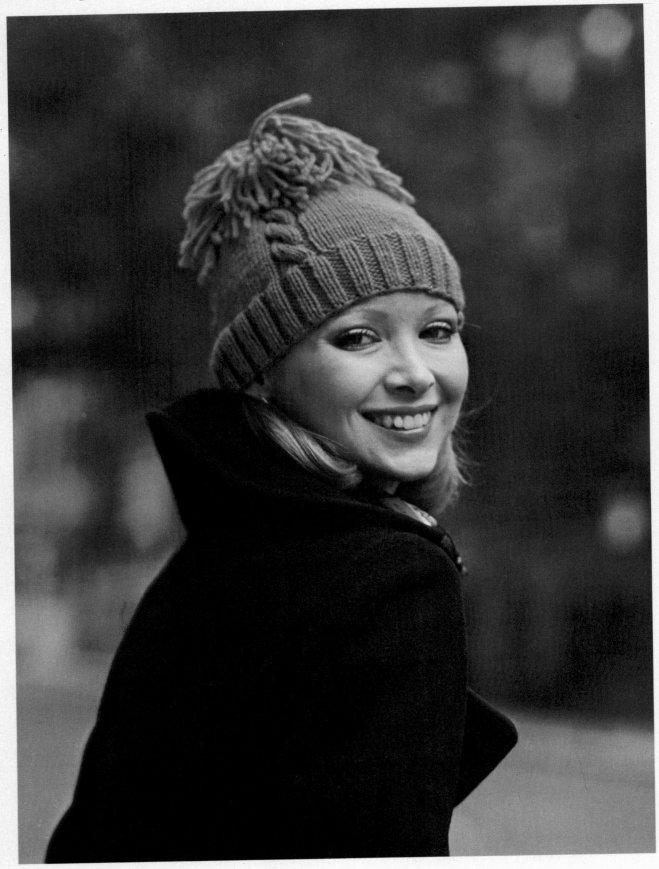

SLEEVELESS JERKIN

Designed and Created by Joe Ann Helms

Instructions are for size 8. Changes for sizes 10, 12, 14, 16 and 18 are in parentheses.

MATERIALS — Brunswick Pomfret Sport or Fore 'N Aft (2-oz) 4(4-4-5-5-5)

NEEDLES: "Susan Bates" No. 5 OR SIZE TO GIVE GAUGE

GAUGE: 6 sts = 1 inch, 8 rows = 1 inch

FINISHED MEASUREMENTS (in inches)

Bust 32(34-36-38-40-42)

Note: Jerkin is shaped at sides. If straight garment is desired, the decreases and increases may be omitted.

Back: Cast on 97(103-109-115-121-127) sts. Work in St St (K 1 row, P 1 row) for 12 rows. P next row on right side of hemline. Beg with a P row continue in St St to 4 inches above hemline. Dec 1 st each side of next row and rep decs every 1 inch 3 times more. Work on 89(95-101-107-113-119) sts until 8 inches above hemline.

Inc 1 st each side of next row and rep incs every 1 inch 3 times more. Work on 97(103-109-115-121-127) sts until 12 inches from beg or desired length to underarms.

Armholes — Row 1: K 1, * P 1, K 1; rep from * 4 times (11 sts in seed st border), K to last 11 sts, K 1, * P 1, K 1; rep from * to end (11 sts in seed st border).

Row 2: K 1, * P 1, K 1; rep from * 4 times, P to last 11 sts, K 1, * P 1, K 1; rep from * to end. Rep last 2 rows until armholes measure 5½(5½-6-6-6½-6½) inches, end with Row 2.

Neck Border — Row 1: Work 11 sts in seed st, K 8(9-10-11-12-13) sts, work next 59(63-67-71-75-79) sts in seed st, K 8(9-10-11-12-13), work last 11 sts in seed st.

Row 2: Work 11 sts in seed, P 8(9-10-11-12-13) sts, work 59(63-67-71-75-79) sts in seed st, P 8(9-10-11-12-13) sts, work 11 sts in seed st. Rep last 2 rows until armholes measure 7(7-7½-7½-8-8) inches, end with Row 2. Bind off all seed sts-sections in pat (knitting the P sts and purling the K sts), all St St sections knitting the sts.

Front: Work same as back.

Finishing: Sew side seams from lower edge to beg of armholes.

Sew 19(20-21-22-23-24) sts from armhole edge of back and front together for shoulder seams. Turn hem to wrong side at hemline and sew in place, taking care not to draw work. Steam lightly.

BABY CARDIGAN

Designed and Created by Joe Ann Helms

Instructions are for Infant Sizes. Changes for Sizes 1, 2 and 3 are in parentheses.

MATERIALS — Brunswick Baby Delf (1 oz) 3(3-4-4) skeins; 8 Buttons

NEEDLES: "Susan Bates" No. 1 and No. 3 OR SIZE TO GIVE GAUGE

GAUGE: 7 sts = 1 inch, 9 rows = 1 inch

FINISHED MEASUREMENTS (in inches)
Chest (buttoned) 20(22½-23½-24½)

Back: With No. 1 needles cast on 68(76-80-84) sts.

Ribbing — Row 1: *K 2, P 2; rep from * to end. Rep Row 1 for 14 rows. Change to No. 3 needles. Work in St St (K 1 row, P 1 row) until 6½(7-7½-8) inches from beg, or desired length to underarms, end with a P row.

Armholes: Bind off 3(4-5-5) sts at beg of next 2 rows.

Next Row: K 2 tog, K to last 2 sts, K 2 tog.

Next Row: Purl.

Rep the last 2 rows twice.

Continue St St on 58(64-66-70) sts until armholes measure 3(3½-4-4½) inches.

Shoulders: Bind off 13(14-15-17) sts at beg of next 2 rows. Place 32(36-36-36) sts on a stitch holder.

Note: For Boys work right front first. For Girls work left front first. Buttonholes will be worked in left front for Boys and in Right Front for Girls.

First Front: With No. 1 needles, cast on 40(44-44-48). For Boys beg with K 2 at front edge; for Girls beg with P 2 at underarm edge and work in K 2, P 2 ribbing for 14 rows.

Next Row: Knit and on Size 2 only, inc 2 sts in row. There are 40(44-46-48) sts on needles.

Next Row For Boys only: P to the last 7 sts, K 7 for front border.

Next Row For Girls Only: K 7 for front border. P to end. Keeping the 7 sts of front border in Garter St (K every row) and remaining sts in St St, work to same length as back to armhole, ending at underarm edge.

Armhole: Bind off 3(4-5-5) sts at beg of next row. Dec 1 st at armhole edge every 2nd row twice. Work on 35(38-39-41) sts until armhole measures 1½(2-2½-3) inches, ending at front edge.

Neck — Row 1: Work 14(16-16-16) sts and place these sts on a stitch holder. Dec 1 st at neck edge *every* row 8 times. Work on 13 (14-15-17) sts until armhole is the same length as back armhole. K 6 rows on all sts for garter st. Bind off. Mark places with pins on front border and rib band for buttons, having first marker ½ inch from lower edge, 7th marker ½ inch from beg of neck (the 8th button will be in center of a 1-inch neckband).

To Work Buttonholes in Second Front, opposite button markers: Beg at front edge K 3 sts, yo, K 2 tog, K 2, work to end. On the next row the yo is worked as 1 st.

Second Front: Work to correspond to First Front, reversing all shaping and working buttonholes opposite markers.

Sleeves: With No. 1 needles, cast on 36(40-44-48) sts. Rib as on back for 10 rows, inc 6 sts evenly across last row. Change to No. 3 needles. Work in St St, inc 1 st each side every 6 rows 5 times. Work on 52(56-60-64) to 7(8-9-10) inches from beg, or desired length to underarms. Bind off 3(4-5-5) sts at beg of next 2 rows. Dec 1 st each side every 2nd row 3(4-10-12) times, *every* row 10(10-5-5) times. Bind off 20 sts.

Finishing: Block lightly, sew underarm, shoulder and sleeve seams. Set in sleeves.

Neckband: With No. 1 needles from right side and beg at front edge, K across sts on holder, pick up 6 sts on shaped neck edge. K across sts on holder, pick up 6 sts on shaped neck edge, K across sts on holder.

Keeping borders as established work remaining sts in K 2, P 2 or K 1, P 1 ribbing for 4 rows, work buttonhole in next row in line with other buttonholes. Work 4 rows more in pat as established. Bind off in pat. Sew buttons on front band opposite buttonholes.

CAP

Designed and Created by Joe Ann Helms

Instructions are for adult size.

MATERIALS — Brunswick Germantown Deluxe or Windrush (4-oz) 1 skein

NEEDLES: "Susan Bates" No. 7 OR SIZE TO GIVE GAUGE. One cable needle and a tapestry needle

GAUGE: (Stockinette Stitch) 5 sts = 1 inch, 6 rows = 1 inch

Cast on 112 sts.

Rib Band — *Row 1:* K 2, P 2; repeat from * to end. Repeat Row 1 for 2 inches.

Body — Row 1 (right side): K 10, * P 1, K 6, P 1; K 20; repeat from * twice; P 1, K 6, P 1, K 10.

Row 2: P 10; K 1, P 6, K 1; P 20; repeat from * twice; K 1, P 6, K 1, P 10.

Rows 3 and 4: Repeat Rows 1 and 2.

Row 5: K 10, P 1, * slip next 3 sts to cable needle, hold at *front* of work, K next 3 sts, K the 3 sts from cable needle (cable twisted); K 20; repeat from * twice, P 1, work cable twist on next 6 sts, P 1; K 10. These are 4 cables.

Row 6: Repeat Row 2.

Row 7: Repeat Row 1.

Row 8: Repeat Row 2. Repeat these 8 rows for pattern (cable is twisted every 8th row) until piece measures approximately 5 inches from beginning, ending with 1 row after a cable twist row.

First Decrease Row: K 8, K 2 tog., * P 1, K 6, P 1, K 2 tog, K 16, K 2 tog; repeat from * twice, P 1, K 6, P 1, K 2 tog, K 8. (1 st is decreased each side of each cable and there are 104 sts on needle). Twisting the 4 cables every 8th row as before and working in established pattern between cables, dec 1 st each side of cables every 6 rows 4 times more. There are 80 sts on needle. On the next right side row, k 2 tog across row. There are 40 sts on needle. Cut yarn, leaving a 12-inch end. Thread end into tapestry needle and run needle through all sts on knitting needle. Draw the stitches together tightly and secure. Sew the two edges together for back seam.

Pompon: See page 29. Wrap remaining yarn around a 4-inch piece of cardboard. Sew pompon to top of cap, allowing ends to fall over top as shown in photograph.

WHITE DRESS WITH BLUE STRIPES

Instructions are for size 8. Changes for sizes 10, 12, 14, 16 and 18 are in parentheses.

MATERIALS — Sport Yarn Weight
Brunswick Fore-'N-Aft (2-oz balls) 8(9-9-10-10-10) White (W) and 2 each Navy (N) and Blue (B)
Placket Zipper
NEEDLES: "Susan Bates" 1 pair each No. 4 and No. 5 OR SIZE TO GIVE GAUGE

GAUGE: 6 sts = 1 inch, 8 rows = 1 inch

FINISHED MEASUREMENTS (in inches)
Lower edge 44(46-48-50-52-54)
Hipline (7 inches below waistline) 35(37-39-41-42-45)
Waistline 27(29-31-33-35-37)
Bust 32(34-36-38-40-42)
Back at shoulders 12½(13-13½-14-14½-15)
Sleeve at underarm 12(12-13-13-14-14)

Note: Length is planned for 24 inches from hemline to waistline. Make any adjustment in length by working more or less inches between dec rows.

Stripe Pattern — Worked in St st, working 20 rows W; 2 rows N; 20 rows W; 2 rows B. Rep these 44 rows for pat for back and front. Carry white loosely along edge of work. Break off N and B when not in use.

Back: With No. 5 needles and W, cast on 132(138-144-150-156-162) sts. Change to No. 4 needles. Work in St st for 1 inch, end with a K row. K next row on wrong side for hemline. Beg with a K row work in striped pat to 3 inches above hemline, end with a P row.
First Dec Row: K 14(15-16-17-18-19), K 2 tog through back lps (K 2 tog b), place marker on needle, K 26(27-28-29-30-31), K 2 tog b, place 2nd marker on needle, K 44(46-48-50-52-54), place 3rd marker on needle, K 2 tog, K 26(27-28-29-30-31), place 4th marker on needle, K 2 tog, K 14(15-16-17-18-19). There are 4 decs in row. Sl markers on every row. Continue pat, decrease 4 sts in a row (by K 2 tog b before first and 2nd marker and K 2 tog after 3rd and 4th marker) every 2 inches 6 times more.
Work on 104(110-116-122-128-134) to 17 inches from hemline, or 7 inches less than desired length to waistline.

Dec 4 sts in a row every 1 inch 6 times. Work on 80(86-92-98-104-110) to 24 inches from hemline, or desired length to waistline and mark. Inc 1 st each side every 4th row 11 times. Work on 102(108-114-120-126-132) to 7½ inches above waistline or desired length to underarms.

Armholes: Bind off 6(6-7-7-8-8) at beg of next 2 rows. Dec 1 st each side every 2nd row 8(9-10-11-12-13) times. Work on 74(78-80-84-86-90) until armholes are 7(7-7½-7½-8-8) inches, end with a K row.
Next Row — Neck and Shoulders: P 24(25-26-27-28-29), place center 26(28-28-30-30-32) on holder, join 2nd ball yarn, work to end. Working each side with separate yarn, bind off from each armhole edge 5(5-5-6-6-7) sts 3 times *and at same time* dec 1 st at neck edges every 2nd row 3 times. Bind off remaining sts from armhole edges.

Front: Work same as back until armhole shaping is completed, end with a dec row 74(78-80-84-86-90) sts.
Neck: P 31(32-33-34-35-36), place center 12(14-14-16-16-18) on holder, join 2nd ball of needed color, work to end. Working each side with separate yarn, bind off 2 sts from each neck edge every 2nd row twice. Dec 1 st at each neck edge every 2nd row 6 times. Work on 21(22-23-23-25-26) to same length as back to shoulders, then shape shoulders as on back.

Stripe Pattern for Cuffs: Worked in K 1, P 1 rib, working 6 rows W; 2 rows N; 6 rows W; 2 rows B. Rep these 16 rows for pat.
Sleeve: With No. 5 needles cast on 66(66-72-72-78-78) sts. Work in rib stripe pat for 26 rows. Change to No. 4 needles and continue in rib stripe pat for 34 rows more, end with a wrong side row. Remainder of sleeve is worked with W. Change back to No. 5 needles. Work in St St inc 1 st each side every 1 inch 3 times. Work on 72(72-78-78-84-84) to 12 inches from beg, or desired length, when cuff is turned back.
Shape Cap: Bind off 6(6-7-7-8-8) at beg of next 2 rows. Dec 1 st each side every 4th row 6 times, every 2nd row 6(6-8-8-10-10) times. Bind off 3 sts at beg of next 4 rows. Bind off 24 sts.
Finishing: Sew left shoulder seam.
Neckband: With No. 4 needle from right side, pick up 1 st in each row to sts on holder. K across sts at back of neck, 1 st in each row to shoulder, 1

st in each st and row on left front neck edge to sts on holder, place a marker on needle, K across sts on holder inc 1 st, place a marker on needle, pick up same number of sts on right neck edge as on left. Sl markers on every row.

Row 1: Rib to marker, sl marker. Rib across center front sts, sl marker, beg with K or P to match st before first marker, rib to end.

Row 2: Work in rib as established. Rep Row 2 for 1 inch, end with a wrong side row.

Next Row: * Rib to 1 st before marker, P 3 tog; rep from * once, rib to end. Keeping rib, work until band measures 1¹/₂ inches. Bind off in rib. Sew right shoulder seam. Set in sleeves. Sew side seams, leaving 3¹/₂ inches below and above waistline open for zipper. Set in sleeves. Sew in zipper.

LACE YOKED AND SLEEVED SLIP-ON

Instructions are for size 8. Changes for sizes 10, 12, 14, 16 and 18 are in parentheses.

MATERIALS — Sport Yarn Weight
Brunswick Icecap (1-oz) 7(7-8-8-9-9)
NEEDLES: "Susan Bates" No. 3 and No. 5 OR SIZE TO GIVE GAUGE
GAUGE: 6 sts = 1 inch, 8 rows = 1 inch

FINISHED MEASUREMENTS (in inches)

Bust 32(34-36-38-40-42)
Back at shoulders 12(12¹/₂-13-13¹/₂-14-14¹/₂)
Sleeve at underarm 12(13-13-13¹/₂-14-14¹/₂)

Back: With No. 3 needles cast on 97(103-109-115-121-127) sts.

Row 1 (right side): K 1, * P 1, K 1; rep from * to end.

Row 2: P 1, * K 1, P 1; rep from * to end.
Rep these 2 rows to 4 inches from beg, end with Row 2. Change to No. 5 needles. Work in St St (K 1 row, P 1 row) to 12 inches from beg, or desired length to underarms.

Armholes: Bind off 9(11-11-12-13-14) at beg of next 2 rows. Dec 1 st each side every 2nd row 4(4-5-5-6-6) times. Work on 71(73-77-81-83-87) until armholes are 6(6-6¹/₂-6¹/₂-7-7) inches.

Neck: Work 22(23-24-25-26-27), place center 27(27-29-31-31-33) on holder, join 2nd ball of yarn, work to end. Working on each side with separate yarn, dec 1 st at neck edges every 2nd

row twice. Work even until armholes measure 7(7-7¹/₂-7¹/₂-8-8) inches.

Shoulders: Bind off from each armhole edge 5(5-5-5-6-6) 3 times, 5(6-7-8-6-7) once.

Front: Work same as back until armhole shaping is completed, end with a wrong side row.

Yoke Pat — Row 1 (right side): K 2(3-5-3-4-2), * yo, K 3 tog, yo, K 5; rep from *, end last rep K 2(3-5-3-4-2).

Row 2: Purl all sts, including yos.

Row 3: Knit.

Row 4: Purl.
Rep last 4 rows twice. Work in St St until armholes measure 3(3-3¹/₂-3¹/₂-4-4) inches.

Neck: Work 25(26-27-28-29-30), join 2nd ball of yarn, bind off center 21(21-23-25-25-27), work to end. Working each side with separate yarn, dec 1 st at neck edges every 2nd row 5 times, shaping shoulders as on back when armholes are same length.

Sleeves: With No. 3 needles cast on 50(52-52-54-58-58) sts. Rib in K 1, P 1 for 4 inches, inc 21(25-25-27-27-29) on last row. 71(77-77-79-81-85-87) sts. Change to No. 5 needles. K 1 row, P 1 row.

Pat — Row 1 (right side): K 2(5-5-3-5-2), * yo, K 3 tog, yo, K 5; rep from *, end last rep K 2(5-5-3-5-2).
Continue in pat (as on back) to 17 inches from beg or desired length to underarm.

Shape Cap: Bind off 9(11-11-12-13-14) at beg of next 2 rows. Dec 1 st each side every 2nd row 2(4-2-4-2-4) times, every 4th row 7(6-8-7-9-8) times. Bind off 3 sts at beg of next 4 rows. Bind off 23 sts.

Finishing: Sew left shoulder seam.

Neckband: With No. 3 needles from right side beg at right back shoulder, pick up 118(118-122-122-126-126) around neck edge including sts on holders. Rib in K 1, P 1 for 8 rows. Bind off in rib. Sew right shoulder including neckband. Sew underarm, shoulder and sleeve seams. Set in sleeves, holding in any extra fullness across top of sleeve. Block between towels.

POPCORN STITCH ZIPPER JACKET, BERET AND MUFFLER

Instructions are for size 8. Changes for sizes 10, 12, 14, 16 and 18 are in parentheses. *Cont. pg. 83*

MATERIALS — Knitting Worsted Weight Yarn

Brunswick Windrush (4-oz skeins) 7(8-8-9-9-10);Separating zipper

NEEDLES: "Susan Bates" 1 pair each No. 5, No. 6 and No. 7 OR SIZE TO GIVE GAUGE

GAUGE: (No. 7 needles) 5 sts = 1 inch, 6 rows = 1 inch

FINISHED MEASUREMENTS (in inches)

Jacket — Bust 32(34-36-38-40-42)
Back at shoulders 12(12^1/$_2$-13-13^1/$_2$-14-14^1/$_2$)
Sleeve at underarm 13(13-14-14-15-15)

JACKET

Pattern Stitch — Worked on a multiple of 6 sts plus 3(7-3-5-3-7).

Row 1 (right side): Knit.

Row 2 And All Even-Numbered Rows: Purl.

Row 3: K 1(3-1-2-1-3), * in next st (K through front lp, K through back lp) twice, sl 4th st on right needle over 3 sts, next st over 2 sts, next st over first st (popcorn — PO made), K 5; rep from * end last rep K 1(3-1-2-1-3).

Row 5: Knit.

Row 7: K 4(6-4-5-4-6), * PO, K 5; rep from *, end last rep K 4(6-4-5-4-6).

Row 8: Purl. Rep these 8 rows for pat. Keep continuity when shaping.

Back: With No. 5 needles cast on 81(85-87-95-99-103) sts.

Row 1 (right side): K 1, * P 1, K 1; rep from * to end.

Row 2: P 1, * K 1, P 1; rep from * to end. Rep these 2 rows for 4 inches, end with Row 2. Change to No. 7 needles and work in pat to 14^1/$_2$ inches from beg, or desired length to underarm, end with a P row.

Armholes: Bind off 6(6-7-7-7-7) at beg of next 2 rows. Dec 1 st each side every 2nd row 4(5-4-7-7-8) times. Work on 61(63-65-67-71-73) until armholes measure 7(7-7^1/$_2$-7^1/$_2$-8-8) inches, end with a P row.

Shoulders: Bind off 6(6-6-7-7-7) at beg of next 4 rows, 6(7-8-7-8-9) at beg of next 2 rows. Place 25(25-25-25-27-27) sts on holder for back of neck.

Left Front: With No. 5 needles cast on 40(42-46-47-52-54) sts. Rib in K 1, P 1 to same number rows as on back. Change to No. 7 needles.

Establish Pat — Row 1: Knit.

Row 2 and All Even Numbered Rows: Purl.

Row 3: K 1(3-1-2-1-3), * PO, K 5; rep from *, end last rep K 2.

Row 8: Purl.

Continue in pat as established to same length as back to armhole, end with a P row.

Armhole: Bind off 6(6-7-7-7-7) at beg of next row.

Dec 1 st at armhole edge every 2nd row 4(5-6-6-9-10) times. Work on 30(31-33-34-36-37) sts until armhole measures 5(5-5^1/$_2$-5^1/$_2$-6-6) inches, end at front edge.

Neck: P 7(7-8-8-9-9) and place these sts on holder, P to end of row.

Dec 1 st at neck edge every 2nd row 5 times. Work on 18(19-20-21-22-23) to same length as back to shoulder, end with a P row.

Shoulder: Bind off 6(6-6-7-7-7) from armhole edge twice. Bind off remaining 6(7-8-7-8-9) from armhole edge.

Right Front: With No. 5 needles cast on and work rib as on left front. Change to No. 7 needles.

Establish Pat — Row 1: Knit.

Row 2: Purl.

Row 3: K 2, * PO, K 5; rep from *, end last rep K 1(3-1-2-1-3).

Complete to correspond to left front, reversing all shaping.

Sleeves: With No. 5 needles cast on 45(45-49-49-51-51) sts. Rib as on back. Change to No. 7 needles.

Inc Row: K 4(4-1-1-1-1), * inc 1 st in next st, K 3; rep from * 9(9-10-10-11-11) times, K to end. P 1 row on 65(65-71-71-75-75) sts.

Pat Row 3: K 2(2-2-2-1-1), * PO, K 5; rep from * end last rep K 2(2-2-2-1-1).

Continue pat as established until sleeve measures 18 inches from beg, or desired length to underarm.

Shape Cap: Bind off 6(6-7-7-7-7) at beg of next 2 rows. Dec 1 st each side every 2nd row 12 times, *every* row 4(4-6-6-8-8) times. Bind off 3 sts at beg of next 2 rows. Bind off 15 sts.

Finishing: Steam pieces lightly, taking care not to flatten popcorn sts. Sew underarm, shoulders and sleeve seams. Set in sleeves.

Neckband: With No. 5 needles from right side, beg at right front edge, pick up 91(91-93-93-

95-95) sts around neck edge, including sts on holders.

Row 1: K 1, * P 1, K 1; rep from * to end. Continue in rib until band measures 3 inches. Bind off knitting. Fold band in half to wrong side and sew to neck edge, taking care not to draw tight. Beg at fold of neckband, sew in zipper.

Beret — Fits All Sizes

With No. 7 needles cast on 10 sts for center top.
Row 1 and All Odd-Numbered Rows: Purl.
Row 2 (right side): K, inc 1 st in each st by K in front, K in back of same st. 20 sts.
Row 4: * K 1, inc 1 st in next st; rep from * to end. 30 sts.
Row 6: * K 2; inc 1 st in next st; rep from * to end. 40 sts.
Row 8: * K 3, inc 1 st in next st; rep from * to end. 10 incs. Continue in this way to inc 10 sts every 2nd (right side rows), with 1 st more between incs on every inc row until there are 170 sts in row. Work 7 rows even.
First Dec Row: * K 15, K 2 tog; rep from * to end. 10 decs. Work 3 rows on 160 sts.
2nd Dec Row: * K 14, K 2 tog; rep from * to end. 10 decs. Work 1 row on 150 sts.
Continue in this way to dec 10 sts every 2nd row, with 1 st less between decs every dec row until there are 120 sts in row. P 1 row.
Next Row: * K 22, K 2 tog; rep from * to end. 115 sts. Change to No. 5 needles. Work in K 1, P 1 rib for 1 inch. Bind off in rib. Sew back seam.

Muffler

With No. 6 needles cast on 49 sts.
Rib in K 1, P 1 for 60 inches, or desired length. Bind off in rib.
Fringe: Wrap yarn around a 10-inch cardboard. Cut at 1 end. Using 2 strands, place fringe (see pg. 21) in first and every 4th st on short ends of muffler. Trim evenly.

HALTER TOP

Instructions are for size 8. Changes for sizes 10, 12 and 14 are in parentheses.

MATERIALS — Brunswick Icecap (1-oz) 4(4-5-5)
NEEDLES: "Susan Bates" 1 pair each No. 4 and No. 6 OR SIZE TO GIVE GAUGE

Crochet Hook: "Susan Bates" Steel No. 2
GAUGE: 6 sts = 1 inch, 10 rows = 1 inch

FINISHED MEASUREMENTS (in inches)

Bust 32(34-36-38)

Front: With No. 4 needles, cast on 84(86-88-90) sts. Rib in K 1, P 1 for 2 inches. Change to No. 6 needles. Continue in rib until 4 inches from beg. Inc 1 st each side every 4th row 4 times, working inc sts in rib. Work on 92(94-96-98) sts until piece measures 8 inches from beg.
Next Row (right side): K, inc 4(8-12-16) sts evenly spaced across row. K 3 rows on 96(102-108-114). Top is worked in Garter Stitch (K every row).
Next Row: K 43(46-49-52), with yarn at *back* sl next 10 sts as to P (be sure yarn at back is loose and work does not pucker), K 43(46-49-52).
Next Row: K all sts.
Rep last 2 rows 3 times.
Next Row: K 4, K 2 tog, K to 10 center sts, sl 10 as before, K to last 6 sts, K 2 tog, K 4.
Dec 1 st each side (5th and 6th sts tog) every 4th row until there are 10(12-14-16) sl st rows in all 10(12-14-16) loose strands at back.
Neck — Next Row: K to 10 center sts, join 2nd ball of yarn, bind off (not too loosely) 10 center sts, K to end.
Work each side with separate yarn. Continue to dec at sides every 4th row (as before) AND AT SAME TIME dec for neck by K the 5th and 6th st from neck edge tog every 2nd row until 9 sts remain at each side. Place sts on stitch holder.
Back: Cast on and work same as front to 8 inches from beg.
K next row for turning ridge. Change to No. 4 needles and rib 1 inch more. With No. 6 needles bind off in rib.
Straps: Slip 9 sts from holder to No. 4 needle. Continue in Garter St (K every row) for approx 15 inches. Bind off knitting.
Finishing: With lower edge of back and front in line, sew side seams. Turn and sew hem at top of back. Try on, cross straps and sew to back as desired. With crochet hook, from right side, work sc on armhole edges to beg of straps, holding in to desired fit.

TURQUOISE MOHAIR SLIP-ON

Instructions are for small size. Changes for medium and large sizes are in parentheses.

MATERIALS — Brunswick Tivolaine (40-gr) 9(10-11)
NEEDLES: "Susan Bates" No. 4 OR SIZE TO GIVE GAUGE
Crochet Hook: "Susan Bates" Size F
GAUGE: 5 sts = 1 inch, 8 rows = 1 inch

FINISHED MEASUREMENTS (in inches)

Bust 32(36-40)
Back at shoulders 12(13-14^1/$_2$)
Sleeve at underarm 12(13-14^1/$_2$)

Pattern Stitch — Worked on a multiple of 11 sts plus 4(2-2).

Row 1 (right side): P 3(2-2), * K 9, P 2; rep from * end last rep P 3(2-2).
Row 2 And All Even-Numbered Rows Through Row 14: K 3(2-2), * P 9, K 2; rep from *, end last rep K 3(2-2).
Row 3: P 3(2-2), K 2, * K 2 tog, yo, K 1, yo, sl 1, K 1, psso, K 2, P 2; rep from *, end last rep P 3(2-2).
Row 5: P 3(2-2), * K 1, K 2 tog, yo, K 3, yo, sl 1, K 1, psso, K 1, P 2; rep from *, end last rep P 3(2-2)
Row 7: P 3(2-2), * K 9, P 2; rep from *, end last rep P 3(2-2).
Row 9: P 3(2-2), * K 2, sl 1, K 1, psso, yo, K 1, yo, K 2 tog, K 2, P 2; rep from * end last rep P 3(2-2).
Row 11: P 3(2-2), * K 4, yo, K 2 tog, K 3, P 2; rep from *, end last rep P 3(2-2).
Row 13: P 3(2-2), * K 9, P 2; rep from *, end last rep P 3(2-2).
Row 15: Purl all sts.
Row 16: Same as Row 2.
Rep these 16 rows for pat, keeping continuity when shaping.

Back: Cast on 81(90-101) sts. P 1 row on right side, K 1 row on wrong side. Beg with Row 1 of pat work to 14 inches from beg, or desired length to underarms.

Armholes: Bind off 4(6-7) at beg of next 2 rows. Dec 1 st each side every 2nd row 3(3-4) times.

Work on 67(72-79) sts until armholes measure 7(7^1/$_2$-8) inches.

Shoulders and Neck: Bind off 7 sts at beg of next 2 rows. 53(58-65) sts.

Next Row: Bind off 7(7-8) sts, work until 7(8-9) sts from bind-off, join a 2nd ball of yarn, bind off next 25(26-29) sts for back of neck, work to end. Work each side with separate yarn.

Next Row: Bind off 7(8-9) sts, work to end. From each armhole edge bind off remaining sts. 21(23-25) sts each shoulder.

Front: Work same as back until armhole shaping is completed. 67(72-79) sts.

Neck: Work 26(28-30) sts, join 2nd ball yarn, bind off center 15(16-19) sts, work to end. Working each side with separate yarn, bind off 2 sts from each neck edge once. Dec 1 st at each neck edge every 2nd row 3 times. Work on 21(23-25) sts each side, shaping shoulders as on back when armholes are same length.

Sleeves: Cast on 59(57-57) sts. P 1 row, K 1 row. Beg with Row 1, work pat as on back. Work 2 rows even.

Next Row: P 3(2-2), insert left needle from front to back under strand between last st worked and next st on left needle, forming a lp on needle, K through back of this lp (1 st increase), continue pat to last 3(2-2) sts, inc 1 st as before, P 3(2-2). Working inc sts in St St (K on right side, P on wrong side), continue pat, inc as before every 4th row 3(3-2) times more, every 2nd row 0(3-6) times. Work on 67(71-75) sts until sleeve measures 4^1/$_2$ inches from beg, or desired length to underarm.

Shape Cap: Bind off 4(6-7) at beg of next 2 rows. Dec 1 st each side every 2nd row 8(7-6) times, every 4th row 4(5-7) times. Bind off 3 sts at beg of next 4 rows. Bind off 23 sts.

Finishing: Sew underarm, shoulder and sleeve seams. Set in sleeves.

Neck Trim: With crochet hook join yarn at neck edge of right shoulder. From right side work 1 row sc around neck edge, spacing sts to keep edge flat, join with a sl st to first sc. Ch 2, do *not* turn.

Rnd 2: Dec in first sc, * ch 4, yo hook, insert hook under front lp at top of dc and in side of dc, yo and draw lp through (3 lps on hook-picot), yo and through 3 lps, sk 2 sts on neck edge; dc in next st; rep from * around. Join to top of first dc and fasten off.

CHECKED EVENING SLIP-ON

Instructions are for size 8. Changes for sizes 10, 12, 14, 16 and 18 are in parentheses.

MATERIALS — Sport Yarn Weight in Metallic (2-oz) 3(4-4-5-5)

NEEDLES: "Susan Bates" 1 pair each No. 3 and No. 5 OR SIZE TO GIVE GAUGE

GAUGE: 6 sts = 1 inch, 8 rows = 1 inch

FINISHED MEASUREMENTS (in inches)
Bust 32(34-36-38-40-42)

Back: With No. 3 needles cast on 94(102-106-114-118-126) sts.
Row 1: K 2, * P 2, K 2; rep from * to end.
Row 2: P 2, * K 2, P 2; rep from * to end.
Rep these 2 rows for 2 inches, inc 2(0-2-0-2-0) sts on last row. 96(102-108-114-120-126) sts. Change to No. 5 needles.
Row 1 (right side): K 3(6-9-12-5-8), * P 10, K 10; rep from *, end last rep K 3(6-9-12-5-8).
Row 2: K the knit sts and P the purl sts. Rep these 2 rows 5 times more (12 rows).
Row 13: P 3(6-9-12-5-8), * K 10, P 10; rep from *, end last rep P 3(6-9-12-5-8).
Row 14: K the knit sts and P the purl sts. Rep last 2 rows 5 times more. (12 rows). Rep these 24 rows for pat. Work to 15 inches from beg, or desired length to underarms.
Armholes: Bind off from each armhole edge 4(4-5-5-6-6) sts twice, 4(4-5-5-5-6) sts once and 2(3-2-3-3-3) sts once. Work on 68(72-74-78-80-84) until armholes measure 2½(2½-3-3-3½-3½) inches.
Neck — Next Row: Work 18(19-19-19-20-21), place center 32(34-36-40-40-42) on holder, join a 2nd ball of yarn, work to end. Working each side with separate yarn, dec 1 st at each neck edge every 2nd row 6(7-7-7-8-9) times. Work on 12 sts until armholes measure 6½(6½-7-7-7½-7½) inches. Bind off 12 sts at each side.
Front: Work same as back until armhole measures 1½(1½-2-2-2½-2½) inches.
Neck: Work 27(28-28-29-30-31), place center 14(16-18-20-20-22) on holder, join a 2nd ball of yarn, work to end. Working each side with separate yarn, bind off 3 sts from each neck edge every 2nd row 4(4-4-5-5-5) times. Dec 1 st at each neck edge every 2nd row 3(4-4-2-3-4)

times. Work on 12 sts each side until armholes are same length as back armholes. Bind off all sts.
Finishing: Sew left shoulder seam.
Neckband: With No. 3 needles from right side pick up 1 st in each row and each st at back of neck, 1 st in each row and each st around front neck edge.
Row 1: Rib in K 2, P 2 (adjusting if necessary to have a multiple of 4 sts).
Rib 4 rows more. Bind off in rib. Sew other shoulder seam.
Armhole Bands: Pick up sts around armhole as on neck. Rib in K 2, P 2, dec 1 st each side on 2nd and 4th row. Bind off in rib. Sew underarm seams. Block between wet towels.

SHADY LANE KNIT AFGHAN

Approximate Size 54 X 66 inches (without fringe)

MATERIALS — Brunswick Germantown Knitting Worsted or Windrush (4-oz balls) 3 each Light Lime (A), Lime (B), Medium Lime (C), Dark Lime (D)
NEEDLE: "Susan Bates" 29-inch circular No. 8 OR SIZE TO GIVE GAUGE

GAUGE: 16 sts (1 rep of pat) = about 3 inches

PATTERN STITCH: Worked on a multiple of 16 sts plus 3 extra sts

Row 1 (right side): K 1, K 2 tog through back lps, (K 2 tog b), * K 13, sl 2 sts as to P, K 1, pass 2 sl sts over K 1; rep from *, end K 13, K 2 tog b, K 1.
Row 2: K 1, * P 1, K 6, yo, K 1, yo, K 6; rep from *, end P 1, K 1.
Rep Rows 1 and 2 for pattern.

AFGHAN

With A, cast on 291 stitches. Repeat the 2 pat rows 4 times (8 rows). Break A. With B, work 8 rows; break B. With C, work 8 rows; break C. With D, work 8 rows; break D. Keeping color sequence as established, work 8 rows with each shade seven times more, then with A work 7 rows more. Bind off as in Row 2 omitting the yos.

Fringe: Wrap D around a 16-inch piece of cardboard. Using eight strands, knot fringe (see pg. 21) in each point of both ends. Trim evenly.

SHAWL — DIAMOND PATTERN

Approximate Size 27″ X 54″ (without fringe)

MATERIALS — Brunswick Icecap (1-oz. skeins) 12.

NEEDLES: "Susan Bates" Size 8 OR SIZE TO GIVE GAUGE

Crochet Hook: "Susan Bates" Size F

GAUGE: diamond across center = 4½ inches diamond in length = 4½ inches

Note: Always sl sts as if to knit.

Cast on 3 sts. Work in St St inc 1 st each side every K row until 21 sts on needle. Beg pat.

Row 1 (right side): Inc 1 st in first st, K 1, yo, sl 1, K 1, psso, K 13, K 2 tog, yo, K 1, inc 1 st in last st. 23 sts.

Row 2 and All Even-Numbered Rows to Row 8: Purl.

Row 3: Inc 1 st in first st, K 3, yo, sl 1, K 1, psso, K 11, K 2 tog, yo, K 3, inc 1 st in last st. 25 sts.

Row 5: Inc 1 st in first st, K 5, yo, sl 1, K 1, psso, K 9, K 2 tog, yo, K 5, inc 1 st in last st. 27 sts.

Row 7: Inc 1 st in first st, K 7, yo, sl 1, K 1, psso, K 7, K 2 tog, yo, K 7, inc 1 st in last st. 29 sts.

Row 8: Purl, inc 1 st in first and last st. 31 sts.

Row 9: Inc 1 st in first st, K 10, yo, sl 1, K 1, psso, K 5, K 2 tog, yo, K 10, inc 1 st in last st. 33 sts.

Row 10 And All Even-Numbered Rows to Row 14: Purl.

Row 11: Inc 1 st in first st, K 12, yo, sl 1, K 1, psso, K 3, K 2 tog, yo, K 12, inc 1 st in last st. 35 sts.

Row 13: Inc in first st, K 14, yo, sl 1, K 1, psso, K 1, K 2 tog, yo, K 14, inc in last st. 37 sts.

Row 14: Rep Row 8.

Row 15: Inc in first st, K 17, yo, sl 1, K 2 tog, psso the 2 tog, yo, K 17, inc 1 st in last st. 41 sts.

Row 16 And All Even-Numbered Rows to Row 22: Purl.

Row 17: Inc in first st, K 1, yo, sl 1, K 1, psso, K 13, K 2 tog, yo, K 3, yo, sl 1, K 1, psso, K 13, K 2 tog, yo, K 1, inc in last st. 43 sts.

Row 19: Inc in first st, K 3, yo, sl 1, K 1, psso, K 11, K 2 tog, yo, K 5, yo, sl 1, K 1, psso, K 11, K 2 tog, yo, K 3, inc in last st. 45 sts.

Row 21: Inc in first st, K 5, yo, sl 1, K 1, psso, K 9, K 2 tog, yo, K 7, yo, sl 1, K 1, psso, K 9, K 2 tog, yo, K 5, inc in last st. 47 sts.

Row 22: Rep Row 8. 49 sts.

Row 23: Inc in first st, K 8, yo, sl 1, K 1, psso, K 7, K 2 tog, yo, K 9, yo, sl 1, K 1, psso, K 7, K 2 tog, yo, K 8, inc in last st. 51 sts.

Row 24 And All Even Rows to Row 28: Purl.

Row 25: Inc in first st, K 10, yo, sl 1, K 1, psso, K 5, K 2 tog, yo, K 11, yo, sl 1, K 1, psso, K 5, K 2 tog, yo, K 10, inc in last st. 53 sts.

Row 27: Inc in first st, K 12, yo, sl 1, K 1, psso, K 3, K 2 tog, yo, K 13, yo, sl 1, K 1, psso, K 3, K 2 tog, yo, K 12, inc in last st. 55 sts.

Row 28: Rep Row 8. 57 sts.

Row 29: Inc in first st, K 15, yo, sl 1, K 1, psso, K 1, K 2 tog, yo, K 15, yo, sl 1, K 1, psso, K 1, K 2 tog, yo, K 15, inc in last st. 59 sts.

Row 30: Purl.

Row 31: Inc in first st, K 17, yo, sl 1, K 2 tog, psso the 2 tog, yo, K 17, yo, sl 1, K 2 tog, psso the 2 tog, yo, K 17, inc in last st. 61 sts.

Row 32: Rep Row 2. One diamond pat has been increased. Rep Rows 17 through 32 for pat having 1 more diamond pat every 32 rows. Work until there are 6 diamond patterns in line at center. Bind off.

Finishing: Steam lightly. From right side, work sc in each bound off st, 3 sc at corner, continue sc on shaped edges, spacing sts to keep edges flat and working 3 sc at corners. Join with a sl st to first sc. Ch 1, turn. Work sc in each sc around, working 3 sc at corners. Join and fasten off.

Rejoin yarn at top of side edge to work from right side, sc in center st of corner, * ch 3, sk 2 sc, sc in next st; rep from * to lower edge, adjust sts if necessary to have ch 3 across sts at point, continue on other side to correspond. Fasten off. Sew in ends. Steam edges.

Fringe: Wrap yarn around a 10-inch cardboard. Cut at one end. Using 6 strands, place fringe (see page 21) in each ch-3 lp on sides. Trim evenly.

LADIES' SLIP-ON WITH CABLE

Instructions are for size 8. Changes for sizes 10, 12, 14, 16 and 18 are in parentheses.

MATERIALS — Sport Yarn Weight
Brunswick Fore 'N Aft Sport or Pomfret Sport Yarn (2-oz balls/skeins) 6(6-7-7-8-8)

NEEDLES: "Susan Bates" 1 pair each No. 3 and No. 5 OR SIZE TO GIVE GAUGE

GAUGE: 6 sts = 1 inch, 8 rows = 1 inch

FINISHED MEASUREMENTS (in inches)

Bust 32(34-36-38-40-42)
Back at shoulders 12(12¹/₂-13-13¹/₂-14-14¹/₂)
Sleeve at underarm 12(12-12¹/₂-12¹/₂-13-13)

Front Cable Pattern — Worked on 14 sts.
Row 1 (right side): P 1, K 12, P 1.
Row 2: K 1, P 12, K 1.
Row 3: P 1, sl next 3 sts to dp needle, hold at *front* of work, K next 3 sts, K 3 from dp needle, sl next 3 sts to dp needle, hold at *back* of work, K next 3 sts, K 3 from dp, P 1.
Row 4: Rep Row 2.
Rep Rows 1 and 2 four times.
Rep from Row 3 (10 rows) for pat.

Back: With No. 3 needles, cast on 96(102-108-114-120-126) sts. Rib in K 1, P 1 for 1 inch. Change to No. 5 needles and continue in rib to 4 inches from beg.
Next Row (right side): P 31(34-37-40-43-46), K 34, P 31(34-37-40-43-46).
Next Row: K 31(34-37-40-43-46), P 34, K 31(34-37-40-43-46).
Rep these 2 rows for pat. Keep continuity when shaping.
Work until 5 inches from beg, end with a wrong side row. Dec 1 st each side of next row and rep decs every 1 inch 3 times more. Work even on 88(94-100-106-112-118) to 9 inches from beg. Inc 1 st each side of next row and rep incs every 1 inch 3 times. Work on 96(102-108-114-120-126) sts to 16 inches from beg, or desired length to underarm, end with a wrong side row.

Armholes: Bind off 6(6-7-7-8-8) at beg of next 2 rows. Dec 1 st each side every 2nd row 6(8-8-9-10-11) times. Work on 72(74-78-82-84-88) until armholes are 7(7-7¹/₂-7¹/₂-8-8) inches.

Shoulders and Neck: Bind off 4(4-4-4-5-5) at beg of next 2 rows.
Next Row: Bind off 4(4-4-4-5-5), work until 10(11-12-13-12-13) sts on needle, join a 2nd ball of yarn, bind off center 36(36-38-40-40-42) sts. Work to end.
Next row: Bind off 4(4-4-4-5-5), work to neck edge, with other ball work to end. Working separately bind off 4(4-4-4-5-5) once, 4(5-6-7-5-6) from each armhole edge once AND AT SAME TIME dec 1 st at neck edges every row twice. 16(17-18-19-20-21) sts for each shoulder.

Front: Cast on and work same as back until ribbing is completed.
Next Row (right side): P 31(34-37-40-43-46), K 10, beginning with Row 1, work cable pat over next 14 sts, K 10, P 31(34-37-40-43-46). Keeping center 14 sts in cable pat and remaining sts as established, decs and incs same as on back. Work even on 96(102-108-114-120-126) to 1 row less than back, ending with a right side row.
Next Row: Work to 12 center sts, place 12 center sts on holder; join a 2nd ball of yarn, work to end. Work each side with separate yarn.
Armhole and Neck — *Row 1:* Bind off 6(6-7-7-8-8), work to 3 sts before neck edge, sl 1 as to K, K 1, psso (neck dec), P 1; with other ball of yarn P 1, K 2 tog, work to end.
Row 2: Bind off 6(6-7-7-8-8), work to 1 st before neck edge, K 1; with other ball of yarn, K 1, work to end.
Continue to shape armhole as on back and keeping 1 st at neck edges P on right side, K on wrong side, continuing to dec for neck (as before) every 4th row 11(11-12-12-12-13) times more, every 2nd row 2(2-2-3-3-3), shaping shoulders as on back when armholes are same length.

Sleeves: With No. 3 needles, cast on 52(52-56-56-58-58) sts. Rib (changing needles) as on back.
Next Row: P 17(17-19-19-20-20), K 18, P 17(17-19-19-20-20).
Next Row: K 17(17-19-19-20-20), P 18, K 17(17-19-19-20-20). Keeping pat as established, inc 1 st each side every 8 rows 10 times, working inc sts by P on right side, K on wrong side.
Work on 72(72-76-76-78-78) until sleeve is 17 inches from beg, or desired length to underarm.
Shape Cap: Bind off 6(6-7-7-8-8) at beg of next 2 rows. Dec 1 st each side every 2nd row 12(12-12-12-10-10) times, every 4th row 3(3-4-4-6-6) times. Bind off 3 sts at beg of next 4 rows. Bind off 18 sts.

Finishing: Sew shoulder, underarm and sleeve seams. Set in sleeves.
Neckband: Slip sts from holder to No. 3 needle to work first row from wrong side.
Inc 1 st in first st, K 1, P 1 to end. 13 sts.
Continue in rib until piece, when slightly stretched will fit around neck edge. Bind off in rib.
Weave to neck edge, then weave bound-off edge neatly under first rib row. Block between towels.

STRIPED RIBBED V-NECKED SLIP-ON

Instructions are for size 8. Changes for sizes 10, 12, 14, 16 and 18 are in parentheses.

MATERIALS — Brunswick Pomfret (2-oz skeins) 4(4-5-5-6-6) Blue (B); 3(3-3-4-4-4) Green (G) and 2 White (W)

NEEDLES: "Susan Bates" 1 pair each No. 2 and No. 4 OR SIZE TO GIVE GAUGE

GAUGE: (Ribbed and Slightly Stretched) 15 sts = 2 inches, 9 rows = 1 inch

FINISHED MEASUREMENTS (in inches)

Bust 32(34-36-38-40-42)

Striped Pattern Stitch — Worked on an uneven number of sts in K 1, P 1 rib in following color sequence: 4 rows B; 2 rows W; 4 rows G; 2 rows W. Rep these 12 rows for pat. Carry colors not in use loosely along edge of work. Back and front are worked in striped pat. Sleeve worked in B with striped cuff.

Back: With No. 4 needles and B cast on 133(139-147-155-163-169) sts.

Row 1 (wrong side): K 1, * P 1, K 1; rep from * to end.

Row 2: P 1 * K 1, P 1; rep from * to end. Counting first 2 rows as part of first B stripe, work to 2 inches from beg, end with a wrong side row.

First Dec Row: K 1, K 2 tog, continue rib to last 3 sts, K 2 tog, K 1.

Continue pat, working 2nd and 3rd sts tog at each end every 12 rows 5 times more. Work on 121(127-135-143-151-157) to 17 inches from beg or desired length to underarm.

Armholes: Bind off 8(8-9-9-10-10) at beg of next 2 rows. Dec 1 st each side every 2nd row 7(8-9-11-13-14) times. Work on 91(95-99-103-105-109) until armholes measure 7(7-7½-7½-8-8) inches.

Shoulders: Bind off 5(5-5-6-6-6) at beg of next 8 rows, 5(6-8-5-6-7) at beg of next 2 rows. Place 41(43-43-45-45-47) on holder.

Front: Work same as back to 16 inches from beg, or 1 inch less than back to armholes, end with a wrong side row.

Neck: Work 60(63-67-71-75-78) sts, place center P st on safety pin, join 2nd ball of yarn, work to end. Work each side with separate yarn.

Row 1 And All Odd-Numbered Rows: K the knit sts and P the purl sts.

Row 2: Rib to 3 sts before neck edge, K 2 tog, K 1, with other yarn K 1, K 2 tog, rib to end.

Keeping 1 st at each side of neck (K on right side, P on wrong side), continue to dec 1 st at each side of neck (as in Row 2) every 2nd row *and at same time* when same length as back to armholes, shape armholes as on back.

Continue to dec for neck every 2nd row until there are 10(11-10-11-11-12) neck decs in all. Dec for neck every 4th row 10(10-11-11-11-11) times, shaping shoulders as on back when armholes are same length.

Sleeves: With No. 2 needles cast on 67(67-71-71-77-77) sts. Work in Striped Pat for 36 rows. Remainder of sleeve is worked with B.

Continue in K 1, P 1 rib, inc 1 st each side every 6 rows 12(12-13-13-14-14) times, working inc sts in rib. Work on 91(91-97-97-105-105) until sleeve measures 17 inches from beg or desired length to underarm.

Shape Cap: Bind off 8(8-9-9-10-10) at beg of next 2 rows. Dec 1 st each side every 2nd row 10(10-12-12-16-16) times, every 4th row 5(5-5-5-4-4) times. Bind off 3 sts at beg of next 4 rows. Bind off 33 sts.

Finishing: Sew right shoulder seam.

Neckband: With No. 2 needles, beg at top of left front shoulder, pick up 1 st in each row to center front having an uneven number of sts , K st from safety pin and mark, pick up same number of sts on right front neck edge as on left, rib across sts at back of neck.

Row 1 (wrong side): P 1, K 1 to center st, P center st, P 1, K 1 to end.

Row 2: Rib to within 3 sts of center st, P 3 tog, K center st, P 3 tog, rib to end.

Row 3: Rib to st before center st, P 3, rib to end. Rep last 2 rows 4 times more. Bind off in rib. Sew left shoulder seam. Set in sleeves. Sew underarm and sleeve seams matching stripes.

GREEN TUNIC SLIP-ON WITH CABLES

Instructions are for size 8. Changes for sizes 10, 12, 14 and 16 are in parentheses.

MATERIALS — Brunswick Germantown Knitting Worsted (4-oz) 4(4-4-5-5)

NEEDLES: "Susan Bates" 1 pair each No. 7 and No. 8

OR SIZE TO GIVE GAUGE
Double/pointed or cable needle

GAUGE: 9 sts = 2 inches, 11 rows = 2 inches

FINISHED MEASUREMENTS (in inches)

Bust 32(34-36-38-40)

Back: With No. 8 needles, cast on 87(91-96-101-106) sts. Work in St St (P 1 row, K 1 row) for 6 rows. K next row on wrong side for hemline, inc 2 sts each side.
Beg with a K row, continue in St St, dec 1 st each side every 4th row 11 times AND AT SAME TIME when 7 inches above hemline, change to No. 7 needles. Work on 69(73-78-83-88) to 11½ inches above hemline, or desired length to waistline and mark. Work to 3½ inches above marker.
Change back to No. 8 needles. Work to 8 inches above waistline marker, or desired length to underarm.

Armholes: Bind off 2(2-3-4-5) at beg of next 2 rows. Dec 1 st each side every 2nd row 2(3-3-3-4) times. Work on 61(63-66-69-70) sts until armholes measure 6(6-6½-6½-7) inches.

Neck and Shoulders: Work 19(19-20-21-21), join a 2nd ball of yarn, bind off center 23(25-26-27-28), work to end. Working each side with separate yarn, dec 1 st at each neck edge *every* row 6 times AND AT SAME TIME when armholes measure 7(7-7½-7½-8) inches, bind off from each armhole edge 6(6-7-8-8) sts once, 7 sts once.

Front: Work same as back to waistline marker. 69 (73-78-83-88) sts. Inc 1 st each side of next row and rep incs every 1 inch 3(3-3-3-4) times AND AT SAME TIME when piece measures 3½ inches above marker change back to No. 8 needles.
Work to same length as back to armholes, or if darts are desired work to ½ inch longer than back.

Armholes: Bind off 4(5-5-6-7) at beg of next 2 rows. Dec 1 st each side every 2nd row 4(4-5-5-7) times. Work on 61(63-66-69-70) until armholes measure 4(4-4½-4½-5) inches.

Neck: Work 22(22-23-24-24) sts, join 2nd ball of yarn, bind off center 17(19-20-21-22) sts, work to end. Working on each side with separate yarn, dec 1 st at each neck edge *every* row 4 times, every 2nd row 5 times, shaping shoulders as on back when armholes are same length.

Bias Neck Facing: With No. 7 needles cast on 14 sts.
Row 1: Inc 1 st in first st, K 11, K 2 tog.
Row 2: Purl.
Rep these 2 rows until approx. 29(29-30-30-30½) inches. Place on holder for any necessary adjustment in length.

Sleeves: With No. 8 needles, cast on 42(44-46-48-50) sts. Work hem and hemline as on back, being sure to inc 2 sts each side 46(48-50-52-54) sts. Beg Pat.
Row 1 (right side): K 17(18-19-20-21); P 2, K 8, P 2; K 17(18-19-20-21).
Row 2: P 17(18-19-20-21); K 2, P 8, K 2; P 17(18-19-20-21).
Row 3: K 17(18-19-20-21); P 2, sl next 4 sts to dp needle, hold at *front* of work, K next 4 sts, K 4 from dp (cable twist), P 2; K 17(18-19-20-21).
Row 4: Rep Row 2.
Rows 5 through 10: Rep Row 1 and 2 three times.
Rep from Row 3 through 10 (twisting cable every 8th row) AND AT SAME TIME inc 1 st each side every 12(12-10-10-8) rows until piece measures approx 8½ inches, end with Row 3 (cable twist).
Next Row: P all sts, discontinuing cable. Continue in St St, inc as before until there are 56(58-62-64-68) sts on needles.
Work even to 14½ inches above hemline, or desired length to underarm.

Shape Cap: Bind off 4(4-5-5-6) at beg of next 2 rows. Dec 1 st each side every 2nd row 10(11-12-13-14) times. Bind off 2 sts at beg of next 2 rows. Bind off remaining sts.

Finishing: Block pieces lightly. Sew darts in front if desired. Assemble.
With right side of neckband to right side of front and cast-on edge at shoulder seam, pin band to front, adjust if necessary, bind off and sew seam. With matching yarn, sew band to front. Turn and sew other edge to wrong side of neck edge. Turn hems to wrong side and sew in place.

GIRL'S SLIP-ON AND CARDIGAN

Instructions are for size 4. Changes for sizes 6, 8 and 10 are in parentheses.

MATERIALS — Brunswick Pomfret Sport or Fore 'N Aft (2-oz) 5(6-7-8) A and 1(1-2-2) B
5 Buttons
NEEDLES: "Susan Bates" No. 3 and No. 5 OR SIZE TO GIVE GAUGE and 1 set dp No. 3
Crochet Hook: "Susan Bates" No. 0

GAUGE: 6 sts = 1 inch, 8 rows = 1 inch

FINISHED MEASUREMENTS (in inches)

Slip-On — Chest 24(26-28-30)
Cardigan Chest (buttoned) 28(30-32-34)

SLIP-ON

Striped Pattern: Worked in St St (K 1 row, P 1 row) as follows: 2 rows B, 4 rows A, 2 rows B, 8 rows A, (2 rows B, 2 rows A) twice. Rep these 24 rows for Striped Pat.
Back: With No. 3 needles and A, cast on 74(78-84-90) sts. Rib in K 1, P 1 for 2 inches. Change to No. 5 needles. Join B, work in stripe pat until piece measures 8(8½-9-9½) inches from beg, or desired length to underarms.
Armholes: Bind off 6(6-8-10) at beg of next 2 rows. Dec 1 st each side every 2nd row 5 times. Work on 58(62-66-70) until armholes measure 4½(5-5½-6) inches.
Shoulders: Bind off 16(18-19-21) at beg of next 2 rows. Place 26(26-28-28) on holder for back of neck.
Front: Work same as back until armholes measure 2½ (3-3½-4) inches.
Neck: Work 23(25-26-28), place center 12(12-14-14) sts on holder, join a 2nd ball of correct color, work to end. Work on each side with separate yarn. Bind off 3 sts from each neck edge once. Dec 1 st at neck edges *every* row 4 times. Work on 16(18-19-21) sts each side to same length as back to shoulders. Bind off sts from armhole edges.
Sleeves: With No. 5 needles and B, cast on 48(50-54-58) sts. Beg at bound-off row of back underarm, count down 12 rows and mark. Beg with same row of striped pat as marked row, work in St St for 12 rows. Continue in striped pat.

Shape Cap: Bind off 3(3-4-4) at beg of next 2 rows. Dec 1 st each side every 2nd row 12(13-14-15) times, *every* row 4 times. Bind off 10 sts.
Finishing: Sew underarm, shoulder and sleeve seams, matching stripes.

Neckband: With dp needles and B, from right side, pick up 86(90-96-100) sts around neck edge, including sts on holders. Join and work in K 1, P 1 rib for 1½ inches. Bind off loosely in rib. Turn band in half to wrong side and tack loosely to neck edge. Steam lightly.

CARDIGAN

With No. 3 needles and A, cast on 78(82-88-94) sts. Rib in K 1, P 1 for 2½ inches, inc 4 sts evenly spaced on last row. Change to No. 5 needles. Work in St St on 82(86-92-98) until piece measures 10(10½-11-11½) inches from beg, or desired length to underarms.
Armholes: Bind off 5(5-5-6) at beg of next 2 rows. Dec 1 st each side every 2nd row 5(5-6-6) times. Work on 62(66-70-74) until armholes measure 5(5½-6-6½) inches.
Shoulders: Bind off 10 sts at beg of next 2 rows, 8(9-10-11) at beg of next 2 rows. Place 26(28-30-32) on holder for back of neck.
Left Front: With No. 3 needles and A, cast on 46(48-52-56) sts. Rib as on back, inc 2 sts on last row. Change to No. 5 needles. Work in St St to same length as back to armhole, end with a P row at armhole edge.
Armhole: Bind off 5(5-5-6) at beg of next row. Dec 1 st at armhole edge every 2nd row 5(5-6-6) times. Work on 38(40-43-46) until armhole measures 3(3½-4-4½) inches, end with a K row at front edge.
Neck: Bind off 10(10-11-12) at beg of next row. Dec 1 st at neck edge *every* row 10(11-12-13) times. Work on 18(19-20-21), shaping shoulder as on right back shoulder when armholes are same length.
With pins mark placement for 5 buttons; first marker 1 inch from lower edge, last ½ inch from neck bind-off, others evenly spaced between.
Right Front: Work to correspond to left front, reversing all shaping and forming buttonholes opposite markers as follows: Beg at front edge, K 3 sts, bind off next 2 sts, K to end. On the following row, cast on 2 sts over the bound-off sts.

Sleeves: With No. 3 needles and A cast on 48(50-52-54) sts. Rib in K 1, P 1 for 2½ inches. Change to No. 5 needles. Work in St St inc 1 st each side every 12(12-12-10) rows 5(5-6-7) times. Work on 58(60-64-68) to 12(12½-13-13½) inches from beg, or desired length to underarms.

Shape Cap: Bind off 5(5-5-6) at beg of next 2 rows. Dec 1 st each side every 2nd row 11(12-13-14) times; *every* row 5(5-6-6) times. Bind off 16 sts.

Finishing: Sew underarm, shoulder and sleeve seams. Set in sleeves.

Neckband: With No. 3 needles and B from right side, beg at right front edge, pick up 86(90-96-102) sts around neck edge, including sts on holder. Rib in K 1, P 1 for 1½ inches. Bind off loosely in rib. Turn band in half to wrong side and sew loosely to neck edge. Tack open ends of neckband tog. With A, from right side, work 1 row sc on front edges. Steam lightly. Sew on buttons.

PINK HALTER WITH LACE PATTERN

Instructions are for size 6. Changes for sizes 8, 10, 12, 14 and 16 are in parentheses.

MATERIALS — SPINNERIN Icecap (1-oz) 6(6-6-7-7) skeins

NEEDLES: "Susan Bates" 1 pair each No. 3 and No. 5 OR SIZE TO GIVE GAUGE Crochet Hook: "Susan Bates" Size E

GAUGE (Pat): 6 sts = 1 inch, 8 rows = 1 inch

FINISHED MEASUREMENTS (in inches)
Bust 30(32-34-36-38-40)

PATTERN STITCH — Worked on a multiple of 8 sts plus 7(5-7-5-7-5) sts.
Row 1 (right side): K 3(2-3-2-3-2), * yo, sl 1 as to K, K 1, psso, K 6; rep from *, end last rep, K 2(1-2-1-2-1).
Row 2 And All Even-Numbered Rows: Purl.
Row 3: K 1(0-1-0-1-0), *K 2 tog, yo, K 1, yo, sl 1, K 1, psso, K 3; rep from *, end last rep yo, sl 1, K 1, psso, K 1(0-1-0-1-0).
Rows 5 and 7: Knit.
Row 9: K 7(6-7-6-7-6), * yo, sl 1, K 1, psso, K 6; rep from *, end last rep K 6(5-6-5-6-5).

Row 11: K 5(4-5-4-5-4), * K 2 tog, yo, K 1, yo, sl 1, K 1, psso, K 3, rep from * end last rep K 5(4-5-4-5-4).
Rows 13 and 15: Knit.
Row 16: Purl.
Rep these 16 rows for Pattern. Keep continuity when shaping.

Back: With No. 3 needles cast on 87(93-103-109-111-117) sts.
Row 1 (right side): K 1, * P 1, K 1; rep from * to end.
Row 2: P 1, * K 1, P 1; rep from * to end. Rep these 2 rows for 12 inches, end with Row 2. Change to No. 5 needles. Work pat for 48 rows (6 inches), end with a wrong side row. Bind off.

Front: With No. 3 needles, cast on 95(101-103-109-119-125) sts. Work rib as on back. Change to No. 5 needles.

Next Row: Work Pat Row 1 over 55(61-63-69-71-77) sts. Place remaining 40(40-40-40-48-48) unworked sts on holder.

Left Front: Work in pat, dec 1 st at neck edge every 2nd row until 48 more pat rows are completed and 24 decs have been made, end with a P row. 31(37-39-45-47-53) sts remain.

Armhole: From armhole edge bind off 4(6-6-8-8-10) sts once, 4 sts once, 3 sts once, 2 sts 2(3-3-3-3-3) times AND AT SAME TIME continue to dec at neck edge as before.

Dec 1 st at armhole edge every 4th row and 1 st at neck edge every 2nd row until 1 st remains. Fasten off.

Right Front: Slip sts from holder to No. 5 needle to work first row from right side, cast on 15(21-23-29-23-29) sts. There are 55(61-63-69-71-77) sts on needle. Complete to correspond to left front, reversing all shaping.

Straps (Make 4): With No. 3 needles cast on 5 sts. Rib in K 1, P 1 for 12 inches. Bind off in rib.
Finishing: Block pieces between wet towels. Sew side seams. Tack cast-on sts of right front under corresponding sts of left front.
Edging: With crochet hook join yarn at lower right front neck edge, spacing sts to keep edges flat work sc on neck and, armholes edges, end at lower left front edge. Ch 1, *do not* turn.

Row 2: Working from *left to right* work sc in each sc for *backward sc.* Fasten off. Sew straps to points of front and to back as desired.

CHERRY COLOR MIDRIFF TOP

Instructions are for size 6. Changes for sizes 8, 10, 12, 14 and 16 are in parentheses.

MATERIALS — Brunswick Sparkletwist (2-oz) 3(3-3-4-4) skeins

NEEDLES: "Susan Bates" No. 4 and No. 5 OR SIZE TO GIVE GAUGE

GAUGE: 6 sts = 1 inch, 8 rows = 1 inch

FINISHED MEASUREMENTS (in inches)
Chest 30(32-34-36-38-40)

Back: With No. 4 needles, cast on 92(98-104-110-116-122) sts. Work in St St (P 1 row, K 1 row) for 12 rows. Knit next row on P side for turning ridge. Beg with a K row continue in St St for 13 rows. K next row on P side. Change to No. 5 needles. Beg with a K row continue St St to 6½ inches from turning ridge, or desired length to beg of cap sleeve, end with a P row.

Cap Sleeves: Inc 1 st each side of next 3 rows. Cast on 6 sts at end of last row. P 1 row. Cast on 6 sts. 110(116-122-128-134-140) sts.

Next Row: (P 1, K 1) 3 times, K to last 6 sts, (K 1, P 1) 3 times. Keeping 6 sts at each side in rib as established and remaining sts in St St work 11 row.

Next Row: Rib 6 sts, inc 1 st in next st, K to last 7 sts, inc 1 st in next st, rib 6 sts.

Continue in this way to inc 1 st after first 6 sts and before last 6 sts every 12 rows twice more. Work on 116 (122-128-134-140-146) sts until cap sleeve measures 6½(6½-7-7-7½-7½) inches from beg.

Neck and Shoulders: Work 47(49-51-53-55-57), join a 2nd ball of yarn, bind off center **22(24-26-28-30-32) sts, work to end.** Working each side with separate yarn, bind off 11(11-12-12-13-13) sts from each armhole edge 3 times 11(13-12-13-12-14) sts once AND AT SAME TIME dec 1 st at each neck edge *every* row 3(3-3-4-4-4) times.

Front: Cast on and work same as back to change of needles. K one row.

Divide For Right and Left Front: P 64(67-70-73-76-79), place the 28(31-34-37-40-43) unworked sts on a holder.

Right Front — Row 1: (P 1, K 1) 3 times, K to end.

Row 2: P to last 6 sts, rib to end.
Row 3: Rib 6 sts, K 2 tog, K to end.
Keeping 6 sts at front edge in rib, dec 1 st for neck edge (by K 2 tog after rib) every 2nd row, (20-21-22-24-25-26) times more; every 4th row 11 times AND AT SAME TIME shape side, cap sleeve and shoulder as on left side of back. Continue rib on 6 remaining sts for 3 inches for ½ back neckband. Place sts on holder.

Left Front: Sl sts from holder to No. 5 needle to work first row from wrong side, then cast on 36 sts on same needle with sts. 64(67-70-73-76-79) sts.

Row 1 (wrong side): (K 1, P 1) 3 times, P to end.
Row 2: K to last 8 sts, sl 1 as to K, K 1, psso, rib to end. Complete to correspond to right front, reversing all shaping.

Bow: With No. 4 needles, cast on 11 sts. Rib in K 1, P 1 for 8 inches. Bind off in rib.

Finishing: Block pieces between wet towels. Sew underarm and shoulder seams. Sew cast-on sts of left front to corresponding sts of right front. Weave ends of back neckband tog and sew lower edge to back neck edge. Turn hem at lower edge at turning ridge and sew in place. Cut elastic to desired measurement and draw through lower hem (casing). Secure ends of elastic. Tie bow and sew to front as shown in photograph.

PERUVIAN AFGHAN AND STOLE

Approximate Size 50″ X 62″ (without fringe).

MATERIALS — Brunswick Aspen or Lochwind (2-oz) 29 for Afghan; 11 for Stole

NEEDLES: "Susan Bates" No. 11 OR SIZE TO GIVE GAUGE

GAUGE: 3 sts = 1 inch, 10 rows = 3 inches

PATTERN STITCH — Worked on a multiple of 4 sts plus 2 sts

Rows 1 and 2: Knit.
Row 3 (right side): K 1, * insert needle in next st as to K, wrap yarn 3 times around needle, draw all wraps through st; rep from * to last st, K 1.
Row 4: K 1, * (with yarn at back, insert needle in next lp as to P, sl to right needle dropping extra 2 wraps) 4 times, forming 4 long sts on right needle, insert left needle from left to right through 4 long

sts and sl back to left needle, insert right needle as if to K through 4 long sts to work them tog, K 1, P 1, K 1, P 1 and drop 4 long sts from left needle; rep from * to last st, K 1.

Rows 5 through 8: Knit.

Row 9: K 1, * insert needle in next st, wrap yarn twice around needle, draw all wraps through st; rep from * to last st, K 1.

Row 10: Knit, dropping extra wraps.

Rep these 10 rows for Pat.

AFGHAN

Cast on 158 sts. Work pat until 20 pats (200 rows) are complete, then rep Rows 1 through 7. Bind off.

Fringe: Wrap yarn around a 16-inch cardboard, cut at 1 end. Using 1 strand place fringe in every st on end (see page 139). Double knot fringe.

STOLE

Cast on 54 sts. Work pat until approx 60 inches long, or desired length, end with Pat Row 7. Bind off.

Fringe: Same as afghan.

CHILD'S LIME DRESS

Designed and Created by Joe Ann Helms

Instructions are for size 4. Changes for sizes 6, 8 and 10 are in parentheses.

MATERIALS — Brunswick Fairhaven Fingering Yarn (1-oz) 7(8-9-10);Buttons

NEEDLES: "Susan Bates" No. 1 and No. 3 OR SIZE TO GIVE GAUGE

Crochet Hook: "Susan Bates" Steel No. 2

GAUGE: 8 sts = 1 inch, 9 rows = 1 inch

FINISHED MEASUREMENTS (in inches)

Lower edge of Skirt 30(31-33-35)
Chest 24(28-30-32)

DRESS

Front: With No. 3 needles cast on 120(124-132-140) sts. Work in St St (K 1 row, P 1 row) for 9 rows, end with a K row. K next row on wrong side for hemline. Beg with a K row, continue in St St to 8 inches from hemline, or approx. 2 inches less than desired length to

waistline. Change to No. 1 needles. Rib in K 1, P 1 until piece measures 16(16¹/₂-17-17¹/₂) from hemline, or desired length to underarm.

Armholes: Keep continuity of rib. Bind off 3(3-4-5) at beg of next 2 rows. Dec 1 st each side every 2nd row 2(3-4-5) times. Work on 110(112-116-120) until armholes measure approx.3(3¹/₂-4-4¹/₂) inches.

Neck: Work 44(45-46-47), join a 2nd ball of yarn, bind off center 22(22-24-26) sts, work to end. Working on each side with separate yarn, bind off 3 sts from each neck edge once. Dec 1 st at each neck edge *every* row 3 times, every 2nd row 8 times.

Shoulders: Bind off from each armhole edge 30(31-32-33).

Back: Work same as front until armholes measure 2¹/₂ (3-3¹/₂-4) inches.

Divide for back opening: Work 55(56-58-60), join a 2nd ball of yarn, work to end. Working on each side with separate yarn, work to same length as back to shoulders.

Shoulders: Bind off from each armhole edge 30(31-32-33) sts. Bind off remaining 25(25-26-27) each side.

Sleeves: With No. 1 needles cast on 82(84-86-90) sts. Rib in K 1, P 1, inc 1 st each side every 16(16-14-14) rows 4(5-6-6) times. Work on 90(94-98-102) until sleeve measures 12(12¹/₂-12¹/₂-13) inches, or desired length to underarm.

Shape Cap: Bind off 3(3-4-5) at beg of next 2 rows. Dec 1 st each side every 2nd row 22(22-23-24) times, *every* row 11(13-13-13) times. Bind off 18 sts.

Finishing: Sew underarm, shoulder and sleeve seams. Set in sleeves. Turn hem to wrong side at hemline and sew in place. Join yarn at top of left side of back opening. From right side, work 1 row sc around neck edge, spacing sts to keep edge flat, sc on right edge of back opening, ch 4, skip ¹/₂ inch on edge for buttonloop, continue sc on right and left edge of opening. Join with a sl st to first st.

Picot Edge: * Sl st in each of 2 sc on neck edge, ch 3, sl st at base of ch 3; rep from * around neck edge. Fasten off.

Steam lightly. Sew button opposite buttonloops.

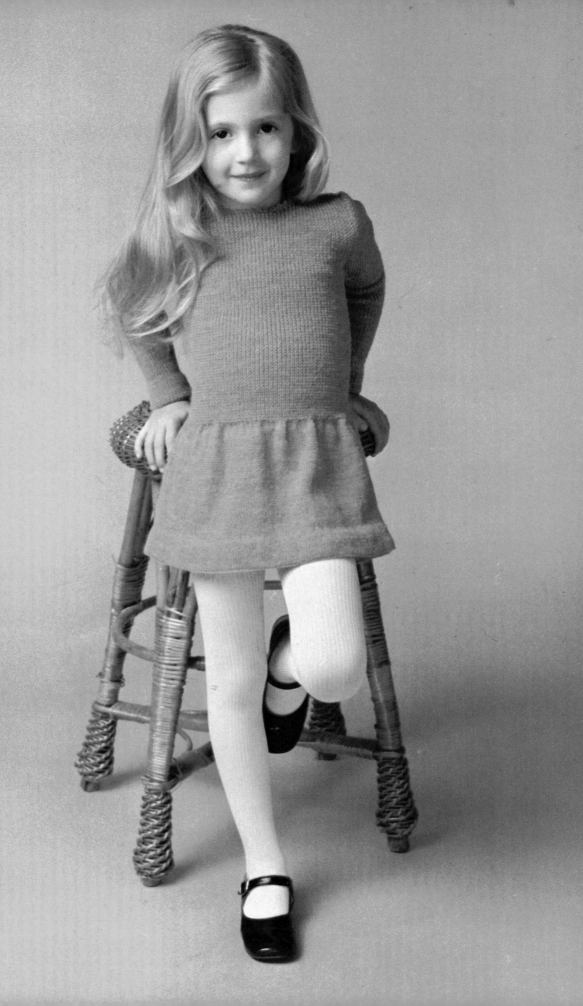

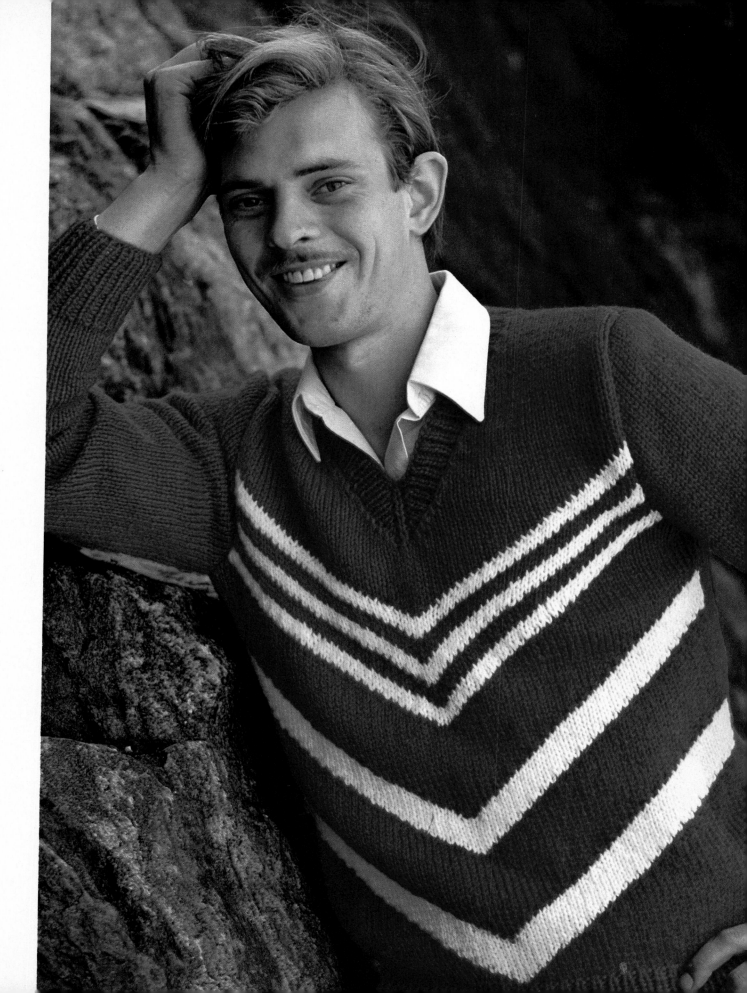

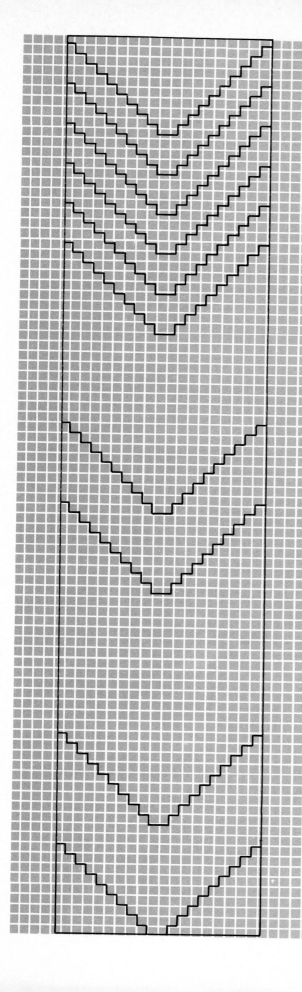

MAN'S RED SWEATER WITH WHITE STRIPES

Instructions are for size 38. Changes for sizes 40, 42, 44, 46, 48 and 50 are in parentheses.

MATERIALS — Brunswick Windrush or Germantown Knitting Worsted (4-oz) 4(4-5-5-5-6-6) MC and 1 CC

NEEDLES: "Susan Bates" 1 pair each No. 7 and No. 9 OR SIZE TO GIVE GAUGE; Bobbins

GAUGE: 9 sts = 2 inches, 6 rows = 1 inch

Note: Wind Bobbins with CC and use a bobbin for each CC diagonal stripe. Use MC from balls. Do not carry yarn across back of work. Cut off balls or bobbins when no longer needed.
When changing colors, pick up color to be used under color previously used, twisting yarns to prevent holes.

FINISHED MEASUREMENTS (in inches)

Chest 38(40-42-44-46-48-50)
Back at shoulders 16(16$^1/_2$-17-17$^1/_2$-18-18-18$^1/_2$)
Sleeve at underarm 15(15-15$^1/_2$-15$^1/_2$-16$^1/_2$-16$^1/_2$-17)

Back: With No. 7 needles and MC cast on 86(90-96-100-104-108-114) sts. Rib in K 1, P 1 for 2$^1/_2$ inches. Place marker between 2 center sts. Change to No. 9 needles.
Row 1 (right side): K to within 1 st of center; join bobbin and K 2; join 2nd ball, K to end.
Row 2: P to 1 st before CC sts, P 4, with other MC ball, P to end.
Beg with Row 3, follow chart (adding or cutting bobbins or balls when necessary) until the back measures 18 inches from beg, or desired length to underarms, end with a wrong side row.
Armholes: Continue to follow chart until all V stripes end at side edges, then work with MC only, AND AT SAME TIME, bind off 4(4-5-5-6-6-7) at beg of next 2 rows. Dec 1 st each side every 2nd row 3(4-5-5-5-7-8) times. Work on 72(74-76-80-82-82-84) until armholes are 9(9-9$^1/_2$-9$^1/_2$-10-10-10$^1/_2$) inches.
Shoulders: Bind off 8 sts at beg of next 4 rows. 5(6-7-8-9-9-10) at beg of next 2 rows. Place 30(30-30-32-32-32-32) on holder.
Front: Work same as back to 1 row less than back to beg of armholes.

Next Row: Work 43(45-48-50-52-54-57), join 2nd ball yarn, work to end.

Armholes and Neck — Next Row: Bind off 4(4-5-5-6-6-7) sts, K to 3 sts of center, sl 1, K 1, psso, K 1; on other side, K 1, K 2 tog, K to end.

Next Row: Bind off 4(4-5-5-6-6-7), P to within 1 st of neck edge, K 1; on other side K 1, P to end. Continue to shape armhole as on back AND AT SAME TIME keeping 1 st at neck edges in Garter St (K every row) dec 1 st each side (as in first dec row) every 2nd row 4 times more, every 4th row 10(10-10-11-11-11-11) times, shaping shoulders as on back when armholes are same length.

Sleeves: With No. 7 needles and MC cast on 40(40-42-42-44-44-46) sts. Rib in K 1 P 1 for 3$\frac{1}{2}$ inches, inc 5 sts evenly spaced on last row. Change to No. 9 needles. Work in St St inc 1 st each side every 8th row 8(8-9-9-10-10-10) times. Work on 66(66-70-70-74-74-76) until 18 inches from beg, or desired length to underarms.

Shape Cap: Bind off 4(4-5-5-6-6-7) at beg of next 2 rows. Dec 1 st each side every 4th row 0(0-1-1-1-1-2) times, every 2nd row 18(18-18-18-19-19-18) times. Bind off 2 sts at beg of next 2 rows. Bind off 18 sts.

Finishing: Sew right shoulder seam.

Neckband: With No. 7 needles and MC from right side, pick up 4 sts in every 5 rows on left front edge, 1 st at center front and mark, pick up same number of sts on right front edge as on left front edge, K across sts on holder.

Row 1: Rib in K 1, P 1 to center front st, P center st, beg with K or P (same as st before center st) rib to end.

Row 2: Rib to st before center st, sl next st to right needle, sl center st to dp needle, hold at *front* of work, sl the last st on right needle back to left needle, insert left needle from back in st on dp needle and sl back to left needle, through back lp, K 3 tog (1 st dec each side of center st), rib to end.

Rep Rows 1 and 2 until band is 1$\frac{1}{2}$ inches, end with Row 2. Bind off in rib. Sew left shoulder, underarm and sleeve seams. Set in sleeves. Block.

MAN'S BELTED JACKET

Instructions are for Size 38. Changes for sizes 40, 42, 44, 46, 48 and 50 are in parentheses.

MATERIALS — Brunswick Aspen (2-oz) 18(19-20-20-22-23-23)

NEEDLES: "Susan Bates" No. 10 and No. 11 OR SIZE TO GIVE GAUGE

GAUGE: 3 sts = 1 inch, 9 rows = 2 inches

FINISHED MEASUREMENTS (in inches)

Chest (including overlap) 43(45-47-49-51-53-55)

Sleeves at underarm 14(14-14$\frac{1}{2}$-14$\frac{1}{2}$-15-15-16)

Back: With No. 11 needles cast on 58(62-64-68-72-76-80) sts. Rib in K 1, P 1 for 2 rows. P 1 row. Work in St St (K 1 row, P 1 row) to 18 inches from beg, or desired length to underarms.

Armholes: Bind off 3(3-3-3-4-4-5) sts at beg of next 2 rows. Dec 1 st each side every 2nd row 3(4-4-5-5-6-6) times. Work on 46(48-50-52-54-56-58) sts until armholes measure 10(10-10$\frac{1}{2}$-10$\frac{1}{2}$-11-11-11$\frac{1}{2}$) inches.

Shoulders: Bind off 4(5-5-5-6-6-6) at beg of next 4 rows, 5(4-5-6-5-5-6) at beg of next 2 rows. Bind off 20(20-20-20-20-22-22) for back of neck.

Left Front: With No. 11 needles cast on 29(31-32-34-36-38-40). Work as on back to 16 inches from beg end with a K row at front edge.

Neck: P 1, P 2 tog, work to end.

Dec 1 st at neck edge (as before), every 4th row 9(9-9-9-9-10-10) times AND AT SAME TIME when same length as back to armhole, shape armhole (at beg of K rows) as on back.

Work on 13(14-15-16-17-17-18) sts until armhole is same length as back to shoulder, then shape shoulder as on back.

Right Front: Work to correspond to left front, reversing all shaping (for neck P to last 3 sts, P 2 tog, P 1).

Sleeves: With No. 11 needles cast on 32(32-32-32-34-34-34). Rib in K 1, P 1 for 2 rows. P 1 row. Work in St St for 10 rows.

Next Row: K 3, inc 1 st in next st, K to last 4 sts, inc 1 st in next st, K 3.

Continue in St St, inc 1 st in 4th st from each end every 14 rows 4(4-5-5-5-5-6) times more. Work on 42(42-44-44-46-46-48) sts to 18 inches from beg, or desired length to underarm.

Shape Cap: Bind off 3(3-3-3-4-4-5) at beg of next 2 rows. Dec 1 st each side every 4th row 5(5-5-5-7-7-8) times, every 2nd row 5(5-6-6-4-4-3) times. Bind off 2 sts at beg of next 2 rows. Bind off 12 sts.

Pockets (Make 2): With No. 11 needles cast on 23 sts for top of pocket. Rib in K 1, P 1 for 2 rows. Beg with a P row, work in St St to 7½ inches from beg. Bind off, leaving an end of yarn for sewing.

Belt: With No. 11 needles cast on 7 sts. Rib in K 1, P 1 to 45 inches from beg, or desired length. Bind off in ribbing.

Collar: With No. 11 needles, cast on 145(145-149-149-153-153-159) sts for outer edge. Rib in K 1, P 1 for 3½ inches.

First Short Row (wrong side): Rib 135(135-139-139-143-143-147), turn.

2nd Short Row (right side): Rib 125(125-129-129-133-133-137), turn.

3rd Short Row: Rib 115(115-119-119-123-123-127), turn.

4th Short Row: Rib 105(105-109-109-113-113-117), turn.

Continue in this way to work 10 sts less every row until 10 short rows in all and 45(45-49-49-53-53-57) sts at center of short rows. Change to No. 10 needles. Rib 1 row on all sts. Bind off as to knit.

Left Front Band: With No. 10 needle, beg at first neck dec, from right side, pick up 1 st in each row on front edge to lower edge. Rib in K 1, P 1 for 2 inches. Bind off in rib.

Right Front Band: Beg at lower edge, pick up sts and complete same as left front band.

Finishing: Sew underarm, shoulder and sleeve seams. Set in sleeves. With bound-off edge of pockets at first St St row of fronts and side edge at 3rd st from underarm seams, weave pockets to fronts. With center back of collar at center back of neck and neck edge of ends at top of front bands, sew collar to neck edges. Block between wet towels.

SQUARE-NECKED — SUMMER TOP

Instructions are for size 8. Changes for sizes 10, 12, 14, 16 and 18 are in parentheses.

MATERIALS — Sport Yarn Weight
Brunswick Icecap (1-oz skeins) 5 (5-6-6-6-7)
1½ inch grosgrain ribbon for facing straps
NEEDLES: "Susan Bates" No. 3 and No. 5 OR SIZE TO GIVE GAUGE
GAUGE: (St st) 6 sts = 1 inch, 8 rows = 1 inch

FINISHED MEASUREMENTS (in inches)

Bust 32(34-36-38-40-42)
Back: With No. 3 needles cast on 114(118-126-128-134-138) sts. K 8 rows for garter st border. Change to No. 5 needles. Work in St St (K 1 row, P 1 row) dec 1 st each side every 8th row 4 times. Work on 106(110-114-122-126-130) until piece measures 6 inches from beg, end with a K row.

Dec Row: P 5(7-9-13-15-17), * P 2 tog, P 3; rep from * 19 times, P to end. 86(90-94-102-106-110) sts. Change to No. 3 needles.

Next Row: K 2, * P 2, K 2; rep from * to end.

Next Row: P 2, * K 2, P 2; rep from * to end.

Rep last 2 rows until piece measures 8½ inches, from beg, ending with a wrong side row and increasing 0(0-1-1-0-0) on last row. Change to No. 5 needles. Work in St St inc 1 st each side every 6th row 6(6-7-6-7-8) times. Work on 98(102-109-115-120-126) until piece measures 17 inches from beg, or approx 4 inches less than desired length to neckline, end with a P row. K 4 rows. Work in St St for 4 rows.

Border — *Row 1 (right side):* K 1(3-1-4-1-4), * (yo, K 2 tog) 4 times, K 3; rep from *, end last rep K 1(3-1-4-1-4).

Row 2 and All Even-Numbered Rows: Purl all sts and yos.

Row 3: K 1(3-1-4-1-4), * yo, K 2 tog, K 4, yo, K 2 tog, K 3; rep from *, end last rep K 1(3-1-4-1-4).

Rows 5 and 7: Rep Row 3.

Row 9: Rep Row 1.

Row 10: Purl.

Work 4 rows St St. Change to No. 3 needles. K next row dec 8 sts evenly spaces. Work in garter stitch for 1 inch, end with a right side row. Bind off as to knit.

Front: Work same as back to bound-off row. 90(94-101-107-112-118) sts.

Next Row: Bind off 18(19-21-23-25-27), K until 8 sts from bind off (strap); bind off next 38(40-43-45-46-48); K until 8 sts from bind-off (strap), bind off remaining sts.

Straps: Using a separate ball of yarn for each strap, continue to work in garter stitch until straps measure approx 10(10-10½-10½-11-11) inches, or desired length. Bind off.

Finishing: Block lightly. Face straps with ribbon. Sew side seams. Tack ends of straps to back.

BROWN KNIT PANTS SUIT FOR BOYS AND GIRLS

Designed and Created by Joe Ann Helms

Instructions are for size 4. Changes for sizes 6 and 8 are in parentheses.

MATERIALS — Brunswick Germantown Knitting Worsted or Windrush (4-oz) 5 (6-7); Jacket Zipper; ¹/₂-inch elastic.
NEEDLES: "Susan Bates" 1 pair each No. 5 and No. 7 OR SIZE TO GIVE GAUGE
Crochet Hook: "Susan Bates" Size F

GAUGE: 5 sts = 1 inch, 7 rows = 1 inch

FINISHED MEASUREMENTS (in inches)
Jacket - Bust or Chest 26¹/₂ (28¹/₂-30¹/₂)
        Back at shoulders 10 (10¹/₂-11)
        Sleeve at underarm 8 (9-9¹/₂)
Pants - Above crotch 17¹/₂ (19¹/₂-20¹/₂)
        Leg at lower edge 13 (14-15)

JACKET

Back: With No 5 needles cast on 60 (64-68) sts. Rib in K 1, P 1 for 2¹/₂ inches, inc 4 sts evenly on last row. Change to No. 7 needles. Work in St St (K 1 row, P 1 row) on 64 (68-72) sts until 10 (10¹/₂-11) inches from beg, or desired length to underarm.
Armholes: Bind off 3 (3-4) at beg of next 2 rows. Dec 1 st each side every 2nd row 4 (5-5) times. Work on 50 (52-54) sts until armholes measure 5¹/₂ (6-6¹/₂) inches.
Shoulders: Bind off 8 sts at beg of next 2 rows; 8 (9-10) at beg of next 2 rows. Bind off 18 sts.
Left Front: With No. 5 needles cast on 31 (33-35) sts. Rib as on back, inc 2 sts evenly on last row. Change to No. 7 needles. Work in St St on 33 (35-37) sts until same length as back to armhole, ending with a P row.
Armhole: Bind off 3 (3-4) at beg of next row, work to end. Dec 1 st at armhole edge every 2nd row 4 (5-5) times. Work on 26 (27-28) sts until armhole measures 4 (4¹/₂-5) inches, ending at front edge.
Neck: Bind off 7 sts at beg of next row. Dec 1 st at neck edge every 2nd row 3 times. Work on 16 (17-18) sts to same length as back to shoulder.
Shoulder: Bind off 8 sts from armhole edge once. Work 1 row even. Bind off 8 (9-10) sts.
Right Front: Work to correspond to left front, reversing all shaping.
Sleeves: With No. 5 needles cast on 36 (40-44) sts. Rib in K 1, P 1, for 1¹/₂ inches, inc 4 sts on last row. Change to No. 7 needles. Work even on 40 (44-48) sts until sleeve measures 13 (13¹/₂-14) inches from beg, or desired length to underarm.
Shape Cap: Bind off 3 (4-4) at beg of next 2 rows. Dec 1 st each side every 2nd row 8 (9-11) times. Bind off 2 sts at beg of next 2 rows. Bind off 14 sts.
Finishing: Sew underarm, shoulder and sleeve seams. Set in sleeves. Steam.
Collar: With No. 6 needles, from right side and beg at right front edge, pick up 72 (76-80) sts around neck edge. Rib in K 1, P 1 for 5 inches. Bind off in ribbing. From right side, work 1 row sc on each front edge, spacing sts to keep edge flat. Sew in zipper so that sc row covers zipper.

PANTS

Right Leg: With No. 5 needles cast on 65 (70-75) sts. Work in St St for 1 inch, ending with K row. K next row on wrong side for hemline. Change to No. 7 needles.
Next Row: K 15 (17-19), place a marker on needle, sl 1 (this will form crease line on right side of work), K 49 (52-55).

Always sl the st after marker on K rows. Beg with a P row, continue in St St, inc 1 st at *beg* of a K row every 7 inches twice AND AT THE SAME TIME inc 1 st at *end* of a K row every 5 inches 3 times. Work on 70 (75-80) sts until leg measures 16 (17-18) inches from hemline, or desired length to beg of crotch, ending with a P row.
Crotch: Dec 1 st at *beg* of next (K) row for *front* edge and *every* K row 3 times then dec 1 st at same edge every 10 rows 4 times AND AT THE SAME TIME dec 1 st at back edge every 2nd row 12 times, every 4th row 5 times. Work even on 46 (51-56) sts until crotch measures 8 (8¹/₂-9) inches, or desired length to waist, ending with a K row. K next row on wrong side for turning ridge for hem. Beg with a K row, continue in St St for 1 inch. Bind off.
Left Leg: Work same as Right Leg, reversing all shaping, placing marker on first K row after 49 (52-55) sts. Dec for *front* edge at *end* of K rows, *back* edge at *beg* of K rows.
Finishing: Sew leg and crotch seams. Sew hems at lower edge of legs. Steam. Cut elastic to desired waist measurement and sew ends together. Turn casing to wrong side over elastic and sew in place.

KNIT CAP AND SCARF

Cap Size 6/8 and 10/12 years. Scarf width approximately 9 inches.

MATERIALS — Brunswick Germantown Knitting Worsted or Windrush (4-oz) 2 skeins Blue (B) and 1 skein each Red (R), Yellow (Y) and Green (G)
NEEDLES: "Susan Bates" No. 5 and No. 7 OR SIZE TO GIVE GAUGE

GAUGE 5 sts = 1 inch, 6 rows = 1 inch

CAP

Striped Pattern: Worked in Reverse Stockinette St (P 1 row, K 1 row). Purl side is right side: 4 rows Y; 4 rows G; 4 rows R; 4 rows B. Rep these 16 rows for pat. Carry colors not in use loosely along edge of work or cut if desired.

Rib Band: With No. 5 needles and B cast on 94 (98) sts. Rib in K 2, P 2 for 3 inches for double band. Change to No. 7 needles.

Crown
Row 1 (right side): With Y, purl, dec 1 st on row. 93 (97) sts. Continue striped pat to 5 (5½) inches from top of ribbing; end with a P row.
First Dec Row: K 3, *K 2 tog, K 17 (18), sl 1, K 1, psso, K 1; rep from * 3 times more, end last rep k 3 instead of K 1, P 1 row.

2nd Dec Row: K 3, *K 2 tog, K 15 (17), sl 1, K 1, psso, K 1; rep from * 3 times more, end last rep K 3 instead of K 1. Continue in this way to dec 8 sts every K row, having 2 sts less between decs every dec row until there are 37 (41) sts on needle.
Next Row: K 2 tog across row, K 1. P 1 row. Rep last 2 rows once. Cut yarns, leave a 14-inch end on last row. Thread end into tapestry needle and run it through sts on needle. Draw together tightly and fasten securely. Sew back seam, matching stripes. Sew in all ends neatly. Turn Rib Band in half as shown in photograph.

SCARF

Striped Pattern: Worked in Garter Stitch (K every row); 4 inches B, Y, G and R. Rep these 16 inches for pat.

With No. 7 needles and B cast on 46 sts. Work in striped pat until there are 13 stripes, or to desired length. Bind off.

SLEEVELESS SLIP-ON WITH BOAT

Instructions are for Size 1. Changes for Sizes 2 and 3 are in parentheses.

MATERIALS — Brunswick Fore-'N-Aft or Pomfret (2-oz) 2(2-3) Blue (MC); 1 White (W) and a few yards Red (R)
NEEDLES: "Susan Bates" No. 3 and No. 5 OR SIZE TO GIVE GAUGE

GAUGE: (St St) 6 sts = 1 inch, 8 rows = 1 inch

FINISHED MEASUREMENTS (in inches)
20(22-24) inches
Note: Boat may be worked in following chart or embroidered in duplicate st before slip-on is assembled.
Front: With No. 5 needles and B, cast on 74(78-82) sts.
Row 1: (wrong side) K 2, *P 2, K 2, rep from * to end.
Row 2: P 2; * K 2, P 2; rep from * to end.
Row 3: Rep Row 1. Drop B.
Row 4: With W, knit.
Row 5: Rep Row 1. Cut W.
Row 6: With B, knit.
Rep Rows 1 through 3, ending on wrong side.
Next Row: Rib 14 sts, dec 1 st, K 44(48-52), rib 14 sts.
Next Row: Rib 14 sts, P 45(49-53), rib 14 sts. Keeping 14 sts each side in rib and remaining sts in St St (K 1 row, P 1 row), work until piece measures 7½(8½-9½) inches from beg, or desired length to underarms.

Armholes: Bind off 10 sts at beg of next 2 rows, 3 sts at beg of next 4 rows.
Dec 1 st each side every 2nd row 1(2-3) times. There are 39(41-43) sts on needle.
Neck: Work 12 sts, place next 15(17-19) sts on holder, join 2nd ball of yarn, work to end. Working each side with separate yarn, bind off 2 sts from each neck edge once. Dec 1 st at each neck edge every 2nd row 3 times. Work on 7 sts until armholes measure 4(4½-5) inches. Bind off sts for shoulders.

Back: Work same as front (omitting neck shaping) until there are 4 rows less on back than on front to shoulder.
Next Row: Work 9 sts, place center 21(23-25) sts on holder, join 2nd ball of yarn, work to end. Bind off 2 sts from each neck edge once. Work 1

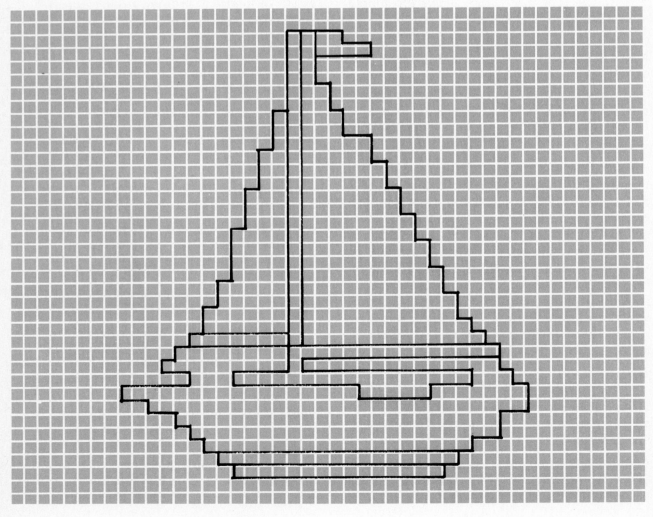

row on 7 sts each side. Bind off for shoulders.
Finishing: Sew left shoulder seam.
Neckband: With No. 3 needles and B, from right side pick up 4 sts on shaped edge of back neck edge, K across sts on holder, pick up 4 sts on shaped edge, pick up 1 st in each row of neck edge, then 1 st in each bound off sts, k across sts on holder, pick up sts on other side of neck to correspond.
Row 1: Rib P 2, K 2, inc across back of neck if necessary to end with K 2.
Row 2: Work rib. Drop B.
Row 3: With W, purl.
Row 4: With W, rib, cut W.
Row 5: With B, purl.
Row 6: With B rib. Bind off loosely in rib. Sew right shoulder seam.
Armhole Bands: With No. 3 needles and B beg at underarm, from right side, pick up 1 st in each st and row around armhole, having a multiple of 4 sts. Work same as neckband. Sew side seams.

BLUE SWEATER WITH DOTS

Instructions are for Size 8. Changes for Sizes 10, 12, 14, 16 and 18 are in parentheses.

MATERIALS — Brunswick Fore 'N Aft or Wintuk Sport (2-oz) 4(5-5-6-6-6) MC and 1 CC.
NEEDLES: "Susan Bates" Size 3 and Size 5 OR SIZE TO GIVE GAUGE
Bobbins
GAUGE: 6 sts = 1 inch, 8 rows = 1 inch.

Note: Wind CC on bobbins or into small balls and work each dot with separate ball. Cut off when not needed leaving a 4-inch end to be woven in. Use MC from ball, carrying yarn on wrong side across dots. When changing colors, pick up color to be used, under color previously used, twisting yarns to prevent holes. Beg each size as indicated on chart, work to center st, work center st ONCE, then follow chart back (left to right) to beg of size. Work 14 rows MC between dots.
Back: With No. 3 needles, cast on 89(95-101-107-113-119) sts.
Row 1: K 1, *P 1, K 1,; rep from * to end.
Row 2: P 1, *K 1, P 1; rep from * to end. Rep these 2 rows for 2 inches. Change to No. 5 needles and continue ribbing to 7 inches from beg. Continue in St St, beg each size as indicated on

chart and inc 1 st each side every 4th row 4 times, beg a new dot when there are sufficient sts between dots. Work 97(103-109-115-121-127) to 10½ inches from beg, or desired length to beg of sleeves, ending with a P row.
Sleeves: Beg new dots when there are sufficient sts, cast on 2 sts at *end* of next 6 rows; 11 sts at end of following 6 rows. Cast on 13(13-15-15-15-15) at end of next 2 rows. There are 201(207-217-223-229-235) sts on needle. Work even until sleeve edge measures 6(6-6½-6½-7-7) inches from last cast-on sts; end with a P row.
Sleeve, Shoulder and Neck Shaping: Bind off 10(12-15-17-19-21) sts at beg of next 2 rows, 7 sts at beg of next 12 rows.
Place a marker at each side of center 37(39-41-43-43-45) sts.
Next Row: Bind off 9 sts, work to marker, place sts between marker on stitch holder for back of neck, join 2nd ball of yarn, work to end. Work on each side with separate yarn. Bind off 9 sts at beg of next row, work remaining sts. Bind off 9 sts at beg of next 4 rows AND AT SAME TIME bind off 3(3-4-4-5-5) sts from each neck edge twice.
Front: Work same as back to beg of shoulder.

Shoulder Shaping: Place a marker at each side of center. 29(29-31-31-33-33) sts.
Bind off 10(12-15-17-19-21) sts at beg of next 2 rows. Bind off 7 sts beg at next row, work to marker, place sts between markers on a stitch holder, join another ball of yarn, work to end. Work each side with separate yarn. Bind off 7 sts at beg of next row, work remaining sts; bind off 7 sts from each sleeve edge 5 times more, 9 sts 3 times AND AT SAME TIME bind off 3 sts from each neck edge 2(2-1-2-2-3) times, 2 sts 0(0-2-1-1-0) times. Dec 1 st at each neck edge every 2nd row 1(2-2-2-2-2) times.
Finishing: Sew top of left sleeve and shoulder.
Neckband: With No. 3 needles from right side, pick up 140(140-146-146-150-150) sts around neck edge, including sts on holders.
Rib in K 1, P 1 for 1½ inches. Bind off in rib. Sew other sleeve and shoulder. With No. 3 needles, pick up 1 st in each row on edge of sleeve. Rib as on neck band and bind off.
Sew underarm and sleeve seams. Sew in all ends neatly.
Block between wet towels.

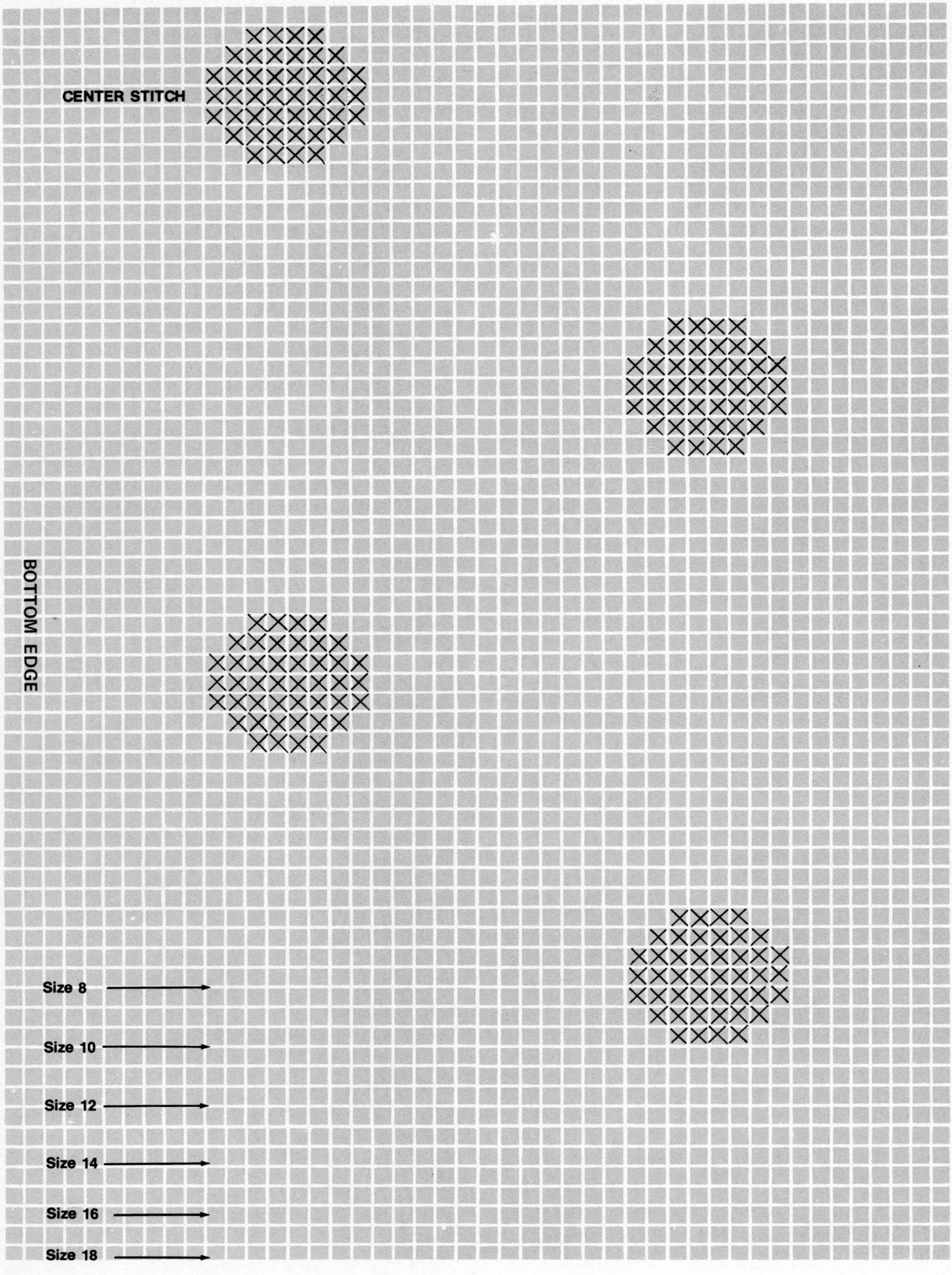

CENTER STITCH

BOTTOM EDGE

Size 8 ⟶

Size 10 ⟶

Size 12 ⟶

Size 14 ⟶

Size 16 ⟶

Size 18 ⟶

WHITE DRESS

Instructions are for Size 8. Changes for sizes 10, 12 and 14 are in parentheses.

MATERIALS — Brunswick Icecap (1 oz) 22(24-25-27) skeins, Round Elastic
NEEDLES: "Susan Bates" Circular No. 4 and 1 pair each No. 3 and No. 4 OR SIZE TO GIVE GAUGE.
GAUGE: (St St) 13 sts = 2 inches, 17 rows = 2 inches

FINISHED MEASUREMENTS (in inches)
Each Side of Front at widest part 7¹/₂(8-8¹/₂-9)
Skirt at lower edge 48(49-50-51)
Pattern Stitch: Multiple of 16 sts and is worked in rnds.
Rnd 1: *K 1, (P 1, K 1) 3 times, yo, K 2 tog, P 1, (K 1, P 1) twice, sl 1 as to P, K 1, psso, yo; rep from * around.
Rnd 2: Work in rib of K 1, P 1 on all sts. Rep these 2 rnds for pat.

SKIRT

With circular needle, cast on 192(192-208-208) sts for skirt waistline. Join, with care not to twist sts on needle. Place a marker on needle to indicate end of rnds and sl marker every rnd. Marker will also indicate center back of skirt. Work in K 1, P 1 ribbing for 2 rnds.
Work in pattern stitch until piece measures 5¹/₂ (5¹/₂-6-6) inches from beg, or desired depth of band.
Remainder of skirt is worked in St St (K all rnds). Knit 1 rnd.
First Inc Rnd: * K 24(24-26-26) sts, insert left point of needle under stand between last st knitted and next st on left end of needle, K in *back* lp of this st (1 st inc); rep from * around. There are 8 incs in rnd and 200(200-216-216) sts on needle. Knit 5 rnds.
Second Inc Rnd: * K 25(25-27-27), inc as before; rep from * around.
Continue in this way, to inc 8 sts in every 6th rnd, having 1 st more between incs every inc rnd until there are 10(11-10-11) inc rnds in all and 272(280-288-296) sts on needle.
Inc every 12th rnd 5 times more. Work on 312(320-328-336) to 25 inches from beg, or desired length.

P next rnd for turning ridge for hem.
K around for 1 inch. Bind off.

TOP

Beg at center back of cast-on-row, count 96(96-104-104) sts. Mark sp between last st counted and next st for center front.
Right Piece: With No. 3 straight needle, beg 3 sts to right of center marking, pick up 1 st in each of 45(45-49-49) cast on sts. Change to No. 4 straight needles. K 1, P to last st, K 1. K next row, inc 3(5-7-9) sts evenly spaced. There are 48(50-56-58) sts on needle.
Next Row: K 1, P to last st, K 1.
Next Row: K 1, K 2 tog, K to last 3 sts, sl 1, K 1, psso, K 1. Continue in this way to dec 1 st each side every 4th row until there are 18(19-23-24) dec rows in all and 12(12-10-10) sts remain. Dec each side every 6th row 4(4-3-3) times. Work on 4 sts until front measures at center 14¹/₂(15-15-15¹/₂) inches or desired length to fit to center back of neck.
Left Piece: With No. 3 needles and beg 48(48-52-52); sts from center front marker, pick up 1 st in each of 45(45-49-49) sts of cast-on row, to within 3 sts of marker. Work same as right side.
Rib Band: On left piece of top with No. 3 needle from right side, on 1 shaped edge *pick up 1 st in each of 3 rows, sk 1 row; rep from * to 4 bound-off sts. Rib in K 1, P 1 for 7 rows. Bind off in rib. On other shaped edge from right side, pick up same number of sts. Rib 7 rows. Bind off in rib.
Work rib bands on right piece in same way.
Finishing: Turn hem to wrong side at hemline and sew in place. Sew ends of top together to form halter top.
Overlap rib band of right piece of top over left piece and tack to cast-on sts at center front. Tack rib bands at underarm edge of fronts to cast-on row.
From wrong side, weave elastic through several rows of pattern band, draw to desired fit, and fasten ends securely.

MEN'S SWEATERS

These two sweaters can be worked in any combination, with crew or V-neck, with or without saddle shoulders. The instructions and materials for both are the same, *but* the gauge is different. Check carefully for the correct gauge before beginning either.

Group A (Fingering Yarn Weight)

MATERIAL — Fairhaven Fingering Yarn or Nylamb (1-oz) 9(10-11-12)
NEEDLES: "Susan Bates" 1 pair each No. 1 and No. 3 OR SIZE TO GIVE GAUGE
1 set double/pointed No. 1
GAUGE: *Beige Sweater* (Pats I and II) 10 sts = 1 inch, 21 rows = 2 inches; *Green Sweater* (Pat) 17 sts = 2 inches, 21 rows = 2 inches

Group B (Sport Yarn Weight)

MATERIALS — Pomfret Sport Yarn or Fore 'N Aft Sport Sayelle (2-oz) 8(9-9-10)
NEEDLES: "Susan Bates" 1 pair each No. 3 and No. 5 OR SIZE TO GIVE GAUGE
1 set double/pointed No. 3

GAUGE: *Beige Sweater* (Pat I and II) 15 sts = 2 inches, 8 rows = 1 inch; *Green Sweater* (Pat) 7 sts = 1 inch, 8 rows = 1 inch

Group C Knitting Worsted Weight

MATERIALS — Germantown Knitting Worsted or Windrush (4-oz) 5(5-6-6)
NEEDLES: "Susan Bates" 1 pair each No. 6 and No. 8 OR SIZE TO GIVE GAUGE
1 set double/pointed No. 6

GAUGE: *Beige Sweater* (Pat I and II) 11 sts = 2 inches, 12 rows = 2 inches; *Green Sweater* (Pat) 11 sts = 2 inches, 12 rows = 2 inches

FINISHED MEASUREMENTS

Chest 39(41-43-45) inches
Sleeve at underarm 15(15³/₄-16¹/₄-17) inches
Instructions are for 3 weights of Brunswick Yarns in sizes 38, 40, 42 and 44.

BEIGE SWEATER

Sizes	Group A 38 40 42 44	Group B 38 40 42 44	Group C 38 40 42 44

PATTERN STITCH I — Worked on a multiple of 3 sts plus 2.

Row 1 (right side): P 2, * K in *back* of next st, P 2; rep from * to end.
Row 2: K 2, * P in *back* of next st, K 2; rep from * to end. Rep these 2 rows for Pattern I

PATTERN II — Cable Pattern

	Group A	Group B	Group C
Row 1 (right side): K.................... sts	16	12	8
Work Pat I over next 5 sts. K............. sts	16	12	8
Row 2: P .... sts	16	12	8
Work Pat I over next 5 sts. P .... sts	16	12	8
Row 3: * Slip to dp needle next .... sts	4	3	2
hold at *back* of work. K next .... sts	4	3	2
K from dp needle .... sts	4	3	2
sl to dp needle next .... sts	4	3	2
hold at *front* of work. K next .... sts	4	3	2
K from dp needle .... sts *	4	3	2

Work Pat I over next 5 sts. Rep between *s once.
Row 4: Rep Row 2.
Rep these 4 rows for Pat II.

	Group A 38 40 42 44	Group B 38 40 42 44	Group C 38 40 42 44
Back: With smaller needles cast on........ sts	154 162 167 174	109 114 121 124	86 89 95 99
Rib in K, P 1 for 2 inches. Rib next row inc evenly spaced .... sts	43 44 45 47	39 40 42 42	22 22 22 24
There are on needle .... sts	197 206 212 221	148 154 163 166	108 111 117 123
Change to larger needles. Work in Pat I .... sts	38 41 41 44	26 26 32 32	17 17 20 23

Sizes	Group A 38 40 42 44	Group B 38 40 42 44	Group C 38 40 42 44
Pat II over .... sts	37 37 37 37	29 29 29 29	21 21 21 21
Pat I over .... sts	47 50 56 59	38 44 41 44	32 35 35 35
Pat II over .... sts	37 37 37 37	29 29 29 29	21 21 21 21
Pat I over .... sts	38 41 41 44	26 26 32 32	17 17 20 23

Keeping Pats as established, work to 15 inches from beg or desired length to underarms.

	Group A 38 40 42 44	Group B 38 40 42 44	Group C 38 40 42 44
Armholes: At beg of next 2 rows bind off. . sts	6 6 7 8	5 5 5 5	4 4 5 5
Dec 1 st each side of next .... rows	6 8 8 8	4 4 4 4	4 4 4 4
Dec 1 st each side every 2nd row .... times	5 5 5 6	5 6 7 7	3 3 3 4
There are on needle .... sts	163 168 172 177	120 124 131 134	86 89 93 97
Work.......... rows	46 50 54 58	40 42 44 48	30 32 36 36
Shoulders: Bind off .... sts	7 7 7 7	7 7 7 7	5 6 6 6
at beg of next.......... rows	10 8 6 4	12 10 4 4	2 10 8 6
Bind off .... sts	8 8 8 8	0 8 8 8	6 0 7 7
at beg of next.......... rows	6 8 10 12	0 2 8 8	8 0 2 4

Bind off remaining sts.

Front: Work same as back until armholes shaping is complete.

	Group A 38 40 42 44	Group B 38 40 42 44	Group C 38 40 42 44
There are on needle .... sts	163 168 172 177	120 124 131 134	86 89 93 97
Work.......... rows	10 8 10 8	8 6 6 6	6 6 8 6
Divide for V-Neck — Next Row: Work .... sts	81 84 86 88	60 62 65 67	43 44 46 48
Slip to holder .... sts	1 0 0 1	0 0 1 0	0 1 1 1

join 2nd ball of yarn, work to end. Dec 1 st at each neck edges on next row and rep decs every

	Group A 38 40 42 44	Group B 38 40 42 44	Group C 38 40 42 44
2nd row .... times	16 16 17 14	11 10 8 10	10 8 9 10
There are on each side .... sts	64 67 68 73	48 51 56 56	32 35 36 37
Dec at neck edges every 3rd row .... times	1 3 3 7	3 5 7 7	1 3 3 3

end at armhole edge.

Shoulder: Continue to dec at neck edges every

	Group A 38 40 42 44	Group B 38 40 42 44	Group C 38 40 42 44
3rd row .... more times	4 4 4 4	3 3 3 3	2 2 2 2

AND AT SAME TIME bind off from each

	Group A 38 40 42 44	Group B 38 40 42 44	Group C 38 40 42 44
armhole edge .... sts	7 7 7 7	7 7 7 7	5 6 6 6
.... times	5 4 3 2	6 5 2 2	1 5 4 3
then .... sts	8 8 8 8	0 8 8 8	6 0 7 7
.... times	3 4 5 6	0 1 4 4	4 0 1 2
Sleeves: With smaller needles cast on ...... sts	72 74 78 80	56 58 60 62	44 46 48 50
Rib in K 1, P 1 for .... inches	2½ 2½ 3 3	SAME AS GROUP A	SAME AS GROUP A
inc across last row.......... sts	14 12 14 12	15 13 17 15	9 13 11 9
There are on needle .... sts	86 86 92 92	71 71 77 77	53 59 59 59

Change to larger needles. Work in Pat I for

	Group A 38 40 42 44	Group B 38 40 42 44	Group C 38 40 42 44
.... rows	4 4 4 4	6 6 6 6	6 6 6 6

Inc 1 st each side of next row and rep incs every

	Group A 38 40 42 44	Group B 38 40 42 44	Group C 38 40 42 44
.... row	4 4 4 4	6 6 6 6	6 6 6 6
.... times	22 25 25 27	16 17 17 20	12 11 12 14
Work on.......... sts	132 138 144 148	105 109 115 110	79 83 85 89

until sleeves measure 19½ inches from beg, or desired length.

	Group A 38 40 42 44	Group B 38 40 42 44	Group C 38 40 42 44
Cap: Bind off .... sts	6 6 7 8	5 5 5 5	4 4 5 5
at beg of next 2 rows. Dec 1 st each side of next rows	16 18 18 18	11 11 13 15	10 10 10 10

Sizes	Group A 38 40 42 44				Group B 38 40 42 44				Group C 38 40 42 44			
Dec 1 st each side every 2nd row........ times	11	12	14	15	10	12	13	13	8	10	10	12
There are on needles .... sts	66	66	66	66	53	53	53	53	35	35	35	35
At beg of next .... rows	8	8	8	8	6	6	6	6	6	6	6	6
bind off .... sts	5	5	5	5	5	5	5	5	3	3	3	3
there are on needle .... sts	26	26	26	26	23	23	23	23	17	17	17	17

Saddle For Shoulder: Work even until saddle fits bound-off sts for shoulder, end with a wrong side row for right sleeve, a right side row for left sleeve.

Front of Neck: From neck edge bind off . . . sts and mark, work to end. Dec 1 st at neck edge on next row. Work 1 row even. Dec 1 st at neck edge on next row. Work on .... sts until piece measures from bound off sts . . inches Place sts on holder.

	Group A 38 40 42 44				Group B 38 40 42 44				Group C 38 40 42 44			
(bind off sts)	12	12	12	12	10	10	10	10	7	7	7	7
(Work on sts)	12	12	12	12	11	11	11	11	8	8	8	8
(inches)	2	2¾	2¾	3	SAME AS GROUP A				SAME AS GROUP A			

Finishing: Block lightly.
Sew saddles to front and back shoulders and across center back.

Neckband: With dp needles from right side and beg at marker, pick up across back of neck.. sts on left front neck edge.................. sts pick up 1 st at center front and mark, pick up on right front edge .... sts join.

	Group A 38 40 42 44				Group B 38 40 42 44				Group C 38 40 42 44			
(back of neck)	45	48	50	53	36	38	37	42	28	29	31	33
(left front)	64	70	72	78	56	60	62	64	40	42	44	46
(right front)	64	66	72	78	56	60	62	66	40	41	44	46

Rnd 1: P 1, K 1 to center front, K center st, P 1, K 1 to end. Continue rib, dec 1 st each side of marked st every row for 1 inch. Bind off in rib, dec as before. Sew in sleeves, then sew underarm seams.

For Crew Neck — Front: Work same as back until armhole shaping is complete. There are on needle............................... sts Work................................... rows end with a right side row.

	Group A 38 40 42 44				Group B 38 40 42 44				Group C 38 40 42 44			
(needle sts)	163	168	172	177	120	124	131	134	86	89	93	97
(Work rows)	45	49	53	57	39	41	43	47	29	31	34	35

Next Row: Work................... sts sl to a st holder next.................... sts Join 2nd ball of yarn, work to end.

	Group A 38 40 42 44				Group B 38 40 42 44				Group C 38 40 42 44			
(Work sts)	69	70	71	72	49	50	53	53	34	35	36	38
(sl to st holder sts)	25	28	30	33	22	24	25	28	18	19	21	21

Shoulders and Neck: From armhole edges bind off .... sts .... times .... sts .... times

	Group A 38 40 42 44				Group B 38 40 42 44				Group C 38 40 42 44			
(bind off sts)	7	7	7	7	7	7	7	7	5	6	6	6
(times)	5	4	3	2	6	5	2	2	1	5	4	3
(sts)	8	8	8	8	0	8	8	8	6	0	7	7
(times)	3	4	5	5	0	1	4	4	4	0	1	2

AND AT SAME TIME dec 1 st at neck edges *every* row .... times every 2nd row .... times

	Group A 38 40 42 44				Group B 38 40 42 44				Group C 38 40 42 44			
(every row times)	7	7	7	7	5	5	5	5	3	3	3	3
(every 2nd row times)	3	3	3	3	2	2	2	2	2	2	2	3

Finishing: Same as V-Neck.

Neckband: With dp needles from right side and beg at marker pick up across back of neck .. sts pick up on left front .... sts

	Group A 38 40 42 44				Group B 38 40 42 44				Group C 38 40 42 44			
(back of neck)	49	50	50	53	36	38	39	40	30	33	33	33
(left front)	28	28	28	28	22	22	22	22	18	18	18	18

Sizes	Group A 38 40 42 44				Group B 38 40 42 44				Group C 38 40 42 44			
K across sts on holder, pick up on right front . . . . sts	28	28	28	28	22	22	22	22	18	18	18	18

Join and work around in K 1, P 1 rib for 1 inch. Bind off in rib. Set in sleeves. Sew underarm seams.

GREEN SWEATER

Sizes	Group A				Group B				Group C			
Back: With smaller needles cast on . . . . sts	142	149	158	165	114	121	127	134	88	92	101	106
Rib in K 1, P 1 for 2½ inches.												
Next Row: Rib . . . . sts	4	4	5	5	4	5	3	4	1	3	5	5
* inc 1 st in next st, rib . . . . sts	6	6	6	6	4	4	4	4	4	4	4	4
rep from *, end last rep rib . . . . sts	4	4	5	5	4	5	3	4	1	3	5	5
There are on needle . . . . sts	162	170	180	188	136	144	152	160	106	110	120	126
Change to larger needles.												
Row 1 (right side): P . . . . sts	3	3	4	4	2	2	2	2	3	5	2	1
* K 4, P 4; rep from * to last . . . . sts	7	7	8	8	6	6	6	6	7	9	6	5
K 4, P . . . . sts	3	3	4	4	2	2	2	2	3	5	2	1
Row 2: K . . . . sts	3	3	4	4	2	2	2	2	3	5	2	1
* P 4, K 4; rep from * to last . . . . sts	7	7	8	8	6	6	6	6	7	9	6	5
K 4, P . . . . sts	3	3	4	4	2	2	2	2	3	5	2	1
Row 3: P . . . . sts	3	3	4	4	2	2	2	2	3	5	2	1

sl next 2 sts to double-pointed needle, hold at *back* of work. K next 2 sts, K 2 from dp needle (cable twist), P 4; rep from *, end last rep cable, P

Sizes	Group A				Group B				Group C			
. . . . sts	3	3	4	4	2	2	2	2	3	5	2	1

Row 4: Rep Row 2. ***Row 5:*** Rep Row 1. ***Row 6:*** Rep Row 2.

Rep these 6 rows for cable pat. Work to 15 inches from beg, or desired length to underarm, end with a wrong side row.

Sizes	Group A				Group B				Group C			
Armholes: At beg of next 2 rows, bind off . . sts	5	6	7	8	6	6	6	7	3	3	6	6
Dec 1 st each side of next 5 rows. Dec 1 st each side of every 2nd row . . . . times	5	5	6	6	3	4	5	5	2	2	3	3
Work on . . . . sts	132	138	144	150	108	114	120	126	86	90	92	98
until armholes measure . . . . inches	8½	9	9½	10	SAME AS GROUP A				SAME AS GROUP A			
Shoulders: At beg of next . . . . rows	8	6	2	14	12	8	4	12	2	10	10	6
bind off . . . . sts	5	5	5	6	6	6	6	7	5	6	6	6
At beg of next . . . . rows	8	10	14	2	0	4	8	0	8	0	0	4
bind off . . . . sts	6	6	6	7	0	7	7	0	6	0	0	7
Place on holder . . . . sts	44	48	50	52	36	38	40	42	28	30	32	34
Front (With Crew Neck): Work same as back until armholes measure . . . . inches	6½	7	7½	8	SAME AS GROUP A				SAME AS GROUP A			
Neck — Next Row: Work . . . . sts	54	56	59	62	44	47	49	52	35	37	37	40
place on holder center . . . . sts	24	26	26	26	20	20	22	22	16	16	18	18

join 2nd ball of yarn, work to end. Working each side with separate yarn, bind off from each neck

Sizes	Group A				Group B				Group C			
edge 2 sts every 2nd row . . . . times	2	3	4	5	2	3	3	4	2	2	2	3
Dec 1 st at each neck edge every 2nd row . . times	6	5	4	3	4	3	3	2	2	3	3	2

shaping shoulders as on back when armholes are same length.

Sizes	Group A 38 40 42 44				Group B 38 40 42 44				Group C 38 40 42 44			

Finishing: Sew shoulder seams.

Neckband: With dp needles from right side, K across sts at back of neck, dec evenly spaced

. . . . sts	4	6	6	6	6	6	8	8	4	4	6	6

pick up 1 st in each st or row on left front neck edge, K across sts on holder, pick up same number of sts on left front edge. Join. Work around in K 1, P 1 rib. Sew underarm and sleeve seams. Set in sleeves. Block between towels.

Front — (With V-Neck): Work same as back until armholes measure . . . . inches — **2 2 2 2** (SAME AS GROUP A) (SAME AS GROUP A)

There are on needle . . . . sts	132	138	144	150	108	114	120	126	86	90	92	98

Divide for V-Neck: Work . . . . sts

	66	69	72	75	54	57	60	63	43	45	46	49

join a 2nd ball of yarn, work to end. Work on each side with separate yarn.

Dec 1 st at each neck edge every 2nd row . . times	12	12	13	13	10	10	10	11	7	8	8	9
every 4th row . . . . times	10	12	12	13	8	9	10	10	7	7	8	8

AND AT THE SAME TIME when same length as back to shoulder, shape shoulders as on back.

Sleeves: With smaller needles cast on . . . . . . sts	72	78	80	80	58	58	58	64	42	45	47	50

Rib in K 1, P 1 for 3 inches.

Next Row: Rib . . . . sts	4	6	7	7	2	2	2	1	3	2	3	2
* in c 1 st in next st, rib . . . . sts	6	5	5	5	3	3	3	3	4	4	4	3
rep between *s . . . . times	8	10	10	10	12	12	12	14	6	7	7	10

inc 1 st in next st, rib to end.

There are on needle . . . . sts	82	90	92	92	72	72	72	80	50	54	56	62

Change to larger needles. Work pat as on back for 4 rows. Inc 1 st each side of next row and rep incs every . . . . rows — **6 6 6 6 | 6 6 6 6 | 4 4 4 4**

(working inc sts in pat) . . . . more times	22	21	23	25	15	18	20	19	15	15	16	15
There are on needle . . . . sts	128	134	140	144	104	110	114	120	82	86	90	94
Shape Cap: At beg of next 2 rows, bind off . sts	5	6	7	8	6	6	6	7	3	3	6	6
Dec 1 st each side every 2nd row . . . . times	11	13	15	16	8	10	11	12	7	9	10	12
every row . . . . times	18	18	18	18	14	15	16	17	12	12	10	10
At beg of next . . . . rows	8	8	8	8	8	8	8	8	4	4	4	4
bind off . . . . sts	5	5	5	5	4	4	4	4	5	5	5	5

Bind off remaining sts.

Finishing: Sew shoulder seams. With dp needles from right side, K across sts at back of neck, dec evenly spaced . . . . sts

	4	6	6	6	6	6	8	8	4	4	6	6
pick up on left front neck edge . . . . sts	80	86	88	92	64	66	70	72	50	52	56	58

pick up 1 st at center front and mark, pick up same number of sts on right front as on left front. Join and mark end of rnds.

Rnd 1: K 1, P 1 to center st; K center st, P 1, K 1 to end. Keeping rib pat, dec 1 st each side of center st until band measures 1 inch. Bind off in rib, dec as before. Sew underarm and sleeve seams. Set in sleeves. Block between towels.

Crochet

The origins of crochet date back to sixteenth century France, where French nuns used hooks for making beautiful lace. In fact, the word "crochet" comes from the French term for hook. The art of crochet was carried by the nuns to Ireland. Here it became very refined; Irish girls skillfully copied many rare old patterns and it became an accomplishment required of well-born young ladies.

In the past, crochet has been usually worked in cotton threads for purely utilitarian items, such as tablecloths, napkins and bedspreads. Today, crocheting can and does employ many various types of threads — for an endless number of attractive garments, as well as wall hangings and other decorative items.

Crochet is a pleasant and very rewarding hobby that needs no previous skills of any kind. The desire to learn, a little time and patience is all that is necessary. Once this craft has been mastered, there are no limits to its many uses. Original creations can be of any desired texture, weight and design.

NEVER TOO YOUNG TO START: Grandmother loved to crochet and now it's time to hand down her skills.

INTRODUCTION TO CROCHET

Fascinated by the useful possibilities of fibers, weavers developed many methods of spinning yarn and thread from wool and cotton. First, the weaver learned to spin the fibers by hand. As the demand for his products increased, he developed the spinning wheel which was the best method prior to the advent of powered machinery.

Once the weaver had the thread, he would weave it into cloth on a loom. Unfortunately, this method required a good deal of space and confined him to a sitting position day in and day out. Portable looms were invented and are still in use in many areas. However, the solution to this problem came with the idea of looping the yarn through itself with the aid of a stick. Hence, knitting and crochet evolved from this technique.

Although modern crochet dates back to sixteenth century France, various crude forms of the art have been found in many earlier societies (as far back as 2000 B.C.). One of these forms was done with a needle similar to a fisherman's needle. Another form was developed from an early mariner's technique of looping without tying a knot. It is thought that weavers combined these

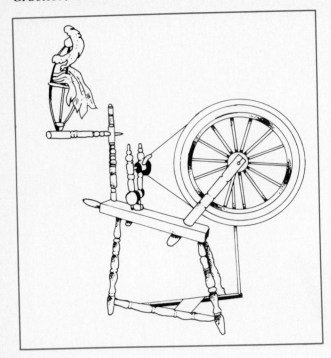

methods in an attempt to find a handier method of weaving. The sticks used in this "hand weaving" became crochet hooks, and then, were eventually smoothed on the ends as knitting needles.

Crochet was refined into a craft during the sixteenth century in French convents, but it was not until the nineteenth century that crochet was recognized as one of the "womanly arts" on the level of popularity with knitting and embroidery. Women fleeing France brought the techniques and the French name "crochet" to England around 1820. A quarter of a century later, crochet was introduced in Ireland as a cottage industry with which people could make a meager living. The rose designs of Irish crochet were used in edgings, tablecloths and beautiful delicate blouses sold all over the world. Unfortunately, the modern machine copies have lost much of the delicacy and beauty of the original handmade crochet.

During the Victorian era, many American women decorated the interior of their homes with crocheted bedspreads, tablecloths, lampshades, and antimacassars. Crochet was again in danger of being a lost art prior to the sudden revival of handmade clothing and purses as part of fashion in the last decade.

There are many reasons for the renewed interest in crochet. New yarns, the use of larger needles and the slick designs have given crochet a whole new look. The Granny Square has become part of the new style in skirts, tops and purses. Afghans have regained popularity, bringing the Granny Square back to its original purpose. Designers have applied crochet stitches to a range of items from cardigans and fashionable clothes to rugs and delicate edgings. For many people, crochet stitches are easier to learn than knitting because mistakes are easier to correct. Also crochet designs are easier to create than knitting designs.

LEFT-HANDERS

As most crochet patterns and instructions are drawn for right-handed people, it was once thought that "left-handers" had a special problem in learning the art. Experience has taught that this case does not always hold true. Left-handed people can learn to crochet from the same instructions as right-handed people. One method is to employ the use of a mirror to reflect the image of the illustration in the opposite way that it was drawn.

A help in learning for left-handers is that crochet is an ambidextrous craft in that it utilizes both hands equally; one to hold the crochet hook, the other to hold the guide yarn. This will make crocheting much easier in the long run. Many of the problems that the left-hander feels are the same problems felt by right-handers — the lack of dexterity and the feeling of tension. The awkwardness will ease as one becomes familiar with crochet hooks. The beginner will feel the tension relax as crochet becomes a habit rather than a conscious thought process.

TIPS ON LEARNING

The crochet novice should consult the Primer on Crochet found in this chapter for the rudiments. As with any art form, crochet basics are generally simple. Without a solid knowledge of these basics, the intricate designs and patterns soon become impossible to comprehend. Therefore, it is imperative to obtain a thorough understanding of the knotting and stitching techniques.

First, the basic techniques will be fully described; then advanced methods will be discussed. At the completion of these, you will be able to produce as simple or as elaborate designs as you wish.

GLOSSARY OF ABBREVIATIONS
USED IN CROCHET

ch . . . . chain	sl . . . . slip
sc . . . . single crochet	sk . . . . skip
dc . . . . double crochet	rnd(s) . . . . round(s)
hdc . . . . half double crochet	beg . . . . beginning
trc . . . . treble crochet	'' . . . . inches(es)
dtr . . . . double treble crochet	in(s) . . . . inch(es)
tr tr . . . . triple treble crochet	tog . . . . together
st(s) . . . . stitch(es)	tch . . . . turning chain
yo or o(s) . . . . yarn over(s)	pat . . . . pattern
inc(s) . . . . increase(s)	MC . . . . Main Color
dec . . . . decrease(s)	CC . . . . Contrasting Color
sp(s) . . . . space(s)	rep . . . . Repeat
lp(s) . . . . loop(s)	

Symbols and Terms
Used for Crochet

SYMBOLS

* (Asterisk): Indicates that work following the * is to be repeated the number of times indicated *in addition* to the first time.

* to *: Indicates that work between *s is to be repeated the number of times indicated *in addi-*

** (Double Asterisk): Used in the same way as * (Asterisk).

† (Dagger): Used in same way as * (Asterisk).

()Parentheses: Indicate that what is enclosed in the () must be repeated the number of times indicated after the ().

[] Brackets: Indicate that what is enclosed in the [] must be repeated the number of times indicated after the [].

TERMS

Work Even: Work without increasing or decreasing any stitches.

Mark Stitch: Tie a contrasting colored thread or place a safety pin on stitch.

Mark Row: Tie a contrasting colored thread or place a safety pin at beg or end of row.

The Multiple of a Pattern Stitch: This is the number of stitches which is necessary to work one repeat of a pattern.

Afghan Stitch: A crochet stitch which forms square boxes.

Motif: A complete crochet design used in creating larger items.

Gauge: The number of rows and the number of stitches equivalent to 1 inch.

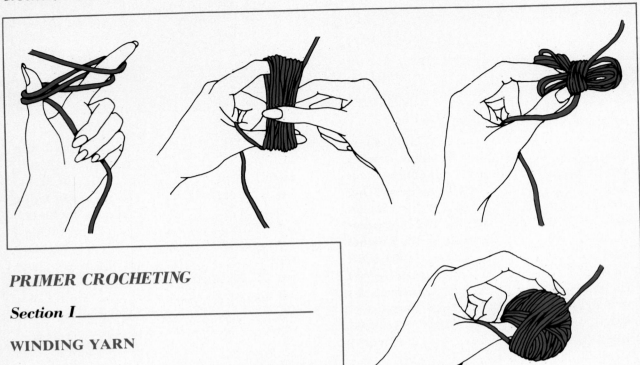

PRIMER CROCHETING

Section I

WINDING YARN

(To draw working end from center). Yarns in skeins (except pull skeins) must be wound into balls before they can be used. Open a skein; slip the coils over the back of a chair or sit down and slip them over your knees. Break and discard the knotted piece of yarn holding the coils together. Take one end of the strand from the skein. Leaving a 12-inch end, wind yarn ten times around thumb and index finger of left hand forming a figure eight. Remove from fingers; fold in half and hold folded piece at center with thumb and second finger of left hand. Wind yarn loosely around thumb and two fingers fifteen times. Keeping thumb at center, remove yarn from fingers; turn ball one quarter turn. Continue to turn ball in order to keep a round shape. Be sure that the 12-inch end remains free. Wrap loosely until skein is converted into a pull ball. Wind final end around several wraps; secure with a knot. Draw yarn from center for working.

HOLDING THE CROCHET HOOK

There are two ways in which a crochet hook can be held. Choose the method that is most comfortable.

Method 1: Hold hook with the right hand at top. Grasp the hook between thumb and index finger at the flat surface of the hook shank; or, 2 inches from hooked end.

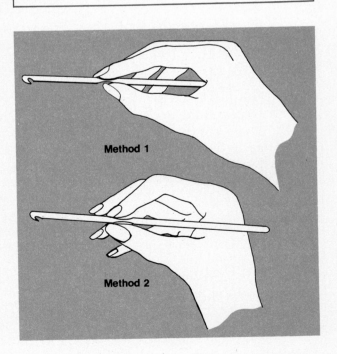

Method 2: With the right hand, hold hook as if it were a pencil. Grasp it between thumb and index finger at the flat surface of the hook shank; or, 2 inches from hooked end.

MAKING A FOUNDATION CHAIN (ch)

Step 1: Make a slip knot about 2 inches from end of yarn. With right hand insert hook in knot, forming a loop on hook.

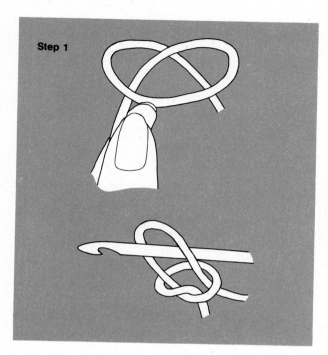

Step 2: With index finger of left hand draw yarn to fit hook shank — *not tightly.* Hold slip knot between thumb and 3rd finger. Pass long end (attached to ball) over the index finger, under the middle finger and over the ring finger. Grasp yarn with little finger and hold against palm. You will learn to control the yarn so that it will slide easily under the fingers.

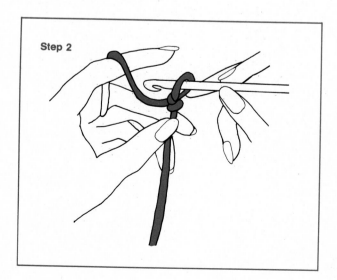

Step 3: Hold hook with point down. Pass yarn over hook. Catch yarn with hook.

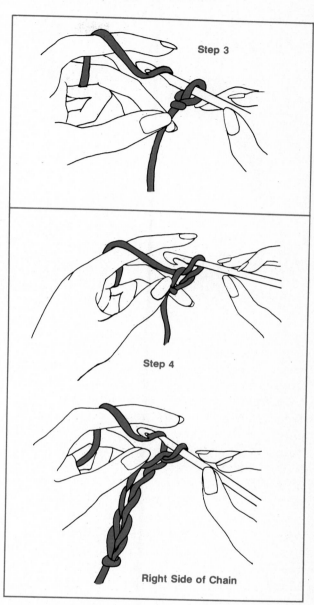

Step 4: Draw yarn through loop, making a new loop on hook. One chain has been made. Repeat Steps 3 and 4 for desired number of chains. After making several chain stitches, move thumb and middle finger up on chain so as to hold the last chain close to the hook. On the right side there will be two top strands and one bottom strand.

SINGLE CROCHET (sc)

Make a foundation chain of 21 chain stitches. *Do not* count loop on hook.

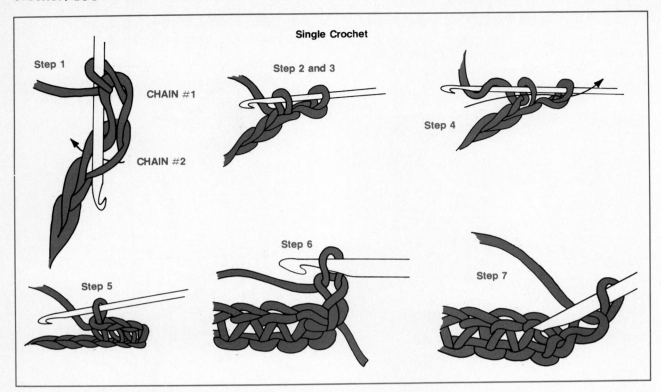

Single Crochet

Step 1

CHAIN #1

CHAIN #2

Step 2 and 3

Step 4

Step 5

Step 6

Step 7

Step 1: Insert hook in middle of the second chain from hook so that two top strands lie on top of hook and one strand lies below hook.

Step 2: Pass yarn over hook, catch yarn with hook.

Step 3: Draw yarn through chain. There are 2 loops on hook.

Step 4: Pass yarn over hook, catch yarn with hook, draw through both loops. One single crochet has been worked.

Step 5: Insert hook in next chain. Repeat Steps 2 through 5 in each chain. There are 20 sc in row. Look at stitches to see how they are formed. Chain 1 before turning at end of every sc row to raise the work to the correct level for the next sc row. The chain does *not* count as a stitch.

Step 6: Turn work from right to left; the yarn will remain at back of work.

Step 7: Insert hook under 2 strands of first sc (this is the last sc of previous row), draw yarn through stitch. Catch yarn and draw through 2 loops on hook. The first sc has been worked on Row 2. Work 1 sc in each sc. Again there are 20 sc in the row. Chain 1 and turn.

Notice how the first and second rows look. Continue to work rows of sc until there are 20 rows. Do *not* chain at the end of the last row.

To Fasten Off: Cut yarn, leaving a 4-inch end. Pull cut end through loop on hook.

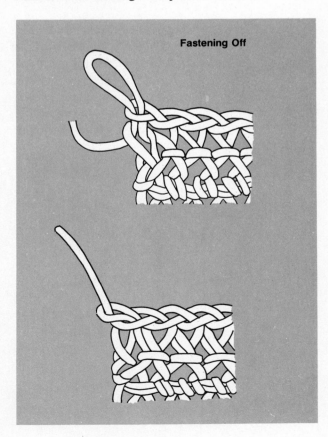

Fastening Off

Single Crochet

Half Double Crochet

HALF DOUBLE CROCHET (hdc)

Make a foundation chain of 22 chains. Do *not* count loop on hook.

Steps 1 and 2: Pass yarn over hook once, insert hook under two top strands of third chain from hook.

Step 3: Pass yarn over hook, catch yarn with hook, draw yarn through chain. There are 3 loops on hook.

Step 4: Pass yarn over hook, catch yarn with hook.

Step 5: Draw yarn through 3 loops on hook. One hdc has been worked.

Work 1 hdc in each chain. There are 20 hdc in the row. Look at stitches to see how they are formed. Chain 2 before turning at end of every hdc row to raise the work to the correct level for the next hdc row. The chain 2 does *not* count as a stitch.

Step 6: Turn work from right to left.

Step 7: Yarn over hook, insert hook under 2 strands of first hdc, yarn over hook, draw yarn through stitch. Yarn over hook, draw yarn through 3 loops on hook. The first hdc has been worked on Row 2. Work 1 hdc in each hdc, *do not* work in the chain 2 at end of the row. Again there are 20 hdc in row. Chain 2 and turn. Notice how the two rows compare. Continue to work rows of hdc until there are 16 rows hdc. Fasten off same as for single crochet.

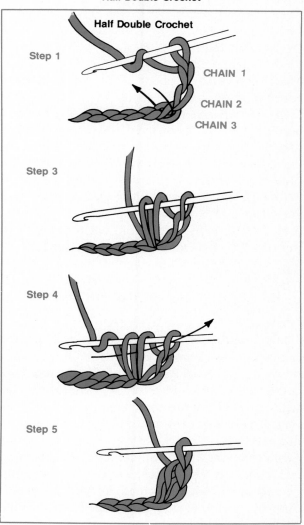

Half Double Crochet

Step 1

CHAIN 1
CHAIN 2
CHAIN 3

Step 3

Step 4

Step 5

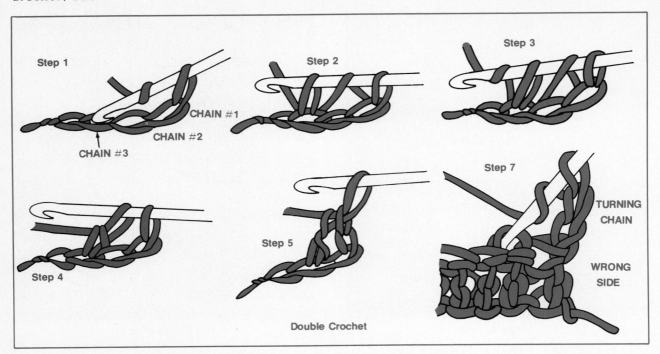

Double Crochet

DOUBLE CROCHET (dc)

Make a foundation chain of 21 chains. *Do not* count loop on hook.

Step 1: Pass yarn over hook once, insert hook under 2 top strands of third chain from hook.

Step 2: Pass yarn over hook, catch yarn, draw yarn through chain. There are 3 loops on hook.

Step 3: Pass yarn over hook.

Step 4: Catch yarn, draw through 2 loops. There are 2 loops on hook.

Step 5: Pass yarn over hook, catch yarn, draw through 2 loops. One dc has been worked. Work 1 dc in each chain. Counting the chain 2 at beginning of row as 1 dc, there are 20 dc. Look at stitches and compare with the hdc. The dc is one loop higher.

Chain 2 before turning at the end of every dc row to raise the work to the correct level for the next dc row. The chain 2 at end of each row always counts as the first dc of the following row. This will be called the turning chain.

Step 6: Turn work from left to right; yarn will remain at back.

Step 7: Skip the first dc of previous row. Inserting hook under 2 top strands, work 1 dc in the 2nd dc and in each dc to the end. Work the last (the 20th dc) in the top of the chain 2 (the turning chain).

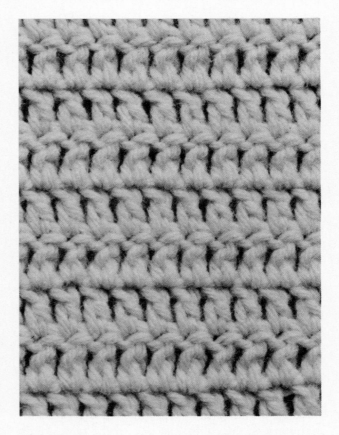

Continue to work rows of dc until there are 14 dc rows. Always skip the first dc of the completed row and always work a dc in the top of the turning chain at end of row.

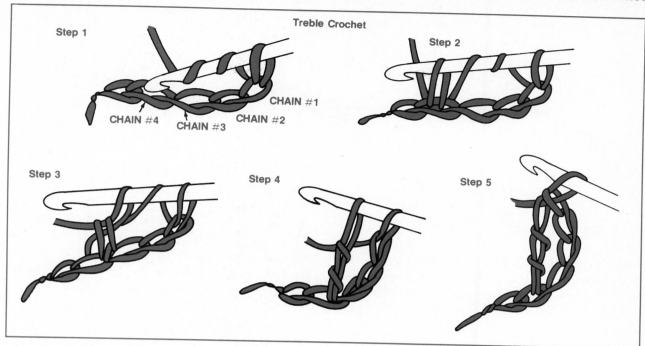

Treble Crochet

Step 1 · Step 2 · Step 3 · Step 4 · Step 5

CHAIN #4 · CHAIN #3 · CHAIN #2 · CHAIN #1

Treble Crochet

Step 1: Pass yarn over hook twice, insert hook under 2 top strands of fourth chain from hook.
Step 2: Pass yarn over hook, catch yarn, draw yarn through chain. There are 4 loops on hook.
Step 3: Pass yarn over hook, catch yarn, draw yarn through 2 loops. There are 3 loops on hook.
Step 4: Pass yarn over hook, catch yarn, draw yarn through 2 loops. There are 2 loops on hook.
Step 5: Pass yarn over hook, catch yarn, draw yarn through 2 loops. One tr has been worked.

Work 1 tr in each chain. Counting the ch 3 at the beginning of the row as 1 tr there are 20 tr. Look at stitches and compare with the dc. The tr is one loop higher. Ch 3 before turning at end of every tr row to raise the work to the correct level for the next tr row. The chain 3 at end of row always counts as the first tr of the following row and is called the turning chain. The following rows are worked the same as the dc rows. Continue to work rows of tr until there are 10 tr rows. Fasten off.

TREBLE CROCHET (tr)

Make a foundation chain of 22 chains. Do *not* count loop on hook.

DOUBLE TREBLE CROCHET (dtr)

A double (dtr) is worked by passing yarn over the hook three times. Insert the hook in the fifth chain stitch and take off 2 loops four times. Chain 4 before turning at end of rows.

Slip Stitch

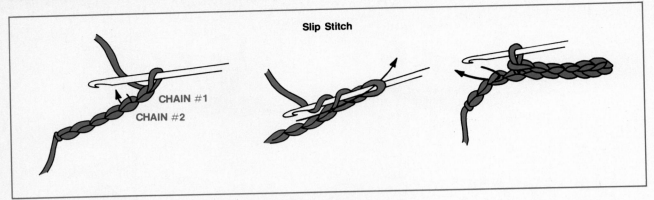

CHAIN #1
CHAIN #2

SLIP STITCH (sl st)

Make a foundation chain of 13 stitches.
Step 1: Insert hook in second chain from hook, catch yarn and draw through chain and also through loop on hook. One sl st has been worked. Work a sl st in each chain to the end. There are 12 sl sts in the row. Fasten off.

HEIGHT OF BASIC STITCHES

To observe the difference in heights of the basic stitches, make a chain of 34 stitches. * Sl st in sec- ond ch from hook, sc in next ch, hdc in next ch, dc in next ch, tr in next ch, dtr in next ch, tr in next ch, dc in next ch, hdc in next ch, sc in next ch, sl st in next ch; rep from * twice more. Fasten off.

FORMING A CIRCLE

A circle can be made in any size. Make a chain of the required number of stitches.
Step 1: Insert hook in first chain. Be sure the chain is not twisted.
Step 2: Work one sl st.

TOP

BOTTOM

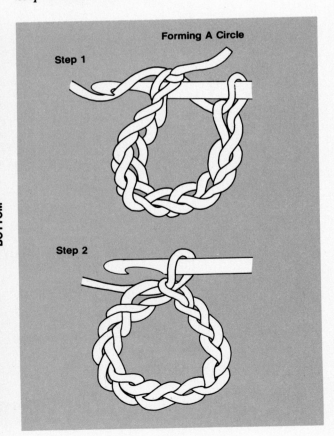

Forming A Circle

Step 1

Step 2

MAKING FRINGE

Cut a piece of cardboard the same width as desired for the fringe length. Wrap yarn loosely around cardboard; cut at one end. Use the num-

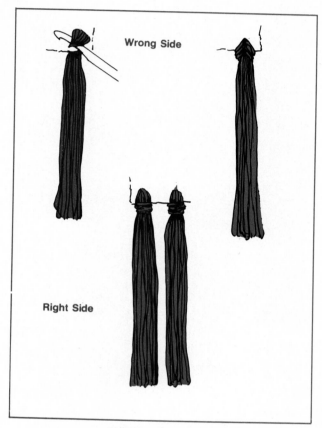

Single Knot Fringe

Double Knot Fringe

Triple Knot Fringe

ber of strands in instructions or as desired. Fold strands in half. Insert crochet hook from wrong side into stitch or row to be fringed. Draw folded loop through stitch or row. Draw cut ends (beginning and end of yarn strands) through loop and pull to tighten. Knot will be on right side.

MAKING TASSELS

Around a piece of cardboard cut to specified measurements, wrap yarn the number of times required in the instructions. Draw a piece of the same yarn under the loops at the top of the cardboard and tie the strands together. Cut the loops at the bottom of the cardboard. Cut a small piece of the same yarn. Wrap it tightly several times around the strands about one inch from the fold. Tie the ends together and draw them to the middle of the tassel.

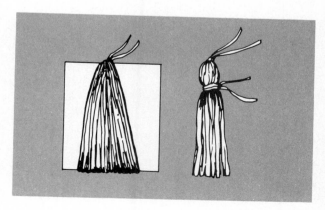

Section II

GAUGE

Every set of crochet instructions calls for a specific gauge. The stitch gauge is the number of stitches which equals 1 inch; the row gauge is the number of rows which equals 1 inch. The gauge is determined by the weight of the yarn, the size of the crochet hook used and the way the yarn is controlled (called the tension).

The size of a garment is based on mathematical calculations according to the gauge given. Before beginning the project, always check the gauge by making a sample piece using the yarn and crochet hook recommended.

Making a Sample Piece: Chain the number of stitches required to measure 4 inches (multiply the stitch gauge by 4). Then add the number of chain stitches necessary for the turning chain. This will equal the number of chains for the foundation chain. Work 4 inches according to the row gauge given. Fasten off.

Measuring Stitch Gauge: Place sample right side up on a flat surface. Do not stretch; if necessary, pin to keep flat. Place tape measure in a straight line across stitches as shown. Place pins at beginning of tape, at 1-inch and at 2-inch markings, even if the pin does not come between two stitches.

4 Rows = 1 Inch

4 Stitches = 1 Inch

Remove tape; unpin. Holding work, count stitches between the first 2 pins; make a note; count stitches between the first and third pin. This gives the number of stitches which equals 2 inches. If this is an uneven number of stitches do not disregard the ½ stitch per inch. If there are fewer stitches to an inch than the gauge given, the work is too loose and a smaller size hook should be tried. If there are more stitches to an inch, the work is too tight and a larger size hook should be tried. The size of the hook used is *not* important; the correct gauge is *very* important. Never try to change the gauge by working tighter or looser.

Gauge shows 4 stitches = 1 inch, 4 rows = 1 inch.

Measuring Row Gauge: With sample in same position, place tape measure as shown. Place pins at beginning of tape, at 1-inch and 2-inch markings. Count rows and make note.

INCREASING

Single Crochet: Work 2 sc in one stitch.

Half Double Crochet: Work 2 hdc in one stitch.

Double Crochet: *At the beginning of a row,* work 1 double crochet in *first* double crochet (the double crochet which is usually skipped at the beginning of a row). *Within a row* work 2 dc in any

2 Single Crochets in 1 Stitch

stitch. *At end of row,* work 2 double crochet in the last double crochet, then work 1 double crochet in the top of the turning.

Treble Crochet and Double Treble Crochet: Work the same as in Double Crochet.

DECREASING

Single Crochet: Draw up a loop in each of the next 2 sts, yo and draw loop through all 3 loops on hook.

Half Double Crochet: Yarn over hook; insert hook in next stitch and draw loop through; yarn over hook again; insert hook in next stitch and

Increase 1 Double Crochet at Beginning of Row; Increase 1 Double Crochet Within Row; Increase 1 Double Crochet at End of Row.

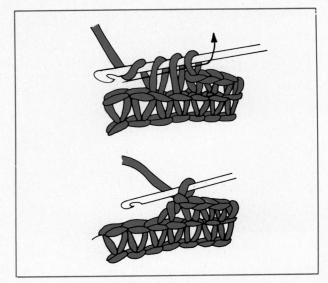

Decreasing Single Crochet

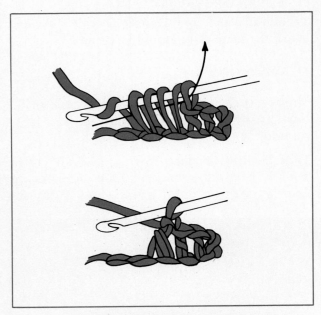

Decreasing Half Double Crochet

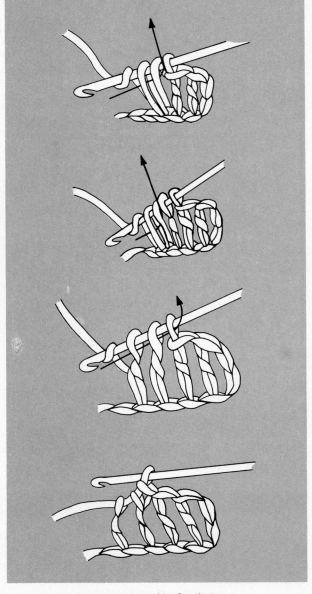

Decreasing Double Crochet

draw loop through (5 loops on hook). Yarn over hook and draw loop through all 5 loops.

Double Crochet: Yarn over hook; insert hook in next stitch and draw yarn through stitch; yo hook and draw through 2 loops, (2 lps remain on hook). Yarn over hook, insert hook in next stitch; draw yarn through stitch; yarn over, draw through 2 loops; yarn over, draw through 3 loops. *At the beginning of row,* if turning chain is counted as first stitch always skip first st as usual; work decrease over second and third stitch. *At*

end of row, work decrease over the last 2 stitches then work in the turning chain.

Treble Crochet: Yarn over hook twice; insert hook in next stitch and draw yarn through stitch (4 loops on hook). Yarn over and draw through 2 loops; yarn over and draw through 2 again (2 loops remain on hook). Yarn over twice, insert hook in next stitch; yarn over and draw yarn through stitch (5 loops on hook). Yarn over and draw through 2 loops; yarn over and draw through 2 loops again; yarn over and draw

Decreasing Treble Crochet

through 3 loops. *At beginning and end of row, work same as for a double crochet decrease.*

JOINING A NEW STRAND OF YARN

There should never be a knot in the work. If there is a knot in the ball of yarn, cut it out; if new yarn is needed, join as follows. With the yarn being used, work the stitch until there are 2 loops on hook. Drop yarn and with new strand complete the stitch. With crochet it is best *not* to join new yarn at the beginning of a row unless it is necessary for a color change.

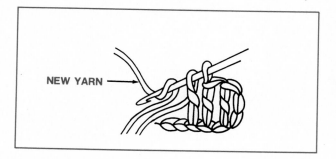

NEW YARN

RIBBING STITCHES

Method 1: Slipper Stitch — Worked vertically

Chain the number of stitches for desired depth of ribbing.

Slipper Stitch (Lower Edge)

Foundation Row: Work sc in second chain from hook and in each chain to end.

Ch 1, turn at end of every row.

Row 1: Through *back* loop only, work 1 sc in each sc. Repeat Row 1 for desired length of ribbing. Fasten off.

Method 2: Post Stitch and Single Crochet Stitch

To Work the Post Stitch: Yarn over, insert hook from *front* (No. 1 on diagram) in space to right of single crochet and from *back* (No. 2 on diagram) in space to left of same stitch. The hook is behind the *post* of the single crochet. Always skip the stitch behind the Post Stitch (PS).

Chain an even number of stitches.

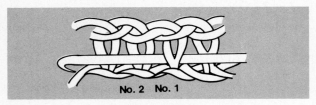

To Work Post Stitch

Foundation Row: Single crochet (sc) in second chain from hook and in each chain to end.

Chain 1, turn at end of every row.

Row 1: Sc in first st, * PS around next st, sc in next st; repeat from * to end.

Row 2: Sc in each st.

Row 3: Sc in first st, * PS around next PS 2 rows below, sc in next st; repeat from * to end. Repeat last 2 rows for desired depth of ribbing.

Post Stitch and Single Crochet

Front and Back Post Stitch

Method 3: Front and Back Post Stitch Worked in Single Crochet

Pattern is worked on an even number of stitches.

Row 1: From front, insert hook in space after first sc and to front at left of second sc (hook is behind *post* of 2nd sc), draw yarn through and complete sc — a Front Post Stitch (FPS), * from back, insert hook in space to left of post stitch just worked, then to back over post of next st (hook is in *front* of third sc). Draw yarn through and complete sc — a Back Post Stitch (BPS). From front, insert hook to left of post just worked and to front at left of next post and complete FPS. Repeat from *, ending FPS around last post stitch. Sc in space to left of last FPS. Ch 1, turn.

Row 2: Insert hook from back to front over first post and complete BPS, * insert hook under 2 crossed strands of next post stitch (do *not* insert hook completely under post) and complete FPS. BPS around next post. Repeat from * ending BPS around last post stitch, sc in space to left of last BPS. Ch 1, turn.

Row 3: Begin at * of Row 2 and work pattern ending FPS around last post stitch, sc in space to left of last post stitch.

Repeat Rows 2 and 3 for pattern.

MEASURING WORK

Always lay article to be measured on a flat surface. Measure at center of work with a ruler or heavy tape measure.

Measuring Armhole: With a colored thread, mark last row before first armhole row. Run thread for 3 inches across row into body of work. Lay work on a flat surface. Measure up in a straight line from colored thread.

BLOCKING

Careful blocking often makes the difference between a beautiful crocheted garment and a non-professional looking one. *The most important elements are time and patience. Never hurry!* There are three acceptable methods for blocking.

Method 1: Blocking pieces separately
As many actual measurements as possible should

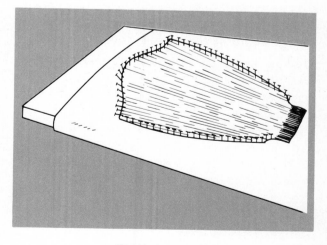

Blocking separately

be taken. Lay the piece wrong side up flat on a padded pressing surface. (Old table pads, a table or the floor may be used.) With rustproof T-pins, pin edges to padded surface (about every ¼ inch) stretching to desired measurements. Lay a wet cloth (sheeting or terry cloth wrung out in cool water) over the piece. Using moderately hot iron, pat the iron all over cloth, allowing steam to go through cloth. A steam iron may be used. Do not run iron back and forth over cloth as in ordinary pressing. Do not allow weight of iron to rest anywhere on piece. Leave pieces pinned until thoroughly dry. Remove pins. After making seams, steam them. It is advisable to fold large symmetrical pieces in half, block to within 1 inch of fold; let dry before removing pins; and, steam out fold. When two pieces are alike (fronts or sleeves), pin them together for blocking to keep the two pieces same size. *Do not* block ribbed borders or raised pattern stitches.

Method 2: Blocking after Finishing
In cold water, immerse two terry cloth towels large enough to cover the garment. Wring the towels as dry as possible. Lay one towel on blocking board or floor space. Lay garment on moist towel and cover with the other moist towel. Allow to dry thoroughly but take care to check within one-half hour to make certain the thumbtacks are rustproof.

Note: If garment requires stretching, twist tissue paper into long strips and place inside center of sleeves, along shoulders and inside of all seams. Press in *rustproof* thumbtacks an inch apart just inside the tissue-paper ridge, beginning at shoulder. Stretch or ease the armhole to proper size, keeping desired bust or chest measurement. The garment may be steamed slightly through top terry towel to hasten drying, but do *not* press.

Method 3: Blocking Acrylics after Finishing
Carefully wet entire garment, taking care to keep hands under garment so that it will not stretch. Lay it flat on a large dry towel and roll up that towel. Squeeze out extra moisture. Place another dry towel on a flat surface. Lay garment carefully on towel. Pat into desired shape and correct measurements. Leave until dry.

SEWING SEAMS

Method 1: Backstitch
Pin right sides of pieces together. Keep edges

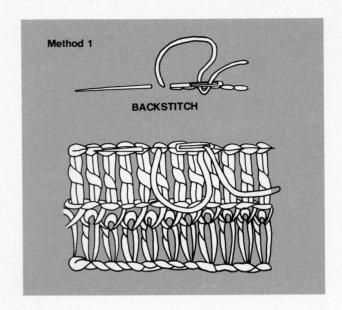

even, match rows and adjust the width of seams for proper fit. Fasten ends securely. Backstitch the seam using small stitches. Be careful not to draw stitches too tightly. Seam should be as elastic as the crocheted pieces.

Method 2: Lacing Stitch for Vertical Seams
This is worked from right side. Use lightweight yarn to match or two plies of the original yarn. Stitches will be joined at top of each row and rows will be matched. Join yarn for seaming at top stitch of the piece to be secured. Then join with a tacking stitch to top of corresponding stitch of other piece. Run small stitches in and out of post of same stitch. Tack top of next stitch of the two pieces together. Continue in this way to bottom of seam. Tack bottom of last row together and fasten yarn on wrong side.

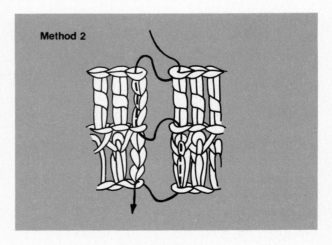

Lacing Seams

SET IN SLEEVES

Method 1: First seam shoulders, sides and sleeves. With wrong side of garment showing, divide armhole into four equal parts using pins as markers. With right side of sleeve showing, divide and mark cap of sleeve into four equal parts. With right side of sweater and sleeve together, pin sleeve-cap to armhole matching four pins. Between four sections add additional pins. Join sleevecap to sweater using backstitch for seam and easing in any fullness.

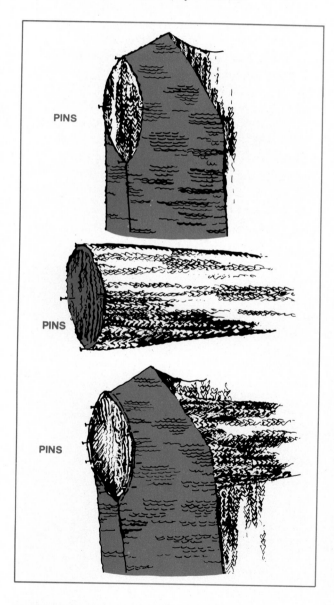

Method 2: Sew Shoulder Seams
With right side of sleeve cap and armhole together, pin center of bound-off stitches at top of sleeve cap at shoulder seam. Slip stitches at beginning of sleeve cap matching slip stitches of armhole. East remainder of cap to fit armhole. Backstitch sleeve to armhole.

MAKING POMPONS

Step 1: Cut two cardboard circles 1¹/₂ inches in diameter for small pompon; 2 inches for medium; 3 inches for large. Cut hole in middle of the circles. Cut strand of yarn 6 yards long.

Step 2: Thread the cut ends into a blunt tapestry needle. Place circles together. Draw the needle through center, over the circles and through the loop formed by the fold in the yarn. Continue to wrap yarn over the circles and through the hole until yarn fills the center and the circles are completely covered.

Step 3: With sharp scissors, cut between the circles at the outside edge.

Step 4: Between the circles, wind two strands of yarn about 8 inches long. Tie securely.

Step 5: Remove circles. Attach pompons with yarn used for tying. Trim pompon evenly.

Note: If this length is not long enough to cover the circle, use a second length. If the original length is cut too long, it will fray.

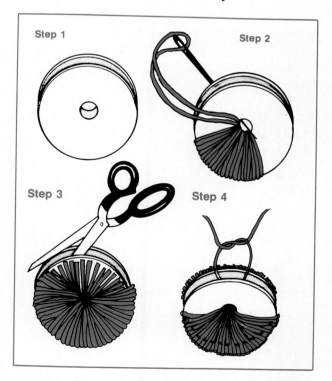

PROJECT — LADIES' HAT (See page 181 for hat you can make now)

ADVANCE CROCHET

Section III

BUTTON AND BUTTONHOLE BANDS

Bands may be worked separately, then sewn to fronts; or, worked on the fronts after they have been completed. Buttonholes may be worked when the front is being made. Work the front or band for the buttons first and mark as explained below.

Separate Horizontal Bands for Round Neck: There are two bands to be worked for a round neck garment.

Button Band: Chain the number of stitches necessary for desired width of band.
Foundation Row: Work sc in second ch from hook and in each ch to end. Ch 1, turn.
Row 1: Work 1 sc in each sc, ch 1, turn. Rep Row 1 until band is correct length to fit from lower edge of front to beginning of neck. Pin to front and check fit to be sure that band will neither draw front or cause it to sag. Fasten off.
To Mark For Buttons: With safety pins, mark a place in the center of band as follows; when a neckband is to be added, allow for the last button to be placed in the center of the neckband; when a neckband is not to be used, place first marker 1/2 inch below top of band, last marker 1 inch from lower edge. Divide space between pins evenly for desired number of buttons and mark each space. These pins will be guides for making buttonholes. A completed front for buttons should be marked in same way.

Buttonhole Band: Chain the same number of stitches as on button band. Work the same number of rows as on button band to the first marker. Consider size of button to be used.
Next Row: Depending on size of button to be used work 1 sc in each sc until there are several sc at center unworked. Skip these center stitches; chain the same number of stitches as the skipped st; work sc in each stitch to end of row.
Next Row: Work sc in each sc and sc in each chain. Continue in this manner working a buttonhole to correspond to each marker. There should be the same number of rows between buttonholes as between markers. Fasten off. Pin and sew bands to fronts.

Crocheted On Vertical Bands for Round Neck: Measure the front to know if it should be held in

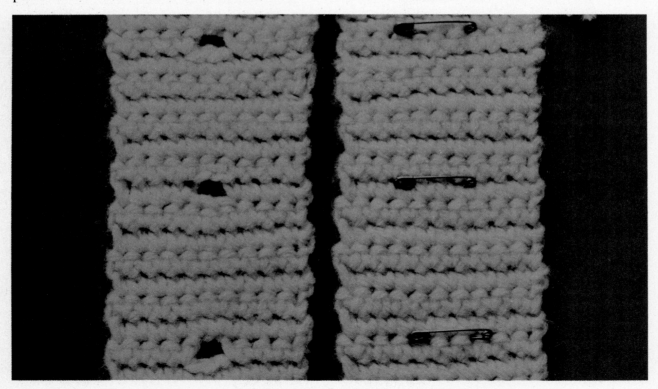

Mark for Buttons with Safety Pins; Work Buttonholes to Correspond With Pins.

or pulled down for correct measurement. Divide the front into sections with pins; first into halves, then into fourths.

With the right side up (beginning at neck edge of left front for ladies, lower edge of right front for men) work sc across first section. Measure to be sure the measurement is one fourth the entire measurement. If too long, rework with fewer sc; if too short, rework with more sc. Continue to check; rework this section if necessary.

When correct measurement has been achieved, continue to work each section with the same number of sc to lower edge, or neck edge. Ch 1, turn.

Row 2: Work 1 sc in each sc. *(Do not* tighten or loosen work.) Ch 1, turn.

Repeat Row 2 until band is desired width. (There should be uneven number of rows in band.)

To Mark For Buttons: See instructions for horizontal buttonhole band worked separately.

Buttonhole Band: Beginning at lower edge for ladies, neck edge for men, work same number sc on front as on button band. Work 1 row less than one-half the number of rows (an even number) on button band.

Next (Center) Row: Work 1 sc in each sc to beginning of first marker. Skip several sc (depending on size of button to be used), chain same number of stitches as the skipped stitches. Continue in this way to work a buttonhole to correspond to each marker, then work to end of row. Ch 1, turn.

Next Row: Work 1 sc in each sc and each chain. Ch 1, turn.

Rep Row 2 until there are the same number of rows on both sides of buttonhole row. Fasten off.

Crochet On Vertical Bands for V-Neck: Garment must be assembled. Place a marker on both fronts at first neck decrease. Divide front from lower edge to marker and work sc on right front edge the same as on crocheted Vertical Bands for Round Neck. Make a note of the number of sc. Continue sc on neck edge to shoulder. (Count stitches and make note.) Work sc across back of neck. Continue sc on left front, having same number of stitches between shoulder and neck marker and same number of stitches between

neck marker and lower edge as on right front. Ch 1, turn.

Row 2: Work sc in each sc. Ch 1, turn.
Repeat Row 2 until there is 1 row less than desired number of rows for width of band. (Make an even number of rows.)

Marking for Buttons: With safety pins mark places (on right front band for ladies, left front band for men), one marker ½ inch below first neck decrease and another marker 1 inch from lower edge. Divide space between for desired number of buttonholes and mark each space.

Next Row: Work sc in each sc to beginning of first marker, skip several st (depending on size of button) chain same number of stitches as skipped stitches, continue in this way to work a buttonhole over each marker, then work to end. Ch 1, turn.

Next Row: Work 1 sc in each sc and each chain. Ch 1, turn. Repeat Row 2 until there is the same number of rows on both sides of buttonhole row. Fasten off.

MAKING BUTTONS

Plastic Ring Button: Use size ring smaller than desired size for button, usually ⅜-inch ring.

Use a fine or medium-weight yarn or only 2 plies of a 4-ply yarn. Make a slip knot and place on hook. Work sc around entire ring until it is completely covered (count number of sts and use same number on every button). Cut yarn, leaving an end for sewing on button.

Thread end into a tapestry needle and draw under each sc. Pull tightly so top edge will turn to center of ring. Secure the end with a few stitches. Sew to garment through center of button.

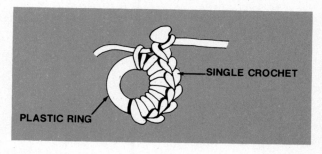

Ball Button: Using yarn as for plastic ring button, ch 3. Join with a slip st to form a ring.
Rnd 1: Work 6 sc in ring.
Rnd 2: 2 sc in each sc. (12 sc).

Rnd 3: * Sc in next sc, 2 sc in next sc; repeat from * around. 18 sc. Continue to inc 6 sts in every rnd to approximate size for top of button. Work 1 rnd even. Stuff with yarn, cotton or button mold. Work around skipping every 2nd st until ball is tightly closed. Fasten off and secure end with a few stitches. Cut yarn, leaving an end for sewing.

WORKING WITH COLORS FROM A CHART

When reading a chart, start at the bottom and read to the top. When working right side rows, read chart from right to left. When working wrong side rows, read chart from left to right.

Method 1: Carry the color not in use across *back* of work. *On right side rows,* work up to the last stitch of first color; work the next (last stitch of first color) to its last step, retaining last loops on hook; take first color to left, work off loops with second color.

On wrong side rows, take last color to right instead of left and work off loops with new color (be sure color not in use remains on wrong side of work).

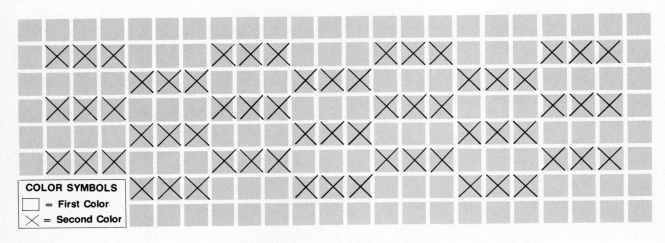

COLOR SYMBOLS
☐ = First Color
✕ = Second Color

Color Crocheting (Carry Color Across Back)

Right Side

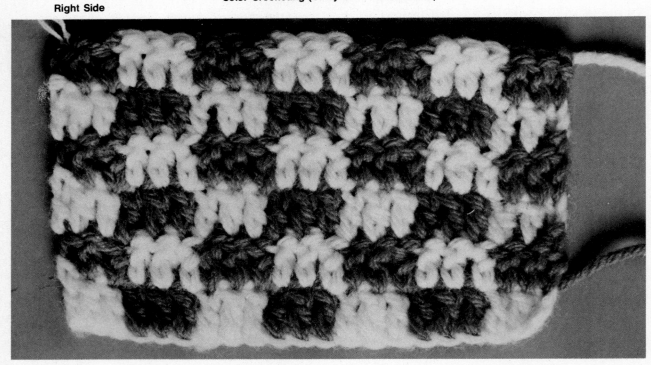

Wrong Side

Method 2: Work over color not in use. Make chain of first color. Hold first color to be used in left hand, lay second color along chain. Following chart, work over second color to last stitch of first color. Work next (last) stitch to last step of first color. Retaining loops on hook, drop first color, pick up second color and work off loops with second color. Work second color stitches over first color. Change colors in the same way.

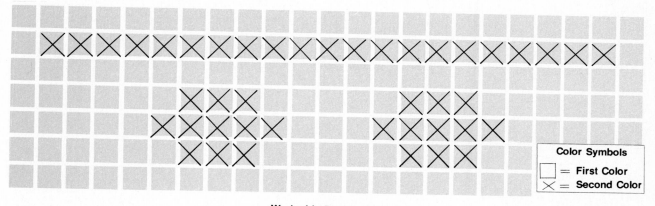

Color Symbols

☐ = First Color
✕ = Second Color

Worked in Double Crochet

Right Side

Wrong Side

Color Crocheting (Working Over Color)

Right Side

Color Crocheting (Cutting Color Not In Use)

Wrong Side

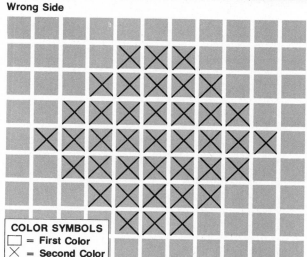

COLOR SYMBOLS
☐ = First Color
✕ = Second Color

Worked in Double Crochet

Method 3: Cut color when not in use. Make chain of given color. On right side row, work to last st of first color; work next (last) stitch to last step; retaining loop on hook, drop color to back (wrong side); cut yarn, leaving an end to be woven in later. Leaving the end on wrong side, work off loops with second color.

On wrong side rows, work to last stitch of color, drop color to front (wrong side); cut yarn, leaving the end on wrong side. When work is complete, weave ends neatly into matching color stitches.

PROJECT — MAN'S SWEATER (See page 187 for a sweater you can make now)

Section IV

AFGHAN STITCH OR TUNISIAN CROCHET

This stitch looks very much like knitting, however it is actually a crochet stitch. Patterns are formed by two basic stitches, the knit stitch and the purl stitch. Easy to work, this stitch can be used for flat work, such as afghans, bedspreads or table mats. Garments of any type from the very simple to the most elaborate can be shaped easily. The afghan stitch has an excellent weave or body for wearing apparel such as coats, suits and dresses.

Basic Afghan Stitch (Knit Stitch): A special needle called an afghan hook is required. Make a chain of desired length.

Row 1 — First Half: Skip first chain, * insert hook through *top* loop only of next chain. Yarn over hook, draw yarn through chain, forming a loop on hook. Retain loop on hook (1 Knit Stitch). Repeat from * across foundation chain. There will be same number of loops on hook as the number of chains.

Row 1 — Second Half: Yarn over hook and draw through first loop. * Yarn over and draw through 2 loops. Repeat from * across row until there is one loop on hook. This loop is the first stitch for the next row. *Do not* turn work.

Row 2 — First Half: Insert hook in second upright stitch or vertical bar, yarn over hook. Draw loop through vertical bar, forming a loop on hook. Retain loop on hook. Continue across row, drawing up a loop through each vertical bar. (If flat work is being made, draw up a loop through front and back bar of last stitch to give a firm edge.)

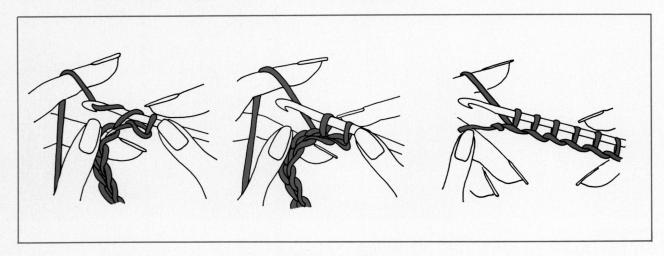

Row 1 — First Half

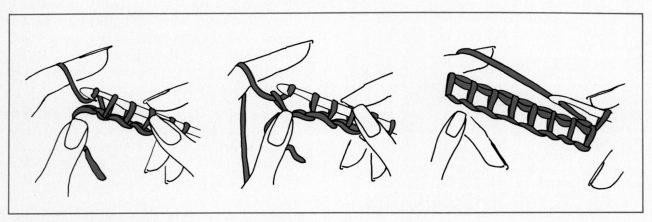

Row 1 — Second Half

Row 2 — Second Half: Same as second half of Row 1. Repeat Row 2 for pattern.

To Bind off: Slip stitch across row as follows: *Draw up loop in vertical bar as usual, then draw loop also through the loop on the hook. Repeat from * across row. Break yarn and draw through last loop.

To Decrease: Decreasing is always worked on the first half of a row. Work the second half of the row in the usual manner.

At beginning of row: Insert hook under second and third vertical bar and draw up *one* loop.

At end of row: Insert hook under second and third vertical bar from end of row and draw up one loop, then draw up *one* loop in last vertical bar.

Within a row: Insert hook under two vertical bars and draw up *one* loop.

To Increase: This is always made on the first half of a row. Work second half of row in usual way.

At beginning of a row: Draw up a loop in first vertical bar (the bar which is usually skipped).

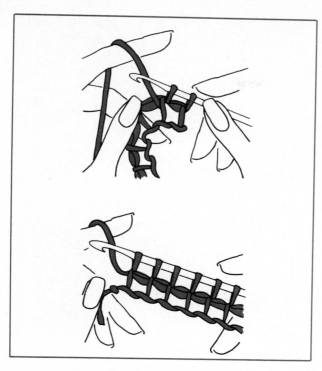

Row 2 — First Half

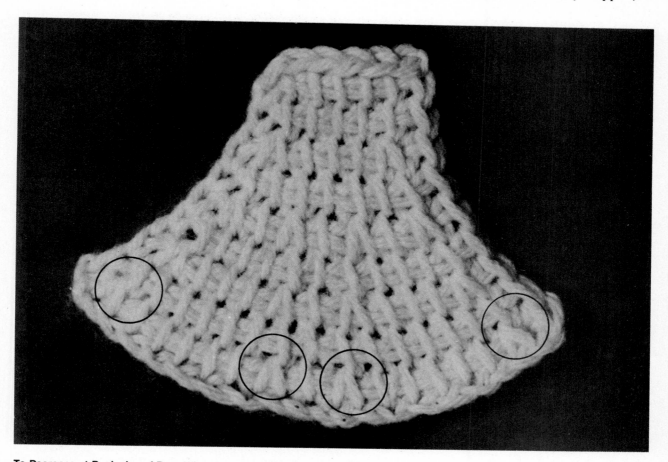

To Decrease at Beginning of Row, Within the Row and at the End of the Row

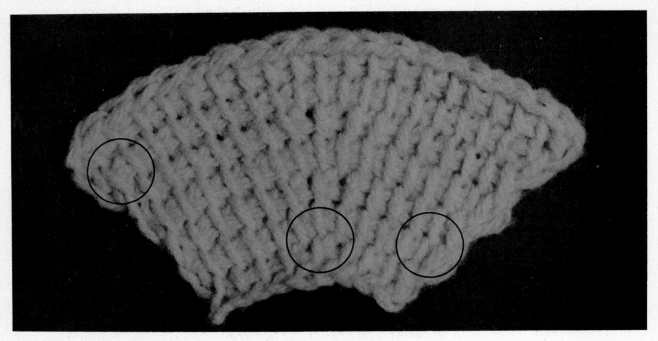

To Increase at Beginning of the Row, Within the Row and at the End of the Row.

At end of a row: Draw up a loop in front and a loop in back of last bar.

Within a row: Pick up a loop in the horizontal strand between 2 vertical bars (the chain stitch).

Purl Stitch: Make a chain of desired length.

Row 1 — First Half: Skip first chain. * Bring yarn forward, with yarn in front of hook, insert hook through top loop of next chain, yarn over hook. Draw yarn through chain. Retain loop on hook (1 Purl Stitch). Repeat from * across foundation chain.

The Purl Stitch — Row 1 — First Half

The Purl Stitch

Row 1 — Second Half: Same as Row 1 — Second Half of Basic Afghan Stitch.

Row 2 — First Half: * Bring yarn forward. Insert hook in second upright stitch or vertical bar, complete Purl Stitch; continue across row, working a Purl Stitch through each vertical bar.

Row 2 — Second Half: Same as Row 1 — Second Half. Always bind off in pattern (Purling the stitches).

Knit 1 and Purl 1 Ribbing: Make a chain of an uneven number of stitches.

Row 1 — First Half: Skip first chain, * knit 1 in next chain, purl 1 in next chain. Repeat from *, ending purl 1 in last chain.

Row 1 — Second Half: Work same as Second Half of Basic Afghan Stitch.

Row 2 — First Half: Skip first vertical bar, * knit 1 in next vertical bar, purl 1 in next vertical bar. Repeat from *, ending Purl 1 in last vertical bar.

Row 2 — Second Half: Same as Second Half of Row 1. Repeat Row 2 for pattern. Bind off in pattern.

Knit 1, Purl 1 Rib

Smocked or Seed Stitch: Make a chain of an uneven number of stitches.

Row 1 — First Half: Skip first chain, * knit 1 in next chain, purl 1 in next chain. Repeat from * ending purl 1 in last chain.

Row 1 — Second Half: Work same as Second Half of Basic Afghan Stitch.

Row 2 — First Half: Skip first vertical bar, * purl 1 in next vertical bar, knit 1 in next vertical bar. Repeat from *, ending knit 1 in last vertical bar.

Row 2 — Second Half: Same as Second Half of Row 1. Repeat these 2 rows for pattern working in vertical bars instead of chains on Row 1. Bind off in pattern.

Smocked Stitch

Smocked-Tweed Afghan Stitch: With Color A, chain an uneven number of stitches. * With A, pick up loops in Smocked Afghan Stitch. Join B. With B, work off loops.

With B, pick up loops in Smocked Afghan Stitch (alternating with stitches of previous rows). With A, work off loops. Repeat from * for pattern stitch. Bind off in pattern.

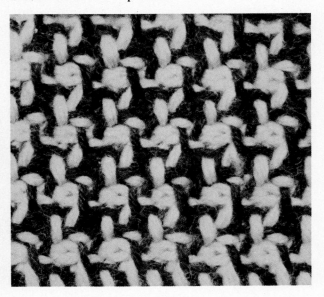

Smocked-Tweed Afghan Stitch

Basic Afghan Stitch with Star Stitch: Make a chain of an uneven number of stitches. Work Basic Afghan Stitch for desired number of rows.

Star Stitch Row 1 — First Half: Chain 3, draw up

Basic Afghan Stitch with Star Stitch

a loop in 2nd and 3rd chain from hook, draw up a loop in each of next 3 bars, yarn over and draw through all loops on hook. Chain 1 tightly to form eye of star, * draw up a loop in eye of star, a loop in back of last loop of last star, in same vertical bar as last loop of last star and in each of next 2 bars, yarn over and through all 6 loops on hook. Chain 1 tightly to form eye of star. Repeat from * to end. There will be one-half the number of stars (less 1 stitch) as the number of vertical bars.

Star Stitch Row 1 — Second Half:
Ch 2, turn work. Work 1 hdc in eye of first star, * 2 hdc in eye of next star. Repeat from *, end 1 hdc in top of ch 3 of last star. Ch 1, turn work.

Afghan Stitch Row 1 — First Half:
Retaining all loops on hook, draw up a loop between first 2 hdc, * draw up a loop between next 2 hdc. Repeat from * to last hdc, skip last hdc, draw up a loop in top of ch 2. There will be the same number of loops on hook as original number of loops. Work off loops. Continue to work Basic Afghan Stitch and Star Stitch Rows as desired. Bind off.

Basic Afghan Stitch with Worked-In Design: On all rows, read chart from right to left. The first and second half of 1 row afghan st = 1 row on chart.

Joining Colors — On First Half of Row:
Pick up the designated number of loops of first color shown on chart. Join next color, pick up specified number of loops in this color, etc. When the same color appears with no more than 3 stitches of another color between, the first ball may be carried across the back — however, *never* across more than 3 stitches. Join new balls of same color, if necessary.

On 2nd Half of Row:
Work off loops with matching color until there is one st left of the color. Change colors, picking up yarn to be used under color previously used, thus twisting colors to prevent hole in work. New color will be drawn through 1 loop of previous color and 1 loop of new color.

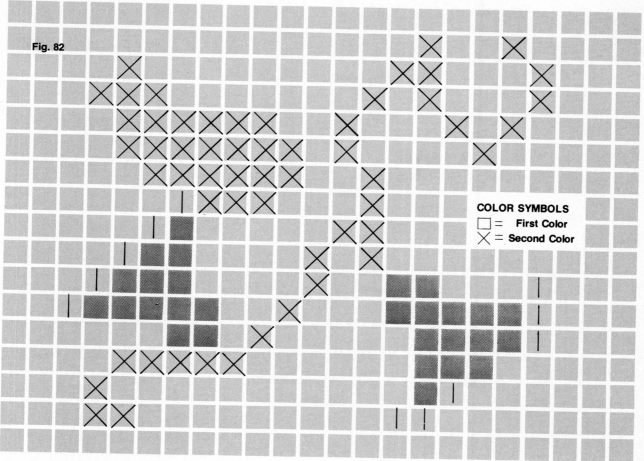

Fig. 82

COLOR SYMBOLS
☐ = First Color
✕ = Second Color

Basic Afghan Stitch with Worked-In Design: 1 Row Afghan Stitch = 1 Row on Chart

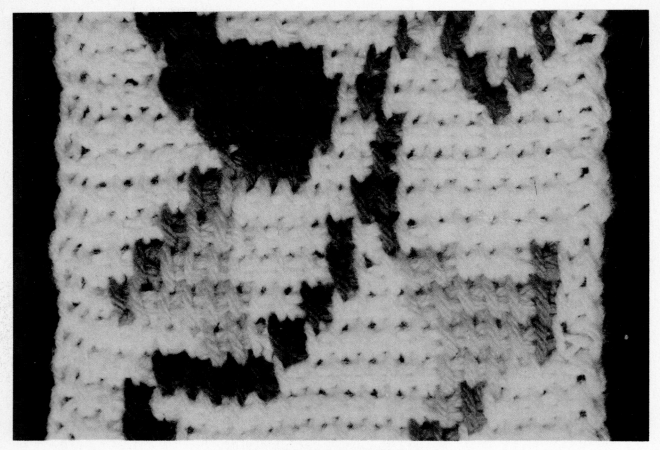

Basic Afghan Stitch with Worked-In Design

When a color is no longer needed, break off, leaving an end long enough to be woven in on the wrong side.

Basic Afghan Stitch with Cross Stitch: Make a chain of given number of stitches. Work Basic Afghan Stitch for given number of rows. Bind off. Following the steps in the illustrations below, work the Cross Stitch design as shown.

PROJECT — AFGHAN SHOULDER BAG

(See page 181 for shoulder bag you can make now)

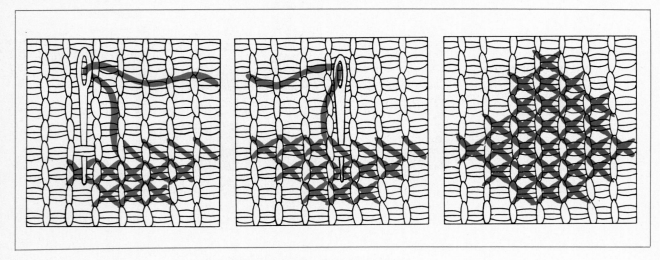

Basic Afghan Stitch with Cross Stitch

PROFESSIONAL CROCHETING

Section V

BODY MEASUREMENT CHARTS

Misses'

Misses' patterns are designed for a well-proportioned and developed figure.

Size	6	8	10	12	14	16	18	20
Bust	30½	31½	32½	34	36	38	40	42
Waist	23	24	25	26½	28	30	32	34
Hip	32½	33½	34½	36	38	40	42	44
Back Waist Length	15½	15¾	16	16¼	16½	16¾	17	17¼

Women's

Women's patterns are designed for the larger, more fully mature figure.

Size	38	40	42	44	46	48	50
Bust	42	44	46	48	50	52	54
Waist	35	37	39	41½	44	46½	49
Hip	44	46	48	50	52	54	56
Back Waist Length	17¼	17⅜	17½	17⅝	17¾	17⅞	18

Girls'

Girls' patterns are designed for the girl who has not yet begun to mature.

Size	7	8	10	12	14
Breast	26	27	28½	30	32
Waist	23	23½	24½	25½	26½
Hip	27	28	30	32	34
Back Waist Length Approx.	11½	12	12¾	13½	14¼
Height	50"	52"	56"	58"	61"

Children's

Size	1	2	3	4	5	6
Breast or Chest	20	21	22	23	24	25
Waist	19½	20	20½	21	21½	22

Back Waist

	1	2	3	4	5	6
Length Approx.	8¼	8½	9	9½	10	10½
Height	31"	34"	37"	40"	43"	46"
Finished Dress Length	17"	18"	19"	20"	22"	24"

Babies'

Babies' sizes are for infants who are not yet walking.

Age	Newborn (1-3 months)	6 months
Weight	7-13 lbs.	13-18 lbs.
Height	17"-24"	24"-26½"

Boys'

These size ranges are for growing boys and young men who have not yet reached full adult stature.

Size	7	8	10	12	14
Chest	26	27	28	30	32
Waist	23	24	25	26	27
Hip (Seat)	27	28	29½	31	32½
Neck	11¾	12	12½	13	13½
Height	48	50	54	58	61

Mens'

Men's patterns are sized for men of average build.

Size	34	36	38	40	42	44	46	48
Chest	34	36	38	40	42	44	46	48
Waist	28	30	32	34	36	39	42	44
Hip (Seat)	35	37	39	41	43	45	47	49
Neck	14	14½	15	15½	16	16½	17	17½

TAKING BODY MEASUREMENTS

1. Around the fullest part of the bust (with undergarments as worn); hold tape a little higher in back; take care to hold tape snugly but not tightly.

2. Around the natural waistline.

3. Around hips at fullest part; usually 7 inches below waistline for Misses' sizes, 9 inches for Women's sizes.

4. Across back of shoulders from armhole to armhole.

5. Across back from armhole to neck.

6. Lengthwise from waistline to underarm (1 inch below armpit).

7. From waistline to back of neck to give shoulder slant.

8. Around upper arm for sleeve.

9. From wrist to armpit for long sleeve.

10. From waistline to desired length for skirt.

WORKING FROM INSTRUCTION BOOKS

Numerous yarns are *interchangeable,* provided the same stitch gauge can be achieved with each. The yarns may be of the same type, both smooth or both nubby, or they may be of different types, one smooth and one nubby. If they are of different types the garment will have a different appearance, so the desirability should be considered when interchanging yarns. It is advisable also when interchanging yarns to compare the *yardage* of balls or skeins of both yarns; they may vary according to manufacture, temperature and humidity. Do *not* compare weight of balls or skeins of yarn; equal weight does *not* mean equal length. It is necessary to know the number of yards called for in the instructions (not the number of balls or skeins). Acquire not only the exact number of yards, but also an extra amount of yarn to assure enough to finish the work satisfactorily.

Usually the finished measurements are given at the beginning of the instructions. These measurements are the body measurements with an allowance for the fit of garment, depending on the style. If these measurements correspond to body measurements, plus the allowance you desire (at least 2 inches more than body measurements), you can select the desired size and follow the instructions.

If the measurements are not given, divide the number of stitches at bustline (back and front or fronts) by the gauge (number of stitches which equals 1 inch). Do the same for the waistline. You will then have the bustline and waistline measurements upon which the book's instructions are based.

Note: The body measurements as given in tabulation states that for sizes 10, 12, 14, bustline measurements are 32½, 34, 36 inches and waistline measurements 25, 26½, 28 inches.

A slip-on with back and front alike, no shaping for waistline and worked in single crochet

Instructions read as follows: Directions are written for size 10. Changes for sizes 12 and 14 are in parentheses.

Gauge: 6 sc = 1 inch, 8 rows = 1 inch
Back: Chain 105 (109-115) to measure 17½ (18¼-19¼) inches. *Foundation Row:* Work 1 single crochet (sc) in 2nd chain from book and in each chain (ch) to end. There are 104 (108-114) sc in row. Ch 1 and turn at end of every row. Continue to work in sc until piece measures 12 inches from beginning, or to desired length to underarm.

To arrive at bust measurement, divide 104 (108-114) sts by 6. This will give 17¼ (18-19) inches for ½ bust measurement, or 34½ (36-38) inches for total bust measurement. An extra 2 inches has been added to body bust measurement for this style of garment.

If *measurements* check and the extra allowance of 2 inches over body bust measurement is satisfactory, begin work.

If measurements do not check but size is in same range as book size (Misses', Women's, etc.), add or subtract the number of stitches equal to the number of inches to be added or subtracted to the original chain.

Example: If body bust measurement is 31½ inches and a 2-inch allowance is satisfactory, ½ inch should be subtracted from both back and front. Three chain or ½ of 6 chain would be subtracted from back and also from front. With 101 sc on each piece divided by 6 sc (which equals 1 inch), we have 16¾ inches or a 33½-inch bust measurement (a 2-inch allowance over body bust measurement).

If body bust measurement is 33½ inches, add 3 sc or ½ inch to back and also to front. Then garment bust measurement will be 35½ inches, again 2 inches over body measurement.

If a pattern stitch is used, be sure the multiple of sc is correct.

Slip-on with back and front alike, but with fitted waistline

Instructions read as follows: Directions are written for size 10. Sizes 12 and 14 are in parentheses.

Gauge: 6 sc = 1 inch, 8 rows = 1 inch
Back: Chain 97 (101-107) to measure 16 (16¾-17¾) inches. *Foundation Row:* Work sc in 2nd chain from book and in each chain to end. There are 96 (100-106) sc in each row. Ch 1 and turn at end of every row. Continue to work in sc decreasing 1 sc each side every 6 rows 8 times.

Work even on 80 (84-90) sc until piece measures 7 inches from beginning, or desired length to waistline; mark.

To arrive at waistline measurement, divide the 80 (84-90) sc by 6 (the number of sc which equals 1 inch). This will give 13¼ (14-15) inches for one half waistline or 26½ (28-30) inches for total measurements, again 2 inches extra added.

If a larger waistline measurement is desired, work fewer decreases and space them farther apart. If a smaller waistline measurement is desired, work more decreases and reduce spaces between them.

When changing the instructions, write the changes in the instruction book. Circle or underline all the correct numbers to follow. This will prevent the use of any wrong numbers.

Terms Used in Crochet Instruction Books: Example in crochet armholes. Work slip stitch in each of 6 stitches. Chain and turn. This means that the 6 stitches at the beginning of the row must be worked over but will be omitted on the next row; the 6 stitches at the end are left unworked for armhole shaping. These 6 stitches at each end are called the "bound off" stitches. This requires only one row.

Decrease or increase one stitch each side: This means you must follow the basic instructions for decreasing or increasing, depending on the stitch being used, such as single crochet, double crochet, treble crochet, etc.

BEING YOUR OWN DESIGNER

How To Make The Correct Size Without Taking Body Measurements: Sometimes it is difficult to take your own or another's body measurements. Select a garment from your own or the other person's wardrobe that fits just the way the crocheted garment should fit. You can measure this and get all the important measurements; bust, hips, shoulder width, underarm seam length, sleeve width and length and any other necessary measurements. Make a note of all measurements.

How To Make The Correct Size When Taking Body Measurements: Take as many body measurements as possible. Make a note of each measurement. Decide if a tight or loosely fitted garment is desired. Take into account the style

and type to be made. Make a swatch using the yarn for garment and the size crochet hook recommended for desired gauge or texture. Make a note of the gauge. This often requires experimentation of designer.

For An Average Slip-on For Misses' and Teens' Sizes. Add 1 inch over bust measurement for back and 1 inch for front, add ¼ inch for each seam, more if a loosely fitted slip-on is desired.

For An Average Slip-on For Women's Sizes: Add 1 inch to back, 2 inches to front and ¼ inch for each seam; more if a loosely fitted slip-on is desired. Also, front may be made 1 inch longer than the back and a ½-inch underarm bust-line dart may be sewn in before assembling slip-on.

For A Man's Slip-on: Chest measurement is used plus ¼ inch for each seam unless a looser fitting garment is desired.

For Children's Clothes: Garment should be loosely fitted; add 1 or more inches to back and front.

For An Average Cardigan for Misses' and Teens' Sizes: Add 1 inch over bust measurement to back; ½ inch plus width of borders and seams to each front, or more to fronts if a loosely fitted cardigan is desired.

To Figure Correct Number of Stitches and Rows For Each Measurement: Secure graph paper if possible. Figure instructions by multiplying the width measurement by the number of stitches which equals 1 inch; the length measurement by the number of rows which equals 1 inch. Place all information on graph paper; or draw outline of each piece and place information on the outline of each piece to be made.

To Figure Shaping For Slip-on (Back and Front Alike, Round Neck, No Back Opening, Long Sleeves)

Back or Front Armhole: Subtract the number of stitches needed for the shoulder measurement from the total number of stitches at underarm. This gives the number of stitches to be bound off and decreased for armhole shaping. Usually one-half the number of stitches are bound off for the two armholes or one-fourth for each armhole. The remainder of stitches are decreased every row or every second row, depending on the number of stitches being used and the number of times it is necessary to decrease. Usually with single crochet and half double crochet, the

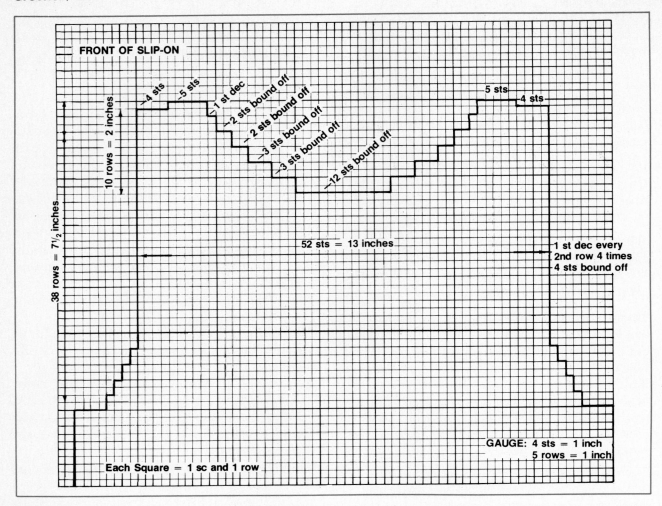

FRONT OF SLIP-ON

10 rows = 2 inches

38 rows = 7½ inches

−4 sts
−5 sts
1 st dec
−2 sts bound off
−2 sts bound off
−3 sts bound off
−3 sts bound off
−3 sts bound off
−12 sts bound off
5 sts
4 sts

52 sts = 13 inches

1 st dec every
2nd row 4 times
4 sts bound off

GAUGE: 4 sts = 1 inch
5 rows = 1 inch

Each Square = 1 sc and 1 row

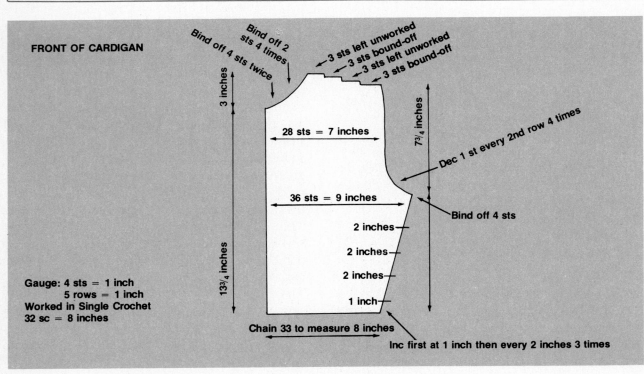

FRONT OF CARDIGAN

Bind off 4 sts twice
Bind off 2 sts 4 times
3 sts left unworked
3 sts bound-off
3 sts left unworked
3 sts bound-off

3 inches

28 sts = 7 inches

7¾ inches

Dec 1 st every 2nd row 4 times

36 sts = 9 inches

Bind off 4 sts

13¾ inches

2 inches
2 inches
2 inches
1 inch

Gauge: 4 sts = 1 inch
5 rows = 1 inch
Worked in Single Crochet
32 sc = 8 inches

Chain 33 to measure 8 inches

Inc first at 1 inch then every 2 inches 3 times

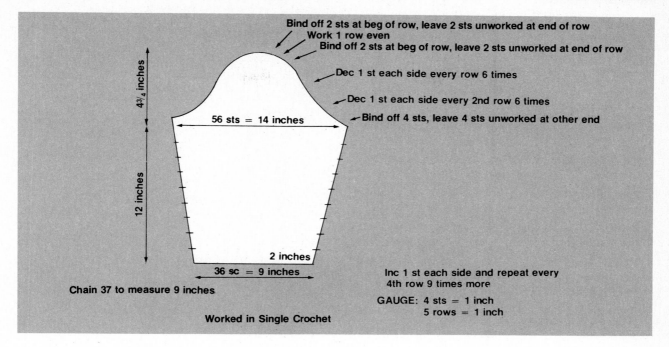

Bind off 2 sts at beg of row, leave 2 sts unworked at end of row
Work 1 row even
Bind off 2 sts at beg of row, leave 2 sts unworked at end of row
Dec 1 st each side every row 6 times
Dec 1 st each side every 2nd row 6 times
Bind off 4 sts, leave 4 sts unworked at other end

56 sts = 14 inches

4³/₄ inches

12 inches

2 inches

36 sc = 9 inches

Chain 37 to measure 9 inches

Inc 1 st each side and repeat every 4th row 9 times more
GAUGE: 4 sts = 1 inch
5 rows = 1 inch

Worked in Single Crochet

decreases are made every second row. When double crochet or higher stitches are used, the decreases are made *every* row. If the number is not even, the extra stitches are placed in the bound-off stitches.

Example: The Gauge is 4 stitches = 1 inch, 5 rows = 1 inch. There are 70 stitches in last row before armhole shaping. Shoulders: 70 − 48 = 22 to bind off and decrease; therefore, work a slip stitch in each of 6 sts at beginning of row, work to last 6 sts, chain and turn. Decrease 1 stitch each side every row or every 2nd row 5 times.

Back Shoulders: Two-thirds of the number of stitches are usually allowed for the shoulders; one-third for back of neck. However, if shoulders are wider more stitches may be needed; if narrower, less stitches. Also, if there is no zipper opening, neck will need more stitches so that it will fit easily over head and will require more stitches. Also, shoulders should have at least a 1-inch (5 rows = 1 inch) slant. Neck should be at least 5 inches (20 stitches). Thus, 48 − 20 = 28 stitches for shoulders or 14 stitches for each shoulder. Use 3 rows for shaping. Work a slip stitch in each of the first 5 stitches, work to last 5 stitches. Chain and turn. Repeat the last row once. Work a slip stitch in each of the first 4 stitches, work to the last 4 stitches, chain and

turn. There are 14 stitches bound-off for each shoulder and there are 20 stitches left for back of neck.

When the slip-on is finished, a neckband can be added. The neck can also be finished without a neckband.

Front of Neck: Usually begins 2 inches below first row of shoulders. Subtract the number of stitches equal to 3 inches (center front stitches) from the number of stitches left after armhole shaping. If number does not divide evenly, add extra stitches to center-front number. Divide remaining number of stitches by two (gives number of stitches at each side of center stitches). Subtract the number of stitches of one shoulder from number of stitches at one side of center stitches. The remaining stitches have to be bound off or decreased before shoulder shaping is completed.

Example: 48 stitches on needle; 4 stitches = 1 inch, 5 rows = 1 inch. 48 − 12 = 36. 36 ÷ 2 = 18 stitches at each side of center stitches. 18 − 14 = 4 stitches to be bound off or decreased at one side of neck. One stitch is decreased at neck edge every second row 4 times, using 8 rows or 1¹/₂ inches. Then the 14 stitches are worked and the shoulder is bound off as on one side of back.
Sleeves: Determine the width desired at wrist (be sure it will stretch to go over hand) and multiply by stitch gauge. Subtract number at wrist from

number to be used at underarm. From total length to underarm, subtract at least 3 inches; all increasing should be completed at this point. Divide the number of stitches to be increased by two, as 1 stitch will be increased at each side on increase rows. Multiply the number of inches allowed for increases by the row gauge. Now divide number of rows by the number of times necessary to increase. If this is not even, adjust by alternating number of rows between increases.

To Shape Cap: There are many methods used, depending on the style of the garment and present-day styles. At the top of the cap there can be from 2 to 5 inches bound-off. When the length is finished to the underarm, the same number of stitches are bound off as on the back armholes. The length of the sleeve cap must be worked to fit into the size of the armhole.

Example: Width of Sleeve is 14 inches at underarm. Gauge is 4 stitches = 1 inch, 5 rows = 1 inch ($14 \times 4 = 56$ stitches). There are 4 stitches bound-off at each side of armhole ($56 - 8 = 48$ stitches).

At top of sleeve leave 4 inches ($4 \times 4 = 16$ stitches). Subtract this number of stitches from last number ($48 - 16 = 32$ stitches).

Just before ending cap to round top of cap, bind off the number of stitches which equals approximately $^{1}/_{2}$ inch (2 stitches) for the number of rows which equals approximately $^{1}/_{2}$ inch (2 rows); ($2 \times 2 = 4$ stitches). Subtract this number of stitches from the last number ($32 - 4 = 28$ stitches). Therefore 28 stitches must be decreased in a given number of rows, or 14 stitches at each side.

Armholes are 7 inches (in straight line) from first armhole bind-off to beginning of shoulder on both back and front or 14 inches around.

From total of 14, subtract the 4 inches across top ($14 - 4 = 10$). Now subtract the 1 inch at each side made from other bind-off. ($10 - 2 = 8$). There are two sides to sleeve cap ($8 \div 2 = 4$). Row gauge is 5 rows = 1 inch ($4 \times 5 = 20$). Therefore, there must be 20 rows of decreases; 28 stitches to decrease, or 14 times to decrease.

(See KNITTING, Pg. 46 For Methods of Translating Formulas.)

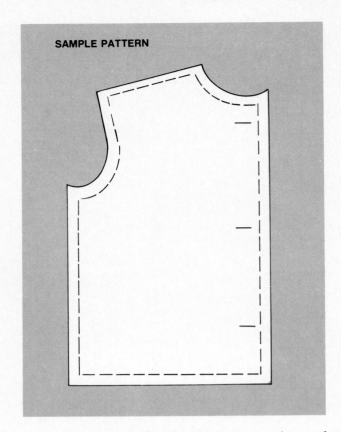

SAMPLE PATTERN

Using a Commercial Pattern: A very advanced and yet easy method is to select a commercial dressmaking pattern of the correct size for the style garment planned.

Select a suitable yarn and stitch; make a sample piece to acquire the desired texture. Gauge is *not* important in this particular instance. Examine the pattern and select the necessary pieces (extra facings, etc. can be put aside). After careful checking for all lengths and widths, hems and seam allowances should be cut off. Vertical darts should be basted into pattern unless they are desired in the crochet garment. This is seldom necessary. As you work, lay piece on pattern and follow shaping by working increases, decreases or slip stitches.

If pieces are found to be slightly inaccurate when finished, block a little larger than pattern; then cut, allowing for seam — the crochet will not rip. Place several rows of machine stitching $^{1}/_{4}$ inch in from cut edges. Sew seams by hand or machine. If desired, cut edges may be bound with bias tape.

Crocheted Garment from Sample Pattern

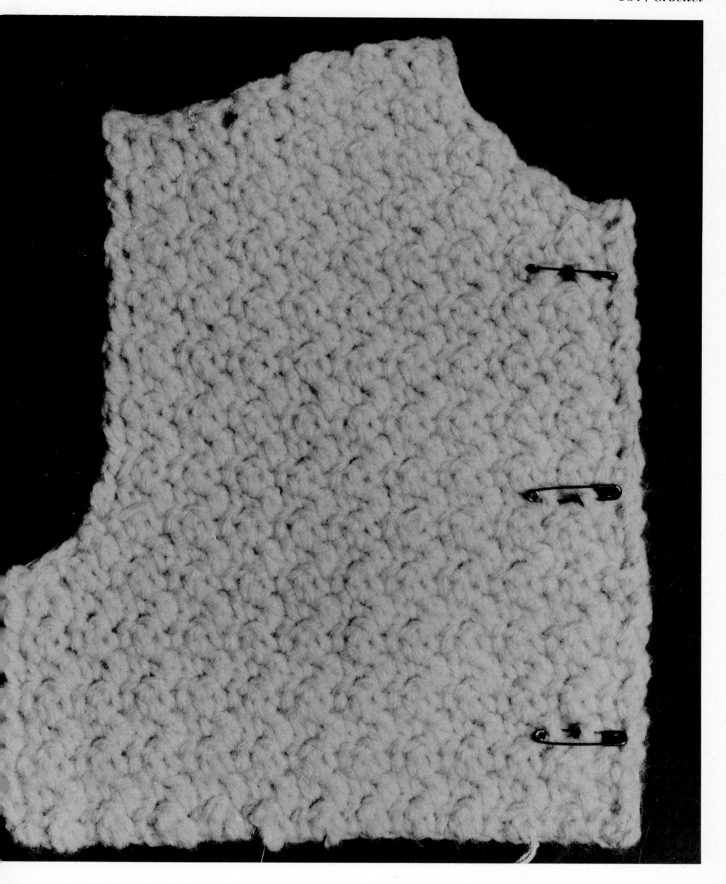

Section VI

A knowledge of knitting is required for this section. You will need to know the basic knitting stitches and techniques before beginning.

PICKING UP STITCHES ON FRONT EDGES (FOR KNIT BAND)

Number of stitches given: Use size needle recommended. Divide one front in half, place pin at this point. Divide in fourths, then in eighths, placing pins. Divide into smaller sections, if desired. Divide the number of stitches to be picked up by the number of sections. With the right side of work on top, begin at the lower edge of right front for men, at the neck of left front for women. Insert needle in stitch (one or one-half stitches from edge) and draw a loop through. When front has no decreases, stay in same stitch or line. If there are decreases, stay in far enough so that there are no holes. Pick up the number of stitches for one section. Check to be sure that there are no holes and that the line is straight. Then continue with same number of stitches in each section and work to desired width. When picking up stitches on other front, begin at top or lower edge as necessary; pick up as on first front. If ribbing is used, bind-off in rib pattern.

Number of stitches not given: Make a small sample to determine type and appearance of knitting desired. Divide front into sections and pick up stitches of first section as explained above. Work pattern to be used for 1 inch. If work is satisfactory, rip and pick up all sections. If work is too full, reduce number of stitches. When satisfied that work will lie flat, proceed for entire front. If ribbing is to be used, be sure to stretch and block first section before ripping work as rib should be stretched out.

DETERMINING NUMBER OF STITCHES TO PICK UP FOR ROUND-NECK RIB BAND

Make a sample piece with yarn and needles to be used. Take measurement on 3 inches. Neckband must go easily over the head. Multiply the number of inches required (Misses' sizes are usually 18 to 20 inches without stretching) by the number of stitches which equals 1 inch. This equals the necessary number of stitches to pick up around the neck. Pick up this number, spacing as evenly as possible, and work to desired width. Bind-off loosely in pattern.

Rib Band on Crochet

Section VII

CROCHETING WITH SEQUINS

String Sequins On Yarn: Hold one strand of sequins with right side of sequin (inside of cup) toward ball of yarn. Tie thread on which sequin is strung around yarn (do *not* tie yarn around thread). Slide sequin carefully over knot onto yarn. String no more than one strand (usually 1,000 sequins) onto yarn at one time. When additional sequins are needed, cut yarn 4 inches from last st worked (always at end of a row) and slide 1 more strand onto yarn.

Crocheting Sequins: A sequin may be placed in any stitch. The swatch shown has been made by placing a sequin in every 2nd stitch (sc) and alternating sequins on every sequin row. It is worked as follows: Make a chain of an even number.

Foundation Row (right side): Work sc in 2nd chain from hook and in each chain to end. These will be an uneven number of sc. Ch 1, turn.

Row 1 (wrong side): Sc in first sc, * insert hook in next sc, draw loop through (there are 2 loops on hook), slide one sequin close to work, (sequin is on right side of work), complete sc, sc in next sc; repeat from * to end. Ch 1, turn.

Row 2: Work sc in each sc. Ch 1, turn.

Row 3: * Sc in each of 2 sc, place sequin in next sc, sc in next sc; repeat from * ending row sc in each of last 2 sc.

Row 4: Same as Row 2.

Repeat these 4 rows for pattern. Do *not* place a sequin in first or last stitch of a row.

Care of Sequins: Before seaming, if sequin will fall in seam, cut it away carefully *(do not cut yarn)* with scissors; seam as usual. Never use an iron or steam on a garment with sequins. Sequin garments can be blocked between wet towels as follows: Saturate a bath towel and wring out as much water as possible. Lay on flat surface. Turn garment inside out (sequins are inside of garment). Place on towel and smooth into place. Then pat garment out to size. Saturate another towel and wring out. Place on top of garment. Leave until practically dry. Turn to right side, shake gently, be sure no moisture clings to sequins. Lay on a dry flat surface until completely dry. Hand wash gently in warm water with mild detergent. *Do not* machine wash or dry-clean.

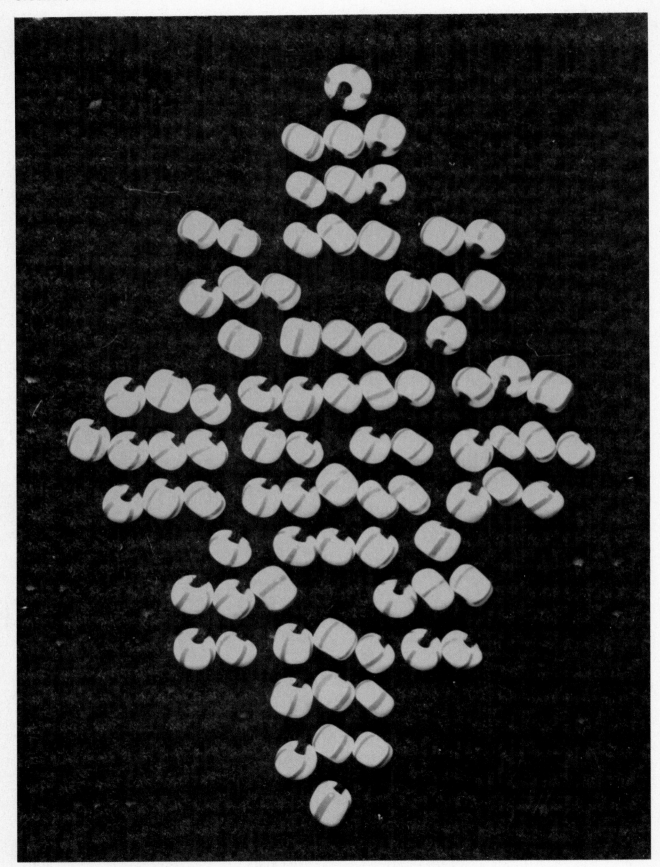

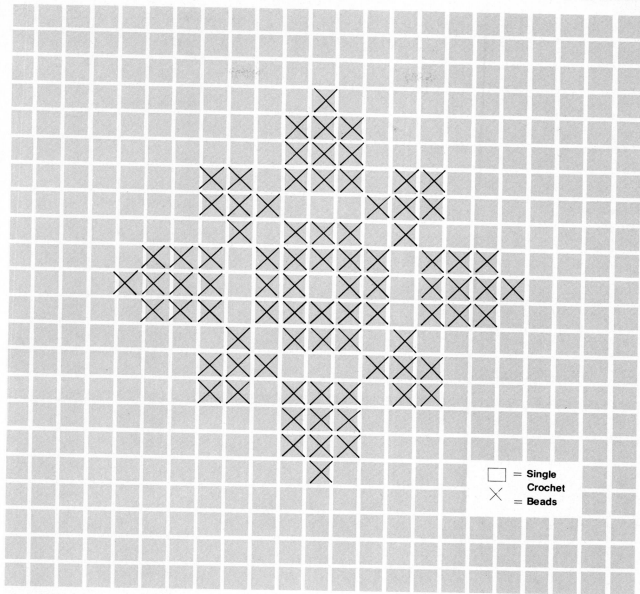

= Single Crochet

X = Beads

CROCHETING WITH BEADS

To String Beads: Use yarn of the size that will almost fill the hole of the beads. When beads are already strung on thread, string to yarn as described for sequins. When beads are not on thread, use tapestry needle and yarn for stringing. When more than one color or type of bead is to be used, string each color or type on separate ball of yarn; or count from chart the correct number of each to be used in a row and string in this order. When using more than one ball of yarn with beads, break off ball if it will not be needed for several rows.

Crocheting With Beads Following A Chart: All chart rows show *only* the wrong side rows or the rows on which beads are worked. The plain rows between beaded rows are not shown. Read all rows shown from right to left.

Working a row from wrong side and following chart, work a single crochet in each stitch to first bead, insert hook in next single crochet and draw a loop through. Slide bead close to work and complete the single crochet (the bead will be on the right side of work). Continue across row, following chart.

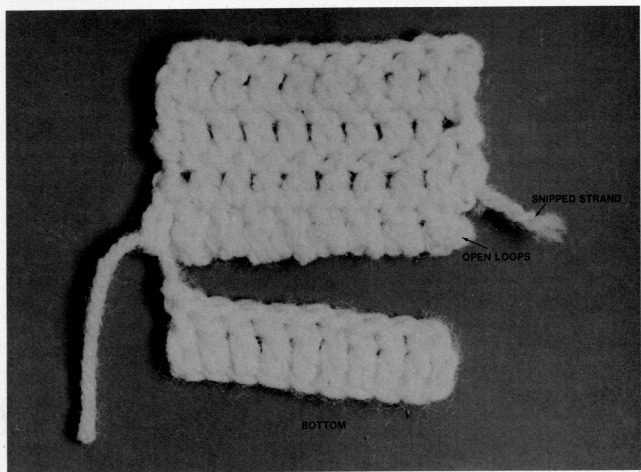

ALTERATIONS BY HAND — TO SHORTEN

Separate the crochet piece horizontally: If seams have been made, rip seams to 1 inch above desired length. Snip thread of turning chain section to be removed.

Pick out lower end of cut strand. There will be a loop at bottom of row of piece to remain for desired length. Pull picked out strand and rip to end of row. Carefully pick out end stitch. There will be open loops at lower edge of main section. Join same color yarn at beginning of row (¹/₂ cut strand is at this end). Chain to form turning

chain. Insert hook through open loops of a stitch and work a slip st. Work a slip st through loops of each stitch to end and fasten off. Resew seams.

To Lengthen: Work over the slip-stitch row with any stitch or color desired for a border.

ALTERATION BY MACHINE

A basic knowledge of sewing is necessary to alter a crochet garment. Turn garment inside out and baste to proper size. Work two rows of stitching as close as possible to basting. Trim excess material, leaving ¹/₄- to ¹/₂-inch seams. If desired, seams may be bound with bias tape.

SECTION VIII (Extra Know-How)

WOVEN CROCHET

This is a combination of crochet and weaving.

First the basic fabric is made: This is a mesh fabric that can be made with any of the basic crochet stitches, depending on the texture desired. A very good background or fabric is made with a knitting worsted-weight yarn, treble crochet with chain 1 between trebles. In making this fabric to give a firm stitch, it is advisable to insert the hook into the treble crochet of the previous row instead of the 2 top strands of the treble. Fabric can be made of any color and woven with different colors to form a plaid stripe. Rows of different colors can be used for making fabric and when woven in a given order, patterns such as houndstooth, checks and plaids can be obtained.

To weave, use the number of strands which will fill but not crowd the opening of the mesh. (Usually 3 strands for fabric as described above.) Cut the strands 10 inches longer than length of row to be woven. Thread correct number of strands into a blunt tapestry needle.

Vertical Weaving: Leaving a 5-inch end, weave over first chain 1 of first row; under first chain 1 of 2nd row, over first chain 1 of 3rd row and continue in this way to last row. Leave ends. Adjust work so that it is correct length. Weave under 2nd chain 1 of first row, over 2nd chain 1 of 2nd row, under 2nd chain 1 of 3rd row and continue in this way, having strands alternate with first row of weaving. Continue to alternate rows until fabric is completely covered. Weave in loose ends on wrong side, or if desired use for fringe for afghan, scarf, etc. by knotting ends over chain.

EDGINGS

Backward half double crochet: *Do not* turn at end of last row, ch 2. Working from left to right, work a half-double crochet in 2nd and then in each stitch.

Backward single crochet is worked in same way, beginning row with chain 1 and working in every stitch.

(For More Elaborate Edgings for Many Uses, See Pg. 179.)

CROCHET PROJECTS

EDGINGS FOR MANY USES

MATERIALS — Lilly Size 50 Crochet Cotton
CROCHET HOOK: "Susan Bates" Steel No. 10

Note: The edgings may be made of any weight of cotton or yarn adjusting size of crochet hook.

No. 2

Row 2: Dc in same dc with ch-4, *sk 1 dc, in next dc work dc, ch 1, dc; (shell) rep from *, ending shell under turning ch. Ch 5, turn.
Row 3: Sl st in 2nd dc of shell, *sl st in first dc of next shell, ch 5, sl st in 2nd dc of same shell; rep from *, end sl st in 3rd ch of ch-4. Fasten off.

No. 3

No. 1

EDGING 1

Make a chain of a multiple of 10 plus 7 ch.
Row 1 (right side): Dc in 4th ch from hook and in each ch to end. There will be a multiple of 10 dc plus 5 dc, counting ch-3 at beginning of row as 1 dc. Turn.
Row 2: *Sc in each of 5 dc, sk 2 dc, 7 dc in next dc, sk 2 dc; rep from *, ending sc in each of last 5 dc. Turn.
Row 3: * Sk 1 sc, sc in each of next 3 sc, sk 1 sc, dc in next dc, ch 1) 6 times, dc in next dc; rep from * ending sk 1 sc, sc in each of next 3 sc. Ch 1, turn.
Row 4: * Sk 1 sc, sc in next sc, ch 1, sk 1 sc, (dc in next dc, ch 2) 6 times, dc in next dc, ch 1; rep from * ending sk 1 sc, sc in next sc. Fasten off.

EDGING 2

Make chain of an uneven number of sts.
Row 1: Dc in 5th ch from hook, *ch 1, sk 1 ch, dc in next ch; rep from * to end, Ch 4, turn.

EDGING 3

Make a chain of a multiple of 13 plus 11 chain.
Row 1 (right side): Dc in 4th ch from hook and in each ch to end. There will be a multiple of 13 dc plus 9 dc, counting ch-3 at beg of row as 1 dc.
Row 2: *(Ch 5, sk 2 dc, sl st in next dc) 3 times, ch 7, sk 3 dc, sl st in next dc; rep from *, ending (ch 5, sk 2 dc, sl st in next dc) twice, ch 5, sk 2 dc, sl st in 3rd ch of ch at beg of row 1. Turn.
Row 3: Sl st in each of first 2 ch of ch-5, sc in same ch-5 lp, ch 5, sc in next ch-5 lp, ch 5, sc in next lp, *ch 2 (dc in next lp, ch 1) 4 times, dc in same lp, ch 2, sc in next lp, (ch 5, sc in next lp) twice; rep from *, ending ch 2, sc in next lp, (ch 5, sc in next lp) twice. Ch 3, turn.
Row 4: *Sc in next lp, ch 3, sc in next lp, ch 2, 3 dc in next dc (ch 3, sk 1 dc, 3 dc in next dc) twice, ch 2; rep from *, ending sc in next lp, ch 3, sc in next lp, sc in last sc. Fasten off.

EDGING 4

Make a chain of a multiple of 6 plus 4 chain.
Row 1 (right side): Sc in 2nd ch from hook and in each ch to end. There will be a multiple of 6 sc, plus 3 sc.
Row 2: *Ch 5, sk 2 sc, sc in next sc; rep from * to end. Turn.

No. 4

Row 3: Sl st in each of 2 ch, sc in same sp (center of sp), *ch 5, sc in next sp; rep from * to end. Turn.

Note: To work a cluster (yo hook twice), draw up a lp in next ch-5 sp, yo and draw through 2 lps, yo and draw through 2 lps, retain unworked lps on hook) 3 times, yo and draw through 4 lps on hook — cluster made.

Row 4: Sl st in each of 2 ch, sc in same sp, *ch 3, cluster in next sp, ch 4, cluster in same sp, ch 3, (dc in next sp), twice; rep from *, ending cluster in next sp, ch 4, cluster in same sp, dc in each of last 2 sps. Ch 3, turn.

Row 5: * In sp between next two clusters, work (tr, ch 1) 4 times, then work 1 more tr in same sp, dc between next 2 dc; rep from * end dc in last sp. Turn.

Row 6: *(Ch 3, sc in next ch-1 sp) 4 times, ch 3, sc in next dc; rep from *, ending ch 3, sc in top of turning ch. Fasten off.

EDGING 5

First Rose: Ch 7, join with a sl st to form a ring. Rnds are worked from right side.

Rnd 1: Ch 6, dc in ring, (ch 3, dc in ring) 6 times, ch 3, join with a sl st to 3rd ch of ch-6. There are 8 ch-3 loops.

Rnd 2: Ch 1, under each ch-3 lp work sc, 3 dc, sc. 8 petals.

Rnd 3: Insert hook from back in same lp as last petal and to back in lp of first petal (hook is in front of dc), work a sl st around the dc, ch 6, *work sl st around next dc, ch 6; rep from * 6

times, ending sl st around first dc again. There are 8 ch-6 lps.

Rnd 4: Ch 1, under each ch-6 lp work sc, 7 dc, sc, join with a sl st to first sc. Fasten off.

Second Rose: Work first 3 rnds same as First Rose.

Rnd 5 (Join 2 roses together): Ch 1, under first ch-6 lp work sc, 4 dc, insert hook from wrong side in 4th (center dc) of petal of first rose and work a sl st, complete petal of second rose; join next petal of first and second rose in same way. Complete second rose. Continue to make roses and join to last one for desired length. There will be 2 petals free at top and lower edge of each rose, 6 petals free on first and last rose.

Finishing Rows

Row 1: Join cotton in 4th (center) dc of first free petal of first rose, sc in same place with joining, ch 7, sc in center dc of next petal of first rose, ch 7, sc over joining of first and second rose, ch 7, continue across top of roses, ending sc in 2nd free petal of last rose. Ch 9, turn.

Row 2: Sc in first ch-7 lp, * ch 7, sc in next ch-7 lp; rep from *, ending ch 7, sc under turning ch-9, sc in first sc. Ch 9, turn.

Row 3: Rep row 2, ending sc under turning ch. Ch 9, turn.

Rep last row once or to desired depth. Ch 1, turn.

Last Row: Work 7 sc in each ch-7 lp. Fasten off.

EDGING 6

Chain 10, join with a sl st to form a ring.

Row 1: Ch 3, 7 dc in ring (shell), ch 4, sc in ring. Ch 5, turn.

Row 2: Sc in ch-4 lp, ch 4, sk 1 dc, sc in next dc, ch 5, sk 5 dc, sc in next dc. Ch 3, turn.

Row 3: 7 dc in ch-5 lp (shell), ch 4, sc in next lp, ch 4, sc under turning ch. Ch 5, turn.

Row 4: Sc in first lp, ch 4, sc in next lp, ch 4, sk 1 dc, sc in next dc, ch 5, sk 5 dc, sc under turning ch. Ch 3, turn.

No. 5

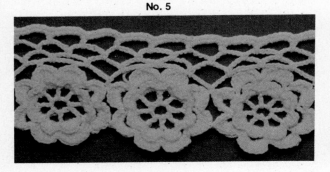

No. 6

Row 5: 7 dc shell in ch-5, (ch 4, sc in next lp) twice; ch 4, sc under turning ch. Ch 5, turn.

Row 6: Sc in first lp, (ch 4, sc in next lp) twice, ch 4, sk 1 dc, sc in next dc, ch 4, sk 2 dc, sc in next dc, ch 4, sk 2 dc, sc in top of turning ch. Ch 4, do *not* turn, sc in sp between shells, ch 4, sc in sp between next shells. Turn.

Row 7: Ch 6, sl st in 4th ch from hook (picot made), ch 2, sc in next lp, *ch 6, picot, ch 2, sc in next lp; rep from * 4 times more, (ch 4, sc in next lp) twice. Ch 5, turn.

Row 8: Sc in first lp, ch 5 sc in next lp. Ch 3, turn.

Row 9: 7 dc shell in ch-5 lp, ch 4, sc under turning ch. Ch 5, turn.

Row 10: Sc in first lp, ch 5, sk 1 dc, sc in next dc, ch 5, sk 5 dc, sc in top of turning ch. Ch 2, sl st in first picot. Ch 3, turn. Rep from Row 3 for pat.

ROLL BRIM HAT

Approximate head size — 22 inches
MATERIALS — Brunswick Fore 'N Aft or Wintuk Sport Yarn (2-oz) 1 ball
CROCHET HOOK: "Susan Bates" Size F OR SIZE TO GIVE GAUGE

GAUGE: 4 hdc = inch, 11 rows = 4 inches

Crown: Chain 5, Join with a sl st to form a ring.
Rnd 1: Ch 2, work 9 hdc in center of ring. Join with sl st to top of ch 2, 10 hdc counting ch 2 as 1 dc.
Rnd 2: Ch 2, hdc in same st, 2 dc in each hdc. Join with a sl st to top of ch-2. 20 hdc. Each rnd begins with ch-2 and counts as 1 hdc and is joined with a sl st to top of ch-2.
Rnd 3: Ch 2, 2hdc in next st, * 1 hdc in next st, 2 hdc in next st; rep from * around. Join. 30 hdc.
Rnd 4: Ch 2, hdc in next st, 2 hdc in next st, * hdc in each of 2 sts, 2 hdc in next st; rep from * around. Join. 40 hdc.
Rnd 5: Ch 2, hdc in each of 2 sts, 2 hdc in next st, hdc in each of next 3 sts, 2 hdc in next st; continue around inc 1 hdc in every 4th st. Join. 50 hdc.
Rnd 6: Ch 2, hdc in each of next 8 sts, 2 hdc in next st, hdc in each of 9 sts, 2 hdc in next st, continue around, inc 1 hdc in every 10th st. Join. 55 hdc.
Rnd 7: Inc 1 hdc in every 11th st. Join. 60 hdc.
Rnd 8: Inc 1 hdc in every 10th st. Join. 66 hdc.
Rnd 9: Inc 1 hdc in every 11th st. Join. 72 hdc.
Rnd 10: Inc 1 hdc in every 9th st. Join. 80 hdc.
Rnd 11: Inc 1 hdc in every 10th st. Join. 88 hdc. Check head measurement. If too large, decrease hdc, if too small, increase hdc to desired size. Work even to 6¾ inches from center top.
Next 2 rnds: Work through *front* lp only, work hdc in each hdc. Join.

Brim: Work all rnds thru *front* lps.
Rnd 1: Work 2 hdc in every 3rd st, hdc in last st. 118 hdc.
Rnd 2: Ch 2, hdc in each of 2 hdc, 2 hdc in next st * hdc in each of 10 hdc, 2 hdc in next st; rep from * 9 times more, hdc in each st to end. Work 4 rnds even. Fasten off.

SHOULDER BAG (Afghan Stitch with Lion)

Approximate Size — 14 x 16 inches

MATERIALS — Brunswick Germantown Knitting Worsted or Windrush 2 MC and 1 each A and B.

AFGHAN HOOK: "Susan Bates" 12-inch SIZE I OR SIZE TO GIVE GAUGE

GAUGE: 4 sts = 1 inch, 7 rows = 2 inches

Pattern: Afghan Stitch with Worked-In Design Following Chart (see pg. 159).

Front: With A chain 56 to measure 14 inches. Work in Basic Afghan Stitch of 6 rows. Cut A. With MC work in Afghan Stitch following chart for 44 rows. Cut MC.
With A work in Basic Afghan Stitch for 6 rows. Bind off.

Back: Work same as front or omit design if desired. *Handle:* With A chain 8. Work in Basic Afghan Stitch for 66 inches or until piece fits around sides and bottom of bag, then continue for 22 inches more for handle. Bind off.

Finishing: Overcast strap to each side, matching centers, tops and bottoms. Back handle with 1-inch wide ribbon to a point 2 inches below top of bag. Measure, cut and sew lining to match bag and Blind Stitch it in around top edge. If desired, sides of bag can be backed with iron-on interfacing for added stiffness before lining.

COLOR SYMBOLS
☐ = Main Color
X = A
O = B

MAN'S CROCHET CARDIGAN — *Long Sleeves or Sleeveless*

Instructions are for Size 38. Changes for Sizes 40, 42, 44, 46 and 48 are in parentheses.

MATERIALS — Brunswick Germantown Knitting Worsted or Windrush (4-oz) 6(6-7-7-7-8) for Cardigan with Sleeves; 5(5-7-7-7-8) for Sleeveless Cardigan

CROCHET HOOK: "Susan Bates" Size E and G OR SIZE TO GIVE GAUGE

GAUGE: (Rib) 4 sc = 1 inch, 3 ridges = 2 inches

FINISHED MEASUREMENT (in inches): *Chest 38(40-42-44-46-48)*

Fronts And Back

Rib Band: With G hook chain 11 to measure 2¹/₂ inches.

Row 1: Sc in 2nd ch from hook and each ch to end. 10 sc. Ch 1, turn at end of every row.

Row 2: Through *back* lp only, sc in each sc. Rep row 2 until there are 44(46-48-51-54-56) ridges or 88(92-96-102-108-112) rows. Ch 1, turn.

Body

Row 1: Across top edge of rib, work 3 sc across each ridge. There are 132(138-144-153-162-168) sc. Ch 1, turn.

Row 2: Sc in each sc, inc across row 0(0-2-1-0-0) sc. Ch 1, turn.

Row 3: Sc in each of 132(138-146-154-162-168) sc. Ch 1, turn.

Rep Row 3 to 16 inches from beg, or 2 inches less than desired length to underarms. Do *not* ch 1 at end of row.

Dec Row: Draw up a lp in each of first 2 sts, yo and through 3 lps on hook (1 st dec), ch 1, sc in each sc to last 2 sc, work dec, ch 1, turn. Work 1 row even, do *not* ch 1, turn.

Rep last 2 rows 3 times more. There are 124(130-138-146-154-160) sc. Divide for fronts and back. Work 28(30-32-34-36-38) sc for one side of front, sl st in each of next 4 sts for underarm, ch 1, sc in each of next 60(62-66-70-74-76) sc for back, sl st in each of next 4 sts for underarm, ch 1, sc in each of last 28(30-32-34-36-38) sc for other side of front.

Front Armhole and Neck Shaping: Work 1 row even on sts of 1 side of front, do *not* ch 1, turn.

Dec 1 st at armhole edge and 1 st at front (neck) edge on next row. Rep last 2 rows once. There are 24(26-28-30-32-34) sc in row. Keeping armhole edge even continue to dec at front edge every 2nd row 8(9-10-11-12-13) times more. Work on 16(17-18-19-20-21) sts until armhole measures 7³/₄(8-8¹/₄-8¹/₂-8³/₄-9) inches, end at front edge.

Shoulder (Front)

Row 1: Work across 10(10-12-12-12-14) sts, ch 1, turn.

Row 2: Work to front edge.

Row 3: Work across 5(5-6-6-6-7) sts, ch 1, turn.

Row 4: Work to front edge. Fasten off.

Back Armhole: Join yarn in first sc of back, to work first row from same side as first row of front. Ch 1, work sc in each sc of back. Do *not* ch 1 at end of row. Dec 1 st each side as on front. There are 56(58-62-66-70-72) sts. Work even to same number of rows as front armhole to beg of shoulder.

Shoulders (Back)

Row 1: Sl st in each of 5(5-6-6-6-7) sc, sc in each sc to last 5(5-6-6-6-7) sts. Turn.

Row 2: Sc in each sc. Turn.

Row 3: Rep row 1. Turn.

Row 4: Rep row 2. Turn.

Row 5: Sl st in each of 6(7-6-7-8-7) sc, sc in each sc to last 6(7-6-7-8-7) sc. Fasten off. There are 16(17-18-19-20-21) sts for each shoulder; 24(24-26-28-30-30) for back of neck.

Other Side of Front: Join yarn at underarm edge of back to work first row from same side as first row of the other front. Work so as to correspond to first side, reversing all shaping.

Sleeves

Cuff: Work rib band same as for body until there are 12(12-13-13-14-14) ridges or 24(24-26-26-28-30) rows. Ch 1, turn.

Row 1: Across top of rib work 3 sc in each ridge until there are 36(36-36-36-42-42) sc, then work 0(0-2-2-0-0) sc in last ridge. Ch 1, turn.

Continue in sc rows, inc 1 st each side every 4 rows 5(6-6-7-6-7) times. Work on 46(48-50-52-54-56) sc to 19 inches from beg, or desired length to underarm.

Shape Cap: Sl st in each of 2 sc, sc in each sc to last 2 sc. Turn. Dec 1 st each side *every* row, 14(15-16-17-18-19) times. Fasten off.

Finishing: Sew underarm, shoulder and sleeve seams. Set in sleeves.

Front Bands: See Crochet on Vertical Bands for V Neck, page 148.

Using Size E hook and beg at bottom of right front edge work 2 rows sc around entire neckline. Mark for desired number of buttonholes on left front.

Next Row: Work buttonholes as explained. Work 2 rows more of sc. Fasten off. Sew buttons opposite buttonholes.

For Sleeveless Cardigan, work same as Cardigan omitting sleeves.

To Finish Armholes: Work 2 rows sc around each armhole, holding to desired fit.

CROCHET NET BAG

MATERIALS — Lily Soft Sheen
CROCHET HOOK: "Susan Bates" Steel Size 1 OR SIZE TO GIVE GAUGE

GAUGE: 4 ch-6 loops = 3 inches

Chain 8, sl st in first ch to form a ring.
Rnd 1: Ch 4, 1 dc in ring, * ch 1, 1 dc in ring; rep from * 12 times more, ch 1; join in 3rd ch of ch-4. 15 sps.
Rnd 2: Sl st in first sp, * ch 3, sc in next sp; rep from * 12 times more, ch 3, sc in same place as sl st. 15 lps.

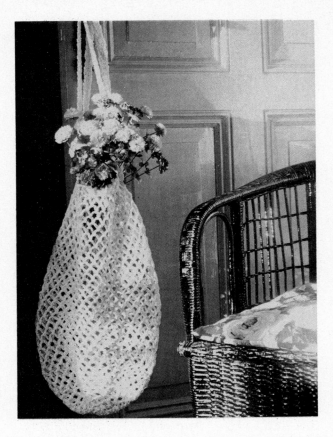

Rnd 3: Sl st to center of first lp, *ch 4, 1 sc in next lp; rep from * 13 times more, ch 4, sl st to center of first lp. 15 lps.
Rnds 4 and 5: *Ch 5, 1 sc in next lp; rep from * 13 times more, ch 5, sl st to center of first lp. 15 lps.
Rnd 6: * Ch 5, 1 sc in next lp, ch 5, 1 sc in same lp; rep from * 14 times more, ch 5, sl st to center of first lp. 30 lps.
Rnd 7: * Ch 5, sc in next lp; rep from * 25 times more, ch 5, sl st in center of first lp. 30 lps.

Rep Rnd 7, 3 times more.
Rnd 11: Same as rnd 7 chaining 6 instead of 5 for each lp.

Rep Rnd 11 until 44 rnds in all, or to desired length. Fasten off.
Cord: Ch 6, 1 dc in 4th ch from hook, 1 dc in each of next 2 ch. 4 dc. Ch 3 at beginning counts as 1 dc. Ch 3, turn.
Row 2: 1 dc in each of 2nd and 3 dc, 1 dc in turning ch. Ch 3, turn.

Rep Row 2 until about 24 inches long. Fasten off.

Lace cord through lps at top of bag. Sew ends together.

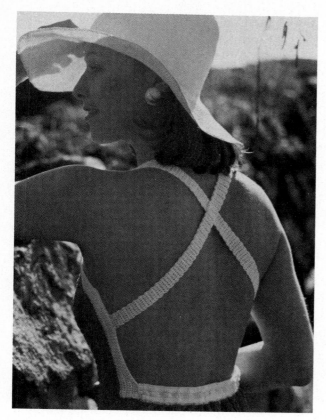

SUN DRESS

Instructions are for size 36. Changes for sizes 38, 40 and 42 are in parentheses.

MATERIALS — Brunswick Windspun (1-oz) 20(22-24-26) A and 4 B; Elastic ½ inch wide, 1 yard

CROCHET HOOK: "Susan Bates" Size F OR SIZE TO GIVE GAUGE

GAUGE: 20 sts = 4 inches, 18 rows = 4 inches

Instructions are for dress approximately 26 inches from lower edge to waist. To lengthen add extra length before first dec row. To shorten work 2 rows less between dec rows required number of times.

FINISHED MEASUREMENTS (in inches)

Width at lower edge 59(59-64-64)

Width at waistline 35(36-38½-40) to be held in with elastic across back to desired width.

Front: Chain 150(150-162-162) loosely to measure 30(30-32-32) inches.

Row 1 (right side): 1 dc in 3rd and each remaining st of chain: 149(149-161-161) dc. Ch-2 at beginning of row counts as first dc. Ch 1, turn.

Row 2: Sc in each dc, sc in top of turning ch-2. 149(149-161-161) sc. Ch 2, turn.

Row 3: Dc in 2nd dc and each of next 3 dc, * skipping sc row, yo, insert hook *around* next dc in first row and work dc (Post Stitch — PS), sk next sc on 2nd row (behind PS) and work 5 dc; rep from * to end. Ch 1, turn.

Row 4: Sc in each st. Ch 2, turn.

Row 5: Dc in 2nd and each of next 3 sc, * dc around PS in 2nd row below, sk next sc, work 5 dc; rep from * to end.

Rep Rows 4 and 5 for pat. Work until 8 rows from beginning, end with a sc row. Ch 2, turn.

First Dec Row: *Note: Dec 4 dc across row as follows:* 1 dc in center of the 3rd and the 8th 5-dc stripe from each end of piece.

To dec: Yo hook, insert hook in next st, yo and draw up a lp, yo and through 2 lps; yo, insert hook in next st, yo and draw up a lp — 4 lps on hook, yo and through 2 lps, yo and through 3 lps. There will be 1 dc less in each dec stripe after every dec row. Rep dec row every 8th row (every 4th dc row) 3 times more, having 1 dc between PS in each of 4 dec stripes. Work 7 rows even.

Fifth Dec Row: Work first two 5-dc stripes, work PS, sk 1 dc, work PS, sk *3 sts* on sc row, 1 dc in each of 5 dc, continue pat dec 3 more sts in same way. Work 7 rows even, with care to sk *2 sc* behind 2 PS.

Sixth Dec Row: Work first two 5-dc stripes, work PS around 2 PS, sk 2 sts on sc row, 1 dc in each of 5 dc, continue pat dec 3 more sts in same way; 125(125-137-137) sts. Rep last 6 dec rows once more; 101(101-113-113) sts. *Dec 1 dc each side, (dec in first and last 5-dc stripe only), every 4th row (2nd dc row) 3(2-4-2) times;* 95(97-105-109) sts. Work even until 26 inches or desired length from beginning to waistline, end with dc row. Mark for waistline. Leave off 6 sts each side as follows: Sl st loosely across first 6 dc, ch 1, 1 sc in each st to within 6 sts of end. Ch 2, turn.

Top: Work even in pat on 83(85-93-97) sts for 6(6½-6½-7) ins, end with a dc row.

Leave off 3 sts each side of each of 6 rows as follows: Turn.

Row 1: Work 1 sl st loosely in each of first 3 sts, work sc to within 3 sts of end, sl st in next st. Ch 1, turn.

Row 2: Sk sl st, work 1 sl st loosely in each of next 3 sts, work pat to within 3 sts of end, sl st in next st. Ch 1, turn.

Rep last 2 rows twice more. Fasten off.

Back: Same as Front until 1 row less than front to waistline, end with sc row. Ch 2, turn. Work pat row dec 1 dc in center of each 5-dc stripe. Fasten off A. With B, work 7 rows sc for waistband. Fasten off.

Border for Top of Front: From right side, beginning where 6 sts were left off at waistline, work 1 row sc around top (keeping work flat and increasing at corners if necessary) to waistline on other side. Ch 1, turn. Work 6 more rows sc, increasing at corners where necessary. Fasten off.

Shoulder Straps (Make 2): With B, ch 7. Work 6 sc on ch. Ch 1, turn, 1 sc in each sc. Ch 1, turn.

Buttonhole: 1 sc in each of 2 sc, ch 2, sk 2, 1 sc in each of 2 sc. Ch 1, turn. Work 1 sc in each sc and each ch. 6 sc. Continue even in sc until strap measures about 24(25-25-26) inches. Fasten off.

Finishing: Sew side seams, sewing edge of waistband on back to adjoining edge of front border. Make casing for elastic on wrong side of back waistband. Steam lightly.

Sew 2 small buttons on wrong side of front border to attach shoulder straps. Insert elastic in casing and sew one edge to side seam. Button on straps and try on dress. Adjust elastic to fit and pin to other seam with safety pin. Cross straps at back and pin in desired position. Remove dress and sew free edge of elastic and straps as pinned. If desired join B on front of skirt at top of first raised ridge, from right side, work 1 row sc along ridge from waistline to lower edge, keeping work flat. Ch 1, turn. Work 2 or 4 rows more. Fasten off.

SHOULDER BAG

Approximately 9 x 6 inches

MATERIALS — Lily Cotton, four ³/₄-inch Rings, Lining

CROCHET HOOK: "Susan Bates" Aluminum Size 1 OR SIZE TO GIVE GAUGE

GAUGE: 7 dc = 1 inch, 3 rows = 1 inch

Chain 105 loosely for *side* edge.

Row 1 (right side): Dc in 4th ch from hook, dc in each remaining ch; 103 dc (ch-3 at beginning of row counts as 1 dc). Ch 3, turn.

Row 2 (Open-work Row): Dc in 2nd dc, *ch 1, sk 1 dc, dc in next dc; rep from * 49 times more, dc in top of turning ch. 50 openwork sps, 2 dc each side. Ch 3, turn.

Row 3: Dc in 2nd dc, * dc in next sp, dc in next dc; rep from * across row, end dc in next dc, dc in top of turning ch-3. 103 dc. Rep last 2 rows 15 times more. 16 open-work rows and 17 dc rows. Fasten off.

Turnback: Place piece on flat surface with wrong side up and open-work stripes running vertically. Folding along center of 9th sp from top, fold top to wrong side and pin.

Chains for Handle and to secure fold: Beg at right edge insert hook through 8th sp (directly below fold), and through 10th sp (directly behind 8th sp), join thread and work sl st, ch 6 inches. Fasten off. Rep in each of 15 remaining open-work rows.

Fold remainder of piece in half for bag, having lower edge under turnback and just below fold. Sew or crochet side edges together, with care to leave edges of turnback free.

Handle: Ch 16 inches loosely. Work 1 dc row, 1 open-work row and 1 dc row as for bag. Fasten off.

Finishing: Cover rings with 1 row sc if desired. Draw first 8 chs through a ring; attach end of chs to 2nd ring.

Draw remaining 8 chs through 3rd ring; attach end of chs to 4th ring.

Draw handle through 2nd and 4th rings and sew ends together.

Line bag if desired.

CROCHET TOP

This top can be made to fit up to size 12 or larger if desired. See instructions below.

MATERIALS — Brunswick Icecap (oz.) 4 each A and B

CROCHET HOOK: "Susan Bates" Steel No. 2 OR SIZE TO GIVE GAUGE

GAUGE: 7 sc = 1 inch, 13 rows = 2 inches, 7 dc = 1 inch, 6 rows = 2 inches

Take body measurement just below bust. Multiply number of inches obtained by 7 and chain this number of sts, plus 1.

Example: If body measurement is 30 inches, multiply 30 by 7, obtaining 210. Chain 210 sts loosely enough to measure 30 inches; ch 1 more st for turning.

With A, chain required number of sts as above. Always use an even number of chs plus 1 for turning.

Pattern

Row 1 (right side): Sc in 2nd and in each remaining ch. Ch 1, draw up lp and drop it from hook (it is advisable to slip small safety pin through lp to prevent ripping). Mark first row for right side.

Row 2: Working from same side as last row, join B with sl st in *back* lp of first sc, ch 1, sc in same place, sc in *back* lp of each sc to within 1 sc of end, draw up a lp in *back* lp of last sc, drop B, draw dropped A lp through 2 lps on hook to complete sc. With A, ch 1, turn.

Row 3: With A, sc in *front* lp of each sc to end. Ch 1, drop lp.

Row 4: Working from same side as last row, insert hook in *back* lp of first sc, with B draw up a lp, ch 1, sc in *back* lp of same sc, sc in *back* lp of each sc to within 1 sc of end, draw up lp in last sc, drop B, draw dropped A lp through 2 lps on hook. With A, ch 1, turn. Rep Rows 3 and 4 until about 4 inches from lower edge, end with pat Row 4. Fasten off both colors.

Bra Top: Work on 108 sts only at center of piece, leaving same number of sts free at each side as follows: Subtract 108 sts from total number of sts on piece. Divide this figure by 2. This will give the number of sts to leave free for each half of back.

Note: For larger than size 12 work on 114-116 sts.

Row 1: With wrong side of last row facing you, skip sts of one-half of back, join A with sl st in *front* lp of next sc, ch 2 (for first dc), 1 dc in *front* lp of each of next 107 sc. 108 dc. Ch 1, drop lp from hook.

Row 2: Working from same side as last row, join B in top of first ch 2, ch 2, 1 dc in *back* lp of 2nd and each dc to within 1 dc of end, yo, draw up a lp in *back* lp of last dc, yo and through 2 lps, then insert hook in A lp and draw this lp through 2 lps on hook; drop B. Ch 2, turn.

Row 3: With A, dc in *front* lp of 2nd and each dc, end dc in top of ch-2. Ch 1, drop A.

Row 4: Working from same side as last row, with B, sl st in first st of ch-2, sl st in top of same ch-2, ch 2 for first dc, 1 dc in *back* lp of each remaining dc to within 1 dc of end, yo, insert hook in *back* lp of last dc, yo and through 2 lps, insert hook in A lp and draw this lp through 2 lps on hook; drop B. Ch 2, turn.

Rep rows 3 and 4 until 15 dc rows in all, end with an A row. Fasten off both colors.
Note: For larger than size 12 work 17-19 rows.

Shoulder Straps and Edging (Make 2): With A, ch 7, dc in 3rd ch from hook, dc in each remaining ch. 6 dc (ch-2 at beginning of row counts as 1 dc). Ch 2, turn.

Row 2: Dc in 2nd and each of next 3 dc, dc in top of turning ch. Ch 2, turn.

Rep row 2 until 28-32 inches from beginning, or long enough to go around one upper edge of back and side edges of bra top with additional length to tie around neck.

Front Strap: With A, ch 7. Work in dc for 13 rows. Fasten off.

Finishing: Beginning at center back, pin edge of one shoulder strap to upper edge of back and side of bra top, stretching shoulder strap slightly; leave remainder of strap to tie around neck. Sew on strap. Sew on other strap to correspond. Sew lower edge of front strap over bra top and sew other edge at same place on wrong side.

With A, beginning on right side, work 3 rows sc on left back edge and short end of shoulder strap, keeping edge flat. Mark position of desired number of buttons. Work 3 rows sc on right edge to correspond working buttonloops on 2nd row, opposite markers for buttons as follows: Ch 3, sk 3 sc, sc in next sc; on 3rd row work 3 sc over each ch-3 to complete buttonholes.

TRIANGLE CROCHET SHAWL

Approximate size at long edge 70 inches; each side 48 inches, not including fringe

MATERIALS — Brunswick "Fore-'N' Aft Sport (2-oz), 5 Blue (Main Color), 3 Green, 2 Red, 2 Yellow, 2 White

Note: Use main color for small motifs and for fringe. Use all colors in desired combination for octagonal motifs.

CROCHET HOOK: "Susan Bates" Size F OR SIZE TO GIVE GAUGE

GAUGE: Octagonal Motif = 3 inches across — 3½ inches from point to point

Note: Work all rnds from right side.
Octagonal Motif: With desired color chain 8, sl st in first ch to form ring.
Rnd 1 (right side): Ch 2, work 15 dc in ring; join with sl st in top of ch 2; 16 dc, counting ch 2 as first dc.
Rnd 2: Ch 3, sk next dc, 1 dc in next dc, *ch 3, yo, inserting hook into same dc as last st was worked in, yo and draw up a lp, yo and thru 2 lps; sk next dc, yo, insert hook into next dc, yo and draw up a lp, yo and thru 2 lps, yo and thru 3 lps; rep from * 6 times more ch 3, sl st in top of first dc; 8 ch-3 sps. Fasten off.
Rnd 3: Join another color with sl st in any ch-3 sp, ch 3, work (2 dc, ch 3 for point, 3 dc) all in same sp; *(3 dc, ch 3, 3 dc) all in next ch-3 sp; rep from * 6 times more, sl st in top of first ch-3; 8 points with 6 dc between points. Fasten off.
Second Motif: With desired color work first 2 rnds as for first motif. Fasten off.
Rnd 3: Joining Rnd
Work as for rnd 3 of first motif repeating from *4 times (6 points made); join to first motif as follows: 3 dc in next (7th) ch-3 sp, ch 1, join with sl st in center of a ch-3 lp (point) on first motif (see A on chart), ch 1, 3 dc in same sp on 2nd motif; 3 dc in next sp on 2nd motif, ch 1, sl st in center of next ch-3 lp on first motif (B on chart), ch 1, 3 dc in same sp on 2nd motif. Complete rnd; join with sl st. Fasten off.

Third Motif: Same as 2nd motif, joining last 2 points to first motif at points C and D as indicated on chart, finish rnd.
Fourth Motif: Same as 2nd motif, joining last 2 points to 2nd motif at points E and F, finish rnd.
Fifth Motif: Work as before until 4 points have been completed, join next 2 points to points G and H on 3rd motif, last 2 points to points I and J on 2nd motif, finish rnd.
Sixth Motif: Work as before, joining last 2 points to 3rd motif at points K and L.

Continue in this manner until 17 rows in all, having 1 more motif in each succeeding row — 17 motifs in last row. 153 motifs in shawl.

Flower motifs are all made with Main Color and are used to fill in square sps between octagonal motifs, including the 16 sps between motifs in last row.
Flower Motif: With Main Color ch 5, sl st in first ch.
Rnd 1: Ch 1, work 8 sc in ring, sl st in first sc.
Rnd 2: Joining Rnd — Ch 2, join with sl st in any corner of a small square sp (at joining of motifs) ch 2, 1 sl st in each of next 2 sc, *ch 2, sl st in next corner of square, ch 2, 1 sl st in each of next 2 sc; rep from * twice more. Fasten off. 136 flower motifs. Steam lightly.
Fringe: Wind Main color around 9-in cardboard. Cut at one end — 18-in strands.

Leaving long edge (last row) free, knot 6 strands in each ch-3 lp (point) on short sides. Trim evenly.

BLUE SHAWL

Approximately 28 inches by 88 inches, not including fringe

MATERIALS — Mohair Yarn (40-gr), Pale Blue, 2; Turquoise, 2; Dark Blue, 2; Navy Blue, 2
CROCHET HOOK: "Susan Bates" Size G OR SIZE TO GIVE GAUGE
GAUGE: 3 loops = 4 inches, 5 rows = 4 inches

With Navy Blue, chain 128 loosely.
Row 1: 1 sc in 8th ch from hook, *ch 8, sk next 5 ch, 1 sc in next ch; rep from * 19 times more; 21 lps.
Row 2: Ch 8, 1 dc in first lp, *ch 8, 1 dc in next lp; rep from * 19 times more.

Rep Row 2 for entire shawl, working colors in following sequence: 4 more rows Navy Blue; 6 rows in all — change to Pale Blue at end of last row by working off 2 lps of last sc with Pale Blue; break Navy and tie short ends of both colors.

With Pale Blue work 5 rows in all. Change to Navy and work 5 rows; work 2 rows Dark Blue; 6 rows Turquoise; 2 rows Navy; 2 rows Dark Blue; 6 rows Pale Blue; 3 rows Dark Blue; 1 row Navy; 6 rows Turquoise; 2 rows Dark Blue; 2 rows Pale Blue; 3 rows Navy; 6 rows Turquoise; 1 row Navy. Mark last row for center. Continue for other half, working stripes in reverse order, end with 6 rows Navy. Fasten off. Weave in all ends.

Fringe: Wind Navy around 7-in wide cardboard. Cut at one end — 14-in strands. Knot 8 strands in each lp on each short end of shawl. Trim evenly.

CROCHET TABLECLOTH

Approximate Size 50 x 50 inches, including edging

MATERIALS — Lily Catlou
CROCHET HOOK: "Susan Bates" Steel Size 5 OR SIZE TO GIVE GAUGE

GAUGE: Each motif = 3 inches square
Note: All motif rounds are worked from right side.

Motif: Chain 6, join with sl st in first ch to form ring.

Rnd 1 (right side): Ch 3 (for first dc), work 2 dc in ring, * ch 5, 3 dc in ring; rep from * twice more, ch 5, sl st in 3rd ch (top) of first ch-3.
Note: Work into *back* lp of sts unless otherwise stated.

Rnd 2: Ch 3, working into *back lp of sts,* work 3 dc in next dc (center dc of group), 1 dc in next dc, * ch 6, sk ch 5, 1 dc in next dc, 3 dc in next (center) dc, 1 dc in next dc; rep from * twice more, ch 6, join with sl st to top of first ch-3, 4 ch-6 sps and four 5-dc groups.

Rnd 3: Ch 3, 1 dc in next dc, 3 dc in center dc, 1 dc in each of next 2 dc, *ch 4, work 1 sc *around 2-ch lps,* ch 4, 1 dc in each of next 2 dc, 3 dc in center dc, 1 dc in each of next 2 dc; rep from * twice more, ch 4, 1 sc around *2 ch-lps,* ch 4, sl st in top of ch-3.

Rnd 4: Ch 4, sk 2 dc, work 3 dc in center dc *through both* lps, ch 4, sk 2 dc, 1 sc in next dc, * ch 6, 1 sc in next dc, ch 4, sk 2 dc, 3 dc in center dc through *both* lps, ch 4, sk 2 dc, 1 sc in next dc; rep from * twice more, ch 6, 1 sl st in joining st (same place as first sl st).

Rnd 5: Ch 7, * 1 dc in first dc, ch 5, sk 1 dc, 1 dc in next dc, ch 4, 7 dc in ch-6 lp, ch 4; rep from * 3 times more, end last rep 6 dc in ch-6 lp, sl st in 3rd ch of ch-7.

Rnd 6: Ch 8, *sk next lp, work — 3 dc, ch 5, 3 dc — all in next (center) lp, ch 5, sk next lp, 1 dc in each of next 7 dc, ch 5; rep from * 3 times more, end last rep 1 dc in each of 6 dc, sl st in 3rd ch of ch-8. Fasten off.

Make 256 motifs. Sew them together from wrong side, 16 motifs in height and 16 motifs in width.

Edging

Rnd 1: From right side, with lp on hook, work 1 dc in each dc of *last dc group before any corner,* work — ch 3, 3 dc in center ch of corner, ch 3 — 1 dc in each of next 3 dc (work all corners in this way), *ch 5, 1 dc in each of 7 dc, ch 5, 1 dc in each of 3 dc, ch 3, 2 dc at joining, ch 3, 1 dc in each of 3 dc; rep from * to corner, work corner as before; continue around in this manner, end ch 5, sl st in first dc.

Rnd 2: Ch 4, sk 1 dc, 1 dc in next dc, ch 3, 1 dc in first dc of 3-dc corner group, ch 1, sk 1 dc, 1 dc in next dc, ch 3, 1 dc in next dc, ch 1, sk 1, 1 dc in next dc; *ch 6, work 7-tr group in next 7 dc as follows: yo hook twice, insert hook in next dc, yo and draw up a lp — 4 lps on hook, yo and draw thru 2 lps, yo and draw thru 2 lps — 2 lps on hook, † yo hook twice, insert hook in next dc and draw up a lp, yo and draw thru 2 lps, yo and draw thru 2 lps, retain remaining lps on hook; rep from † 5 times more, yo and draw thru remaining 8 lps on hook; ch 6, 3 dc ch 2 — 1 dc in next dc, ch 1, 1 dc in next dc — at joining, ch 2, 3 dc; rep from first * until last 7-tr group before corner has been completed, ch 6, 1 dc in next dc, ch 1, sk 1, 1 dc in next dc, ch 3, 1 dc in next dc, ch 1, sk 1, 1 dc in next dc, ch 3, 1 dc in next dc, ch 1, sk 1, 1 dc in next dc; rep from * around, end ch 6, sl st in 3rd ch of ch-4.

Final Rnd: **Note:** Sc to be worked around ch spaces and in *both lps* of sts. 1 sc in ch-1 sp (between 2 dc), ch 3, 1 sc in same sp, 3 sc in next sp, — 1 sc, ch 3, 1 sc — in next (corner) sp, 3 sc in next sp, 1 sc, ch 3, 1 sc in next ch-1 sp, * 7 sc in next sp, ch 3, 1 sc in first ch of ch-3 for picot, 1 sc in tr group, 7 sc in next sp, 1 sc in each of 3 dc, 2 sc in next sp, — 1 sc, ch 3, 1 sc — in ch-1 sp at joining, 2 sc in next sp, 1 sc in each of 3 dc; rep from * around, working corners as for first corner, join with sl st to first sc. Fasten off.

CHILD'S CROCHET SKIRT, SHORTS AND CAP

Instructions are for size 2. Changes for sizes 4 and 6 are in parentheses.

MATERIALS — Brunswick Fore-'N' Aft Sport (2-oz) 3(4-4) A and 2B
CROCHET HOOK: "Susan Bates" Size F OR SIZE TO GIVE GAUGE

GAUGE: 9 sts = 2 inches, 10 rows = 3 inches
FINISHED MEASUREMENTS (in inches)
Skirt - Waist 22(23-24)
       Length 8(9-10)
Shorts - Waist 22(23-24)
        Hips 23(24-26)

Note: Use 2 strands for foundation chains; then work pat with 1 strand.

SKIRT

Back: With 2 strands A, chain 67(73-79) to measure 11(11½-12) inches. Fasten off 1 strand of yarn and continue with 1 strand only.
Pattern
Row 1 (right side): Sc in 2nd ch from hook and in

each ch to end, working off 2 lps of last sc with B to change color. Fasten off A. 66(72-78) sc. Ch 2, turn. (Ch-2 counts as first dc of row).
Row 2: Dc in 2nd and each sc across row, working off last 2 lps of last dc with A. 66(72-78) dc. Fasten off B. With A, ch 1, turn.
Row 3: Sc in each dc, end sc in top of turning ch-2. Ch 2, turn.
Row 4: Dc in 2nd and each sc across row. Ch 1, turn.

Rep Rows 3 and 4 for pat. Work pat until 8 rows from beg, end with dc row. Ch 1, turn.
First Dec Row: Work until 10(11-12) sc, draw up a lp in each of next 2 sts, yo and through 3 lps on hook (1 st dec), work next 10(11-13) sc, dec 1 st as before, work next 18(20-20) sc, dec 1 st, work 10(11-13) sc, dec 1 st, finish row. 62(68-74) sc. Ch 3, turn.

Work 3 rows even, end with dc row. Ch 1, turn.
Second Dec Row: Work until 9(10-11) sc, dec 1 st, work 9(10-12) sc, dec 1 st, work 18(20-20) sc, dec 1 st, work 9(10-12) sc, dec 1 st, finish row. 58(64-70) sc. Ch 3, turn.

Continue in this way, decreasing 4 sts every 4th row 2(3-4) times more, keeping 18(20-20) sts between 2nd and 3rd dec and having 1 st less between other decs after each succeeding dec row. 50(52-54) sts. Work even until about 7½(8½-9½) inches, or desired length to waistline, end with dc row. Ch 1, turn. Work 1 row sc, decreasing, if necessary to desired waist measurement. Work 2 more rows sc, end on right side. Fasten off.

Front: Same as back.

Bib: With wrong side of front facing, sk first 16(16-17) sc. Join B in next sc and ch 2, 1 dc in each of next 17(19-19) sc, working off 2 lps of last sc with A. Fasten off B. 18(20-20) dc. With A, ch 1, turn.
Row 2: Sc in each dc, end 1 sc in turning ch, working off 2 lps with B. Fasten off A. With B, ch 2, turn.
Row 3: Dc in 2nd and each remaining sc, working off 2 lps of last sc with A. Fasten off B. With A, ch 1, turn.

Rep Rows 2 and 3 until 5 rows from beg of bib, end with dc row. With A, ch 1, turn.
Row 6 (Inc Row): Sc in first dc, 2 sc in next dc, sc

in each st to within 2 sts of end, 2 sc in next dc, sc in turning ch. 20(20-22) sc. Work as before until 7(8-9) B rows in all, or desired length, ending with B row. Fasten off.

Border: From right side, with A work 1 row sc on left edge of bib, working 1 sc in edge of each sc row, 2 sc in edge of each dc row, 3 sc in corner, 1 sc in each st along top, 3 sc in corner, sc to lower edge as on first side. Fasten off.

Row 2: Beg in first sc, from right side with A work 1 sc in *back* lp of each sc, 3 sc in corners. Fasten off.

Rep Row 2 once more. Sew side edges of border to adjoining edge of skirt.

Shoulder Straps: Join A at left top corner of bib, ch 2, 1 dc in each of next 3 sts. 4 dc for left strap. Ch 2, turn, work dc on these 4 sts until strap measures about 12½(12½-14½) inches, or desired length. Ch 4, turn. Sl st in last dc, for buttonloop, ch 1, turn, work 6 sc over buttonloop. Fasten off. Make right strap to correspond.

Pocket: With 1 strand A ch 11(12-13). Work 1 row sc, changing to B. Work pat with stripes as on bib until 7(7-9) rows, end with sc row. With A work 2 rows sc around 4 sides of pocket as for border of bib, working 3 sc in each corner.

Finishing: Sew on pocket as illustrated. Steam lightly. Sew 2 buttons on back of skirt at waist for shoulder straps.

SHORTS

Right Leg: With A chain 57(59-63).

Row 1 (right side): Sc in 2nd and each ch, changing to B at end of row. Break A. 56(58-62) sc. Ch 2, turn.

Row 2: With B work dc to end. Change to A, break B.

With A work 1 row sc, inc 1 st each side. 58(60-64) sc. Continuing in pat, work 1(1-3) rows, end with dc row.

Crotch: Sl st loosely across first 4 dc for front of crotch, work sc to within 2 sts of end, leaving 2 sts free for back crotch. Mark *beg* of row for front; *end* of row for back.

Continue in pat, dec 1 st at *back* edge every 4th row 4(4-5) times, and *at the same time,* dec 1 st at *front* edge every 8th(8th-6th) row 2(2-3) times. 46(48-50) sts. Work even until about 6¼(6¾-7¼) inches above crotch, or desired length to waist, end on right side. Ch 2, turn.

Short Rows

Row 1: Work until 26(26-28) dc, sc in next st, sl st in next st, turn.

Row 2: Sk sl st, work sl st in each of next 6 sts, work sc to end. Ch 2, turn.

Row 3: Work until 14(14-16) dc, sc in next st, sl st in next st, turn.

Row 4: Same as Row 2.

Work 3 rows sc. Fasten off.

Left Leg: Work same as right leg reversing all shaping.

Finishing: Sew leg seams. Sew front, back and crotch seams.

Bib: Mark 9th(9th-10th) st at each side of center front seam at waist. Beg at marker, from wrong side with B, work 18(18-20) dc across center front. Change to A, ch 1, turn.

Beginning with Row 2 of Bib for Skirt, follow instructions to end of Skirt.

CAP

Triangle: With 1 strand A, ch 17.

Row 1: Work 16 sc on ch. Ch 2, turn.

Continue in pattern, as on skirt, until 8 rows from beg, end with dc row. Ch 1, turn.

Dec 1 st each side of next row. Rep dec each side every 2nd row 4 times more. 6 sts. Ch 2, turn. Work 1 row dc. Ch 1, turn. Dec 3 sts across row. 3 sc. Ch 2, turn.

Last Row: Yo, draw up a lp in 2nd sc, yo and through 2 lps, yo, draw up a lp in last sc, yo and through 2 lps, yo and through 3 lps. Fasten off.

Make 2 more triangles with A; 3 with B. Sew triangles together along side edges, alternating A and B to form cap. From right side, with A work 3 rows sc on lower edge of cap; join. Fasten off.

Peak: From right side, with A work 1 hdc in each st on lower edge of any 3 triangles, inc 3 sts evenly spaced on edge of center triangle, sl st in next st. Turn.

Row 2: Sk sl st, sl st in each of next 3 sts, 1 hdc in each hdc to within 4 hdc of end, sl st in next st. Turn.

Rep Row 2 five times more. Fasten off. From right side, work 1 row sc on edge of peak. Fasten off.

CROCHET BABY PANTS

Instructions are for Size 1. Changes for Size 2 are in parentheses.

MATERIALS — Brunswick Winspun (1-oz) 2 skeins MC, 1 skein A and small amount of B or desired Color. ½ inch Elastic and Round Elastic

CROCHET HOOK: "Susan Bates" Steel No. 0 OR SIZE TO GIVE GAUGE

GAUGE: 11 sc = 2 inches, 13 rows = 2 inches

Striped Pattern: 2 rows MC, 6 rows A, 2 rows MC, 2 rows A, 2 rows MC, 2 rows B, 2 rows MC, 2 rows A, 2 rows MC, 6 rows A. Carry color loosely along edge of work, when not in use. With MC chain 51 (55) to measure 9 (10) inches for top of back.

Row 1: Sc in 2nd ch from hook and in each ch to end. 50 (54) sc Ch 1, turn at end of every row.

Row 2: Sc in each sc. Draw A through loop on hook, drop MC. Continue working rows of 50 (54) sc until stripe pat is complete. Cut A and B. Continue with MC only until there are 30 (34) rows from beg.

Next Row: Draw up a lp in each of first 2 sts, yo and through 3 lps on hook (1 st dec), sc in each st to last 2 sts, dec 1 st. Rep last row until 14 sts remain, ch 7 (9) at end of row, turn.

Next Row: Sc in 2nd ch from hook and in each of next 5 (7) ch, sc in next 14 sc; join a short length of yarn at beg of last row, ch 6 (8) and fasten off short length, sc in each of 6 (8) ch, ch 13 (13), turn.

Next Row: Sc in 2nd ch from hook and next 11 ch, sc in each sc, join short length at beg of last row and ch 12 (12) and fasten off short length, sc in each of 12 ch. There are 50 (54) sc in row.

Front: Work same number of rows as on back, with stripes corresponding to stripes on back. Fasten off.

Finishing: Sew side seams. From right side with MC work 1 row sc around top edge. Join with a sl st to first sc.

Beading Row: Ch 4, *sk 1 sc, 1 dc in next sc, ch 1; rep from * around, join with a sl st to 3rd ch of ch-4. Ch 1.

Next Row: Work 2 sc in each ch-1 sp. Join and fasten off.

From right side, work 2 (3) rnds sc around leg openings, and if desired work last row over round elastic. Cut elastic to desired size, draw through beading row. Sew ends together.

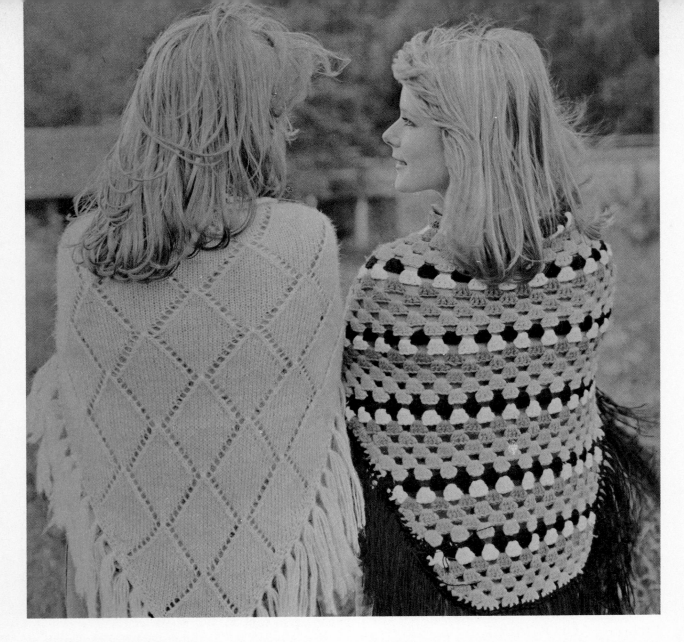

SHAWL IN GAY COLORS

Approximate Size 24 X 56 inches (without fringe)

MATERIALS — Brunswick Fore-'N-Aft Sport (2-oz balls) 1 ball each of 5 colors; 3 balls extra of desired color for fringe

CROCHET HOOK: "Susan Bates" Size F OR SIZE TO GIVE GAUGE

GAUGE: 3 groups and 6 ch = 4 inches, 3 rows = 2 inches

Work stripe Pattern as desired. When changing color draw new color through lp on hook, turn, cut color not in use.

Chain 206 to measure 57 inches for neck edge.

Row 1: Tr in 4th ch from hook and in each of next 2 ch (4 tr = 1 group - gr), * ch 2, sk 1 ch, tr in each of next 4 ch; rep from * to end. 41 grs.

Row 2: Turn. Sk 1 tr, dc in next tr, ch 1, * 4 dc in next ch-2 sp, ch 2; rep from *, end 4 dc in last ch-2 sp, ch 1, sk 2 tr, dc in next tr. 40 grs. Rep Row 2, having 1 gr less in every row until there are 6 grs in row. Fasten off. Weave in ends.

Finishing: Join yarn at beg of foundation row, work dc around entire shawl, spacing sts to keep edges flat and working 3 dc at all corners, and, having same number of dc on each side. Join with a sl st to first dc. Fasten off.

Fringe: Wrap yarn around a 7-inch cardboard. Cut at one end. Using 3 strands, place fringe (see page 139) in every 2nd dc on sides. Trim evenly.

HUSMODE

NR 12 · 13 mars 1972 · PRIS 1:95 (inkl moms) Das

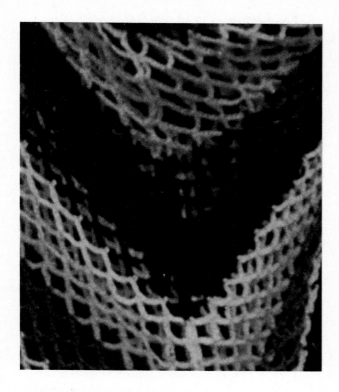

CROCHET SHAWL

Approximate Size 51 inches square

MATERIALS — Brunswick Wintuk Sport or Fore 'N Aft (2-oz), 3 Black (MC) and 1 each of 5 colors. Red (A), Cherry (B), Blue (C), Green (D) Yellow (E) or desired colors
CROCHET: "Susan Bates" Size F OR SIZE TO GIVE GAUGE

GAUGE: (stretched slightly) 1 lp = 1 inch, 2 rows = 1 inch

Striped Pattern: 7 rows MC (Black), 2 rows each A, B, C, D, E, A, B and 8 rows MC, 2 rows each E, B, A, C, D, B, 7 rows MC. Total of 48 rows.

Shawl

With MC chain 9. Join with a sl st to form a ring. Work in Striped Pattern as follows:
Rnd 1: *Ch 9, sc in ring; rep from * twice. Ch 4, tr in ring. 4 lps.
Rnd 2: (Ch 9, sc in next lp, ch 9, sc in same lp) 3 times, ch 9, sc in next lp, ch 4, tr in same lp. 8 lps.
Rnd 3: (Ch 9, sc in next lp, ch 9; sc in next lp, ch 9, sc in same lp for corner) 3 times, (ch 9, sc in next lp) twice, ch 4, tr in same lp. 4 corners, 12 lps.

Rnd 4: Ch 9, sc in next lp, ch 9, sc in next lp, ch 9, sc in next lp, ch 9, sc in same lp (for corner) 3 times, (ch 9, sc in next lp) 3 times, ch 4, tr in same lp with last sc. 16 lps.

Note: When changing colors draw new color through lp on hook. Cut color not in use.

Continue in striped pattern, always working 2 sc in corner lps and having 1 lp more between corners every rnd until there are 192 lps around on 48th rnd and 48 lps on each side. Fasten off.

Edge
Rnd 1: Join MC in loop after a corner lp, ch 5, in same lp work (tr, ch 1) 3 times, then work 1 more tr in same lp, ch 1, sc in next lp, ch 1; * in next lp work 5 tr with ch 1 between trs, ch 1, sc in next lp, ch 1; rep from * to corner, in corner lp work 9 tr with ch 1 between trs; ch 1; rep from * around and join with a sl st to 4th ch of ch-5.

Sl st in first ch-1 sp.
Rnd 2: Ch 6, tr in ch-1 sp between 2nd and 3rd tr, ch 2, tr in same sp, ch 2, in next sp work tr, ch 2, tr; ch 2; tr in last ch-1 sp (6 tr over 5 tr), *ch 2, sc in next sc, ch 2, tr in sp between first and 2nd tr, ch 2, (in next sp work tr, ch 2, tr, ch 2) twice, in sp between 4th and 5th tr work 1 tr (6 tr worked over 5 tr); rep from * to corner, in corner work (tr in next sp, 2 tr in next sp) 4 times; rep from * around. Join with a sl st to 4th ch of ch-6.
Rnd 3: Work dc and ch 4 in each ch-2 sp, sc in each sc. Join with a sl st to first sc. Fasten off.

CROCHET BAG

Approximate Size 16 x 19 inches

MATERIALS — Brunswick Fairhaven or Windspun (1-oz) 3 White (A) and 4 Green (B), Lining Material
CROCHET HOOK: "Susan Bates" Size E OR SIZE TO GIVE GAUGE

GAUGE: 1 motif = 4 inches square

First Motif: With A chain 8, join with sl st to first ch to form a ring. Ch 3 (to count as 1 dc).
Rnd 1 (right side): Work 23 dc in ring, join with sl st to top of ch-3. 24 dc. Ch 3, do *not* turn.
Rnd 2: 1 dc in each of next 5 dc, *ch 4, 1 dc in each of next 6 dc; rep from * twice more, ch 4, sl st in top of ch-3. Ch 3, do *not* turn.

Rnd 3: 1 dc in next dc, *ch 2, sk 2 dc, 1 dc in each of 2 dc, 8 dc in ch-4 sp, 1 dc in each of 2 dc; rep from * twice more, ch 2, sk 2 dc, 1 dc in each of 2 dc, 8 dc in last sp, join and fasten off.

Rnd 4: From right side, join B in 7th dc in any 12-dc group, 1 sc in same st, *ch 6, 1 sc in next ch-2 sp, *turn,* working over ch, work 3 sc in ch-6 lp, *turn,* (ch 6, sc in same ch-2 sp, turn, 3 sc in last ch-6 lp, turn) 3 times, ch 4, sk next 5 dc, 1 sc in each of next 2 dc; rep from * 3 times more, end 1 sc in last dc, join with sl st to first sc. Do *not* turn.

Rnd 5 (right side): *5 sc in each of 2 B lps, 2 sc, ch 5, 2 sc in next lp (corner), 5 sc in each of next 2 lps, sk 2 sc*; rep between * s 3 times more, end sl st in first sc. Fasten off.

2nd Motif: Work first 4 rnds as for first motif.

Rnd 5 (right side): Rep between * s of rnd 5 of first motif twice, 5 sc in each of next 2 lps, 2 sc in next (corner) lp, hold first motif behind 2nd motif (wrong sides together), ch 2, sl st in center ch of ch-5 lp of first motif, ch 2, 2 sc in same corner sp of 2nd motif, (2 sc in next lp of 2nd motif, sl st in center st of corresponding lp on first motif, 2 sc in same lp of 2nd motif) 4 times, 2 sc in next lp on 2nd motif, ch 2, sl st in center st of ch-5 lp, ch 2, 2 sc in same lp, finish rnd as before, join. Fasten off. Continue in this way until 7 motifs have been joined.

8th Motif: Work first 4 rnds as before.

Rnd 5: 5 sc in each of 2 B lps, 2 sc in first (corner) lp, (with wrong sides together) ch 2, sl st in center ch of ch-5 lp of 7th motif, ch 2, 2 sc in same corner lp of 8th motif, continue to join motifs to next corner, as before, work to 3rd corner, then work across lower edge, joining to top edge of first motif, finish rnd forming circle of 8 motifs.

2nd Circle — First Motif: Work first 4 rnds, then join one edge of motif to free right edge of first motif in first circle as follows:

Rnd 5: 5 sc in each of 2 B lps, 2 sc in first corner lp, ch 2, sl st in center of ch-5 lp at upper right corner of first motif in first circle, ch 2, 2 sc in first corner lp of motif, continue to next corner, joining motifs as before, finish rnd.

2nd Motif: Work first 4 rnds, then join top edge of motif to lower edge of last motif made and to adjoining side edge of 2nd motif in first circle as follows:

Rnd 5: 5 sc in each of 2 B lps, 2 sc in first corner lp, ch 2, sl st in center of ch-5 lp at lower right corner of last motif made, ch 2, 2 sc in same corner lp, continue joining top and side edge to 3rd corner, finish rnd.

Continue in this way until there are 8 motifs in 2nd circle, joining lower edge of last motif to top edge of first motif. Rep 2nd circle until 4 circles in all.

Finishing: Fold bag so that there are 16 motifs for front; 16 for back. Sew lower edge securely with B, leaving top edge free for opening.

Border: From right side, with B work sc around top opening keeping work flat by working about 20 sc on edge of every motif (sk every 3rd st), do *not* join. Continue around in sc until border measures 3 inches, sl st in next st and fasten off. Fold border to wrong side and sew last sc row to first sc row.

Handles: (Make 2) With B ch 7, 1 sc in 2nd and each ch to end. 6 sc.

Row 2: Ch 1, turn, 1 sc in each sc. Rep row 2 until about 14 ins, or desired length. Fasten off.

Sew on handles as illustrated. Line bag.

LIMELIGHT AFGHAN

Approximate Size 51 X 64 inches

MATERIALS — Brunswick Germantown Knitting Worsted or Windrush (4-oz) 6 Dark (D), 5 Light (L) and 1 medium (M)

CROCHET HOOK: "Susan Bates" Size F OR SIZE TO GIVE GAUGE

GAUGE: Each motif = 4¼ inches square
Note: All motif rounds are worked from right side.

Flower Motif (Make 90): With M chain 7, join with a sl st to form a ring. Ch 1.

Rnd 1: Work 8 sc in ring, draw L thru lp on hook, cut D, join L with a sl st to first sc, ch 4.

Rnd 2: (Yo hook, draw up a lp in same st) 3 times, yo and through 7 lps on hook — a cluster made, ch 3, cluster in same st, * ch 1, dc in next st, ch 1, in next st work cluster, ch 3, cluster; rep from * twice more, ch 1, join with a sl st to 3rd ch of ch-4. Ch 3.

Rnd 3: Dc in ch-1 sp before first cluster, ch 1, in ch-3 sp, work cluster, ch 3, cluster (corner), * ch 1,

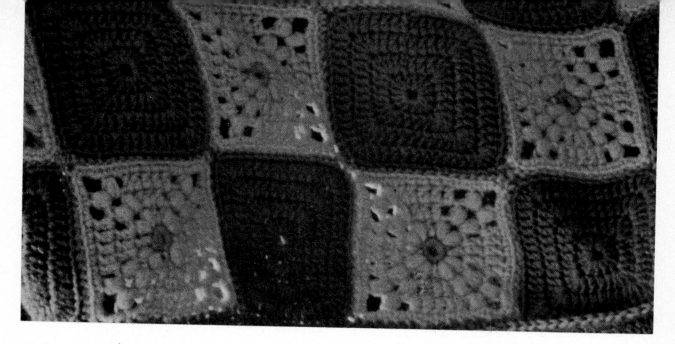

dc in next ch-1 sp, dc in next dc, dc in next ch-1 sp, work corner in next ch-3 sp; rep from * twice, ch 1, dc in next ch-1 sp. Join with a sl st to top ch-3. Ch 3.

Rnd 4: Dc in next dc, dc in next ch-1 sp, ch 1, in corner, work cluster, ch 5, cluster, * ch 1, dc in next ch-1 sp, dc in each of next 3 dc, dc in next ch-1 sp, ch 1, in corner work cluster, ch 5, cluster; rep from * twice, ch 1, dc in next ch 1 sp, dc in next dc. Join. Ch 1.

Rnd 5: Work sc in each dc, each ch-1 sp, each cluster and 5 sc in ch-5 sp. Join with a sl st to first sc. Fasten off. Sew in ends.

Plain Motif (Make 90): With D ch 4.

Rnd 1: Work 15 dc in 4th ch from hook, join with a sl st to top of ch-4 (16 dc).

Rnd 2: Ch 3 (counts as 1 dc), dc in each of next 2 sts, 5 dc in next st, * dc in each of the next 3 sts; 5 dc in next st, rep from * twice more. Join with a sl st to top of ch-3.

Rnd 3: Ch 3, dc in each of next 4 sts, 5 dc in next st (corner), * dc in each of next 7 sts, 5 dc in next st (corner); rep from * twice more, dc in each of next 2 sts. Join.

Rnd 4: Ch 3, dc in each of next 6 sts, 5 dc in next st, * dc in each of next 11 sts, 5 dc in next st; rep from * twice more, dc in each of next 4 sts. Join and fasten off.

Finishing: Steam squares lightly. Make 6 strips of 15 motifs alternating motifs, beginning and ending with a flower motif. Make 6 strips beginning and ending with a plain motif.

To Join Motifs: With right side of a flower and plain motif together, over cast-motifs taking up top lps only and matching sts. Over-cast strips together in same way, alternating the strips as shown in photograph.

Edge: With D from right side, work hdc around entire afghan, spacing sts to keep edges flat and work 3 hdc in each corner. Join, *do* not turn.

Rnd 2: Work hdc in each st with 3 hdc in each corner st. Join and fasten off.

EVENING DRESS

Instructions are for size 10. Changes for sizes 12, 14 and 16 are in parentheses.

MATERIALS — Brunswick Delf Baby Yarn (1 oz) 30(30-34-34). Zipper for back opening
CROCHET HOOK: "Susan Bates" Size 1 Steel OR SIZE TO GIVE GAUGE

GAUGE: Motif = 4¼ inches square. Pattern — 7 dc = 1 inch, 15 rows = 4 inches

FINISHED MEASUREMENTS (in inches)
Bust 34(36-38-40)
Hipline 36(38-40-42)

Note: Dress is worked to approximately 40 inches from underarm to lower edge; with borders and blocking 42 inches finished; make any desired change in length before first dec row, or between dec rows.

Motif: Chain 6, join with sl st to first ch to form a ring. Ch 3 (counts as first dc).

Rnd 1 (right side): 23 dc in ring, join with sl st to 3rd ch of ch 3: 24 dc. Ch 3, turn.

Rnd 2: 1 dc in each of next 2 dc, ch 1, sk 1 dc, 1 dc in each of next 3 dc, *ch 3 (corner sp), 1 dc in *same st* as last dc, 1 dc in each of next 2 dc, ch 1, sk 1 dc, 1 dc in each of next 3 dc; rep from * twice more, working last dc of last rep in same place as first ch-3, ch 3, sl st in top of first ch-3. Ch 3, turn.

Rnd 3: * 2 dc, ch 3, 2 dc — all in ch-3 corner sp, 1 dc in each of 3 dc, 1 dc in ch-1 sp, 1 dc in each of 3 dc; rep from * 3 times more, end last rep 1 dc in each of 2 dc, sl st in top of ch-3. Ch 3, turn.

Rnd 4: 2 dc, ch 1, sk 1, 5 dc, * 2 dc, ch 3, 2 dc — all in corner sp, 5 dc, ch 1, sk 1, 5 dc; rep from * twice more, 2 dc, ch 3, 2 dc in last corner, 2 dc; join. Ch 3, turn.

Rnd 5: 4 dc, * 2 dc, ch 3, 2 dc in corner, 7 dc, 1 dc in ch-1 sp, 7 dc; rep from * 3 times, end last rep 1 dc in sp, 2 dc, join. Ch 5, turn.

Rnd 6: Sk next 2 dc, 1 dc in next dc, ch 2, sk 2, 7 dc, * 2 dc, ch 3, 2 dc in corner, 7 dc, ch 2, sk 2, 1 dc, ch 2, sk 2, 7 dc; rep from * twice more, 2 dc, ch 3, 2 dc in corner, 6 dc, sl st in 3rd st of ch-5. Sl st in next ch-2 sp. Ch 5, turn.

Rnd 7: Sk 2 sl sts and 1 dc, 7 dc, *2 dc, ch 3, 2 dc, 7 dc, ch 2, 1 dc in next sp, ch 2, 1 dc in next sp, ch 2, sk 2 dc, 7 dc; rep from * 3 times more, end last rep 7 dc, ch 2, 1 dc in next sp, ch 2, sl st in 3rd st of ch-5. Fasten off. Make 44 motifs in all.

Dress Front: Sew 6 motifs together to form a strip, sewing through *both* loops of sts from wrong side, from center ch of corner to center ch of next corner, match sts. Make 3 strips. Sew 3 strips together for skirt border. Work across top of border as follows: Make lp on hook, from wrong side work * 1 dc in corner sp, then working in *front* lp of st, work 1 dc in each of 9 dc, 3 dc in first sp, 2 dc in 2nd sp, 3 dc in 3rd sp, 1 dc in each of 9 dc, 1 dc in corner sp; rep from * across, end 2 dc in last corner sp; 169 dc. Ch 3, turn.

Pattern

Row 1 (right side): Working in *front* lp of sts, 1 dc in 2nd and each dc across, end 1 dc in top of turning ch; 169 dc. Ch 1, turn. Mark this row for beginning of pat.

Row 2: Working in *both* lps, 1 sc in first dc, *ch 3, sk 2 dc, 1 sc in next dc; rep from *, end 1 sc in top of ch-3. 56 lps. Ch 3, turn.

Row 3: 3 dc in each lp, end 2 dc in last lp, 1 dc in sc; 169 dc. Ch 3, turn.

Row 4 (wrong side): Rep Row 1.

Rows 5 and 6: Rep Rows 2 and 3.

Continue to rep Rows 1, 2 and 3 for pat. Work until 15(15-12-18) rows pat, end with pat row 3. Ch 3, turn.

Dec Row: Pat row 1 — Work until 23 dc from beg, yo, insert hook in *front* lp of next st and draw up a lp, yo and draw through 2 lps, yo, draw up a lp in next st — 4 lps on hook, yo and draw through 2 lps, yo and draw through 3 lps (1 dc decreased), * work 22 dc, dec 1 dc as before; rep from * 4 times more, finish row; 163 dc.

Note: Decs are always worked on Row 1 of pat — a plain dc row.

Continue to dec 6 sts evenly spaced across row every 9th(9th-12th-15th) row 2(4-3-2) times more; every 6th(6th-9th-9th) row 5(2-2-2) times; 121(127-133-139) sts. Work even until about 35 inches from lower edge of border, or 7 inches less than desired finished length, end with a dc row. Fasten off.

Back: Same as front until desired length for lower edge to back opening. Leave center st of row free for opening, working each half separately to correspond to front.

Finishing: Sew side seams. Sew 8 motifs together forming strip. With center of strip at center front of dress, pin strip to top of dress. On larger sizes work 1 or 2 rows sc or dc on each short edge to fit top of dress. Sew on strip as illustrated.

Border: Work 1 row dc on neck edge from wrong side, working 28 dc on edge of each motif as on top of skirt border. Ch 3, turn. Work 2nd row dc working in *front* lp of sts. Fasten off.

Edging: From right side join yarn with sl st in first st, * ch 4, sk 2, sl st in next st; rep from * to end. Fasten off.

Work Border and Edging on lower edge of skirt in same way.

Shoulder straps (Make 2): Chain about 16 inches or length required, plus 2 inches. Work 8 dc in 4th ch from hook, 1 dc in each ch to within 1 ch of end, 9 dc in last ch, continue around working 1 dc in each st on other side of ch, sl st in first ch-3.

Edging: * Ch 4, sk next 2 dc, sl st in next dc; rep from * around entire strap. Fasten off. Steam lightly, stretching to 42 inches in length. With ends inside dress sew on straps adjusting as required. Sew in zipper.

WOMAN'S SLEEVELESS COAT

Instructions are for Size 12. Changes for Sizes 14, 16, 18, 44, 46 and 48 are shown in parentheses.

MATERIALS — Brunswick Germantown Knitting Worsted or Windrush (4-oz) 6(6-7-7-7-8-8)
CROCHET HOOK: "Susan Bates" Size G OR SIZE TO GIVE GAUGE

GAUGE: 7 sc = 2 inches, 6 pat rows = 2 inches

FINISHED MEASUREMENTS (in inches)
Bust 36(38-40-42-44-46-48)
Lower Edge 48(49-50-51½-54-55)

Pattern Stitch: Worked on an uneven number of sts. Chain an even number.
Foundation Row: Sc in 2nd ch from hook and in each ch to end.
Row 1 (right side): Ch 2, sk first st, dc in next st, dc in skipped st (cross st made) * sk next st, work cross st; rep from * ending dc in last st. (Ch 2, does *not* count as a st). Rows 2, 3 and 4; Ch 1, sc in each st. Rep these 4 rows for pat.
Back And Fronts: Chain 168(172-176-180-184-188-192) loosely to measure 48(49-50-51½-52½-54-55) inches. Work foundation row. 167(171-175-179-183-187-191) sc. Work in pat st for 7 rows.
Next Row: Sc in each of 20(20-21-21-22-22-23) sts, draw up a loop in each of next 2 sts, yo and through 3 lps on hook (1 st dec), place a marker in dec for dart, sc in each of next 40(41-41-43-43-45-45) sts, dec, place marker in dec, sc in each of next 39(41-43-43-45-45-47) sts, dec, place marker in dec, sc in each of next 40(41-41-43-43-45-45) sts, dec, place marker, sc in each of last 20(20-21-21-22-22-23) sts. There are 4 markers — 4 sts dec.

Continue in pat, working decs directly over decs of previous row every 8th row (4th pat row) 9(8-7-7-6-6-5) times more.

Work even on 127(135-143-147-155-159-167) sts to 27 inches from beg or 2 inches less than desired length to underarm (for drop when blocked or washed), end with pat row 1. Divide for fronts and back.
Next Row: Sc in each of 30(32-34-35-37-38-40) sts for front, sl st in each of next 4 sts for under-arm, sc in each of next 59(63-67-69-73-75-79) sts for back, sl st in each of next 4 sts for underarm, sc in each of 30(32-34-35-37-38-40) sts for front.
Front
Armhole: Working on sts of 1 front only dec 1 st at armhole edge *every* row 4 times. Work on 26(28-30-31-33-34-36) until armhole measures 5(5¼-5½-5¾-6-6¼-6½) inches, ending at armhole edge.
Neck: Work to within 6(6-7-7-8-8-9) sts of front edge, turn.
Dec 1 st at neck edge every row 4(5-5-5-5-6-6) times. Work on 16(17-18-19-20-21) until armholes measure 7½(7¾-8-8¼-8½-8¾-9) inches ending at neck edge.
Shoulder: Work to within 6(7-8-9-10-10-11) sts of end of row. Turn.
Row 2: Work to neck edge. Ch and turn.
Row 3: Work to within 5 sts of end of last row, turn.
Row 4: Work to neck edge. Fasten off.
Back: Join yarn in first st of back to work first row from same side as first row of front armhole. Dec 1 st at armhole edges *every* row 3 times. Work on 53(57-61-63-67-69-73) to same length as front to shoulder.
Shoulder
Row 1: 1 sl st in each of 6(7-8-9-10-10-11) sts, pat to last 6(7-8-9-10-10-11) sts. Turn.
Row 2: Work even.
Row 3: Sl st in each of 5 sts, pat to last 5 sts. Turn.
Row 4: Work even.
Row 5: Rep Row 3. There are 21(23-25-25-27-29-31) sts for back of neck.
Front: Join yarn in first st. Work to correspond to other front, reversing all shaping.
Finishing: Sew shoulder and underarm seams. From right side, beg at lower right front edge, work sc on front edge to beg of neck, spacing sts to keep edge flat. Ch 1, turn. Work 3 rows of 1 sc in each sc, ch 1, turn at end of every row. Beg at neck edge work same number of sc on left front edge, then work 3 more rows of sc on edge. Fasten off.

From right side, beg at right front neck edge, of band, work sc around neck, spacing sts to keep edge flat and holding neck to desired fit. Ch 1, turn. Work 1 or 2 rows of 1 sc in each sc as desired.

From right side work 1 row sc on lower edge and 2 rows sc around armholes.

Scallop Trim: Join yarn at lower right front edge, *ch 3, dc in same st, sk 2 sts, sc in next st; rep from * on front, around neck, on other front and lower edge. Join with a sl st and fasten off.

Work trim around armholes.

Make a buttonloop on right front at neck edge, sew button on left front.

CROCHET DRESS

Instructions are for size 12. Changes for sizes 14, and 16 are in parentheses.

MATERIALS — Brunswick Pomfret Sport Yarn (2-oz) 11 (12-13), Round Elastic

CROCHET HOOK: "Susan Bates" Size E OR SIZE TO GIVE GAUGE

GAUGE: 5 sts = 1 inch, 7 rows = 2 inches

FINISHED MEASUREMENTS (in inches)

Bust 36 1/2(38-41)
Hipline 38(40-42)

Pattern Stitch: Worked on a multiple of 3 sts plus 2 extra st.

Foundation Row: Dc in 4th chain from hook and in each ch to end. 98(104-110) dc, counting ch-3 at beg of row as 1 dc. Ch 3, turn (counts as first dc of next row).

Row 1 (wrong side): Sk first dc, dc in next dc, * yo hook insert hook from front to back to front around 3rd dc (hook is behind 3rd dc) draw up a lp and complete dc (dc worked around post of dc - PS), dc in each of next 2 dc, * PS around post of next dc, dc in each of next 2 sts; rep from *, end dc in last dc, dc in top of ch-3. 98(104-110) sts. Ch 3, turn.

Row 2: Sk first dc, PS around next dc, * dc in next dc, PS around each of next 2 dc; rep from *, end PS around last dc, dc in top of turning ch. Ch 3, turn. Rep Rows 1 and 2 for Pat. Keep continuity when shaping.

Back: Chain 100(106-110) to measure approx 20(21-22) inches.

Work Foundation Row as above. 98(104-110) sts. Continue in pat to 18 inches from beg, or 6 1/2 inches less than desired length to waistline.

Next Row: Sk first st, yo, draw up a lp in next st, yo and thru 2 lps on hook, yo, draw up a lp in next st, yo and thru 2 lps, yo and thru 3 lps (1 st decreased), continue pat to last 3 sts, decrease 1 st, dc in top of turning ch. 1 st decreased each side. Continue pat, decreasing 1 st each side (as above) every 4th row 4 times more. Work on 88(94-100) sts to 24 1/2 inches, or 1 1/2 inches less than desired length to waistline and mark for waistline. Work even to 8 1/2(9-9 1/2) inches above marked waistline, or desired length to underarm.

Armholes: Sl st in each of 3(4-4) sts, work pat to last 3(4-4) sts.

Decrease 1 st each side *every* row 3(4-5) times. Work on 76(78-82) sts until armholes measure 7(7 1/2-8) inches.

Shoulders: * Sl st across 7(7-8) sts, work pat to last 7(7-8) sts, turn. Rep last row once.

Front: Work same as back to 5 inches above waistline marker 88(94-100) sts. Ch 3, turn.

Next Row: Work 2 sts in first st (1 st inc), continue pat to last st, 2 sts in last st, dc in top of turning ch. (1 st inc each side).

Continue pat, inc 1 st each side every 1 inch 3 times more. Work on 96(102-108) until 9(9 1/2-10) inches above waistline marker.

Armholes: Sl st in each of 4(5-5) sts, work to last 4(5-5) sts. Turn.

Dec 1 st each side *every* row 6(7-8) times. Work on 76(78-82) until armholes measure 5 inches.

Neck: Work 21(22-24) sts, place marker, skip center 34 sts; join 2nd ball of yarn, work to end. Working on each side with separate yarn, decrease 1 st at each neck edge *every* row 7(8-8) times AND AT SAME TIME when armholes measure same length as back armholes, shape shoulders as on back.

Bow: Chain 6. Sc in 2nd and each ch to end. Ch 1, turn. Work rows of 5 sc, ch 1 at end of every row until piece measures 15 inches from beg. Fasten off. Make a 2nd piece to measure 17 inches from beg.

Finishing: Sew shoulder and sleeve seams. If desired, turn 1 inch hem around neck edge and sew in place. Turn 1/2 inch hem around armholes and sew in place. Turn 1 inch at lower edge and sew for hem. Cut two lengths of round elastic to desired waist measurements. Weave strands over and under pattern at waistline. Secure ends. Make a bow of two strips (as shown in photograph). Sew at waist as desired.

CROCHET CLUSTER POINT AFGHAN

Approximate Size 50 X 63 inches (without fringe)

MATERIALS — Brunswick Germantown Knitting Worsted (4-oz) 5 each of Saffron (S), and Burnt Orange (B), 4 each of Persimmon (P) and Orange (O)

CROCHET HOOK: "Susan Bates" Size F OR SIZE TO GIVE GAUGE

GAUGE: 4 sc = 1 inch, 26 rows = 6 inches

Cluster Pattern: Worked in 1 stitch. Yo hook, draw up a lp in st, yo hook, draw up a lp in same st twice more, yo and through 7 lps on hook.

Note: In Row 1 of pat st, 5 sc are worked in 1 st. This has a tendency to spread, pulling the next st so tight that it seems to disappear. Be sure *not* to skip this tight st.

Afghan

With S chain 296 to measure 50 inches.

Row 1 (wrong side): 3 sc in 2nd ch from hook, * sc in each of next 9 ch, sk 2 ch, sc in each of next 9 ch, 5 sc in next ch; rep from *, end last rep 3 sc in last ch. Ch 1, turn.

Rows 2 and 3: 2 sc in first st, * sc in each of next 10 sts, sk 2 sts, sc in each of next 10 sts, 3 sc in next st (center st of point); rep from *, end last rep 2 sc in last st. Ch 1, turn.

Row 4 (Cluster Row): Cluster in first st, * (ch 1, sk 1 st, cluster in next st) 5 times, sk 2 sts, cluster in next st, (ch 1, sk 1 st, cluster in next st) 5 times, ch 1, sk 1 st, cluster in next stitch (center of point); rep from *, ending cluster in last st. Ch 1, turn.

Row 5: 3 sc in first cluster, * sc in each of next 9 sts (1 st in cluster and 1 st in each sp between clusters), sk 2 clusters at center of V, sc in each of next 9 sts, 5 sc in cluster at top of point; rep from *, end 3 sc in last cluster. Ch 1, turn.

Rows 6 and 7: Rep Row 2 and 3. Cut S. * With P rep Row 2 three times, then rep Rows 4 through 7 once *. Cut P. With O rep between *s once. Cut O. With B rep between *s once. Cut B. Keeping color sequence as established, rep Row 2 three times, then Rows 4 through 7 with each color 5 times more. Piece will measure approx 61 inches. With S rep the 7 rows once more. Fasten off.

Finishing: From right side, beg at foundation chain with S, work sc on side edge of S stripe, spacing sts to keep edge flat. Draw P through lp on hook, cut S. Continue in this way to work sc on side edge, matching colors. Beg at last row work sc on other side to correspond.

Fringe: Wrap B around an 8-inch cardboard. **Using 8 strands, place fringe at points of ends.**

ROSETTE BABY BLANKET

Approximate Size 20 x 26 inches (including border)

MATERIALS — Brunswick Delf Baby Yarn or Windspun (1-oz). 8 White (A) and 7 Green (B)
CROCHET HOOK: "Susan Bates" Size D OR SIZE TO GIVE GAUGE

GAUGE: 1 Motif = 3 inches square

Work all rounds from right side.
First Motif: With A ch 10, join with sl st to first ch to form a ring. Ch 1.
Rnd 1: Work 24 sc in ring, sl st in first sc.
Rnd 2: * Ch 3, sk 2 sc, 1 sc in next sc; rep from * around (8 ch-3 lps) Ch 1.
Rnd 3: * 1 sc, 1 hdc, 3 dc, 1 hdc, 1 sc — all in next loop (petal made) rep from * around, working last sc of last petal in first ch 1.(8 petals).
Rnd 4: * Ch 4, keeping ch behind petal work 1 sc between last sc of petal and first sc of next petal; rep from * around (8 lps) Ch 1.
Rnd 5: * 1 sc, 1 hdc, 5 dc, 1 hdc, 1 sc — all in next lp; rep from * around, end last sc of last petal in first ch-1.
Rnd 6: Work as for rnd 4, chaining 5 instead of 4 for each loop. Ch 1.
Rnd 7: * 1 sc, 1 hdc, 6 dc, 1 hdc, 1 sc — all in next lp; rep from * around, end last sc of last petal in ch-1. Fasten off A.
Rnd 8: Join B with sl st between 2 center dc of any petal, ch 1, sc in same place, *ch 5, working between 2 center dc of next petal, work 2 hdc, ch 3, 2 hdc, ch 5, 2 hdc, ch 3, 2 hdc — all in same place for corner, ch 5, 1 sc between 2 dc at center of next petal; rep from * 3 times more, end last rep ch 5, sl st in first sc. Fasten off.
2nd Motif: Work first 7 rnds as before. Fasten off A.
Rnd 8: Join B and work same as Rnd 8 until first 2 corners have been completed, end ch 5, 1 sc in center of a petal, ch 5, — 2 hdc, ch 3, 2 hdc in center of next petal, join to edge of first motif as follows: hold first motif behind 2nd motif with wrong sides together, ch 2, sc in ch-5 lp of first motif, ch 2, 2 hdc, in corner of 2nd motif, ch 1, sc in ch-3 lp of first motif, ch 1, 2 hdc in corner of 2nd motif, ch 2, sc in next ch-5 loop of first motif, ch 2, sc in center of next petal on 2nd motif, ch 2, sc in next lp on first motif, ch 2, 2 hdc, in center of next petal of 2nd motif, ch 1, sc in next ch-3 lp on first motif, ch 1, 2 hdc in same corner of 2nd motif, ch 2, sc in ch-5 lp of first motif, ch 2, 2 hdc, ch 3, 3 hdc in corner of 2nd motif, ch 5, join with sl st in first sc of 2nd motif. Fasten off. Continue in this way until 8 motifs have been joined for First Strip.

2nd Strip: Work first motif until first corner on rnd 8 has been completed, ch 5, sc in center of next petal, ch 5, 2 hdc, ch 3, 2 hdc, in next corner, holding motif in front of first motif of first strip (wrong sides together), ch 2, sc in ch-5 lp of first motif in strip, ch 2, continue to join edges until next ch-5 corner lps are joined, complete 3rd corner and finish rnd.

Work 2nd motif until 7 rnds have been completed.

Rnd 8 — Joining: Join B at center of any petal, ch 1, 1 sc in same place, ch 5, 2 hdc, ch 3, 2 hdc, in center of next petal, ch 2, sc in free ch-5 lp at lower right edge of first motif, ch 2, 2 hdc, ch 1 in corner of 2nd motif, continue to join upper edge of 2nd motif to lower edge of first motif and side edge of 2nd motif to side edge of 2nd motif in first strip, complete 3rd corner and finish rnd.

Continue in this manner until 6 strips of 8 motifs each have been joined.

Border
Rnd 1: With B from right side work 1 sc in any ch-5 corner lp, * ch 3, 1 sc in next ch-3 lp, ch 3, 1 sc in ch-5 lp, ch 3, 1 sc in next ch-5 lp, ch 3, 1 sc in ch-3 lp, ch 3, 1 sc over joining sc between next 2 ch-5 lps; rep from * along edge, end ch 3, 1 sc in corner lp; rep from first * around, end ch 3, sl st in first sc.
Rnd 2: Ch 1, — 1 sc, ch 1, 1 sc all in same st as sl st (corner), * ch 1, 1 sc in center st of ch-3, ch 1, 1 sc in next sc*; rep between *s to corner, work ch 1, 1 sc, ch 1, 1 sc in corner; rep from first * around, increasing at corners as before, end ch 1, sl st in first sc.
Rnd 3: Ch 1, 1 sc, ch 1, 1 sc in ch-1 corner sp, * ch 1, sk 1 sc, 1 sc in next ch-1 sp; rep from * to corner, ch 1, 1 sc, ch 1, 1 sc in ch-1 corner sp, ch 1, 1 sc in next ch-1 sp, continue around, increasing at corners, as before, end ch 1, sl st in first sc.

Rep rnd 3 three times more, or to desired width of border. Fasten off.

Steam lightly. If desired, line blanket with same color as B.

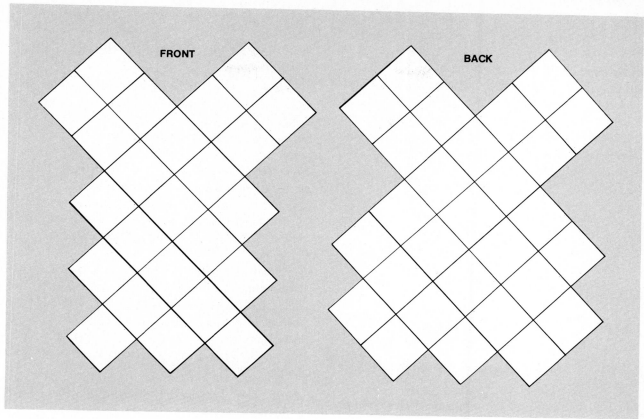

FRONT   BACK

CROCHET SHORT SLEEVE SWEATER

Instructions are for Small, Medium and Large Sizes. Changes for sizes are made by changing Size of Crochet Hook. Instructions are written for Small Sizes. Changes for Medium and Large Sizes are in parentheses.

MATERIALS — Brunswick Windspun (1-oz) 7 MC and 1 skein each of 7 desired colors
CROCHET HOOK: "Susan Bates" Size E for Small Size; Size F for Medium Size and Size G for Large Size OR SIZE TO GIVE GAUGE

GAUGE: Square (Size E Hook) = 4 inches square, Square (Size F Hook) = 4½ inches square, Square (Size G Hook) = 5 inches square

FINISHED MEASUREMENTS (in inches):
Bust 33(37½-41)

Note: Work all rnds from right side.

Motif: Use 2 colors and black. With first color ch 5, join with a sl st in first ch to form a ring. Ch 3 (counts as first dc).

Rnd 1: 2 dc in ring, *ch 3, 3 dc in ring; rep from * twice more, ch 3, join with a sl st to 3rd ch of first ch-3. Ch 6 (first dc and first ch-2 lp).
Rnd 2: *Sk 3 dc, work 3 dc, ch 3, 3 dc in ch-3 sp for corner, ch 2; rep from * twice, 3 dc, ch 3, 2 dc in last corner. Break first color, tie in 2nd color and join by working sl st in 4th ch of ch-6 sp. Ch 3. (Always change color by working sl st with new color for joining).
Rnd 3: 2 dc in first sp, *ch 2, 3 dc, ch 3, 3 dc in corner sp, ch 2, 3 dc in next sp; rep from * twice, ch 2, 3 dc, ch 3, 3 dc in corner sp, ch 2, sl st in 3rd ch of ch-3. Ch 6.
Rnd 4: 3 dc in next sp, *ch 2, 3 dc, ch 3, 3 dc in corner (ch 2, 3 dc in next sp) twice; rep from * twice; ch 2, 3 dc, ch 3, 3 dc in last corner, ch 2, 2 dc in next sp; break yarn; tie in MC and work sl st in ch-6 sp. Ch 3.
Rnd 5: 2 dc in first sp, ch 2, 3 dc in next sp, *ch 2, 3 dc, ch 3, 3 dc in corner, (ch 2, 3 dc in next sp) 3 times; rep from * twice, ch 2, 3 dc, ch 3, 3 dc in corner, ch 2, 3 dc in last sp, ch 2, sl st in 3rd st of ch-3. Fasten off.

Make 52 square, using colors as illustrated or as desired for first 4 rnds. Always use MC for last rnd.

Finishing: Arrange squares as given on charts, see page 227. Sew squares together for front and back, using an overcast st and sewing from wrong side through *back* loop of sts. Sew shoulder and side seams, leaving neck and armhole opening free. From right side, work 3 rows sc around neck, keeping work flat.

METALLIC CROCHET TOP

Instructions are for size 8-10. Changes for size 12-14 are in parentheses.

MATERIALS — Sport Yarn Weight Metallic Yarn

CROCHET HOOK: "Susan Bates" Size F OR SIZE TO GIVE GAUGE

GAUGE: 3 shell patterns = 4¼ inches, 9 rows = 3 inches

FINISHED MEASUREMENTS (in inches)
Bust 34 (37)

Pattern Stitch: Worked on a multiple of 8 chain plus 2 extra chain.

Back: Chain 98 (106) loosely.

Row 1 (right side): Sc in 2nd ch from hook, * sk 3 ch, work — 1 dc, ch 1, 1 dc, ch 1, 1 tr, ch 1, 1 dc, ch 1, 1 dc — all in next ch (shell made), sk 3 ch, 1 sc in next ch; rep from * across ch, end with sc in last ch; 12 (13) full shells. Ch 4, turn (counts as first dc and ch-1).

Row 2: Dc in first sc, ch 2, * 1 sc in center st (tr) of shell, ch 2, — 1 dc, ch 1, 1 dc — all in next sc, ch 2; rep from * across row, end 1 sc in center st of last shell, ch 2, 1 dc, ch 1, 1 dc in last sc. Ch 4, turn.

Row 3: 1 dc, ch 1, 1 dc in first ch-1 sp between 2 dc, 1 sc in next sc, *1 shell in next ch-1 sp, 1 sc in next sc; rep from * across row, end 1 dc, ch 1, 1 dc, ch 1, 1 dc in last ch-4 sp — 11 (12) full shells, plus ½ shell each side. Ch 1, turn.

Row 4: Sc in first dc, * ch 2, 1 dc, ch 1, 1 dc in next sc, ch 2, sc in center st of shell; rep from * across row, end last sc in ch-4 sp. Ch 1, turn.

Row 5: Sc in first sc, * shell in next ch-1 sp, sc in next sc; rep from * to end; 12 (13) shells. Ch 4, turn.

Rep rows 2, 3, 4 and 5 for pat. Work until about 14 inches from beg., or to desired length to underarm, end on wrong side with pat Row 4. Turn.

Armholes: Leave off 1 pat each side as follows: Sl st loosely across first 8 sts, ch 1, 1 sc in next sc, shell in next ch-1 sp, continue pat until 10 (11) shells, end with sc; leave last pat free for other armhole. Turn.

First Dec Row: Sl st loosely to within 1 st of center of first shell, ch 1, sc in center tr of shell; *ch 2, 1 dc, ch 1, 1 dc in next sc, ch 2, sc in center of next shell; rep from * across row, end sc in center of last shell — ½ pat decreased each side. Ch 1, turn.

Next Row: Sc in first sc, work shell in ch-1 sp between next 2 dc, continue pat until 9 (10) full shells, end sc in last sc. Turn.

Second Dec Row: Rep first dec row. Ch 1, turn.

Next Row: Sc in first sc, continue pat, end sc in last sc. 8 (9) full shells. *This completes armhole shaping.* Ch 4, turn.

Work 11 (15) rows even, end with Pat Row 4. Ch 1, turn.

Neck and Shoulders: Row 1 (right side): Work 3 full shells, end with sc. Turn.

First Dec Row: Sl st loosely to within 1 st of center of first shell, ch 1, 1 sc in center tr of shell, ch 2, work even to end — ½ pat dec at neck.

Work 1 row even. Dec ½ pat at neck edge on neck row, work to end (2 pats). Work 2 (0) rows even and fasten off — about 7 (7¾) inches above underarm.

From right side sk next 2 (3) pats of last long row for neck, join yarn in next sc, ch 1, 1 sc in same st, work 3 shells, end with sc. Finish to correspond to other side.

Front: Same as Back until armhole shaping is completed. Work 3 (7) rows even, end with Pat Row 3. Ch 1, turn. Shape Neck and Shoulders as for Back, working even on 2 pats for each shoulder until armholes are same length as back. Fasten off.

Finishing: Sew side and shoulder seams. From right side, work 2 rows sc around neck and armhole edges, keeping work flat, or holding in to desired size. Work 1 row sc around lower edge. Steam lightly.

ROUND TABLE MAT

Approximate Size 15-inch diameter

MATERIALS — Lily Mercerized Bedspread Cotton

CROCHET HOOK: "Susan Bates" Steel Size 2 OR SIZE TO GIVE GAUGE

GAUGE: 15 sc = 2 inches

Chain 6, join with sl st to first ch to form a ring. Ch 3, turn.

Rnd 1: 11 dc in ring, join with sl st to 3rd ch of ch-3. 12 dc (ch 3 counts as 1 dc). Ch 9, do not turn. *All* rnds are worked from the right side.

Rnd 2: 1 tr in same place as sl st, ch 3, *work group of — 1 tr, ch 3, 1 tr, ch 3 — all in next dc; rep from * 10 times more, end join last ch 3 with sl st to 6th ch of ch-9. 24 ch-3 sps. Ch 3.

Rnd 3: 2 dc in same st as sl st, *ch 1, 3 dc in next tr; rep from * 22 times more, ch 1, sl st in top of ch-3. 24 groups. Ch 7.

Rnd 4: 1 dc in ch-1 sp between first and 2nd group, *ch 4, 1 dc in next sp; rep from * around, end ch 4, sl st in 3rd ch of ch-7. 24 lps. Ch 1.

Rnd 5: 4 sc in each loop, sl st in first sc. 96 sc.

Rnd 6: Sc in same st as sl st, 1 sc in each of next 10 sc, 2 sc in next sc (inc) * 11 sc, 2 sc in next sc; rep from * 6 times more. 104 sc, join. Ch 1.

Rnd 7: 1 sc in each sc. Join with sl st to first sc and ch 1 at beginning of all sc rnds.

Rnd 8: Inc 1 sc in 7th sc, then in every 13th sc 7 times, finish rnd. 112 sc.

Work 1 rnd even.

Rnd 10: Inc 1 sc in every 14th sc 8 times. 120 sc. Work 1 rnd even.

Rnd 12: Inc 1 sc in 7th, then in every 15th sc 7 times, finish rnd. 128 sc, join. Ch 3.

Rnd 13: 2 dc in same st as sl st, * ch 1, sk 3 sc, 3 dc in next sc; rep from * around, end ch 1, join in top of ch-3; 32 sps.

Rnd 14: Sl st in first sp, ch 3, 2 dc in same sp, * ch 2, 3 dc in next sp; rep from *, end ch 2, join.

Rnd 15: Same as Rnd 14, but ch 3 instead of ch 2 between groups. 32 groups and 32 sps. Ch 1.

Rnd 16: 1 sc in same st as sl st, 1 sc in each of next 2 dc, * 3 sc in next sp, 1 sc in each of 3 dc; rep from * around, end 3 sc in sp, join. 192 sc.

Rnd 17: Inc 1 sc in every 48th sc 4 times 196 sc.

Rnd 18: Inc 1 sc in 24th sc, then in every 49th sc 3 times, finish rnd. 200 sc.

Inc 4 sc in each of next 5 rnds, spacing incs between incs of previous rnd 220 sc. Join. Ch 3.

Rnd 24: Work as for rnd 13. 55 sps.

Rnd 25: Work as for rnd 14.

Rnd 26 and 27: Work as for rnd 15.

Rnd 28: Work as for rnd 16. 330 sc.

Work 6 rnds sc, increasing if necessary to keep work flat, join.

Final Rnd: Work sc working from left to right, for backward sc. Join and fasten off.

Steam lightly.

FILET BRIM HAT

MATERIALS — Brunswick Icecap (1-oz) 4 skeins

CROCHET HOOK: "Susan Bates" No. 2 OR SIZE TO GIVE GAUGE

GAUGE: 13 sc = 2 inches,
13 rows = 2 inches

To Begin: Ch. 6. Join with a sl st to first ch to form a ring.

Rnd 1: 8 sc in ring.

Rnd 2: 2 sc in each sc (16 sc).

Rnd 3: * Sc in sc, 2 sc in next sc; rep from * around (24 sc).

Rnd 4: * Sc in each of 3 sc, 2 sc in next sc; rep from * around (32 sc).

Rnd 5: Sc inc 1 st in every 4th sc (40 sc).

Rnd 6: Sc, inc 1 st in every 5th sc (48 sc).

Continue in this way to inc 8 sts every rnd having 1 st more between incs in each rnd until there are 72 sc in rnd.

Rnd 10: Sc in each sc.

Inc 8 sts in each of next 3 rnds (96 sc).

Rnd 14: Sc in each sc.

Inc 8 sts in each of next 2 rnds. (112 sc).

Rnd 17: Sc in each sc.

Inc 8 sts in each of next 2 rnds (128 sc).

Rnd 20: Ch 4 (counts as 1 dc and ch-2), sk 1 sc, dc in next sc, (sk 1 sc, ch 2, dc in next sc) 6 times, ch 2, sk 2 sc, dc in next sc, sk 1 sc, ch 2, dc in next sc) 7 times, ch 2, sk 2 sc, dc in next sc; rep from * end ch 2, (sk 1 sc, ch 2, dc in next sc) 3 times, ch 2, join with a sl st to 2nd of ch-4. (60 mesh — 180 sts).

Rnds 21 through 34: Follow chart beg each rnd ch 4 and end with sl st in 2nd ch of ch-4.

Rnd 35: Sc in same st with joining, 2 sc in ch-2 sp, continue working sc in dc, 2 sc in ch-2 sp and skipping every 3rd dc around. (160 sc).

Rnds 35 thru 38: Sc in each sc.

Rnd 39: Sc around inc 1 st every 10th sc (176 sc).

Rnd 40: Sc, inc 1 st in every 11th st (192 sc).

Inc 16 sts in each of next 3 rnds. (240 sc).

Rnds 44 through 49: Sc in each sc.

Rnd 50: * Sc in each of 13 sc, draw up a lp in each of next 2 sc, yo and through 3 lps on hook (1 st dec), rep from * around. (224 sc).

Rnd 51 through 53: Sc in each sc.

Rnd 54: * Sc in each of 12 sc, dec 1 st; rep from * around. (208 sc).

Rnd 55 and 56: Sc in each sc.

Rnd 57: * Sc in each of 11 sc, dec 1 st; rep from * around. (192 sc).

Rnd 58 through 61: Sc in each sc.

Rnd 62: * Sc in each of 10 sc, dec 1 st; rep from * around. (176 sc).

Work 2 rnds even. Join with a sl st to first sc and fasten off.

Double brim as shown in photograph and tack if desired.

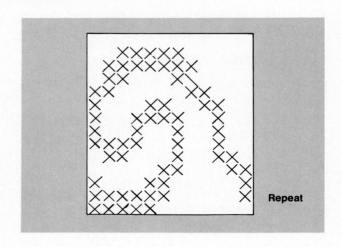

Repeat

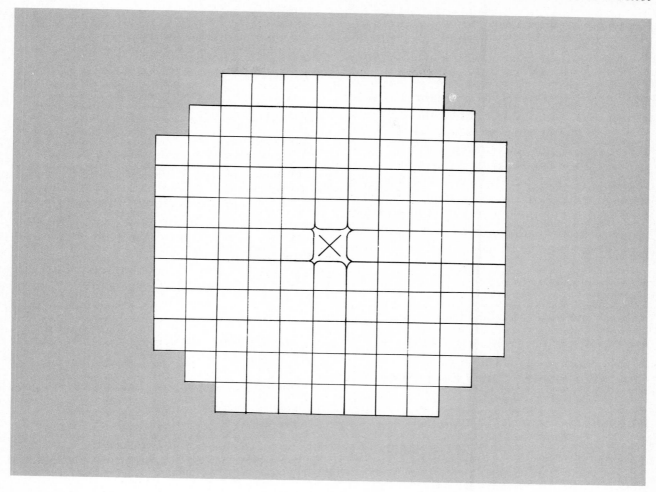

CHILD'S PONCHO

Instructions are for Small and Medium Sizes. Changes in Size are made by changing size of crochet hook. Instructions are for Small Size. Change for Medium Size is in parentheses.

MATERIALS — Brunswick Germantown Knitting Worsted or Windrush (4-oz). One each of Orange (O), Yellow (Y), Gold (G), and White (W), Pale Green (PG) and Dark Green (DG)
CROCHET HOOK: "Susan Bates" Size F for Small; Size G for Medium Size OR SIZE TO GIVE GAUGE

GAUGE: Motif (Size F Hook) = 3¼ inches square, Motif (Size G Hook) = 3¾ inches square

FINISHED MEASUREMENTS (in inches): 36 (42) inches square.

Note: Work all rounds from right side.
Motif: With one color chain 4, join with a sl st to first ch to form a ring. Ch 3 (counts for first dc).
Rnd 1: Work 1 dc in ring, *ch 3, 3 dc in ring; rep from * twice more; ch 3, 1 dc in ring, join with a sl st to 3rd ch of ch-3. Ch 3.
Rnd 2: Dc in next dc, * 2 dc, ch 3, 2 dc in ch-3 (corner sp), dc in each of next 3 dc; rep from * twice more, 2 dc, ch 3, 2 dc in corner sp, dc in last dc, join. Ch 3.
Rnd 3: Dc in each of next 3 dc, *2 dc, ch 3, 2 dc in corner sp, dc in each of next 7 dc; rep from * twice more, 2 dc, ch 3, 2 dc in corner sp, dc in each of next 3 dc, join. 44 dc, plus 4 ch-3 corner sps. Fasten off. Make 108 motifs, using assorted colors.

Finishing: Arrange motifs as on chart, using colors as desired and omitting center motif (marked "X" on chart) for opening of neck. Sew motifs together from center ch of corner sp to center ch of next corner sp, matching sts, and sewing from wrong side with an overcast stitch through top loop of sts.

Important: To make neck opening large enough, sew the 8 seams which terminate at neck edge to last dc before corner ch, leaving all ch-3 corners free for neck opening.

From right side, with desired color, work 1 row sc around neck, working 1 sc in each dc and 2 or 3 sc in each ch-3 at seams as required, join. Work 2nd sc row if desired, working 1 sc in each sc, join and fasten off. From right side, work 1 row sc around entire outer edge, working 1 sc in each st on straight edges, 3 sc in each outer corner; to keep work flat,on inner corner draw up a loop in last st of square and first st of next square and work off as 1 sc. Steam lightly if desired.

HAT WITH BRIM

Approximate Head Size 20 Inches

MATERIALS — Brunswick Fore 'N Aft or Wintuk Sport (2-oz) 1 ball
CROCHET HOOK: "Susan Bates" Size E OR SIZE TO GIVE GAUGE

GAUGE: 5 sc = 1 inch, 5 rnds = 1 inch

Crown: Chain 3, join with a sl st to form a ring. Ch 1. Mark end of rnds.
Rnd 1: Work 9 sc in center of rnd.
Rnd 2: 2 sc in each sc. 18 sc.
Rnd 3: * Sc in 1 sc, 2 sc in next sc (1 st inc); rep from * around. 27 sc.
Rnd 4: *Sc in each of 2 sc, 2 sc in next sc; rep from * around. 36 sc.
Rnd 5: * Sc in each of 3 sc, 2 sc in next sc; rep from * around. 45 sc.
Rnd 6: Sc in each sc. 45 sc.
Rnd 7: Inc 1 st in every 5th st. 54 sc.
Rnd 8: Inc 1 st in every 6th st. 63 sc.
Rnd 9: Sc in each sc. 63 sc.
Rnd 10: Inc 1 st in every 7th st. 72 sc.
Rnd 11: Inc 1 st in every 8th st. 81 sc.
Rnd 12: Sc in each sc. 81 sc.
Rnd 13: Inc 1 st in every 9th st. 90 sc.
Rnd 14: Inc 1 st in every 10th st. 99 sc.

Work even until crown measures 7½ inches from beg.

Brim

Row 1: Inc 1 st in every 3rd st. 132 sc.
Row 2: Sc in each of 36 sts, mark last st, sc in each

of next 60 sc, mark last st. Turn. From now on work back and forth in rows.
Row 3 (wrong side): Sc in each st to marker, sc in each of next 5 sts, sl st in next st. Turn. Mark end of each row.
Row 4: Sc in each sc to marker at other side, sc in each of next 5 sts, sl st in next st. Turn.
Row 5: Sc in each sc to marker, sc in each st to 5 sts after end of Row 3, sl st in next st. Turn.
Row 6: Sc in each sc to marker, sc in each st to 5 sts after end of Row 4, sl st in next st. Turn.
Row 7 (wrong side): Work sc across brim sts, across sts at back, across sts of brim again then over 5 more sts, sl st in next st. Turn. Rep rows 4 through 7 twice more.
Last Row: Sc in each st around. Join with a sl st to first sc. Fasten off. Turn up Brim. Trim as desired.

CROCHET BEDSPREAD TRADITIONAL ELEGANCE

Approximate Size 72½ x 87 inches (without fringe)

MATERIALS — Lily Mercerized Crochet Cotton, Art. 65, Size 20, 51 skeins
CROCHET HOOK: "Susan Bates" Steel, Size 9 OR SIZE TO GIVE GAUGE

GAUGE: Each square = 7¼ inches square

Note: Work in *back* loop of each st throughout.
Square: (Make 120). Chain 8 for center. Join with sl st to first ch to form a ring.

Rnd 1: * 1 sc in each of next 2 ch, ch 3; rep from * 3 times more. Do not join, continue in rounds.
Rnd 2: Sc in each of next 2 sc, * sc in next ch, ch 3, sk 1 ch, sc in next ch (corner made and 2 sts increased), sc in each of next 2 sc; rep from * twice more, sc in next ch, ch 3, sk 1 ch, sc in next ch.
Rnd 3: Sc in each of next 3 sc, * sc in next ch, ch 3, sk 1 ch, sc in next ch, sc in each of next 4 sc; rep from * twice more; to finish rnd work sc in next ch; ch 3, sk 1 ch, sc in next ch. Work last corner for end of rnd. All rnds end in this way.
Rnd 4: 5 sc, * work corner, 6 sc; rep from * twice more, work last corner to finish rnd.
Rnd 5: Picot Rnd: 3 sc, ch 4, sl st into same place as last sc made (picot); 4 sc, * work corner, 4 sc, 1 picot, 4 sc; rep from * twice more, finish rnd.
Rnd 6: Keeping picots on right side, 9 sc, * work

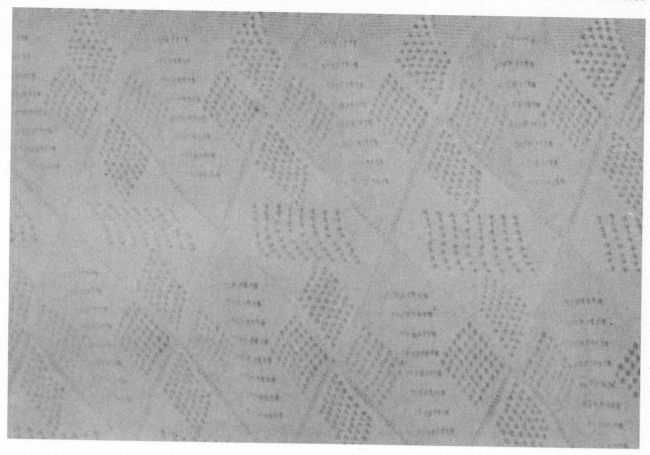

corner, 10 sc; rep from * twice more, finish rnd.

Rnd 7: 3 sc, picot, 4 sc, picot, 4 sc, * work corner, 4 sc, picot, 4 sc, picot, 4 sc; rep from * twice more, finish rnd.

Rnd 8: 13 sc, * work corner, 14 sc; rep from * twice more, finish rnd.

Rnd 9: 3 sc, (picot, 4 sc) 3 times, * work corner, 4 sc, (picot, 4 sc) 3 times; rep from * twice more, finish rnd.

Rnd 10: 17 sc, * work corner, 18 sc; rep from * twice more, finish rnd.

Rnd 11: 3 sc, (picot, 4 sc) 4 times, * work corner, 4 sc, (picot, 4 sc) 4 times; rep from * twice more, finish rnd.

Rnd 12: 21 sc, * work corner, 22 sc; rep from * twice more, finish rnd.

Rnd 13: 3 sc (picot, 4 sc) 5 times, * work corner, 4 sc, (picot, 4 sc) 5 times; rep from * twice more, finish rnd.

Rnd 14: 25 sc, * work corner, 26 sc; rep from * twice more, finish rnd.

Rnd 15: 3 sc, (picot, 4 sc) 6 times, * work corner, 4 sc, (picot, 4 sc) 6 times; rep from * twice more, finish rnd.

Rnd 16: 29 sc, * work corner, 30 sc; rep from * twice more, finish rnd.

Rnd 17: 3 sc, (picot, 4 sc) 7 times, * work corner, 4 sc, (picot, 4 sc) 7 times; rep from * twice more, finish rnd.

Rnd 18: 33 sc, * work corner, 34 sc; rep from * twice more, finish rnd.

Rnd 19: 7 sc, (picot, 4 sc) 5 times, picot, 8 sc, * work corner, 8 sc, (picot, 4 sc) 5 times, picot, 8 sc; rep from * twice more, finish rnd.

Rnd 20: 37 sc, * work corner, 38 sc; rep from * twice more, finish rnd.

Rnd 21: 11 sc, (picot, 4 sc) 4 times, picot, 12 sc, * work corner, 12 sc, (picot, 4 sc) 4 times, picot, 12 sc; rep from * twice more, finish rnd.

Rnd 22: 41 sc, * work corner, 42 sc; rep from * twice more, finish rnd.

Rnd 23: 15 sc, (picot, 4 sc) 3 times, picot, 16 sc, * work corner, 16 sc, (picot, 4 sc) 3 times, picot, 16 sc; rep from * twice more, finish rnd.

Rnd 24: 45 sc, * work corner, 46 sc; rep from * twice more, finish rnd.

Rnd 25: 19 sc, (picot, 4 sc) twice, picot, 20 sc, * work corner, 20 sc, (picot, 4 sc) twice, picot, 20

Crochet / 238

sc; rep from * twice more, finish rnd.

Rnd 26: 49 sc, * work corner, 50 sc; rep from * twice more, finish row.

Rnd 27: 23 sc, picot, 4 sc, picot, 24 sc, * work corner, 24 sc, picot, 4 sc, picot, 24 sc; rep from * twice more, finish row.

Rnd 28: 53 sc, * work corner, 54 sc; rep from * twice more, finish rnd.

Rnd 29: 27 sc, picot, 28 sc, * work corner, 28 sc, picot, 28 sc; rep from * twice more, finish rnd.

Rnd 30: 57 sc, * work corner, 58 sc; rep from * twice more, finish rnd.

Rnd 31: 8 sc, (picot, 6 sc) 7 times, picot, 9 sc, * work corner, 9 sc, (picot, 6 sc) 7 times, picot, 9 sc; rep from * twice more, finish rnd.

Rnd 32: 61 sc, * work corner, 62 sc; rep from * twice more, finish rnd.

Rnd 33: 10 sc, (picot, 6 sc) 7 times, picot, 11 sc, * work corner, 11 sc, (picot, 6 sc) 7 times, picot, 11 sc; rep from * twice more.

Working corners as before, rep 8 picots on each side every 2nd rnd twice more, keeping picots directly above each other. Work 1 rnd without picots, sl st in next st, fasten off.

Finishing: Sew or crochet squares together, having 10 squares in width, 12 squares in length.

Edging: From right side, beginning at right top corner of spread, work 1 dc, ch 2, 1 dc in corner, * ch 1, sk 1 sc, 1 dc in next sc; rep from * to next corner; work around in this manner, end sl st in first dc; continue *across top edge only,* working 1 sc in each dc and in each ch-1. Fasten off.

Fringe: Fringe side and lower edges only. Cut 4 threads each 9 inches long. From wrong side, beginning at top of side edge, fold strands in half and draw folded end through ch-1 sp (from right to wrong side), draw cut ends through loop and tighten. Rep in every 3rd ch-1 sp on sides and lower edge, knotting 2 tassels into corner sps. Using 4 strands of one tassel and 4 strands of next tassel, make a knot ¾ inches from edge of spread. Continue around.

CROCHET CAP

Approximate size for 6 to 8 years (10 to 12 years)

MATERIALS — Brunswick Germantown Knitting Worsted (4-oz) 1 skein each of 4 or 2 colors as desired

CROCHET HOOK: "Susan Bates" Size F and Size G OR SIZE TO GIVE GAUGE

GAUGE: 7 hdc = 2 inches, 3 rows = 1 inch

Crown: Made in 4 sections and is worked in hdc. Always work hdc between hdc of previous row. Ch 2, turn at end of every row, but *do* not count ch as 1 st.

First Section: With G Hook and desired color, chain 20 (22) to measure 6 (6½) inches for lower edge.

Row 1: Hdc in 3rd ch from hook and in each ch to end. 18 (20) hdc. Ch 2, turn.

Row 2: Work hdc between sts 2 (3) times, 2 hdc between next 2 sts (1 st inc),   (hdc between next 2 sts) 4 times, 2 hdc between next 2 sts 3 times, (hdc between next 2 sts) 4 times, 2 hdc between next 2 sts, (hdc between next 2 sts) 2 (3) times, hdc between last hdc and ch-2. There are 23 (25) hdc. Ch 2, turn.

Work 11 (13) rows of 23 (25) hdc. Ch 2, turn. Place marker on 12th (13th) st from end of center of row.

First Dec Row: (Yo, draw up a lp in next sp, yo and through 2 lps) twice, yo and through 3 lps, (1 st dec), continue pat to 2 sps before center st, dec 1 st, work hdc in next sp, dec 1 st, pat 2 last 2 sps, dec 1 st. 4 decs in row.

Next Row: Work even.

Rep last 2 rows until there are 3 (5) sts in row. *On larger size only,* dec 1 st each side of next row. Fasten off.

Make 3 more sections in same way, using colors as desired. Sew sections together.

With F hook and desired color from right side, work 1 sc in each st. Join with a sl st to first sc. Fasten off.

Peak: Mark off 23 (25) sts for peak so that center of peak will be at center of 1 color section. Join same color as on lower border.

Row 1: From right side work sl st in each of 2 sts, *sc in each of next 2 sts, 2 sc in next st; rep from * to last 2 sc marked for peak. Turn.

Row 2: Sl st in each of 2 sts, * sc in each of next 3 sts, 2 sc in next st; rep from * to last 2 sc, turn.

Continue to sl st over first 2 sts at *beg* of every row and leave 2 sts unworked at *end* of every row until there are 7 rows in all on peak. Fasten off. From right side, work 1 row sc around peak, rounding side edges. Fasten off.

CROCHET AFGHAN

Approximate Size 50 x 50 inches

MATERIALS — Brunswick Fore-'N' Aft Sport or Pomfret (2-oz.) 16 skeins

CROCHET HOOK: "Susan Bates" Size F OR SIZE TO GIVE GAUGE

GAUGE: 1 Motif = 4 inches square

Note: Work all rnds from right side.

Flower Motif (Make 72): Chain 5, join with a sl st to first ch to form a ring.
Rnd 1: *Ch 5, 1 sc in ring; rep from * 4 times (5 lps).
Rnd 2: In first lp *work sc, ch 1, 4 dc, ch 1, 1 sc, (1 petal made); in next lp; rep from * 3 times more; 5 petals.
Rnd 3: *Ch 6, keeping ch behind petal work 1 sc between last sc of petal and first sc of next petal; rep from * 4 times more.
Rnd 4: * 1 sc, ch 1, 6 dc, ch 1, 1 sc in lp; rep from * 4 times more.
Rnd 5: *Ch 7, work 1 sc between petals as on Rnd 3; rep from * 4 times more.
Rnd 6: Sl st in lp, ch 3, (counts as 1 dc), 7 dc in lp, *8 dc in next lp; rep from * 3 times more, join with sl st to 3rd ch of ch-3 (40 dc).
Rnd 7: Ch 3, inserting hook through *back* lp of each st work 1 dc in each of next 9 dc, *ch 5 for corner, 1 dc in each of next 10 dc; rep from * twice more, ch 5, sl st in 3rd ch of ch-3, fasten off.

Plain Motif (Make 72): Chain 5, join with a sl st to first ch to form a ring.
Rnd 1 — Cluster Rnd: Ch 3, yo hook twice, draw up a lp in ring — 4 lps on hook; (yo and through 2 lps) 3 times, ch 3, *yo hook twice, draw up a lp in ring — 4 lps on hook, (yo and through 2 lps) twice; yo hook twice, draw up a lp in ring — 5 lps on hook, (yo and through 2 lps) twice, yo and through 3 lps to complete cluster, ch 3; rep from * 6 times more, join with sl st to top of first cluster; 8 clusters and 8 ch-3 sps.
Rnd 2: Ch 3, 4 dc in ch-3 sp, *5 dc in next sp; rep from * 6 times more; sl st in 3rd ch of ch-3 (40 dc).
Rnd 3: Ch 3, inserting hook through *back* lp of each st work 1 dc in each of next 9 dc, *ch 5 for corner, 1 dc in each of next 10 dc; rep from *

twice more, ch 5, sl st in 3rd ch of ch-3. Fasten off.
Finishing: Join motifs, having 12 in width and 12 in length, alternating plain and flower motifs as illustrated and sewing together from wrong side through back lp of sts.

CROCHET BERET

Head Size Approximately 20/22 inches

MATERIALS — Brunswick Wintuk Sport or Pomfret (4-oz) 2 balls or skeins
CROCHET HOOK: "Susan Bates" Size F OR SIZE TO GIVE GAUGE

GAUGE: 9 dc = 2 inches, 7 rnds = 3 inches

Crown: Chain 4. Join with a sl st to form a ring.
Rnd 1: Ch 3, 13 dc in ring, join with a sl st to top of ch-3. 14 dc counting ch-3 as 1 dc.

Rnd 2: Ch 3, dc in same st with ch-3, 2 dc in each st around. Join each rnd with a sl st to top of ch-3. 28 dc.
Rnd 3: Ch 3, 2 dc in next st, *dc in next st, 2 dc in next st; rep from * around. 42 dc.
Rnd 4: Ch 3, dc in next st, 2 dc in next st, * dc in next st, 2 dc in next st; rep from * around. 56 dc.
Rnd 5: Ch 3, dc in each of next 2 sts, 2 dc in next st, * dc in each of next 3 sts, 2 dc in next st; rep from * around. 70 dc.

Continue in this way to inc 14 sts every rnd, having 1 st more between incs each rnd until there are 10 sts between incs. There are 168 dc in rnd and diameter measures approximately 10½ inches.

Work 3 rnd even.
First Dec Rnd: * Work 10 sts, draw up a lp in each of next 2 sts, yo and through 3 lps on hook (1 st dec); rep from * around. Join. (14 dec).
2nd Dec Rnd: * Work 9 sts, dec; rep from * around. Join.

Continue in this way to dec 14 sts every rnd, having 1 st less between decs each rnd until there are 6 sts between decs.
Headband: Work 6 rnds of one sc in each st. Join and fasten off.
Trim: Chain 13. Work 12 sc on chain . Fasten off, leaving an end for sewing. Fold in half and sew to top of crown.

Hook Arts

Over the centuries people have used textiles to ornament themselves and their houses, and as a result, many techniques for making lacy knotted braids, fabrics and edgings have developed. The simplest methods of knotting were known from the time of the early Mediterranean civilizations when fishermen knotted coarse nets and horsemen made ropes and reins of strong fibers.

During the Renaissance in Europe, lace-making grew to an extremely skilled and important art. For centuries, two styles of handmade lace were made in Italy, Belgium and France. These developed into highly specialized types in each country and region. The basis for most laces is either *Point,* which is worked with a needle over a net base, or *Pillow,* which is worked with the end of the piece anchored to a pillow and the thread carried in bobbins that are braided together.

Today there are few people with the time for such intricate work — even the fine European laces are now made on machines. Mostly in use today is a collection of techniques and types of lacy work requiring only a few simple tools and the knowledge of one or two easy stitches. Several of these laces require a slight knowledge of crochet for joining the strips or pieces made on needles or looms.

The oldest and most intricate one of these lace techniques is tatting, which will be explained in this chapter. A small shuttle and very fine thread

The perfect introduction to creative handiwork for children is Horse Reins Knitting.

are used to create lovely edgings for collars, hand towels and handkerchiefs. Hairpin lace, jiffy-lace and daisy-loom are all moderately simple ways of creating large lace-like areas suitable for afghans and simple garments. Horse reins braid is really a form of knitting that dates back to a time when all strings, shoestrings and related items had to be made by hand. It is especially amusing to children and a fine way to introduce them to hand work. Many attractive items can be made by laying lengths of horse reins in spirals and joining them with needle and thread as in a hooked rug.

These hook arts are what ladies used to call "pick-up work," meaning that a piece of it could be kept in a purse and picked up from time to time. It still serves well for this purpose as there are no intricate patterns requiring the concentration necessary in knitting or crochet. Another bonus to this type of handwork is that, with the exception of tatting, it will not look different even though several people work on it. For bazaars, children's and senior citizens' groups, it is an ideal community project. Each person can make a strip or a group of daisies which can all be joined by one person who crochets. In many cases, scrap yarn can be used in a gloriously colorful afghan, scarf or horse reins rug. Supplying a group of people with the equipment for any of these techniques is not as expensive as planning large sewing projects requiring machines and cutting tables.

Macramé is another knotting technique which can produce a sort of lace. This art spread to Europe from North Africa and became the hobby of sailors the world over. Macramé has developed so much over the centuries that it is explained in a separate chapter.

TATTING

Tatting, a form of creative knotting, is a distant cousin of macramé. While the basic tatting knot looks like the macramé Lark's Head Knot, the knots are developed in a very different way. Basically, tatting is the formation of rings and half rings of knots arranged to produce various designs. This form of lace-making looks very delicate, but is actually very strong.

Tatting is actually a rather difficult craft to explain with words and pictures. A friend who has worked with tatting will be able to teach this skill much faster.

Materials: The two basic needs for tatting are a tatting shuttle, which is available at needlework counters, and crochet cotton, size 20 or 30. Tatting shuttles are available with or without the hook end. In the beginning it is much easier to learn on a shuttle without the hook, using a crochet hook to pull the thread through the joinings. It is also much easier to practice with a piece of heavy cord and a knitting needle until the basic tatting knot has been mastered.

Winding The Shuttle: For a shuttle that has a removable bobbin, simply remove the bobbin and wind it just a bit over three quarters full. If the bobbin is not removable, wind the thread around the center of the shuttle.

The Basic Tatting Knot

Tatting is made up of one simple knot, called the Double Stitch, worked over and over.
Step 1: Bring the cord over the top and around the back. **Fig. 1.**
Step 2: Bring the cord over, around the back, over the top and through the loop. **Fig. 2.** Pull the knot into place. **Fig. 3.**
Repeat Steps 1 and 2 for the Double Stitch Knot.

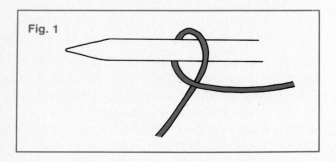

Fig. 1

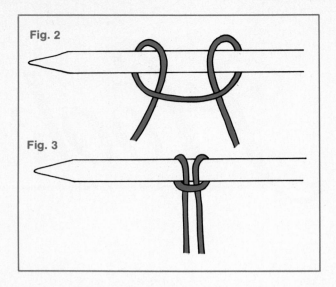

Fig. 2

Fig. 3

Learning To Use A Shuttle. When working, always have the thread coming from the back of the shuttle.
Step 1: Unwind about 15 inches of shuttle thread. Position the shuttle between the thumb and forefinger of the right hand. Then take the thread end between the thumb and forefinger of the left hand and spread the thread over the remaining left hand fingers. **Fig. 4.**

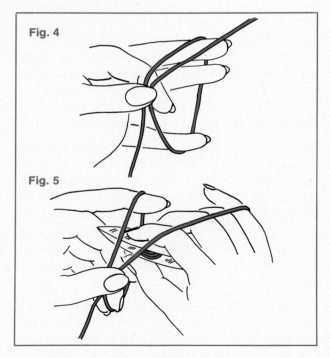

Fig. 4

Fig. 5

Step 2: With the shuttle still in the right hand, pass the thread under the right hand fingers and over the hand.

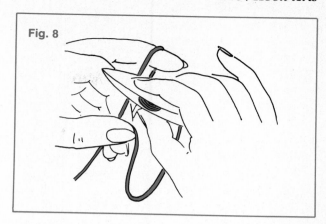

Step 3: Pass the shuttle under the ring thread on the left hand. **Fig. 5.**

Step 4: Pass the shuttle over the ring thread. **Fig. 6.**

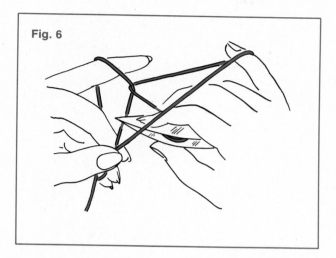

Step 5: Pull the shuttle thread tightly and drop the middle left hand finger so that the loop turns over.

Step 6: While holding the shuttle thread taut, raise the middle left hand finger to the original position. **Fig. 7.** Hold the loop firmly in place. The first half of the knot is now complete.

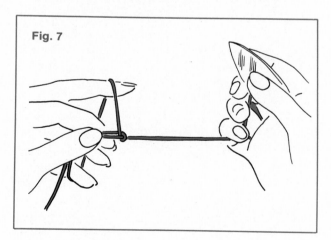

Step 7: The second half of the knot is the same as the first, but worked in reverse. Let the shuttle thread fall slack; then pass the shuttle over the ring thread **(Fig. 8),** back under the ring thread and over the shuttle thread.

Step 8: Pull the shuttle thread tightly and hold it in place as you slacken the ring thread and tighten it again.

MAKING PICOTS AND RINGS

In tatting, the picot serves both as a decoration and as a method of connecting the rings. To form a picot, work a complete Double Stitch, leave about ¼ inch of thread unworked and then work a second complete knot. **Fig. 9.** Slide the knots together to complete the picot. **Fig. 10.** Picots can be worked as often as needed. **Fig. 11.** When the ring has been completed, pull the shuttle thread to tighten into place. **Fig. 12.** Start new ring.

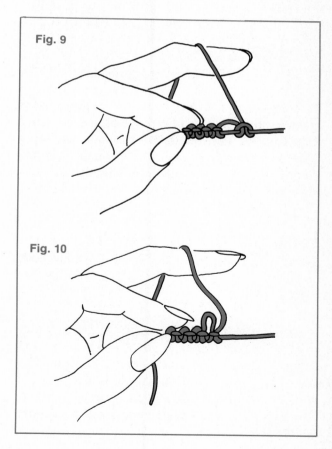

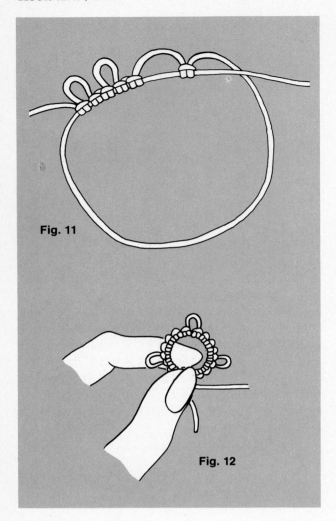

Fig. 11

Fig. 12

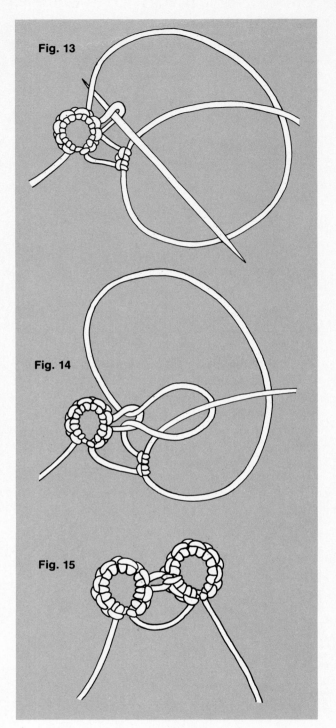

Fig. 13

Fig. 14

Fig. 15

Joining Rings: Insert the shuttle point or a crochet hook in the last picot of the previous ring. **Fig. 13.** Pull the thread through, making a hole large enough through which you can pass the shuttle. **Fig. 14.** Draw the thread tightly and continue working to complete the second ring. **Fig. 15.**

Joining New Threads: Always join the new thread at the base of a ring. When work has been completed, weave the threads under on the reverse side.

Working With Two Threads: A much wider range of tatting designs is possible when working with two threads. The best known technique is to use a ball of cord and the shuttle thread. Tie the thread ends of the ball and the shuttle together. Use the ball for working the knots and the shuttle for making the rings.

HAIRPIN LACE

Hairpin lace, which can best be described as easy and elegant, is a form of crochet that requires a very inexpensive loom available at most needlework counters. There are two types of hairpin lace looms. One type has crossbars at both ends and is adjustable. The other type has one rounded end and a bar at the opposite end. This type is not adjustable, but is available in different sizes. When working with this type of loom, always work with the rounded section at the top.

Materials: Hairpin lace loom, 4 inches width. Crochet hook, size J. Knitting worsted.

Step 1: Remove the bottom cross bar. Make a slip loop to equal half the width of the loom, and place the loop on the left prong of the loom. **Fig. 16.**

Step 2: Bring the yarn around the right side of the loom to the back. **Fig. 17.** Center the slip loop, pick up the yarn and pull it through the loop. **Fig. 18.** Remove hook from the loop.

Step 3: Working from the back, insert the hook in the dropped loop. **Fig. 19.** Turn the loom toward you from right to left, passing the yarn around the loom back, ch 1 **(Fig. 20),** sc in left front loop. **Fig. 21.** Drop loop from hook. Repeat Steps 2 and 3 for pattern.

Joining Strips: Join the strips together by weaving the loops from one side through loops from the opposite side. **Fig. 22.**

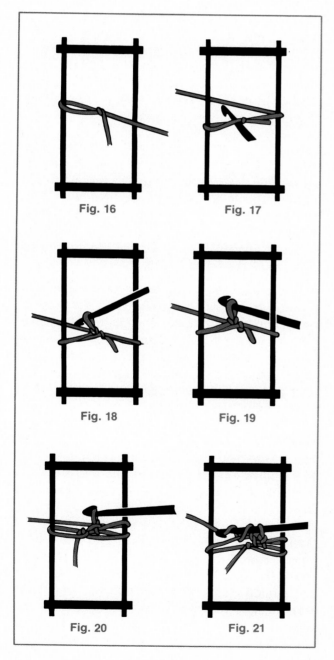

Fig. 16   Fig. 17

Fig. 18   Fig. 19

Fig. 20   Fig. 21

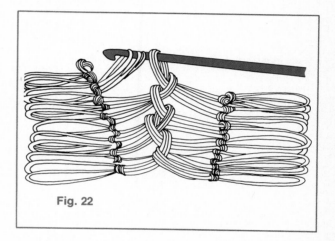

Fig. 22

HELPFUL HINTS ON HAIRPIN LACE

Always count to see that the same number of loops are on each side of the loom, and that each strip that is made has the same number of loops. Work the loops loosely and be sure that one side is not being pulled more tightly than the other. Pulling will cause the center braid to lean to one side.

When the loom has been filled, remove the bottom cross bar and pull off all but the last few completed loops. Replace the cross bar and continue with the work.

Rather than constantly removing the hook, some people find it easier to pass the shank of the crochet hook through the parallel prongs of the loom. Work in whatever fashion that is found to be the most comfortable. The pattern will turn out the same.

Gauge: Measure the gauge on the center braid while the work is still on the hairpin loom.

JIFFY-LACE

Jiffy-lace, also termed broomstick lace, is a new and very beautiful form of crochet that is also very simple and fast.

Materials: Knitting needle, size 50. Crochet hook, size J. Knitting worsted.

Row 1: With the crochet hook, ch 20. Pull up the last loop of the chain and place it on the knitting needle. Holding the knitting needle in the left hand, * insert crochet hook in the next stitch, pull up a loop and place it on the knitting needle. **Fig. 23.** Repeat from * across — 20 loops.

Row 2: * Insert crochet hook through 5 loops, yo.

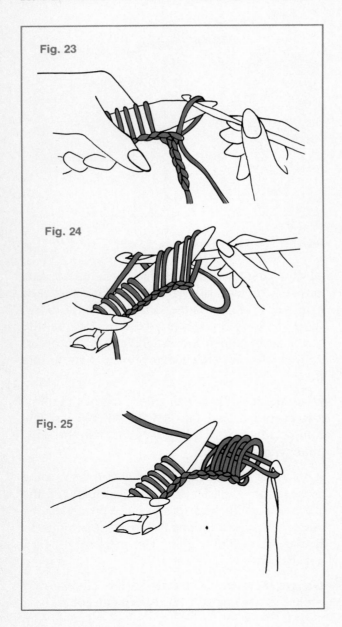

Fig. 23

Fig. 24

Fig. 25

Fig. 24. Pull off the knitting needle. **Fig. 25.** Ch 1, 5 sc in the set of loops — 1 pat complete. Repeat from * across — 20 sc and 4 pats. Do not turn.

Row 3: Pull up the last st and place it on the knitting needle as before. Working in the back loops only, pull one loop through each sc and place it on the knitting needle — 20 loops. Repeat Rows 2 and 3 for pat, end Row 2.

DAISY-LOOM

The Daisy is another easy lace that is made on a special hand loom. They can be used separately as an ornamentation to any knitted or crocheted item, sewn singly onto a piece or joined to form a border. They can also be placed between rows of crochet in creating unique patterns for scarves, afghans and many other items.

The Loom: The Marcia Lynn or Susan Bates Daisy-Loom has twelve spokes, numbered as shown. **Fig. 26.** It also has (on the wrong side) a knob that must be turned to the right in order to release the spokes. This makes them stick out so that yarn can be wound around them. The knob is turned to the left to retract the spokes for easy removal of the finished daisy.

With the right side (without the knob) up toward you, the spokes will be numbered in the order in which you will use them. For medium or heavy-weight yarns such as knitting worsted, cotton rug yarn and synthetic straw, use the basic wind, twice around each spoke. For very fine materials such as baby yarn and bedspread cotton, wind three or four times around.

Making the Daisy: Start by holding yarn at center with left thumb, leaving about 1 inch of yarn end beyond center. Wind up and from left to right around spoke No. 1, then down and from right to left around spoke No. 2; back up and around No. 1 then down and around No. 2 (making a figure 8 so that No. 1 and No. 2 have been covered twice). Then move the yarn to spoke No. 3, around it from left to right, down and around No. 4 from right to left. Wind twice around these two spokes as with spokes No. 1 and No. 2. Then move to spokes No. 5 and No. 6, twice around and move on, until all the spokes

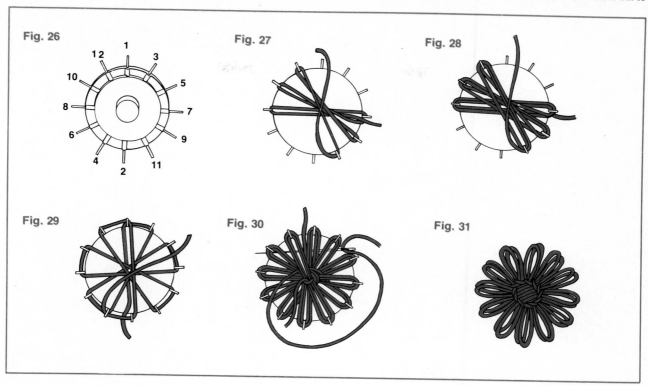

are covered twice around, always moving in the same direction. **Fig. 27.** With a yarn needle, fasten the end securely around the center of the daisy, then cut off and conceal the end.

To finish the center, thread a length of the same or a contrasting color of yarn in a yarn needle and take a few stitches in the center to fasten thread as in embroidery. Insert the needle, from right to left, under the yarn of four spokes and pull the yarn through.*Then insert the needle, from right to left, under the last three of these same spokes and the next spoke to the left (four in all) and pull up stitch *. Repeat between *s until there are thirteen stitches. **Fig. 28.** Fasten the thread and then cut and conceal the ends. Turn the knob to the left to release the daisy. **Fig. 29.**

Slight variations can be made in the daisies by using heavier yarn and working once around each spoke. **Fig. 30.** It is also possible to work once around over two spokes each time. **Fig. 31.**

Joining the Daisies: A simple way of putting daisies together to form a large piece is with a picot joining. This may be worked in the same or a contrasting color of yarn. If knitting worsted or a similar weight yarn is used, work with an aluminum crochet hook size H.

1st Daisy: Make 1 sc in 1 petal of daisy (work sc through as many loops as worked on each spoke),** ch 5, sl st in last sc for picot, * ch 4, sc in next petal, repeat from * twice, repeat from ** all around, cut yarn.

2nd Daisy: Work same as first daisy, sc in 1st loop, ch 2, sl st in corner picot of 1st daisy, ch 2, sl st in last sc of 2nd daisy, * ch 2, sl st in next loop of 1st daisy, ch 2, sc in next loop of 2nd daisy, repeat from * twice, ch 2, sl st in corner picot of 1st daisy, ch 2, sl st in last sc of 2nd daisy, complete 2nd daisy same as 1st daisy, cut yarn.

3rd Daisy: Join 3rd daisy to other side of 1st daisy.

4th Daisy: Join to 2nd and 3rd daisies to correspond. Work and join as many daisies as needed for pattern.

HORSE REINS (*Knitting Knobby or Spool Knitting*)

Using the Knobby: To set up the knitting knobby, thread the end of a ball of knitting worsted (or similar weight yarn) into a yarn needle and pull it down through the center hole of the spool. Leave about a 4-inch tail to hold with the left hand. Bring the ball end of the yarn around the outside of peg No. 1 from right to left. Bring the yarn inside of peg No. 2 and wrap it clockwise once. Continue over to peg No. 3 and wrap from the inside clockwise and onto peg No. 4. The knitting is started after all the pegs have been wrapped. The needle that you will use resembles a crochet hook, but has no hook at the end. **Fig. 32.**

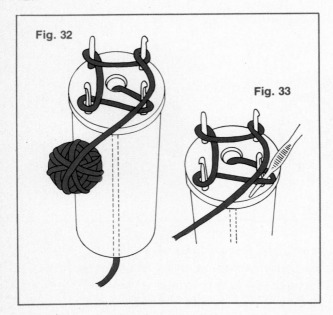

Making the Reins: Hold the knitting knobby in the left hand and bring the yarn around over the loop on peg No. 1. With the needle, pick up the original peg No. 1-loop and cast it over the top thread and over the peg. It is now holding the top thread tightly around the peg. **Fig. 33.** Bring the yarn around across peg No. 2 and cast that bottom loop over with the needle. After each stitch, pull the tail of yarn at the bottom to tighten the stitch. Eventually the knitted rope will start to appear out of the bottom of the spool.

To add yarn or change colors, lay the two yarn ends together and knot. Cut off yarn about ½ inch from the knot. When the knot comes to the top of the spool, be sure to knit it into the center of the rope to hide it.

Casting off at the end is done almost as in actual knitting. Pick up the last loop made and move it over to the peg on the left. Pull the bottom loop on that peg over the peg and over the new loop, then pull it down as usual to tighten it. Move the loop over to the next peg on the left and repeat

the process until there is only one loop. Break off the yarn with about a 3-inch end, which will be pulled through the last loop. Pull it tightly to form a final knot.

Using the Reins: The rope should be joined in a flat spiral for many of the items such as mats and coasters. **Fig. 34.** For some of the toys and for hats, etc., the spiral should be held tightly on the outside while winding so that the whole piece becomes a cup or cone. **Fig. 35.** Such pieces can be shaped over a Styrofoam ball or paper cone for easier and more accurate handling. Use heavy-duty thread and a strong hand-sewing needle to slip stitch pieces together. Make a backstitch or lock stitch every now and then to anchor the work firmly. It is possible to make a durable oval or round bathmat or bedside rug with a sufficient length of horse reins. Coarse jute-type yarns and cotton or synthetic rug yarns are especially suitable for this. Joining should be done with strong thread called carpet thread or carpet warp. A rug can be a perfect winter project for a whole family.

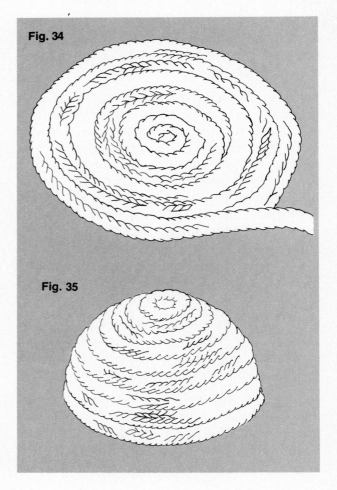

HOOK ART PROJECTS

HAIRPIN LACE EDGINGS

MATERIALS: SUSAN BATES OR MARCIA LYNN, Small Adjustable Hairpin Lace Loom, See Sizes for Individual Edgings, Steel Crochet Hook Size 7, Bedspread Cotton — White or color desired.

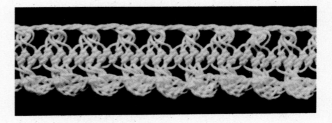

GAUGE: 8 sc each side of loom = 1 inch. Follow directions for making Hairpin Lace.

EDGING #1 — Adjust Loom to 1 inch. Make a strip of lace of desired length, having a multiple of 3 lps on each side of loom.

Edging: Keeping one twist in ech lp throughout, 1 sc thru first 3 lps, * ch 3, 2 dc in same lps, sl st in next 3 lps; rep from * across. Fasten off.

Heading: Join thread with an sc in first 3 lps on other edge of lace, * ch 2, sc thru next 3 lps; rep from * across. Fasten off.

EDGING #2 — Adjust Loom to 1½ inches. Make a strip of lace of desired length having a multiple of 9 plus 7 lps on each side of loom.

Edging — *Row 1:* Keeping 1 twist in each lp throughout, join thread with an sc in first lp, sc in each lp across. Fasten off.

Row 2: Join thread with an sc at beg of last row, ch 3 to count as 1 dc, 1 dc in each sc across. Fasten off.

Row 3: Join thread in top of ch-3 of last row, * ch 3, skip 2 dc, 2 dc in next dc, ch 3, sl st in top of last dc for a picot, dc in same st as last 2 dc, ch 3, skip 2 dc, sl st in next dc, ch 3, skip 2 dc, sl st in next dc; rep from * across. Fasten off.

Heading: Join thread with an sc in first twisted lp on free edge of lace, work 1 sc in each lp across. Fasten off.

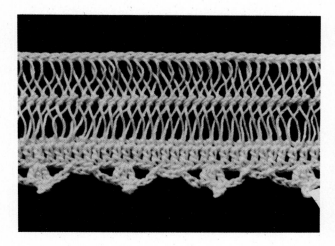

EDGING #3 — Adjust Loom to 2 inches. Make a strip of lace of desired length, having a multiple of 7 plus 4 lps on each side of loom.

Edging: Keeping 1 twist in each lp throughout, join thread with an sc in first 4 lps, ch 3, 2 dc in same lp, ch 5, sl st in 4th ch from hook for a picot, ch 1, 3 dc in same lps, * sc in next 3 lps, ch 3, sl st in last sc for a picot, 3 dc in next 4 lps, ch 5, sl st in 4th ch for a picot, ch 1, 3 dc in same lps; rep from * across. Fasten off.

Heading: Join thread with an sc in first 2 twisted lps on free edge of lace, sc in same lps, * 2 sc in next 2 twisted lps; rep from * across. Fasten off.

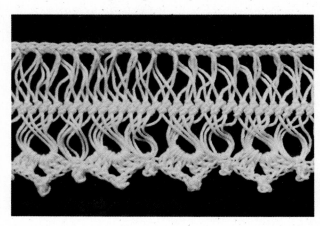

EDGING #4 — Adjust Loom to 1½ inches. Make a strip of lace of desired length, having a multiple of 4 sts on each side of loom.

Edging: Keeping 1 twist in each lp, join thread with an sc in first 2 lps, ch 2, sc in next 2 lps, * draw up a ⅜-inch lp on hook, thread over and thru lp, sc in single lp of last st, draw up another ⅜-inch lp, thread over and thru lp, sc in single lp of last st — double knot st made — sc in next 2 lps, ch 2, (sc in next 2 lps) twice, ch 2, sc in next 2 lps; rep from * across, ending double knot st, sc in next 2 lps, ch 2, sc in next 2 lps. Fasten off.

Heading: Join thread with an sc in first lp on free edge of lace, sc in each twisted lp across. Fasten off.

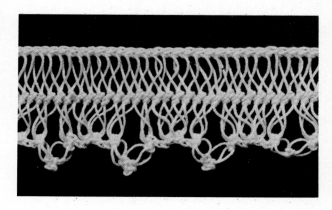

EDGING #5 — Adjust Loom to 2 inches. Make a strip of lace of desired length, having a multiple of 8 plus 4 lps on each side of loom.

Edging: Keeping 1 twist in each lp throughout, join thread with an sc in first 4 lps, * ch 4, sc in next 4 lps, (ch 3, sl st in last sc) 3 times — picot cluster made — ch 4, sl st in next 4 lps; rep from * across. Fasten off.

Heading: Join thread with an sc in first 4 twisted lps on free edge of lace, * ch 4, sc in next 4 lps; rep from * across. Fasten off.

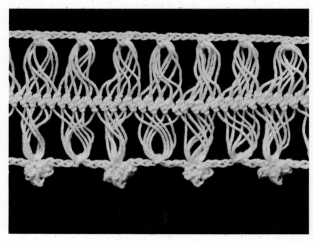

TATTED EDGINGS

Use Lily Tatting and Crochet or Lily Daisy Mercerized Crochet Cotton, Art. 65, Size 30.

TATTING ABBREVIATIONS

R (r) . . . . Ring	S P . . . . . Short Picot
L R . . . . . Large Ring	L P . . . . Long Picot
S R . . . . . Small Ring	Ch . . . . Chain
D or D S . . . . Double	Sp . . . . Space
or Double Stitch	Sep . . . . Separate
P . . . . Picot	Cl . . . . Close

Edging # 1 — Shown on Child's collar. R, 4 d, 3 p sep by 4 d, 4 d, cl r. * ¼ inch space. R, 4 d, join to last p of last r, 4 d, 2 p sep by 4 d, 4 d, cl r. Repeat from * for length desired.

Edging # 2 — Top Row. R, 7 d, p, 5 d, p, 3 d, cl r. R, 3 d, join to last p of last r, 5 d, p, 5 d, p, 3 d, cl r. R, 3 d, join to last p of last r, 5 d, p, 7 d, cl r, turn. Ch, 4 d, p, 4 d, 4 p sep by 3 d, 4 d, p, 4 d, turn. * R, 7 d, join to last p of last r, 5 d, p, 3 d, cl r. R, 3 d, join to last p of last r, 5 d, p, 7 d, cl r, turn. Ch, 4 d, join to corresponding p of opposite ch, 4 d, 4 p sep by 3 d, 4 d, p, 4 d, turn. Repeat from * for length desired.

Edging # 3 — Middle Row. R, 4 d, p, 4 d, 3 p sep by 2 d, 4 d, p, 4 d, cl r, turn. * Ch, 3 d, 4 p sep by 2 d, 3 d, turn. R, 4 d, join to last p of last r, 4 d, 3 p sep by 2 d, 4 d, p, 4 d, cl r, turn. Repeat from * for length desired.

Edging # 4 — Bottom Row. R, 3 d, 3 p sep by 3 d, 3 d, cl r, turn, ¼-inch space. R, 3 d, 3 p sep by 3 d, 3 d, cl r, turn, ¼-inch space. * R, 3 d, join to last p of opposite r, 3 d, 2 p sep by 3 d, 3 d, cl r, turn. ¼-inch space. R, 3 d, join to last p of opposite r, 3 d, 5 p sep by 2 d, 3 d, p, 3 d, cl r, turn. ¼-inch space. R, 3 d, join to last p of opposite r, 3 d, 2 p sep by 3 d, 3 d, cl r, turn. ¼-inch space. R, 3 d, join to last p of opposite r, 3 d, 2 p sep by 3 d, 3 d, cl r, turn. ¼-inch space. Repeat from * for length desired.

LIGHTWEIGHT STOLE

MATERIALS: SUSAN BATES or MARCIA LYNN, 2-inch Hairpin Lace Loom, Crochet Hook B or 1, Baby Yarn or lightweight Fingering yarn — 5 oz. White or color desired, 2 oz. Blue or any contrasting color.

With white, work 9 strips of hairpin lace each having 397 loops on each side of staple. Working on first strip with blue or contrasting color sc through first 5 lps inserting hook through all 5 lps at one time and keeping loops straight. Do not twist, ** ch 5, * sc through next loop but twist loop twice. Repeat from * twice, ch 5, sc through next 5 lps, keeping lps straight. Repeat from ** across strip. Ch 6, sl st in center of strip, ch 6 and work down other side of strip in same way. At end of strip ch 6, sl st in center of strip, ch 6 and fasten off in corner loop.

2nd Strip: Join blue in corner loop, ch 6, sl st in center of strip, ch 6 then work down 1 side. At end of row ch 6, sl st in center of strip, ch 6. You are now ready to join to first strip.

To Join: Sc through first 5 loops of free edge of 2nd strip, ch 2, join to center st of 1st lp of 1st strip (to join: drop lp from hk, insert in st, pull lp through), * ch 2, l sc in each of the next 3 lps of 2nd strip (twist each lp twice), ch 2, join to center st of next lp of 1st strip, ch 2, sc through next 5 lps of 2nd strip, keeping lps straight, ch 2, join to center st of next lp of 1st strip, repeat from * across strip. Work and join all strips as above.

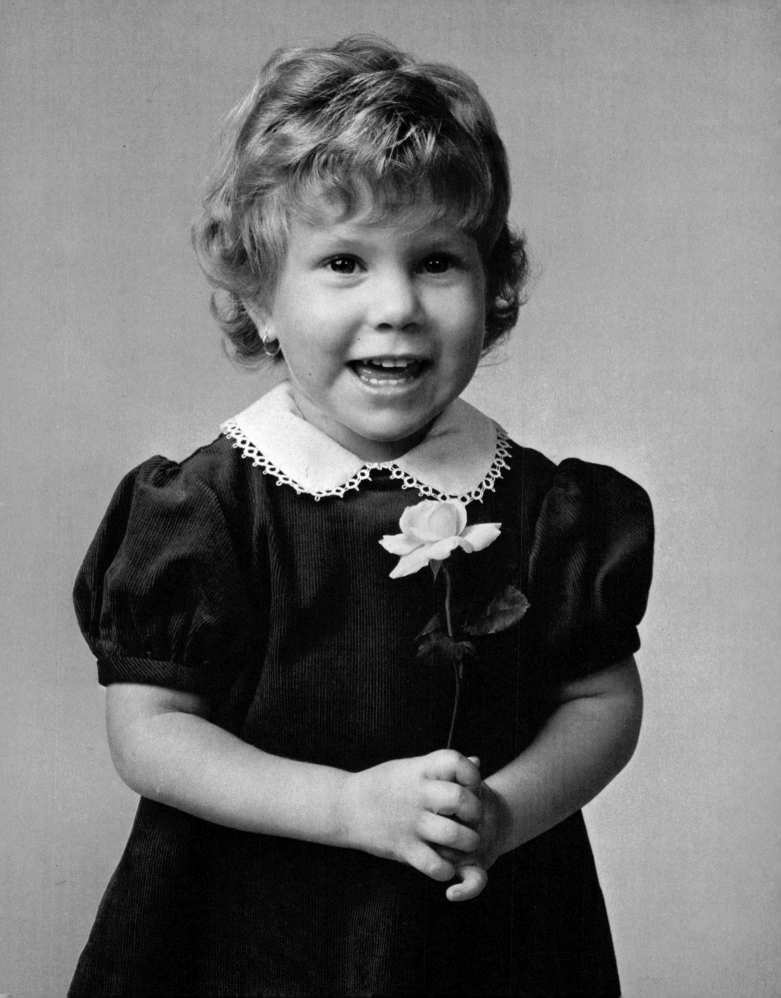

A HAIRPIN HIGHLIGHT

MATERIALS: SUSAN BATES or MARCIA LYNN, Crochet Hook G or 6, 1½-inch Hairpin Lace loom, Knitting Worsted, two 4-oz. skeins each any two contrasting colors.

GAUGE: 5 sc = 1 inch at center of strip

Directions are given for small size (12). Changes for medium (14) and large (16) sizes given in parentheses.

MEASUREMENTS: Width across front at underarm: 18(19,20) inches. Width across back at underarm: 17(18,19) inches.

Back: With darker color work 80 (90, 100) lps on each side of staple. Work 10 (for all sizes) more dark strips. Work 10 (for all sizes) strips contrasting color. This completes strips from lower edge to underarm running horizontally. Work 1 strip contrasting color with 68 (78,88) loops. Work 3 strips dark color and 2 strips contrasting color each with 64 (74,84) loops. This completes strips for armhole.

To Assemble: Always work strips with starting loops on right edge and beginning length of yarn at top. Take 1 dark strip, place 1 contrasting strip above; insert crochet hook in 1st 2 loops of top strip on right edge, insert crochet hook in 1st 2 loops of lower (dark) strip and pull through top strip, insert in next 2 loops of top strip and pull through. Continue in same manner across strips working alternately into top and lower strip until joining is completed. Place a dark strip on top of light strip and join in same manner. Alternating colors continue joining all strips to underarm.

Shape Armhole: Take the strip with 68 (78, 88) loops. Skip 1st 6 loops on last strip, then work joining as before, skipping last 6 loops. Take next color strip with 64 (74, 84) loops; insert hook in 2 loops of top strip, then insert through 4 loops of lower strip and pull through, then join as before working last 4 loops tog. Alternating colors, continue joining all armhole strips.

Front: Work 11 dark strips with 90 (100,110) loops and 10 contrasting strips with 90 (100, 110) loops. Work and mark following strips for neck and armhole shaping: 2 strips 34 (38, 42) loops contrasting color, 2 strips 28 (32, 36) dark color, 2 strips 24 (28, 32) contrasting color, 2 strips 20 (24, 28) dark color, 4 strips 16 (20, 24) contrasting color, 2 strips 16 (20, 24) dark color.

To Assemble: Join strips to underarm in same manner as back.

Shape Neck And Armholes

1st Row: Take 1 strip 34 (38, 42) loops, skip 6 loops on right edge for armhole shaping, then complete joining. Take 2nd 34 (38, 42) loops strip, skip 10 (12, 14) loops for neck, and complete joining skipping last 6 loops at other armhole.

2nd Row: Take 28 (32, 36) strip, insert crochet hook in 2 loops on top strip, insert hook through 4 loops on lower strip and pull through, continue joining loops as before until 10 loops are free on lower strip, * pick up and pull through 3 loops on lower strip, pick up and pull through 2 loops on top strip, repeat from * once, then pick up and pull through 4 loops on lower edge. Take 2nd 28 (32,34) loop strip, pick up 2 loops on top strip, * pick up 2 loops on top strip, pick up and pull through 3 loops on lower strip, repeat from * once, then complete joining in same manner, working last 4 loops tog.

3rd Row: Take next color with 24 (28, 32) loops, work joining even until 10 loops are free on lower strip, then complete same as last row. Take 2nd 24 (28, 32) strip, work joining same as last row working even at armhole edge.

4th Row: Take next color with 20 (24, 28) loops, and join same as last row.
5th Row: Take next color with 16 (20, 24) loops and repeat last row.
6th Row: With next color, repeat last row.
7th Row: Repeat last row.

Finishing: Join front and neck sections together at shoulders same as all joining. Sew side seams with matching colors. Finish all ends. Work a row of sc around each armhole working 4 sc in each stripe, join. Work a row of sc around neck edge working 4 sc in each color stripe and working 2 sc in each st at front neck edge; working 1 sc in each of 2 sts each side at shoulders and 2 sc in each remaining st across back of neck, join.
2nd Row: Sc, 4 dc in same space, skip 3 sc, * sc, 4 dc in next sc, repeat from * all around, join, fasten off.

STRIPED AFGHAN

SIZE: 40 x 60 inches

MATERIALS: SUSAN BATES or MARCIA LYNN Large Adjustable Hairpin Lace Loom Adjusted to 3 Inches, Crochet Hook Size H-8, Knitting Worsted 5 skeins white, 1 skein each of Green, Purple and Peacock.

GAUGE: 9 sc on each side of spine of lace = 5 inches. Use 2 strands of same colored yarn held together throughout.

Each loop of lace has 2 strands of yarn and is counted as 1 loop.

Make 10 strips of White, 3 strips each of Green, Purple and Peacock having 106 lps on each side of loom.

Joinings: Starting at beg of strips and taking care not to twist lps, insert hook in first lp of a White strip, draw first lp of a Green strip through lp of White, * draw next lp of White through Green lp, draw next lp of Green through white lp; rep from * across strips. Secure last lp with cut off strand at end of spine of lace. Join all strips in this manner in following color rotation: White, Purple, White, Peacock, White and Green, end with a Peacock and White strip.

Border: With 2 strands of White, dc in first MrM on free edge of a White strip, ch 1 loosely, dc in dc before the ch-1, dc in same 2 lps, * 1 dc in next 2 lps, ch 1 loosely, dc in dc before ch-1, dc in same 2 lps — 1 par made; rep from * in each group of 2 lps to next corner, make 2 pats in corner 2 lps. Continue across short edge making a pat in each spine of lace and in joining of strips. Work other sides the same, ending with 1 pat in first corner. Join with sl st in first dc. Fasten off.

HAT AND SCARF

MATERIALS: SUSAN BATES or MARCIA LYNN Crochet Hook Jr, 1 Knitting Needle Size 50, Adjustable Hairpin-Lace Loom (adjusted to 4-inch width), 1 Pom-Pon Maker, 4 oz. Knitting Worsted M C (Main Color), 4 oz. Knitting Worsted C C (Contrasting Color).

GAUGE: 4 Patterns = 5 inches, 1 Pattern Row = 1½ Inches.

HAT

Using Adjustable Hairpin-Lace Loom, adjusted to 4-inch width, make 1 strip with contrasting color (C C) of 100 loops on each side of loom. With main color (M C) working always on the right side, work 1 single crochet in each loop of hairpin lace. Pull up last loop and place it on Knitting Needle held in left hand, continue pulling one loop through the back of each sc stitch across. You now have 100 stitches on needle.

Row 2: Insert hook in center of first 5 loops, holding the loops together as one, yo, ch 1, 5 sc. Work * 5 sc in each set of 5 loops, repeat from * across (20 pats). Do not turn.

Row 3: Pull last loop from previous row onto needle, work in back st only, pull yarn through each sc and place on needle. (100 sts)

Repeat Rows 2 and 3 for three full pat rows, end with Row 2, break yarn 12 inches from end of work. Pull yarn through all 100 sts and knot, sew sides together with remainder of this strand. With main color sc in each loop of Hairpin Lace (100 sc). If hat fits, sc in each sc in second row. If a smaller size is required sc in every other sc in second row.

Row 3: Sc in each sc for all sizes. Cut yarn and bind off. Make 3-inch pompon of contrasting color with Pom-Pon Maker.

SCARF

With C C, make Hairpin-Lace strip 200 loops long. With MC do 2 patterns of Jiffy Lace on each side of Hairpin Lace. (Rows 2 and 3 of hat pattern.)

Fringe: Cut six 14-inch lengths MC and fold in half. (Make 16.) Two sets of fringe for each Jiffy-Lace pattern. Cut six 14-inch lengths C C, fold in half. (Make 6). Three sets at each Hairpin Lace end Trim fringe evenly.

THREE-COLOR HAIRPIN BAG

MATERIALS: SUSAN BATES 2-inch Hairpin in Loom, SUSAN BATES Crochet Hook H, Heavy Rug Yarn — 70-yd. skeins, 2 Skeins Purple, 2 Skeins Dark Blue, 2 Skeins Lt. Blue, Belt Buckle, ¾ yd. Lining and stiffening, matching sewing thread.

BAG

Work 4 strips Lt. Blue, 2 strips Purple and 2 strips Dark Blue each with 90 loops on each side of loom. Join strips together, having 1 strip Lt. Blue, 1 strip Dark Blue, 1 strip Purple, 1 strip Lt. Blue, by pulling 2 loops alternately through 1st strip, then through next strip until all loops are joined between strips. The outside edges of Lt. Blue strips are free for joining of gusset and handle.

Handle and Gusset: Work 1 strip Purple and 1 strip Dark Blue each with 140 loops on each side of each strip. Join the 2 strips together by pulling 2 loops through 2 loops, fasten.

Work 1 strip Purple and 1 strip Dark Blue each with 70 loops on each side. Join 2 loops to 2 loops as before.

Finishing: Fold bag over to have 22 loops free for flap, then fold other end so that front of bag is under the 22 loops of flap. (There will be 34 loops for front and 34 loops for back.)

Lining: Cut lining and stiffening the same shape as front and back sections allowing 1/2 inch more on each side for seams for lining section, no seam allowance for stiffening. Cut a section of lining and stiffening for handle and gusset section.

Place end of gusset section of stiffening between front and back of stiffening section and overcast in place. Finish other side of stiffening to correspond. Place gusset of lining between front and back sections of lining sections, pin in place taking 1/2-inch seams. Machine stitch seams. Place lining inside stiffening sections.

Fold hairpin section, join the 140-loop gusset and handle section by pulling 2 loops through 2 loops of the 34 loops of front section, work across handle section, fasten. Complete other side of this handle section by joining to the 34 loops of back section to correspond. Join the 90-loop gusset section to other side in same manner.

Leave the 22 loops free on each side of flap. Work 2 rows of sc across inside top of bag.

Fringe: Cut strands into 11-inch lengths. Take 3 strands of 1 color, fold in half and loop through each strip of flap, working a fringe in following order: 1 Purple, 1 Lt. Blue, 1 Purple, 1 Lt. Blue, 1 Dark Blue, 1 Purple, 1 Dark Blue, 1 Lt. Blue, 1 Purple, 1 Lt. Blue, 1 Purple.

Attach Buckle in position to end of short handle section.

Place lining in position. Turn raw edges under and tack in place.

TWO-TONE JIFFY-LACE HAT AND SCARF

MATERIALS: SUSAN BATES or MARCIA LYNN, 1 Knitting Needle Size 35, Crochet Hook I, Fingering Yarn, 4 oz. Main Color (MC)-Orange, 4 oz. Contrasting Color (CC)-Gold.

With crochet hook, and 1 strand of each color, ch 51. 1 sc in 2nd st from hook, 1 sc in ea. rem. st of ch.

Row 1 Of Jiffy-Lace:

With crochet hook pull up last loop and place it on knitting needle held in left hand. Insert crochet hook in ea st of sc, pull yarn through and place on needle (50 loops). Do not turn.

Row 2: Insert hook in center of first 5 loops, holding these loops tog as one, yo and pull off needle, ch 1, and work 5 sc in first set of loops only. * Work 5 sc in ea set of 5 loops, repeat from * across (10 pats). Do not turn.

Row 3: Pull up last st and place on needle held in left hand. Work in BACK LOOP with crochet hook pull yarn through ea sc of previous row and place on needle (50 loops).

Repeat rows 2 and 3 once more for a total of 2 pat rows ending with row 2.

Cut strand of MC, attach 2nd strand of CC (you now have two strands of CC) ch 2, turn and dc across row, ch 2, turn.

Next Row: Dc across row. Cut 1 strand of CC and attach strand of MC. Repeat rows 3 and then 2 (with 1 strand of MC and 1 strand of CC) until you have 2 rows of Jiffy-Lace pat.

Next Row: Cut strand of CC, attach 2nd strand of MC (you now have two strands of MC) ch 2, turn and dc across row.

Next Row: Dc across row. Cut 1 strand of MC, and attach strand of CC.

Repeat above pat for 60 inches or length desired, ending with a row of sc after last two pat rows of Jiffy-Lace. Weave in ends. Block to 1 inch per pat in both directions.

HAT

With crochet hook ch 91 with 1 strand of each color. 1 sc in 2nd st from hook, 1 sc in ea. rem. st of chain.

Follow pat for scarf until you have completed 4 rows of Jiffy-Lace, 2 rows dc, 4 rows Jiffy-Lace.

Next Row: Dec 1 st in every 10 st.

Next Row: Dec 1 st in every 5th st.

Next Row: Dec 1 st in every 3rd st.

Pull yarn through last row of sts, gather and sew up back seam.

MULTI-COLOR AFGHAN AND PILLOW

MATERIALS: SUSAN BATES or MARCIA LYNN, 1 Knitting Needle — Size 50, Crochet Hook Size K, Knitting Worsted, 32 oz. Yellow, 8 oz. Lt. Coral, 8 oz. Tangerine, 8 oz. Burnt Orange, 8 oz. Orange, 16 inch Pillow Form.

GAUGE: 5 patterns = 5½ inches, 5 pattern rows = 6 inches

Afghan: Size 44 inches x 72 inches approximately, not including fringe. With Yellow ch 200. Pull up last loop and place it on Knitting Needle held in left hand.

Row 1: Insert Crochet Hook in each st of ch, (or sc, in back loop only) pull yarn through and place it on needle. (200 loops)

Row 2: Insert Crochet Hook in center of first 5 loops on Knitting Needle, holding these loops together as one, yo and pull off needle, ch 1, and 5 sc in loop. Work * 5 sc in each set of 5 loops, repeat from * across row (40 patterns). Do not turn. Pull up last st and place it on Knitting Needle.

Repeat Rows 1 and 2 following the colors below:

1st 2 Rows Yellow (above mentioned), 4 Orange, 4 Yellow, 4 Burnt Orange, 6 Yellow, 4 Light Coral, 8 Yellow, 4 Tangerine. 36 Rows (18 pattern rows).

Repeat the above 36 rows twice more for a total of 108 rows (54 pattern rows). Work 2 more rows Yellow (55 pattern rows).

Fringe: Wrap Yellow around a piece of cardboard 6 inches wide, cut yarn at one end to form 12 inch strands. Combine 6 strands for each fringe. Knot fringes in every other stitch across both short ends.

Pillow: Size 16 inches square approximately. With Yellow ch 70. Pull up last loop and place it on Knitting Needle held in left hand. Rows 1 and 2 as for afghan except that you will have 70 loops on your Knitting Needle for 14 pattern sts.

Color scheme as follows:

1st two rows Yellow (1 pat. row)
4 rows each (2 pattern rows each): Orange, Yellow, Burnt Orange, Yellow, Lt. Coral, Yellow, Tangerine.

2 rows Yellow (1 pat. row)

Back Side Of Pillow: Chain 51. Turn, 1 sc in 2nd ch (or sc) from hook and in each ch (or sc) across row (50 sts).

Repeat last row, crocheting in back loop only until you reach 16 inches or length needed to match front of pillow.

With Yellow and wrong sides together work 1 row of sc around 3 sides, insert pillow form and sc around 4th side, fasten off.

Fringe: Wrap Yellow around a piece of cardboard 3 inches wide, cut yarn at one end to form 6 inch strands. Combine 2 strands for each fringe. Knot fringes in every sc around pillow cover.

MOHAIR SCARF AND HAT

MATERIALS: SUSAN BATES or MARCIA LYNN, Knitting Needles Size 35, Crochet Hook Size H, 3½ oz. each Cocoa and Cream Mohair Yarn.

Blocked size for scarf — 10 x 52 inches, one size fits all for hat.

SCARF

With crochet hook and 1 strand each color, ch 40. Pull up last loop and place it on knitting needle held in left hand. Insert hook in ea st of ch, pull yarn through and place on needle. (40 loops). Do not turn.

Row 2: Insert hook in center of first 4 loops, holding the loops tog as one, yo and pull off needle, ch 1 and work 4 sc in first set of loops only. * Work 4 sc in ea set of 4 loops. Repeat from * across, (10 pats). Do not turn.

Row 3: Pull up last st and place on needle held in left hand. Work in BACK LOOP, with crochet hook pull yarn through ea sc of previous row and place on needle (40 loops).

Row 4: Same as 2nd row, drop Cocoa but do not cut.

Row 5: Same as 3rd row but with single strand of Cream only.

Row 6: Knit across row. Turn.

Row 7: Insert hook in 1st 4 loops, pull off needle, pick up Cocoa and with both strands of yarn (1 Cream, 1 Cocoa) pull through, ch 1. Work 4 sc in this group of 4 sts. Insert hook in next group of 4 sts, pull off needle, and work 4 sc in this group. Work 4 sc in ea group of 4 sts across row (40 sc — 10 pats).

Rows 8 & 10: Same as Row 1.

Rows 9 & 11: Same as Row 2. Drop Cream, do not cut.

Row 12: Same as 1st row but work with single strand of Cocoa only.

Row 13: K across row. Turn.

Row 14: Work same as 7th Row, picking up Cream. Repeat these 14 rows 4 times.

Next 11 Rows: Repeat 1st 11 rows. Cut yarn. Block scarf to 10 x 52 inches.

HAT

With 1 strand each color, ch 32. Work pat same as scarf until you have completed 10 pat rows of Jiffy-Lace (about 19 inches), cut yarn. Block to 10 x 20 inches.

Draw 1 long end of piece together for top of hat and with yarn needle and 1 strand each Cocoa and Cream about 20 inches long, sew back seam.

Bows: Cut 6 strands of yarn (3 ea color) 8 inches long and make a bow. Trim ends. Make 4 and sew in position as illustrated.

THE BOLERO VEST WITH METALLIC JIFFY-LACE

Sizes: 8-10, 12-14, 16-18.

MATERIALS: SUSAN BATES or MARCIA LYNN, 1 Knitting Needle Size 50, Crochet Hooks Sizes J and H, 5 (5-6) oz. Knitting Worsted — Beige, 3 Spools Metallic Yarn — Gold (130 yards each).

GAUGE: 9 Pats = 8 Inches, 8 Rows (4 Pats) = 5 Inches.

Note: Entire garment is worked in one piece to underarm using single strand of knitting worsted and double strands of metallic.

Directions are given for Sizes 8-10. 12-14 and 16-18 are in parentheses.

With hook size J, chain 124 (140, 156). Pull up last loop and place it on knitting needle held in left hand. Insert crochet hook in each remaining st of ch. Pull yarn through and place it on needle, 124 (140, 156) loops.

Row 2: Insert crochet hook in center of first 4 loops, holding these loops together as one, yo and pull off needle, ch 1 and work 4 sc in first set of loops only. *Work 4 sc in ea set of 4 loops. Repeat from * across, ending last half of last sc with double strand of metallic yarn.

Row 3: With metallic yarn repeat Row 1, working in BACK LOOP of sc only.

Row 4: Repeat Row 2, ending last half of sc with knitting worsted. Repeat Rows 2 and 3 for pat, working 2 rows with knitting worsted and 2 rows with metallic yarn, until garment measures 12 inches, or length desired to underarm. Divide for Fronts and Back.

Left Front: Work until 20 (24, 28) loops are on needle.

Dec Row: Work 2 sc in each of 2-4 loops groups, then work 4 sc in each of remaining groups of 4 loops, (1 pat.dec).

Next Row: Work until 16 (20, 24) loops are on needle. Sizes 12-14 and 16-18 only repeat dec row. Work on 16 (16, 20) sts, 4 (4, 5) pats until armhole measures 9 (9, 10) inches. Fasten off. Cut yarns. Skip 12 sc (3 pats) all sizes on body for armhole, attach yarn in next sc, pull up a loop in same st, and in each of next 59 (67, 75) sts. Work dec same as on front, but dec on both ends. Work on 13 (13, 15) pats, 52 (52, 60) sts until back measures same as on front. Fasten off. Cut yarn.

Right Front: Skip next 12 sc (3 pats) and work to correspond to left front.

Finishing: Sew shoulder seams.

Edging: Attach knitting worsted on left shoulder seam at front edge, working with H crochet hook, ch 3, * work 3 dc in loop and 1 dc in sc row, repeat from * along left front, 3 dc in corner st at lower edge, 1 dc in each st of starting ch, 3 dc in corner st, work along right front same as left front, 1 dc in each st across back, join with a slip st to 3rd st of ch.

Next Round: Working from left to right *ch 1, skip 1 dc, sc in next dc, repeat from * around, join, cut yarn.

Work same edging around each armhole edge.

THE GREAT TIE SASH SWEATER

Sizes: 10, 12, 14

MATERIALS: SUSAN BATES or MARCIA LYNN, 1 Knitting Needle Size 50, Crochet Hook size 1, 30 (34, 36) oz. Bulky yarn — Yellow.

GAUGE: 5 Pats = 4 Inches, 1 Pat Row = 1¼ Inches

Directions are for Size 10. Sizes 12 and 14 are in parentheses.

BODY

Row 1: Ch 150 (156, 162) for lower edge. With crochet hook pull up last loop and place it on the knitting needle held in left hand. Insert crochet hook in each st of ch, pull yarn through and place on needle. Do not turn.

Row 2: Insert hook in center of first 3 loops, holding the loops together as one, yo and pull off needle, ch 1, and work 3 sc in 1st set of loops only. *Work 3 sc in ea set of 3 loops. Repeat from * across 50, (52, 54) pats. Do not turn.

Row 3: Place last loop on needle. Work in BACK LOOP of each st only. With crochet hook pull

yarn through each sc of previous row and place on needle.

Row 4: Same as Row 2.

Repeat Rows 3 & 4 for pat. Continue in pat for a total of 13 pat rows.

Next Row: Repeat Row 3.

Dec Row: Remove first 6 loops and work 3 sc in set of 6 loops — 1 pat dec. Continue across in pat until 6 loops remain on needle. Remove last 6 loops together and work 3 sc into set of 6 loops — 1 pat dec — 48 (50, 52) pats. Repeat last 2 rows three times more — 42 (44, 46) pats.

Left Front

Row 1: Place last loop on needle. Pull up a loop in next 9 (9, 10) pats — 27 (27, 30) loops.

Row 2: Work scs across row decreasing 1 pat at beg and end of row — 7 (7, 8) pats.

Row 3: Place last loop on needle. Pull up a loop in each sc across.

Row 4: Work scs across row decreasing 1 pat at beg of row.

Repeat Rows 3 & 4 twice more — 4 (4, 5) pats. Work even for 2 more pat rows, fasten off.

Back

Row 1: Sk 3 (4, 4) pats from Left Front for armhole. Draw up a loop in each sc of next 18 pats and place on needle — 54 loops.

Row 2: Work scs across row decreasing 1 pat at beg and end of row — 16 pats.

Work even for 5 more pat rows, fasten off.

Right Front

Row 1: Sk 3 (4, 4) pats from Back for armhole. Draw up a loop in each sc of remaining 9 (9, 10) pats and place on needle — 27 (27, 30) loops.

Row 2: Work scs across row decreasing 1 pat at beg and end of row — 7 (7, 8) pats.

Row 3: Place last loop on needle. Pull up a loop in each sc across.

Row 4: Work scs across row decreasing 1 pat at end of row.

Repeat Rows 3 & 4 twice more — 4 (4, 5) pats. Work even for 2 more pat rows, fasten off.

Sleeve

Ch 39 (42, 42) — wrist edge. Repeat Rows 1 & 2 of Body — 13 (14, 14) pats. Work even for 2 more pat rows.

Next Row: Place last loop on needle, pull up a loop in each sc across.

Inc Row: ** Remove 3 loops and work 4 sc in set of 3 loops ** repeat from ** to ** twice more — 3 sc inc. Continue across in pat until 9 loops remain. Repeat from ** to ** 3 times — 3 sc inc. (Increases will form 2 additional pats in next pat row). Continue in pat for 4 more pat rows. Repeat the 2 rows marked with * once. Continue in pat for 4 more pat rows, fasten off.

Sleeve Cap

Row 1: Sk first 2 pats. Draw up a loop in each sc of next 14 pats and place on needle (42 loops) — 1 (2, 2) pats skipped at end of row.

Row 2: Sc across row decreasing 1 pat at beg and end of row.

Work in pat for 4 more pat rows decreasing 1 pat at beg and end of each row — 4 pats, fasten off. Sew shoulders tog; sew sides of sleeves tog and sew in sleeves.

Border: (Note: All rows are worked from right side.) Attach yarn in any ch on right side of Lower Edge, work 1 sc in each ch across Lower Edge skipping every 4th ch, end with 3 sc in end ch at corner; working up Right Front * ch 2, 1 sc in edge of next sc row, repeat from * across Front; 1 sc in each sc around Neck; work down Left Front the same as for Right Front ending with 3 sc in end ch at lower corner; work across remainder of Lower Edge as before, join with sl st in first sc.

Note: On each Front mark the sc worked in 10th sc from shoulder.

Row 2: Ch 1, sc in each sc around working 3 sc in each lower corner and 3 sc in marked st on Fronts, join with sl st in first sc.

Row 3: Ch 1, sc in each sc around working 3 sc in each lower corner, join with sl st in first sc. Repeat Row 3 twice more, fasten off.

Cuffs: On right side attach yarn at seam, work 1 sc in each ch around skipping every 2nd ch, join with sl st in first sc.

Row 2: Sc in each sc around, join with sl st in first sc.

Repeat Row 2 three times more, fasten off.

Belt: Ch 140, 3 sc in 2nd ch from hook, 1 sc in each remaining ch, end with 3 sc in last ch; continuing back on other side of ch work 1 sc in each ch, end with 1 sc in end ch where first 3 sc were worked, join with sl st in first sc.

Row 2: Ch 1 — do not turn, 1 sc in first sc, 3 sc in next st; continue with scs around both sides of belt working 5 sc in top of other end, end with 3 sc in last st, join with sl st in first sc, fasten off.

SMART! SIMPLE! THE JIFFY-LACE PURSE

MATERIALS: SUSAN BATES or MARCIA LYNN, 1 Knitting Needle Size 35, Crochet Hook Size K, three 70 yd. skeins Rug Yarn.

GAUGE: 1 Pat = 1 inch, 1 Pat Row = 1 inch.

With crochet hook, chain 40, pull up last loop and place on knitting needle held in left hand. Insert hook in ea st of ch, pull yarn through and place on needle, do not turn.

Row 2: Insert hook in center of first 5 loops, holding the loops tog as one, yo and pull off needle, ch 1 and work 5 sc in 1st set of loops only. *Work 5 sc in ea set of 5 loops. Repeat from * across (8 pats). Do not turn.

Row 3: Pull up last st and place on needle held in left hand. Work in BACK LOOP, with Crochet hook pull yarn through ea sc of previous row and place on needle (40 loops). Do not turn. Repeat 2nd and 3rd rows until there are 24 rows of pat ending row 2.

Strap: 48 inches or desired length. Chain 5, sc in second ch from hook, 1 sc in each of next 3 ch, ch 1, turn, * 1 sc in each of next 4 sc inserting hook through both front and back loops, ch 1, turn. Repeat from * until desired length.

Assembling: Counting 8 pat rows for front, 1 pat row for bottom, and 8 pat rows for back, sew strap in to form sides, placing ends of strap against bottom pat row. Purse may be lined with quilted material for padding and body. Snaps may be sewn under flap. Add your favorite pin or clip.

THE TRIANGULAR SHAWL WITH CROCHETED FRINGE

MATERIALS: SUSAN BATES or MARCIA LYNN, 1 Knitting Needle Size 50, Crochet Hook Size K, 8 oz. Sport Yarn.

GAUGE: 5 patterns = 6 inches, 1 pattern row = 1¼ inches

With K Crochet Hook ch 5.

Row 1: With Crochet Hook pull up last loop and place it on the knitting needle held in the left hand. Insert Crochet Hook in each st of ch, pull yarn through and place on needle. (5 loops)

Row 2: Insert hook in center of the first 5 loops on knitting needle, holding these loops together as one, yo and pull off needle, ch 1, 10 sc in loop. Do not turn.

Row 3: Pull up last st and place on knitting needle. Work in BACK LOOP, with crochet hook pull yarn through each sc of previous row and place on needle (10 loops).

Row 4: Insert hook in center of first 5 loops, yo and pull off needle, ch 1, 7 sc, and 8 sc in 2nd set of 5 loops. (15 sc)

Row 5: Repeat Row 3. (15 loops)

Row 6: 10 sc in first set of 5 loops, 5 sc in next set of 5 loops, and 10 sc in last set of 5 loops. The inc will always be made in the first and last sets of 5 loops, as in this row, all patterns in between will have 5 sc. Repeat Rows 5 and 6 until you have 51 patterns (265 sc). Do not cut yarn, pull up a large loop and pull skein through, and start chaining for fringe.

Fringe: With Crochet Hook, ch 12, sc inside of 5 loops, ch 12, sc in picked up st, ch 12, sc in side of sc, continue down to the beginning ch, here put a ch of 12 in the first ch st, sc in next st, ch 12 in the next st, sc in the next st, ch 12 in next st then continue down the other side in same manner to corner. Fasten off.

SQUARE MOTIF JACKET

One size fits all.

MATERIALS: SUSAN BATES or MARCIA LYNN, 1 Knitting Needle Size 35, Crochet Hook Size G, Yarneedle, 14 oz. Knitting Worsted-Blue, 18 oz. Knitting Worsted-White, 6 Buttons 7/8 inch diam.

GAUGE: Each motif with crocheted border — 5 inches square.

Motif: Make 60.

Row 1: With crochet hook and White ch 36. With crochet hook pull up last loop and place it on the knitting needle, insert hook in each st of ch, pull yarn through and place on needle.

Row 2: Insert hook in center of first 3 loops, holding the loops together as one, yo and pull off needle, ch 1, work 3 sc in first set of loops only.

*Work 3 sc, ch 3, 3 sc all in next set of 3 loops — corner pat, (3 sc in next set of 3 loops) twice; repeat from * twice, work corner pat in next set of 3 loops; 3 sc in next set of 3 loops, fasten off. Do not turn.

Row 3: Insert hook in BACK LOOP of last sc, yo with Blue, draw loop through sc and place it on needle, draw up a loop in BACK LOOP of each sc and each ch st at corner and place on needle — 60 loops.

Row 4: (3 sc in next set of 3 loops) twice,* 2 sc, 3hdc, 2 sc all in next set of 3 loops — corner pat, (3 sc in next set of 3 loops) 4 times; repeat from * twice, work corner pat in next set of 3 loops, (3 sc in next set of 3 loops) twice, fasten off.

Center: Thread Yarneedle with 8 inch strand of White; from right side weave needle through single loop of each ch st on first row; draw up the sts tightly and fasten off on wrong side. Fasten ends of rows tog on wrong side.

Crocheted Border: (First Motif Only) On right side attach White in center sc of 2nd pat before any corner, ch 3 — counts as first dc, 1dc in same st, ch 1, 2 dc in center sc of next pat, ch 1, * 2 dc in 2nd st of corner pat, ch 1; sk next st, 1 dc, ch 3, 1 dc all in next st — corner, ch 1, sk next st, 2 dc in next st, ch 1, (2 dc in center sc of next pat, ch 1) 4 times; repeat from * twice, work around corner pat as before, (2 dc in center sc of next pat, ch 1) twice, join with sl st in top of ch 3, fasten off.

Join Second Motif to First Motif in last row as follows: Work same as for First Motif stopping after first dc is made in corner st, ch 1; remove hook, from right side insert hook in center ch at corner of First Motif, draw dropped loop of 2nd Motif through ch, ch 1, 1 dc in same corner st of 2nd Motif; remove hook, from right side insert hook in next ch bet clusters of First Motif, draw dropped loop of 2nd Motif through ch, ch 1, sk next st of corner pat of 2nd Motif, 2 dc in next st; (remove hook, from right side insert hook in next ch bet clusters of First Motif, draw dropped loop of 2nd Motif through ch, ch 1, 2 dc in center sc of next pat of 2nd Motif) 4 times; remove hook, from right side insert hook in next ch bet clusters of first Motif, draw dropped loop of 2nd Motif through ch, ch 1, sk first st of corner pat of 2nd Motif, 2 dc in next st; remove hook, from right side insert hook in next ch bet clusters of First

Motif, draw dropped loop of 2nd Motif through ch, ch 1, sk next st of cornerpat of 2nd Motif, 1 dc in next st, ch 1; remove hook, from right side insert hook in center ch at corner of First Motif, draw dropped loop through ch, ch 1, 1 dc in same corner st of 2nd Motif; ch 1, continue working around 2nd Motif same as for First Motif.

To join motif on 2nd and 3rd sides work same as for first side. Join remainder of motifs according to chart.

Neck: On wrong side attach White in corner space of Left Front Neck, ch 3, 1 dc in same space, * 2 dc in next ch — 1 space — cluster; repeat from * across motif ending with 2 dc in corner space of same motif: 1 cluster in corner space of next motif, continue around neck in this manner ending with 1 cluster in corner space of Right Front.

Row 2: Ch 3 turn, (1 cluster in next space bet clusters) 4 times, * (1 dc in next space bet clusters) twice — 1 cluster decreased; the 2 dc s just made count as 1 cluster, (1 cluster in next space bet clusters) 4 times; repeat from * across; end with 1 cluster in last space, 1 dc in top of turning ch.

Row 3: Ch 3 turn, sk first cluster, (1 cluster in next space) twice, *dec over next 2 spaces, (1 cluster in next space) 4 times; repeat from * across, end with 1 dc in top of turning ch.

Row 4: Ch 3 turn, 1 cluster in space bet dc and first cluster, (1 cluster in next space) 3 times, dec over next 2 spaces, * (1 cluster in next space) 4 times, dec over next 2 spaces; repeat from * across, 1 cluster in next space, 1 cluster in space bet last cluster and turning ch, end with 1 dc in top of turning ch.

Row 5: Ch 3 turn, sk first cluster, (1 cluster in next space) twice, dec over next 2 spaces, * (1 cluster in next space) 4 times, dec over next 2 spaces; repeat from * across, (1 cluster in next space) 3 times, end with 1 dc in top of turning ch.

Row 6: Ch 3 turn, 1 cluster in space bet dc and first cluster, 1 cluster in next space, * dec over next 2 spaces, (1 cluster in next space) 4 times; repeat from * across, end with 1 cluster in space bet last cluster and dc, 1 dc in top of turning ch, fasten off.

Border: On right side of Lower Edge attach White in corner ch where any 2 motifs are joined, ch 3, 1 dc in same st, sk corner dc, (2 dc in next ch 1 space — cluster) 7 times, 1 cluster in corner ch of joining; continue across in this manner to corner; in ch 3 space at corner work 2 dc, ch 3, 2 dc; continue along front edge as before, ending with 1 cluster in corner space of last motif; work 1 cluster in each row along neck edge to within one row from end; in last row at corner work 2 dc, ch 3, 2 dc; continue around top edge of Neck with 1 cluster in space bet clusters; complete other half the same.

Sew buttons to left side as shown. Use natural openings on right side as buttonholes.

CHILD'S TWO-PIECE DRESS

Sizes 6 and 8. Changes for size 8 in brackets.

MATERIALS: SUSAN BATES or MARCIA LYNN, 1 Knitting Needle — Size 35, Crochet Hook Size J, Pom-Pom Maker, 8 oz. White Knitting Worsted, 2 oz. Red Knitting Worsted, 2 oz. Blue Knitting Worsted.

GAUGE: 2 patterns = 1½ inches, 1 pattern row = 1 inch

VEST: Work 2 (front and back)

Row 1: With Crochet Hook and Red ch 33 [39]. Pull up last loop and place it on the Knitting Needle held in the left hand.

Insert Crochet Hook in each st of ch, pull yarn through and place on needle 33 [39] sts.

Row 2: Insert hook in center of first 3 loops, holding these loops together as one, yo and pull off needle, ch 1, * 3 sc in each set of 3 loops, repeat from *. Continue until all the sts are worked off. 11 [13] pats. Cut yarn. Do not turn.

Row 3: With White, work in BACK LOOP of st only, pull yarn through each sc of previous row and place on needle 33 [39] sts.

Row 4: Repeat Row 2. Cut yarn.

Rows 5 and 6: Changing to Blue, repeat Rows 3 and 2. Cut yarn.

Rows 7 and 8: Changing to Red, repeat Rows 3 and 2. Cut yarn.

Rows 9 through 18: Repeat Rows 3 and 2 (alternating colors), ending with Row 2. (9 pat rows in all, 3 pat rows of each color) Fasten off.

Side Panels: With right side facing you and skipping two rows from the top (working from left to right), on right side edge of work, pick up 3 loops in each row.

As in Row 3 place sts on needle and work Rows 3 and 2 once in each color (or wider if needed.)

Strap: With Blue and right side facing you pick up 6 [9] sts from upper lefthand side and work 10 [11] pat rows for strap (Inc or dec as needed for length of strap). Work 2nd side in same manner and sew end of strap to right side of the opposite side. Sew sides together.

Neck and Arm Edge: *Row 1:* Attach Blue yarn at any seam, ch 1, sc around once.

Row 2: Sl st in next sc, ch 1, then back sc (sc worked from left to right instead of right to left) around once. Fasten off.

Bottom Edge: *Row 1:* Attach Blue yarn in any seam, sc in same st, sc in each sc on front and back sides, 3 sc's in each pat row on the side panels, 84 [96] sc. Sl st in next st, ch 1, do not turn.

Row 2: Sc in each sc, dec'ing 3 sts on the front, 3 on the back and 1 on each side panel. 76 [88] st. Sl st in next st, ch 1, do not turn.

Row 3: 1 back sc in each sc around. Fasten off.

SKIRT

Starting at waist, with White chain 96 [108]. Pull up last loop and place it on the knitting needle held in the left hand. Insert crochet hook in each st of ch, pull yarn through and place on needle 96 [108] sts.

Row 2: Insert hook in center of first 3 loops, holding these loops together as one loop, yo, and pull off needle, ch 1, *work 3 sc in each set of 3 loops *. Continue between *s across row until all the sts are worked off. 32 (36) pats. Do not turn. Pull up last loop and place on needle.

Row 3: Pull yarn through each sc of previous row and place on needle working in back loop of st. Inc 6 sts evenly across row. (To inc bring yarn

from left to right around needle and continue pulling yarn through from the next sc and onto needle) 102 [114] sts.

Row 4: And all even rows, repeat Row 2. 34 [38] pats.

Row 5: And all odd rows, repeat Row 3. 108 [120] sts. Repeat Rows 2 and 3 until you have 54 [58] pats (or more if you wish a wider flair). Continue, without inc until you have completed desired length. End with Row 2. Sew seam.

Waist Chain: With double strand make a ch 45 inches long. Run it evenly through the holes at top of skirt. Make 2 pompons and tie to ends of chain.

Hem Chain: With a single strand of Red make a ch long enough to go around bottom of skirt; run through bottom holes of skirt. Do the same with Blue yarn.

CHILD'S BATHROBE

Sizes: 2, 4, 6

MATERIALS: SUSAN BATES or MARCIA LYNN, 1 Knitting Needle Size 35, Crochet Hook Size H, 12 (13-14) oz. Knitting Worsted-Pink, 2 (2-2) oz. Knitting Worsted-White, 3 Snaps

GAUGE: 7 sc = 2 inches, 1 Pat = 1 inch, 1 Pat Row = 1 inch

Note: Garment is worked in one piece.

Directions are given for Size 2. Sizes 4-6 are in parentheses.

Yoke: With Pink, starting at waist, ch 74 (81, 88), 1 sc in 2nd st from hook and in each rem st of ch, ch 1, turn. 73 (80, 87) sc.

Row 2: 1 sc in each sc. Repeat Row 2 until piece measures 1½ (1½, 2) inches from beg.

Divide For Fronts And Back: Next Row — Work across 17(19,21) sc for right front, ch 1, turn. Dec 1 st at armhole edge every row twice (all sizes). Work even on the 15 (17-19) sc until armhole measures 4 (4½,4½) inches, ending at front edge.

Neck and Shoulders: Sl st across 3 (4-5) sc, ch 1, work to end, ch 1, turn. Dec 1 st at neck edge every row 4 (5,6) times. When armhole measures 5 (5$\frac{1}{2}$,5$\frac{1}{2}$) inches, ending at arm edge, sl st across 4 (4,4) sts, work to end, cut yarn.

Back: Skip 4 sc on last long row for underarm. Work across next 31 (34,37) sc, ch 1, turn. Dec 1 st at beg and end of every row twice, work even on the 27 (30-33) sc until back measures same as right front to shoulder.

Shape Shoulders: Sl st across 4 sc, work to within 4 sc, ch 1, turn. Repeat last row once more, cut yarn. 11 (14,17) sc remain for back of neck.

Left Front: Skip 4 sc for other underarm and work to correspond to right front.

Sleeves: With Pink, ch 26 (30,34), 1 sc in 2nd ch from hook and in each remaining st of ch, ch 1, turn. 25 (29,33) sc.

Row 2: 1 sc in each sc. Repeat Row 2 for 8 rows.

Next Row: Inc 1 st at beg and end. Repeat inc row every 8th row twice more 31 (35,39) sc. Work even until sleeve measures 7$\frac{3}{4}$ (9$\frac{3}{4}$,10$\frac{3}{4}$) inches from beg.

Sleeve Cap: Sl st across 2 sts, work to within 2 sts, ch 1, turn. Dec 1 st at beg and end of every row until 9 sts remain (all sizes). Cut yarn.

Sleeve Edge: With White, join yarn on wrong side of work at starting ch. Work 1 sc in each st, 25 (29,33) sc, ch 1, turn.

Row 2: Sc in 1st sc, * skip 1 sc, in next sc work 5 trc, skip 1 sc, sc in next sc, repeat from * across, cut yarn. Sew shoulder seams and sleeve seams, sew sleeves in position.

Neck Edge: Work same edge as on sleeves 33 (37,41) sc.

Jiffy-Lace Skirt: On right side, join Pink in starting ch at waist, inc as follows:

Size 2: In each of the 1st 3 sts, work 3 sc in each st, 2 sc in the next st, * 3 sc in the next st, 2 sc in the next st, repeat from * to last 3 sts, 3 sc in each of the last 3 sts (185) sc.

Size 4: 3 sc in the 1st st, 2 sc in the next st, * 3 sc in the next st, 2 sc in the next st, repeat from * across (200) sc.

Size 6: In each of the 1st 3 sts, work 2 sc in each st, 3 sc in the next st, * 2 sc in the next st, 3 sc in

the next st, repeat from * to last 3 sts, work 2 sc in each of the last 3 sts (215) sc. Do not turn work. Working on right side from left to right, work Jiffy-Lace pattern as follows on the 185 (200-215) sts. With crochet hook, pull up last loop and place on knitting needle held in left hand. *Insert crochet hook in back loop of next sc, pull yarn through and place loop on needle, repeat from * across 185 (200,215) loops. Do not turn.

Row 2: Insert hook in center of first 5 loops, holding these loops tog as one, yo and pull off needle, ch 1, and work 5 sc in first set of loops only. *Work 5 sc in ea set of 5 loops, repeat from * across 37 (40,43) pats. Do not turn.

Row 3: Pull up last st and place on needle held in left hand. Work in BACK LOOP with crochet hook pull yarn through each sc of previous row and place on needle 185 (200,215) loops on needle. Do not turn.

Repeat rows 2 and 3 until skirt measures 19 (21,23) inches ending with row 2.

Border: On wrong side of work, join white and work 1 row of sc, increasing 8 (5,2) sts evenly spaced, ch 1, turn. 193 (205,217) sts.

Row 1: Sc in 1st sc, * ch 5, skip 3 sc, sc in next sc, repeat from * to end. 48 (51,54) ch 5 loops.

Row 2: Ch 5, turn, * sc in 1st loop, 8 dc in next loop, sc in next loop, ch 5, repeat from * across, ending with ch 2, dc in last st.

Row 3: Ch 1, turn, sc in dc of previous row, * (dc, then picot) in each of the next 7 dc of previous row, ending dc in last dc of previous row. (7 picots and 8 dc to each scallop. To make picot, work dc then ch 3, sl st in 1st st of ch just made). Sc in loop between scallops, repeat from * across, ending sc in last space, cut yarn.

Front Edge: Join Pink on right side of lower edge of right front above border and work 1 row of sc up to neck. Do not turn. Work reversed sc. To work reversed sc : ch 1, working from left to right, 1 sc in 1st sc, * ch 1, skip 1, sc in next sc, repeat from * across . Work other side from neck to border, cut yarn.

Tie: Take one end of Pink and one end of White, make a 60 inch ch, lace as illustrated. Sew snaps and ball buttons as illustrated.

Ball Buttons: MAKE 3: Ch 3, join with a sl st to form a ring.

Round 1: 6 sc in ring.

Round 2: 2 sc in each sc (12 sc).

Rounds 3 & 4: 1 sc in each sc, fill cup with yarn.

Dec Round: *Skip 1 sc, sc in the next sc, repeat from * until button is closed, cut yarn.

SHRINK? THINK PINK

Size 8-10

MATERIALS: SUSAN BATES or MARCIA LYNN, Daisy-Loom 2 inch size, Crochet hook F, Light wt. Knitting Worsted, one 4 oz. skein Light Pink, two 4 oz. skeins Hot Pink.

Make 56 Daisies, winding Light Pink twice around each peg. Sew centers with Hot Pink. Follow Daisy-Loom Instructions.

Joining

1st Daisy: Join Hot Pink in any petal of Daisy, sc in same space, * ch 3, sc in next petal, repeat from * 11 times more, cut yarn.

2nd Daisy: Join yarn in any petal, sc in same space, * ch 3, sc in next petal, repeat from * twice more, ch 1, drop loop from hook, working from left to right, sl loop through any ch 3 space of 1st Daisy, ch 1, sc in next petal of 2nd Daisy, * ch 1, drop loop, sl loop through next ch 3 space, ch 1, sc in next petal, repeat from last * once, ch 3, sc in next petal around to complete Daisy, continue in this manner leaving 3 loops free between joinings, until there are 14 Daisies joined. Join last Daisy to 1st Daisy, do not cut yarn. Sl st to 1st ch 3 space, sc in same space, ch 2, sc in next ch 3 space, ch 2, sc in next ch 3 space, ch 2, sc between next 2 Daisies, * ch 2, sc in next ch 3 space, repeat from * twice, ch 2, sc between next 2 Daisies, repeat from 1st * around, join with a sl st to 1st sc.

2nd Round: Sl st to next ch 2 space, sc in same space, * ch 2, sc in next ch 2 space, repeat from * all around, join. Repeat Round 2 twice more, cut yarn.

2nd Daisy Round

1st Daisy: Join yarn in any petal, sc in same space, * ch 3, sc in next petal, repeat from * twice, drop loop from hook, working from left to right, sl loop through ch 2 space directly above previous Daisy, ch 1, sc in next petal, * ch 1, sl loop through next ch 2 space, ch 1, sc in next petal, repeat from * once, ch 3, sc in next petal around to complete Daisy, cut yarn.

2nd Daisy: Join yarn in any petal, sc in same space, * ch 3, sc in next petal, repeat from * twice, ch 1, drop loop, skip 6 ch 3 spaces of 1st Daisy, sl loop through next space, ch 1, sc in next petal, * ch 1, sl loop through next space, ch 1, sc in next petal, repeat from last * once, ch 1, skip 1 ch 2 space, sl loop through next ch 2 space, ch 1, sc in next petal, * ch 1, sl loop through next ch 2 space, ch 1, sc in next petal, repeat from * once, ch 3, sc in next petal around to complete Daisy. Continue in this manner until 14 Daisies have been joined, join last Daisy to 1st Daisy. Continue as before having 4 Daisy Rounds and 3 Mesh Rounds. Divide for Back and Front.

Armholes: Fold work, having 7 Daisies for back and 7 Daisies for front. With right side toward you, join yarn in ch 3 space of daisy, sc in same space, * ch 2, sc in next ch 3 space, repeat from * once, ch 2, sc between next 2 Daisies, * ch 2, sc in next ch 3 space, repeat from last * twice, ch 2, sc between next 2 Daisies, continue this way across 7 Daisies, ch 3, turn. Dec 1 Mesh each side every other row twice.

Neck & Shoulders

Next Row: Work across 6 Mesh, Dec 1 Mesh at neck edge every row twice, work on remaining 4 Mesh until armhole measures 8 inches, cut yarn. Skip 9 Mesh for neck and work other shoulder to correspond. Work Front the same. Sew Shoulders.

Neck Edge: Join yarn at left shoulder and work a row of reversed sc, join, cut yarn. Work same edge around armholes.

Border: Join yarn in ch 3 space of Daisy, sc in same space, * ch 2, sc in next ch 3 space, repeat from * all around, join to 1st sc.

2nd Round: Sl st to ch 2 space, sc in same space, * ch 2, sc in next ch 2 space, repeat from * all around, join. Repeat Round 2 for 6 more Rounds.

THE DAISY COMBO

Hat and Scarf in one

MATERIALS: SUSAN BATES or MARCIA LYNN, Daisy-Loom — 2-inch size, Crochet Hook G, two 4-oz. skeins Knitting Worsted — Any color.

Make 82 Flowers winding yarn twice around each spoke. Follow Daisy-Loom Instructions.

1st Flower: Start with a loop on hook, slip st in petal, * ch 3, slip st in next petal, ch 3, slip st in next petal, ch 5, slip st in next petal, repeat from * around, join in 1st slip st. Cut yarn.

2nd Flower: Always start with a loop on hook, slip st in 1st petal, ch 3, slip st in next petal, ch 3, slip st in next petal, ch 2, slip st in 3rd st of ch 5 loop on 1st flower, slip st in next petal on 2nd flower, * ch 1, slip st in next ch 3 loop of 1st flower, ch 1, slip st in next petal of 2nd flower, repeat from * once, ch 2, slip st in 3rd st of ch 5 loop on 1st flower, ch 2, slip st in next petal on 2nd flower, then complete as 1st flower. Continue in this manner leaving 3 loops free between joinings. Join last flower to 1st flower. Work 3 rounds of 9 flowers in each round of Hat, connecting rounds.

Top Of Hat: Attach yarn in any loop, work 1 sc in each loop. (36 sc). Next Round: Dec 6 sts evenly spaced. (30 sc). Next 2 rounds: Dec all around (8 sc) cut yarn, leaving an 8-inch strand. Thread tapestry needle and pull top together.

Attach 3 rows of 5 flowers each for neck and center of scarf, then add 10 flowers on each of the last 2 rows on each side of the scarf. With double strand of yarn work 1 row of sc around entire garment, working 1 sc in each loop, 1 sc in each connection of flowers, and 3 sc in each corner loop of scarf.

Fringe: Cut strands of yarn 14 inches long. Take 3 strands for each fringe, fold in half, insert crochet hook in sc on end of scarf from wrong side, pull fringe loop through, then pull strands through loop. Pull tight. Work 1 fringe in each sc on each end of scarf.

FIELD O' FLOWERS

Luncheon Set, Size 12 x 18

MATERIALS: SUSAN BATES or MARCIA LYNN, Daisy-Loom 2-inch size, Metal Crochet Hook 1, two 250-Yd. Balls Bedspread Cotton will make 4 Luncheon Mats.

Make 54 Daisies winding 4 times over each spoke, sew centers with double thread. Follow Daisy-Loom Instructions.

Joining: Join thread in any petal of Daisy, sc in same space, ch 5, sc in next petal, *ch 5, sc in next petal, repeat from * 9 times more, ch 5, join to 1st sc, cut thread.

2nd Daisy: Join thread in any petal, sc in same space, ch 5, sc in next petal, *ch 5, sc in next petal, repeat from * once more, ch 2, working from left to right, drop loop from hook, sl loop through 3rd ch of ch 5 of 1st Daisy, ch 2, sc in next petal of 2nd Daisy, ch 2, drop loop, draw through next center ch of ch 5, ch 2, sc in next petal, ch 2, drop loop, draw through next center ch of ch 5, ch 2, sc in next petal, ch 5, sc in each petal around. Continue to join Daisies in this manner leaving 3 loops free between joinings until there are 9 Daisies joined.

2nd Row: Join thread in any petal, sc in same space, ch 5, sc in next petal, *ch 5, sc in next petal, repeat from * once more, ch 2, drop loop, skip 2 ch 5 spaces of previous row, draw loop through center ch of next ch 5, ch 2, sc in next petal, *ch 2, drop loop, draw through next center ch of ch 5 of previous row, ch 2, sc in next petal, repeat from last * once more, ch 5, complete Daisy, cut thread.

2nd Daisy: Join thread in any petal, sc in same space, ch 5, sc in next petal, * ch 5, sc in next petal, repeat from * once more, ch 2, drop loop, skip 6 ch 5 spaces of 1st Daisy, sl loop through center ch of next ch 5, ch 2, sc in next petal, * ch 2, drop loop, sl through next center ch of ch 5, ch 2, sc in next petal, repeat from last * 4 times, ch 5, complete Daisy, cut thread. Continue in this manner until 9 Daisies are joined. Repeat 2nd row until there are 6 rows joined.

Edge: With single thread and right side toward you join thread in any sc, ch 5, sl st in 4th ch from hook, (picot), sl st in center ch of next ch 5 space, ch 5, sl st in 4th ch from hook for picot, sl st in next sc, continue to make a picot in each sc and each center ch of each ch 5 space, and 1 picot in between Daisies all around mat, join, cut thread.

This lovely lace place setting may be enlarged to make an heirloom bedspread or tablecloth. For a tablecloth 54 inches x 72 inches approximately 612 daisies would be needed and for a bedspread single size 60 inches x 108 inches 1,620 daisies would be needed. A simple cloth can be decorated with a daisy edge.

EAR WARMERS

MATERIALS: SUSAN BATES or MARCIA LYNN, Knitting Knobby, Knitting Worsted-size yarn, 37 yds. Purple or color desired, 37 yds. White, Polyester sewing thread, Felt for head band approximately 13 inches x 2½ inches, Felt for 2 circle backings approximately 3 inches in diameter each, Bells for trimming.

Follow directions for making cord.
Make 2 strips of Purple 27 inches long each. Make 2 strips of White 11½ inches each. Make 2 strips — White for ties 19 inches each. Coil and sew Purple strip. Taper and fasten end. Sew White around outside. Make 2. Sew tie strips on circle. Cut 2 strips of felt 12 inches x 1¼ inches or length desired for headband. Sew strips together lengthwise on both edges then sew ends to circles. Cut rounds of felt and sew to backs of circles. Sew on bells as illustrated.

EYEGLASSES CASE

MATERIALS: SUSAN BATES or MARCIA LYNN, Knitting Knobby, Steel Crochet Hook 00, Knitting Worsted-size yarn, 30 yds. White, 5 yds. Orange, 7 inches x 3½ inches Black felt, Polyester sewing thread.

Follow directions for making cord.

Front: Make a White strip 10½ inches long. Fold in half and sew the inner edges tog. Place a marker at fold. Make a 2nd strip 11½ inches long. Fold in half and place marker at fold. Starting at straight edge sew 2nd strip to 1st strip matching markers and easing any fullness around curved edge. Make 3rd strip 13 inches long and sew in same manner as 2nd strip. Make 4th strip 14½ inches long and sew in same manner.

Edge: With right side facing, attach Orange at upper corner work sl sts down side around lower curved edge and up opposite side.

Working across upper edge: * ch 2, sl st in joining of strips, repeat from * across ch 2, join, cut yarn.

Back: Cut felt same size as front section. Over cast to wrong side of front section at inside of border.

Trim: Cut felt ¹/₂ inch x 2 inches. Taper ends and slash for eyelashes. Sew or glue in position.

BOOK MARK

MATERIALS: SUSAN BATES or MARCIA LYNN, Knitting Knobby, Heavy Mercerized Cotton-size yarn, 15 yds. color desired, Polyester sewing thread.

Follow directions for making cord.

Make a strip 20 inches long. Keeping work flat, coil and sew strip until circle measures 1³/₄ inches. On the other end of strip do the same, shaping coil in opposite direction.

STOOL COVER, PLACE MAT AND COASTER

MATERIALS: SUSAN BATES or MARCIA LYNN, Knitting Knobby, Knitting Worsted-size yarn, one 4-oz. skein each Red, White and Navy, Elastic cord, Polyester sewing thread.

STOOL COVER

Follow directions for making cord.

Center: With White make a strip 3¹/₄ yds. long. Coil and sew strip until circle measures 7 inches in diameter (be sure to keep work flat); taper and sew end.

Border: Work a Red strip long enough to fit around outer edge of center. Sew ends tog and sew to center. Continue working in same manner in following color scheme: * 1 round White; 1 round Navy; 1 round White; 1 round Red, repeat from * once; 1 round White and 1 round Navy. Block cover; this should measure about 13 inches in diameter. With White work a strip long enough for 3 rounds approx. 3¹/₂ yds. Sew to cover, taper end and fasten end securely. With elastic thread work a running st on wrong side of last round, adjust to size and fasten ends.

PLACE MAT

With White work a strip 45 inches long. Work same as center of stool cover until center is 4 inches in diameter.

Work border in same manner in following color scheme: 1 round Red; 1 round White; 1 round Navy; 1 round White; 1 round Red; 1 round White and 1 round Navy.

COASTER

With white work a strip 14 inches long. Work same as stool cover until circle is 2 inches in diameter.

Work border in same manner in following color scheme: 1 round Red; 1 round White and 1 round Navy.

PORTRAIT OF A MOUSER

MATERIALS: SUSAN BATES or MARCIA LYNN, Knitting Knobby, Knitting Worsted-Size yarn, 12 yds. White, 1 yd. Black for eyes & whiskers, 3-inch Red for collar, Picture Frame 7 inches x 9 inches with 4³/₄ x 6¹/₂ inches opening, Blue Construction paper 5 inches x 6³/₄ inches, White Glue.

Follow directions for making cord.

Make 2 strips of White — 16 inches and 2 inches. Start 16 inches strip 2¹/₂ inches from left side of construction paper and 3 inches down. Paste horizontally and then coil as illustrated, pasting down carefully as you go along. Paste last 2 inches facing downward for tail. Coil 2-inch strip for face and paste down as shown. Embroider eyes, ears and whiskers as shown, sewing to construction paper. 3 strands of Red for the Collar complete the picture.

THE MOUSE

MATERIALS: SUSAN BATES or MARCIA LYNN, Knitting Knobby, Knitting Worsted-size yarn, 30 Yds. White, 1 yd. Black, 1 pipe cleaner, Kapok for filling, Scrap of Black felt.

Follow directions for making cord.

Make a strip 54 inches long. Tightly coil and sew 1 round. Wrapping over 1 finger, sew 2nd round.

Sew 2 rounds, working over 2 fingers and 1 round over 3 fingers. Section should measure about 2 inches in diameter. Sew 2 more rounds same as last round. Then sew 3 more rounds making each round smaller so that last round will measure about ³/₄ inch across. Fill with kapok and sew opening closed.

Tail: Wind White around a 4-inch length of pipe cleaner gluing each end. When dry sew in position.

Ears: (Make 2.) Cut a section of Black felt ¹/₂ x ¹/₄ inch round 1 long end. Gather opposite end and sew in position.

With Black, embroider eyes and mouth with straight sts.

JOLLY SNOWMAN

MATERIALS: SUSAN BATES or MARCIA LYNN, Knitting Knobby, Yarneedle, Knitting Worsted-size yarn, one 4-oz. skein White, 12 yds. Black, 10 yds. Scarlet, 2 yds. Gold, 1 styrofoam ball 5 inches in diameter, 1 styrofoam ball 3 inches in diameter, Pipe Cleaner, Polyester sewing thread.

Follow directions for making cord.

Body: Make a White strip 5¹/₄ yds. long. Keeping work flat, coil and sew strip until circle measures 4 inches in diameter. Then, pulling strip slightly so that it will cup, continue sewing placing over large styrofoam ball occasionally to be sure it is cupping enough. When about 12 inches remains place over ball, work rem tightly, taper and fasten end securely. Cut off a small portion of ball to keep from rolling.

Head: Make a White strip 3¹/₄ yds. long. Coil and sew until circle measures 2¹/₂ inches in diameter. Continue same as body, using 3-inch ball. Sew to body.

Hat: Make a Black strip 12 inches long.

Crown: Coil and sew until circle measures 1¹/₂ inches in diameter. Work 2 rounds cupping crown. Then work 2 more rounds for brim keeping rounds flat. Sew to head.

Scarf: Make a Scarlet strip 18 inches long. Tie around neck.

With Black, embroider eyes and nose with a French knot (3 times around needle) and 3 buttons (5 times around needle).

Broom: Work a Gold strip for about 8 rounds on Knitting Knobby. Remove from knobby, cut yarn leaving a 12-inch length. Wind Gold 12 times around 2 fingers for top of broom. Remove from fingers and tie one end with an 8-inch length of yarn, cut other end. Thread 2 long ends of tie into yarneedle and draw through center of cord unraveling a few rounds if cord is too long. Then sewing through sts of coil fasten securely. Wind Gold around a 4-inch length of pipe cleaner, gluing both ends. When dry sew one end to top of broom. Sew broom in position.

DOGGY SOAP COVER

MATERIALS: SUSAN BATES or MARCIA LYNN, Knitting Knobby, Pom-Pom Maker, Crochet hook G, Yarneedle, Knitting Worsted size yarn, one 2-oz. skein White, 2 yds. Black, Polyester sewing thread, Elastic cord, 2 Black beads for eyes.

Body Section: Make a strip 62 inches long. Measure 2 inches from one end and fold and sew. Keeping work flat, working around and around sew edges tog for entire length. With elastic thread, work a running st on wrong side of last round. Place over soap, adjust to size and fasten ends securely.

Head and Neck: Ch 4, 7 dc in 1st st of ch, join in ch at beg (8 sts). 2nd and 3rd Rounds: ch 3 (counts as 1 dc), 1 dc in each rem dc, join each round. 4th Round: Ch 3, dc in same space, 2 dc in each rem st, join, cut yarn leaving a 15-inch length for sewing. Thread yarn into yarneedle and sew edge of last rnd to top of one end of body section.

Pompons for Head and Feet: (Make 5.) Cut two 1-yd. lengths. Using small ring, follow directions on POM-POM MAKER Pkg. Sew one pompon to top of head and one on each side. Sew two directly below the crochet section.

Tail: (Make 1.) Cut two 1¹/₂-yd. lengths and use 1 medium and 1 small pompon ring: Sew to opposite end of body section.

Nose: With Black ch 2, 6 sc in 1st st of ch, cut yarn leaving a length for sewing. Thread into yarneedle, draw sts tog and sew in position. Sew eyes in position.